LABOR RELATIONS AND PUBLIC POLICY SERIES

REPORT NO. 5

COLLECTIVE BARGAINING: SURVIVAL IN THE '70's?

Proceedings of a Conference
Sponsored by the Industrial Research Unit and
the Labor Relations Council, Wharton School,
University of Pennsylvania

Edited by

RICHARD L. ROWAN

Associate Professor of Industry
Wharton School of Finance and Commerce
University of Pennsylvania

Published by

INDUSTRIAL RESEARCH UNIT, DEPARTMENT OF INDUSTRY
Wharton School of Finance and Commerce
University of Pennsylvania

Distributed by

University of Pennsylvania Press
Philadelphia, Pennsylvania 19104

THE WHITE HOUSE
Washington

November 17, 1971

The Wharton School of Finance and Commerce can take great pride in the contributions it has made to America's business community and to our nation as a whole. I am pleased to join with you as you celebrate the dual anniversaries of your Industrial Research Unit and the Labor Relations Council, and to congratulate you on the important achievements this occasion marks.

For fifty years the Industrial Research Unit has made industry aware of the changing needs of our work force and of our society. Particularly in the fields of minority policies and collective bargaining, you have helped industry to understand new challenges and to respond to them in a way that attests to the continuing vitality of our free enterprise system.

In the same manner, the Labor Relations Council has provided an important channel for an exchange of ideas between academic and business leaders. Each group is richer for the experience, and improved labor-management relations has been the major beneficiary.

On behalf of all our fellow citizens whom you have helped to serve, you have my best wishes for the rewarding years ahead.

/s/   Richard Nixon

Presented to Dr. Herbert R. Northrup, Director of the Industrial Research Unit and Chairman of the Labor Relations Council, by the Honorable James D. Hodgson, Secretary of Labor, at the dinner meeting of the conference, "Collective Bargaining: Survival in the '70's?" Philadelphia, November 18, 1971.

Foreword

The present volume marks the fiftieth anniversary of the Industrial Research Unit and the twenty-fifth anniversary of the Labor Relations Council at the Wharton School of the University of Pennsylvania. The Wharton Graduate Division is also commemorating its fiftieth anniversary in 1971.

The Industrial Research Unit was established as the Industrial Research Department of the Wharton School in 1921. Its purpose was to undertake "the conduct of systematic research on important social and economic problems of industry for which competence has been gained by persistent specialization." Under the direction of Professors Joseph H. Willits and Anne Bezanson, the Industrial Research Department won an international reputation for its pioneering studies in industrial relations; its analysis of the problems and economics of the coal, textile, hosiery, upholstery, and other industries; its entrepreneurial histories; and later for its research in price history, labor migration and mobility, manpower economics, and productivity. The publications of the Industrial Research Department were issued in a series of major works, in small reports, and in a number of special series. Some of the early studies include the following:

"Skill," by Anne Bezanson. *Quarterly Journal of Economics,* vol. XXXVI, August 1922.

"A Study in Labor Mobility," by Anne Bezanson, Joseph H. Willits, France Chalufour, and Leda F. White. Supplement to *The Annals of the American Academy of Political and Social Science,* vol. CIII, September 1922.

Union Tactics and Economic Change—A Case Study of Three Philadelphia Textile Unions, by Gladys L. Palmer. Industrial Research Study No. 19, 1932.

Effective Labor Arbitration, by Thomas Kennedy. Industrial Research Study No. 34, 1948.

Wage Rates and Working Time in the Bituminous Coal Industry, 1912-1922, by Waldo E. Fisher and Anne Bezanson. Industrial Research Study No. 21, 1932.

"Bituminous Coal," and "Anthracite," by Waldo E. Fisher. Chapters 5 and 6 in *How Collective Bargaining Works.* Twentieth Century Fund, 1942.

"Hosiery," by George W. Taylor. Chapter 9 in *How Collective Bargaining Works*. Twentieth Century Fund, 1942.

Vertical Integration in the Textile Industries, by Hiram S. Davis, George W. Taylor, C. Canby Balderston, and Anne Bezanson. Monograph, 1938.

Labor Mobility in Six Cities, by Gladys L. Palmer assisted by Carol P. Brainerd for the Committee on Labor Market Research. Social Science Research Council, 1954.

Prices in Colonial Pennsylvania, by Anne Bezanson, Robert D. Gray, and Miriam Hussey. Industrial Research Study No. 26, 1935.

Wholesale Prices in Philadelphia—1784-1861, by Anne Bezanson, Robert D. Gray, and Miriam Hussey. Industrial Research Study No. 29, 1936.

Prices and Inflation During the American Revolution, Philadelphia, 1770-1790, by Anne Bezanson. Industrial Research Study No. 35, 1951.

Productivity Accounting, by Hiram S. Davis. Industrial Research Study No. 37, 1955.

The original concept of the Industrial Research Department envisioned a permanent staff of researchers, supplemented when appropriate by members of the teaching faculty of other Wharton departments, and by graduate students and assistants. The Industrial Research Department's publications were produced by a virtual who's who of that period's contributions to labor, personnel, and industrial management studies: C. Canby Balderston, Anne Bezanson, Ewan Clague, J. Frederick Dewhurst, Robert R. Nathan, Hans Neisser, Gladys L. Palmer, George W. Taylor, Alfred H. Williams, and Joseph H. Willits.

World War II necessarily scattered the Industrial Research Department's personnel and many went on to other pursuits. As economic and business knowledge advanced and became more specialized, and funded research through government and foundations became more accessible, research tended to be done more easily within the teaching departments. Morever, in the post-World War II period, the University was extremely short of funds. Accordingly, a decision was made in 1953 to transfer the Industrial Research Department to the Department of Industry, and to transfer also on a permanent basis four persons to the Department of Industry: the late Dr. Gladys L. Palmer, who was appointed Research Professor of Industry; two research associates, the late Miss Miriam Hussey and Mrs. Marjorie Denison, who recently retired after 49 years with the Unit; and Miss Elsa Klemp, statistician. The name of the organization was changed to Industrial Research Unit and Dr. Palmer was named its Director.

Under the direction of Dr. Palmer, the Industrial Research Unit continued as an effective research organization. Dr. Palmer pushed forward with her studies of labor mobility, aided by a substantial grant from the Rockefeller Foundation, as well as grants from other sources. In addition, the Unit continued to perform funded research in the other basic areas where it had gained expertise, particularly studies of industry problems and of industrial relations. Upon Dr. Palmer's retirement in 1965, the Unit was practically dissolved.

In January 1964, Professor Herbert R. Northrup succeeded Dr. George W. Taylor as Chairman of the Department of Industry. The Industrial Research Unit was then largely concerned with final details of the last Rockefeller Foundation grant and with the publication of Dr. Palmer's last book, *The Reluctant Job Changer* (1962). With the need for more stress in the Department on research, and with opportunities for research available, the Industrial Research Unit was seen capable of fulfilling its long-time role to the advantage of all. Accordingly, a decision was made, approved by the Dean of the Wharton School, to revive it, and Professor Northrup assumed the Directorship.

A temporary home in a small building was found and segments of the library were brought together. Mrs. Denison and Miss Klemp were assigned to the Unit to assist in research endeavors, particularly to develop background materials on Negro labor market problems, since discussions were beginning with the Ford Foundation on financing a major effort in this area. "Seed funds" were sought and obtained from industry to support faculty research and to support the development of research proposals. By summer of 1968, the Unit had become again an active, vital organization contributing to knowledge in its traditional areas of competence: industrial relations, labor market, and industry studies. The contemporary publications of the Unit are listed on the back cover of this book.

The Labor Relations Council of the Wharton School was established in 1946 and, except for a one-year interval, its programs have been an integral part of the school's program. Dr. George W. Taylor served as its chairman until 1968 when Dr. Herbert R. Northrup succeeded him. Through the Council, a close cooperation has been maintained over the years between the Industry Department faculty and executives of the member companies. In the monthly seminars, attended by faculty and company members of the Council, many subjects of mutual interest have been discussed. The roster of guest speakers is an impressive one. The monthly seminars have been the heart of the Labor Relations Council, but we believe that other parts of the program have been very important.

Council funds have been used primarily to sponsor research in the field of labor-management relations by faculty members and graduate students. The results have been frequently made available in the form of articles published in numerous journals. The Council has also issued publications under its own auspices. They include the monograph series on Industry-Wide Collective Bargaining published in 1948, the Labor Arbitration Series published in 1952, the book entitled *New Concepts in Wage Determination* published by McGraw-Hill Book Company in 1957, and the volume, *The Negro and Employment Opportunity,* published by the Bureau of Industrial Relations.

There is a third facet of Council activities. Wherever it has seemed that some particular problem of national importance might be clarified by public discussion, the Council has conducted public conferences. For example, in November 1960, at the beginning of what seemed to be a period of economic growth and adjustment to technological change, a conference was held on "Industrial Relations in the 1960's—Problems and Prospects." Serious consideration for holding another public conference was not given until early in 1964 when it became apparent that the most critical and perplexing issue of employer-employee relations had become the provision of equal job opportunities regardless of color. It seemed not only timely but urgently necessary to bring together a group of outstanding men whose experience made them eminently qualified to discuss not only the nature of the problem but the ways and means for resolving it. As a result, a public conference on "Equal Opportunity—The Job Aspect" was held on November 13, 1964. Given the current issues before us, combined with the Council's silver anniversary, the November 1970 conference was an obvious need.

Throughout the fifty-year history of the Industrial Research Unit and the twenty-five year history of the Labor Relations Council, emphasis has been on "the conduct of systematic research on important social and eceonomic problems of industry."

The fascinating complex of problems requiring analysis and the varied interest of faculty and students provide both a never ending source of questions to be solved and questioners desiring to find answers, and should insure a future as interesting, and hopefully, as constructive as the past.

The arrangements for the conference were made by Mrs. Margaret E. Doyle in her usual competent manner and good spirit. The staff of the Industrial Research Unit, including Messrs. Lester Rubin, William Fulmer, Robert Brudno, Kevin Shea, John Morse, Ronald Cowin, Kenneth Bridges, Wayne Williams, Ralph Dereshinsky, Michael Johns, Miss Elsa Klemp, Miss Veronica Kent, Mrs. Marie Spence, Miss Nancy Von, and Mrs. Marie Keeney, performed the innumerable tasks so important to the smooth functioning of any conference. Mrs. Keeney and Miss Klemp also provided excellent editorial assistance. The greatest debt, of course, is owed to the conference participants who were willing to take the time to come to the University and express their ideas in an open forum.

RICHARD L. ROWAN, *Associate Director*
Industrial Research Unit
Wharton School of Finance and Commerce
University of Pennsylvania

Philadelphia
February 1972

Contents

Introduction

This book contains the proceedings of a conference on the challenges to collective bargaining in the 1970's. In addition several articles have been included that are pertinent to the issues discussed. The major emphasis in the conference was on the continued viability of collective bargaining in the face of significant problems. There are five parts of the book which highlight the discussions at the conference.

Part I provides a general introduction to the book. The Honorable James D. Hodgson, Secretary of Labor, responds to the general conference topic, "Collective Bargaining: Survival in the 70's?," by asking: "Are we ready so soon to prepare the eulogy and pay our respects to the short and not-so-happy life of collective bargaining?" George H. Hildebrand considers several aspects of bargaining structure and power, including coalition bargaining, selective strikes, and the impact of inflation on union-management relations.

An examination of collective bargaining and regulatory mechanisms is presented in Part II. John H. Fanning discusses the work of the National Labor Relations Board over the years and finds that the Board in a continuing survey, has done a viable and commendable job of interpreting the National Labor Relations Act, but he thinks that assistance is needed to continue the administrative viability of the Board. Charles J. Morris calls for major changes in the administration of federal labor law and supports new regulatory mechanism based on a court system that can tie together labor laws in the private sector. Francis A. O'Connell makes a strong plea for respect for the law in collective bargaining, and for an NLRB guided by laws, not men, thus differing with the Fanning view. John E. Abodeely discusses the injunctive powers under the Taft-Hartley Act, and questions widening their use as suggested by Morris.

Part III contains several articles pertaining to the strike and its alternatives in both public and private sectors. Benjamin Aaron discusses various questions and issues pertaining to the survival of collective bargaining in those cases where strikes are not tolerated. Kingsley Laffer analyzes the Australian experience under compulsory arbitration and concludes that it has not been a major deterrent to strikes. J. Curtis Counts explains the usefulness and limitations of mediation in the settlement of industrial disputes.

In Part IV several issues pertinent to collective bargaining and industrial relations are discussed. These include: transportation; equal employment opportunity; welfare and pensions; occupational safety and health; and construction.

Herbert R. Northrup examines the record of the Railway Labor Act and finds it wanting, and James E. Burke discusses various facets of collective bargaining in the railroad industry from a union point of view. Edward Shils explores union fragmentation as a major cause of difficulty in the transportation industry. Everett M. Goulard analyzes bargaining difficulties in the airlines industry and the industry's proposal to alter the Railway Labor Act's provisions; and Darold T. Barnum focuses on the problems attendant upon the shift from private to public ownership in the urban transit industry.

The protection of minority rights in collective bargaining continues to be a major factor in industrial race relations. William H. Brown III questions the survival of collective bargaining if it does not protect the rights of minorities and women. Herbert R. Northrup examines the contemporary demand for additional EEOC powers in the context of expanding minority employment rights. Richard L. Rowan reports on a recent investigation to determine the effectiveness of adult basic education programs in the southern paper industry toward improving upgrading of the employed disadvantaged.

Among the most controversial matters in labor relations today are those that relate to welfare payments to strikers and pension benefits. Armand J. Thieblot presents the case against public support for strikers. From the union standpoint, Ray Andrus challenges Thieblot and defends the use of food stamps for strikers. E. S. Willis and Dan McGill analyze problems associated with pensions and collective bargaining.

In 1970, Congress passed the Occupational Safety and Health Act. The major features of this Act, and its likely impact on labor and management, are discussed in a series of articles by Robert D. Moran, Leo Teplow, and Peter Bommarito and Louis S. Belicsky. Moran explains particular sections of the law; Teplow presents a management interpretation of the Act; and Bommarito and Belicsky offer a union response.

The construction industry poses particular problems for collective bargaining and the procurement of minority rights. Arthur A. Fletcher and Michael H. Moskow examine problems pertinent to the establishment of Negro opportunities and wage arrangements in construction.

Part V is concerned with collective bargaining and wage-price guidelines. In a penetrating analysis, W. Allen Wallis explains why he believes the "New Economic Policy" will fail to curb inflation and "reduce the efficiency of the economy and impair individual freedom." Virgil B. Day, a member of the Pay Board, discusses management's role in meeting the problem of inflation control. In a concluding article, A. H. Raskin raises doubts as to whether the "New Economic Policy" can succeed based on both labor's and management's efforts to circumvent the controls and push for as much as possible in terms of increases in wages and prices.

PART I

AN OVERALL LOOK AT THE SURVIVAL OF
COLLECTIVE BARGAINING

The Survival of Collective Bargaining

James D. Hodgson †

It is interesting to recall that 50 years ago, when the Industrial Research Unit was first established, collective bargaining was not a respectable institution. Just 50 years ago, in 1921, the Supreme Court held that nothing in the Clayton Act protected unions against injunctions brought against them for conspiracy in restraint of trade. Collective action was still trying to throw off a conspiratorial mantle. It was not until a few years later that the Railway Labor Act required employers to bargain collectively, and I suppose it was really not until the Wagner Act in 1935 that collective bargaining received the full sanction of law and the mantle of respectability.

Now here we are, some scant 50 years later, discussing the question of whether this rather fledging institution, collective bargaining, can survive! Are we ready so soon to prepare the eulogy and pay our respects to the short and not-so-happy life of collective bargaining?

Perhaps some are. But perhaps also the question about survival is a little premature. Collective bargaining has proved to be an uncommonly hardy plant. It took root in arid and inhospitable soil in the last century. It survived the early attempts to weed it out. After achieving legal status, it survived through storms of adverse public opinion, faulty structural conditions, and the pruning of various regulatory legislation. And, though it is coming under another bout of bad weather today, I suspect it will survive the current storms, too.

Still, I understand the concern. These are times of rapid change and attacks upon all our institutions, and there is no reason to believe that collective bargaining should be an exception. It is, in fact, a vulnerable target. It is highly visible. It is unquestionably messy—sometimes even violent. To the public it is often a nuisance and sometimes a calamity. Its excesses reek of self-interest and unconcern with society. Sometimes it

---

† The Honorable James D. Hodgson is Secretary of Labor.

breaks down, and then we have to drop what we are doing to prop it up.

There is no question that collective bargaining is in trouble and even threatened. But to talk in terms of survival may be just a little melodramatic. Nevertheless, let us take a broad look at it.

The main idea behind collective bargaining is the expectation that out of a struggle between roughly equal economic forces equitable or less acceptable solutions will be forthcoming. Of course, even struggles between equals may be bitter and protracted. Nevertheless, it was thought that even in such circumstances the parties could be left alone to battle themselves into mutual exhaustion without doing much harm to anyone else.

It has not quite worked out that way. A number of things have happened to make some people, at any rate, wonder if the whole idea might have something wrong with it. Let us look at what has happened.

For one thing, both parties to the contest have exhibited a great deal of ingenuity in waging the battle and developing the resources to sustain their positions. I would like to dwell for a minute on this phenomenon.

In a quarter of a century in the aerospace business, I found myself in, but never quite of, the world of physical science. Nevertheless, I osmotically absorbed a few principles of physical science that I came to find had fascinating parallels or applications in the "people world," including the world of collective bargaining. One of the foremost of these principles comes from the structural engineering domain. If a structural problem arises, the engineer solves it by application of a single principle—"either beef-up the structure or lighten the load."

Now how does this apply to collective bargaining? Bargaining presents awesome burdens to its practitioners. Their responsibility is enormous, their tools are limited, and they operate in a setting booby-trapped with every unpleasant manifestation of mischief, guile, and ego. In consequence, a common attitudinal syndrome among bargainers almost everywhere is a belief bordering on the faith of a convert that they, and not their opposite members, lack adequate bargaining power. And here is where our structural engineering principle comes in. The harassed bargainer finds ingenious ways to beef up the structure to add to his own power or to lighten the load—lighten it by crippling the power of the opposition.

Some of this activity is often viewed as just fun and games by the unperceptive. The result of this adaptive reaction pattern over time, however, is to escalate the scope, level, and intensity of the power struggle. Each side seeks ways to increase its power vis-a-vis its opposite number. Coupled with this, each seeks to insulate itself against losses that may accrue from the use of power—from strikes in which it becomes involved.

Someday a Ph.D. dissertation will be written on the emerging range of ways bargaining parties make such adaptations, but just for starters here are some of the ways it is being done. Among unions these ways would include paying strike benefits, promoting community credit support programs, and developing alternate job opportunities for strikers. And, in industry, we would start the list with advance inventory accumulation, mutual assistance pacts, and a range of other cushioning measures.

Now along with the ability of bargainers to insulate themselves against the full effect of the overt use of their power has been another accompanying phenomenon. By now it is almost trite to point out that in recent decades the economy has grown vastly more complex with more interdependent and interlocking parts. We are accustomed to speaking of the "economic system," and it *is* a system in a very real sense. A systems engineer would describe the economy as made up of many sub-systems—communications, transportation, power distribution, manufacturing, any many others—each with its hundreds of component parts and all dovetailing into the rest. And, just as in a space or defense system, trouble in one area can endanger the whole. The overall reliability of any system is the product of the reliability of its individual parts, and the more inter-related the parts, the more likely the system is to break down. Collective bargaining often seems to prove a fairly unreliable part. When it fails today the whole system may be thrown out of kilter.

So we put these two things together—first, the improved ability of parties to cushion themselves against a strike; and second, the widespread effect of certain strikes because of our inter-related economic system. They add up to one thing—less adversity for the parties directly involved and more adversity for the public. It is little wonder that the public is becoming weary and even outraged.

There has been another societal change that has affected the institution of collective bargaining. We are seeing a growing tendency to place more responsibility on the Federal government to make sure that our economic system works and to act to correct it when it is not working properly. This is true not only with regard to bargaining. When a problem exists today, many among the public expect the Federal government to take action—some action, whether legal, quasi-legal, or often even extra-legal—to solve the problem. You know the problem list—cleaning up our air and water, protecting the consumer, curing racial injustice, alleviating urban blight, improving the nation's health, eliminating poverty, and on and on. Among these problems are those of industrial strife stemming from the failure of collective bargaining. Rightly or wrongly, the public expects the Federal government to do something about labor disputes, even if government does not possess the tools. We live in an age when, in spite of complaints against the limitations on individual freedom, we expect even more from government in solving the problems that complexity and bigness and the exercise of freedom itself have created.

There is another element operating here of more recent vintage. Formerly, the public tended to view collective bargaining with a jaundiced eye primarily when its failure resulted in inconvenient or crippling work stoppages. But recently there has emerged a mounting suspicion that in some circumstances at least collective bargaining is working against the public good not only in the area of work stoppages but also in the area of excessive wage settlements that are passed on to the consumer in higher prices. With the advent of our current cost-push inflation, the public is questioning collective bargaining even more intensively than in the past.

So we increasingly see collective bargaining being cast in the devil's role by the public. Today, bargaining results too often in a long and publicized struggle between giants who seem not to care who gets hurt in the process. The public is concluding it is they who suffer. When the economic system is crippled, it is the public that suffers. When inflation results from high wage settlements, it is the public that suffers. So the clamor mounts.

How intense is this mounting clamor? What will be the result?

Probably because of my position at the focal point of government, I may overestimate the intensity of developing public concern. After all, one is apt to overestimate the scope of a storm when one is at its center. On the other hand, nowhere does the accumulated impact of public dissatisfaction and demand for action come together for one to view in totality better than in the Nation's capital. I for one am convinced that the public concern is fast reaching a flood-tide that will require governmental action in the form of legislation in the near future, and it seems to me some action is indeed called for.

In theory, we have two courses. We can scrap collective bargaining for something else, or we can try to improve it. It is hard to see what we can scrap it for. Certainly we will not go back to a system in which only the employer sets the terms of wages, hours, and working conditions by unilateral action. Nor, in spite of present wage-price controls, which the Administration views as temporary, do we want a system in which the government makes the decisions.

Professor Northrup argues, and I think rightly, that experience has shown that compulsory arbitration, as one alternate method to bargaining, is not a solution since it does not insure industrial peace, does not necessarily further the economic or social policies of government, does not reduce manifestations of power, and acts to discourage collective bargaining. I would not quarrel with any of these conclusions.

In fact, when we look at any substitute for collective bargaining, we are apt to come up against insuperable problems. It may well be we must conclude that collective bargaining may be like democracy itself. It is the worst possible system, except for all others.

Sherlock Holmes used to say that when you eliminate all the probable causes for a crime, then whatever remains, no matter how improbable, must be the answer. And when we eliminate all probable substitutes for collective bargaining, then what remains must be the answer. And what remains is retaining collective bargaining and improving it. This is what I believe we must do, and though I admit the difficulties, I do not regard the task as impossible.

Of course, I do not presume to have all the answers here. Really, we are looking to experts such as you to make the major contributions to the long-term improvement of collective bargaining. Yet it seems clear to me that if collective bargaining is really going to survive and continue to serve us, there are some things we must do.

First, and by all means foremost, we must find a way to prevent major strikes that create national emergencies. As I have said, the public will no longer tolerate such strikes, and I think the public should *not* tolerate them. It is easy enough to talk about industrial freedom and the right to strike and all the other clichés that are used to justify these calamitous events, but the fact is the social cost in today's world is simply too high.

Although legally employees of the Nation's railroads, today, have a right to strike, the truth is that the Nation will not tolerate a complete shutdown of our rail system. Thus, we have an anomaly. You recall how often and how swiftly Congress has moved in recent years to prevent rail shutdowns. Last minute congressional action has been our only recourse, and it has been a very poor one. We need something better. We need, I think, a system that at a minimum does two things. It should give the President the tools to deal effectively with these emergencies, and it should at the same time strengthen rather than weaken collective bargaining. As you know, the Administration has proposed such a solution, providing the President with various options, including the "final selector" option which we believe will serve to bring the parties closer together during the entire bargaining process. We are actively pushing for this legislation.

A second thing I think we must do is to perform surgery in industries where the collective bargaining process is not working well. A classic example is the construction industry. Here we have been obliged to move in with a program of self-administered wage restraints. To date the program has been working surprisingly well. At last count, the program had reduced the number of construction strikes to one tenth of what they were a year ago. Wage settlements, which had been averaging 16 percent annually before the program was initiated, since that time have been around 10 percent.

This has been a remarkable achievement, and perhaps it augurs well for our current effort at national wage-price controls, since both efforts share many of the same concepts—flexible guidelines, participation by the parties affected, and voluntary compliance with sanctions available if needed. But even so, no one should conclude that such a mechanism provides a long-time solution to the problems of bargaining in the construction industry. The more fundamental problem appears to lie in the fragmentation of bargaining units. Perhaps the trouble will never be cleared up until we are able to restructure markedly bargaining within the industry.

There is also a wide range of things that can be done by both management and labor away from the bargaining table to make collective bargaining less painful and more fruitful when they get down to it. You are, of course, familiar with these things. They range from a continuing dialog on specific problems to, as in a few industries, a prearrangement for voluntary arbitration—a device not without appeal even to labor leaders like Mr. Meany. The point, of course, is that with no suitable alternative available to replace collective bargaining, both management and labor have much to gain in improving the bargaining process. They have done some things already; I am convinced they could do much more. As the pressures of public discontent and the prospect of increasing government intervention mount, I believe they will.

I would like to add a final prescription: greater understanding on the part of everyone—labor, management, and the public— of certain economic facts related to the bargaining process. All of us need to be made aware, for example, of the actual effect of economic changes made in bargaining on national inflationary trends and on international competitive survival. We need to understand how bargaining can serve and how it can hinder productivity. We need to be aware of its role in re-distributing income and even its place in social reform. Some of this information is already available but not generally known. Much of it, I am sure, is still unknown. Misinformation, misunderstanding, and simple ignorance now becloud the issues and inflame our passions whenever the subject of collective bargaining comes up for discussion.

This adds up to a big job of education and research. And I think it reasonably certain that in the unlikely event any of us are around 50 years from now, we may still be discussing the problems of collective bargaining. It will be much changed, of course, and I hope much improved. But both bargaining and its problems will still be with us.

Bargaining Structure and Relative Power

George H. Hildebrand †

In what follows, I propose to consider three recent shifts in the balance of bargaining power between unions and managements in the United States. One involves an effort by certain unions to enlarge the scope of negotiations by forming coalitions of separate bargaining units. The second concerns the substitution of "selective" for industry-wide strikes by one of the leading unions in the railroad industry. The third involves the impacts of seven years of inflation upon union demands and management resistance.

I. Coalition Bargaining

Probably the most dramatic attempt to alter the balance of bargaining power in recent years has been the movement for coalition bargaining mounted by the Industrial Union Department of the AFL-CIO during the period 1962-1968. The campaign extended over a broad range of industries, among them petroleum refining, nonferrous metals, chemicals, metal products, electrical equipment, and food processing. Several very prominent firms have been involved.

In each instance, the initial target situation was one in which a multi-plant concern had been conducting separate negotiations with several different locals, frequently affiliated with more than one international union. As I have pointed out elsewhere,

> The initial object of a coalition is to enlarge the scope of bargaining beyond the limits of each of the existing units—*without, however, technically replacing either the units themselves or the unions recognized to be their respective bargaining agents.*[1]

Put a little differently, the goal of a coalition is to bring about unilaterally an enlargement of the scope of negotiations and of decision-making to embrace a fragmented group of bargaining units that hitherto had negotiated separately; and to accomplish this while leaving these separate units technically intact.

---

† George H. Hildebrand is Maxwell M. Upson Professor of Economics and Industrial Relations, Cornell University.

Typically, coalitions have emerged in the following contexts. In the first, the employer has several competing plants, each with a different local belonging to the same national union, and with a separate agreement for the particular plant. This was a situation confronted by an early coalition directed against bargaining in Standard Oil of Ohio. Where it occurs, the employer has the advantage of being able to substitute among alternative sources of supply, which enables him to take local strikes more effectively, and to bargain successfully to recognize differences in wages and other conditions according to locality, to the disadvantage of the locals and their parent organization, as they see the matter.

The second situation is a variant of the first: here there is more than one parent international. Each suffers from incomplete jurisdiction, rivalry with the other organizations, inability to mount companywide strikes, and the risk of being undercut because it cannot effectively "take wages out of competition." This roughly describes the situation confronting the coalition in General Electric and Westinghouse. Only a carefully coordinated common strategy among the unions can overcome these inherent weaknesses of fragmented bargaining.

In the third situation, the basic problem for the unions is the vertical integration of the company—in the case of copper, from mine to concentrator to smelter to refinery to fabricating plant. At any one stage, the problem is as in our first case: substitute plants under the control of the same employer, with local bargaining. But with vertical integration combined with separate bargaining, the employer is better able to take strikes at any link in the chain. If the mines and smelters are closed, he can buy metal for his fabricating plants in the open market, avoiding a complete shutdown of operations. If the finishing plants are struck instead, the mines can continue to produce either for stock or for sale in the open market. In basic steel, the technical circumstances are quite similar, but because the industry has been organized by a single large union that bargains companywide, there is no problem of strike effectiveness devolving from the fact of vertical integration. By contrast, in nonferrous there is such a problem from the union point of view. Its solution requires a coalition of monumentally complex character, as in fact was put together by the United Steelworkers back in 1967 after this organization had absorbed the former Mine-Mill Union.

Finally, there is the case of the conglomerate producing company, for example, Union Carbide. Within given lines of production, some plants in such a concern will be substitutes for one another. But the very existence of a broad array of products will bring about diversity in technology and in occupational requirements. Add fractional bargaining to this mixture and the result will be a complex bargaining system in which the employer is likely to have the initiative. No local union is likely to be strong; indeed, no national union is either. Thus the incentive for concerted action will be present and acutely felt, though putting together a combination will be unusually difficult.

Over the past five years ample opportunity became available to test the strategy and tactics of coalitions in the courts and before the NLRB. Although I lack space to develop them fully, the following now seem to be relatively settled points of law.

First, as the Board found in the *Philps Dodge* case,[2] it is "nonmandatory" that negotiations be conducted on a basis broader than the established bargaining unit. To insist, as the Respondents did in that case, that the employer bargain companywide and therefore beyond the scope of the established units, and to strike in behalf of this demand, were violations of Section 8(b)(3) of the Act.

Second, the parties have a duty to execute local settlements once reached, even if other units remain without agreemnts.[3] In short, it is violative of the Act for a party to a system of local agreements to follow an all-or-nothing strategy as regards a return to work in any one unit in which settlement separately has been achieved. This, of course, denies to the coalition a central element in the typical strategy of such combinations.

Third, an employer is within his rights to try to preserve a system of local bargaining, provided he observes his own obligations under the law. Thus, he can insist that the bargaining be confined to the scope of the established unit whose agreement is before the parties for renegotiation. But he cannot refuse to undertake such negotiations simply because the union's bargaining team may include persons belonging to other unions or from "outside" of the unit as such.[4] And if the employer can also show that he has bargained to an impasse on mandatory items, he may lock out the particular plant as part of his strategy for countering a coalition.

Finally, in view of the foregoing it seems clear that the Board will continue to emphasize the scope of existing bargaining units except where the parties themselves agree to change that scope. This was not so clear in 1968, when the Board decided over the employer's opposition in the *Libbey-Owens-Ford* case that separate self-determination elections could be directed over the question of whether the locals involved should now be represented by an established multi-plant unit for other locations of the same company.[5] The company successfully contested the majority view in Federal District Court, but the Board obtained a reversal in the Court of Appeals, and the Supreme Court denied certiorari. The elections were then held, but thereafter the company refused to bargain with the enlarged unit in order to test the majority view of the Board's powers in disputed cases involving changes in the scope of a unit.

During the pendancy of a complaint on this aspect of the matter, Mr. Edward B. Miller became Chairman of the NLRB. By his joining the earlier minority members, a new majority emerged that found that the Board should not have made the earlier "clarification" of the original certification, nor have conducted the ensuing elections. In the Chairman's own words, "the principle which the Board so boldly announced in 1968 has proved to have extremely limited utility." [6] However, he was careful to distinguish his majority colleagues' position—that statutory authority was lacking for the Board's original order—from his own—that the authority was available to merge units but was inappropriately used in this instance, where the parties' relationships had been long established.

As matters now stand, the record of the various coalitions is a spotty one. It has not proved possible to compel the enlargement of the scope of a negotiating unit where the employer is opposed to the move. This is not to say that the employers have not had to pay a high economic price, both to withstand long strikes and to obtain ultimately separate settlements of those disputes. Rather it is to say that as things have turned out, the law now leans heavily against the more obvious forms of coalition strategy. In the legal sense, then, the balance of bargaining power is not likely to shift in the near term.

But to those who would seek such a shift *de facto,* a subtler strategy still remains open: this is to try gradually to narrow down the spread between the expiration dates in the separate agreements. Eventually a companywide strike then would become feasible, whereupon the negotiations can be made interdependent even though they remain legally separate. In this way uniformity in settlement terms at the end of a dispute can be approached although the integrity of the separate units is left free from direct attack.

Thus the apparent failure of several coalitions should not be taken to mean that negotiating scope ultimately cannot be enlarged because unit scope has successfully been preserved. In turn, this means that it is still possible legally to shift the center of negotiating gravity from the plant to the entire company. And where this difficult exercise can be successfully executed, a shift in the locus of union power also seems a likely next step. The national office would gain relative to the locals. Parallel national unions would acquire incentive to merge. And where a dominant national organization has provided successful leadership to a coalition involving weaker nationals as well, its prestige, influence, and ability to expand are all likely to grow. By the same token, all of these tendencies together would diminish the bargaining power of those multi-plant companies that now have fractional local systems. These concerns would lose the ability to resist strikes by substituting one plant for another, and therewith the means for preserving major inter-plant differences in their local agreements.

The logical extension of the concept of coalition bargaining is from all company plants within the United States and Canada to those owned by the same firm overseas. Although nothing lasting so far has emerged from this interesting conception, the possibility has been discussed in recent years for automobiles, chemicals, textiles, and radio-tv sets. Superficially, it seems plausible to argue that if wage uniformity is "fair" for all automobile workers in the United States, it is equally so for those throughout the world. The more interesting question is whether the automobile workers in the plants abroad would actually want wage parity with their brethren in the United States. Would they press equalitarianism to this extreme?

I doubt it. Competitive economic analysis tells us that the principal reason for international differences in wages is differences in the economic productivity of labor. If, then, an international coalition were to be proposed, the first item on the agenda would be wage standards. If the U. S. level were proposed, the more astute foreign bargainers would quickly point out that this would serve as a protectionist device for the U. S., by equalizing wages but not unit labor costs throughout the industry—with attendant sizable loss of jobs abroad. But anything less than international wage uniformity for the industry would require the acceptance of the "competition of cheap foreign labor"—hardly an attractive goal for an American union. And so I conclude that a proposed international coalition would founder at once on the shoals of wage policy. If it could survive this passage, its course toward effective strike control for all competing plants anywhere in the world still would be perilously difficult to carry out. In turn this is indeed fortunate for industrial workers in the developing countries in particular, for otherwise their jobs would be at forfeit.

II. Selective Strikes on the Railroads

The unspoken and unexamined premise of the foregoing discussion is that a coalition of separate bargaining units to enlarge the scope of negotiations will increase the relative bargaining power of the union, to the disadvantage of the employer. Otherwise why would the coalition be undertaken?

But at this point we encounter a paradox: if the premise is correct, how are we to interpret the recently judicially recognized right of the United Transportation Union to strike selectively against any of some 170 railroad carriers who are joined together for multi-employer bargaining? Presumably the UTU switched to the tactic of striking selectively because it believed that this would increase its power to attain its objectives. Collaterally, by fighting these strikes vigorously in the courts, the carriers must have reasoned that the tactic would weaken their own position. Yet the tactic itself calls for substituting selective strikes for a mass stoppage of the whole industry—in short, partial disintegration of a coalition, at least so far as strikes are concerned. By contrast, the ability to mount a companywide strike is the central tactical argument for a coalition itself.

Fortunately, there is a way out of this dilemma. On the railroads, a selective strike already involves an entire company rather than a subdivision thereof. Within the struck carrier, there is no counterpart to the substitute plants of the multiplant manufacturer. In consequence, the UTU is already in a position to impose companywide strikes upon as many carriers as it chooses, to the same effect as that arduously sought by an industrial coalition in pursuit of simultaneous expiration dates for its separate contracts. Accordingly, the carrier's normal revenues can be completely cut off. If it stands out for any length of time, its losses can be enormous and it will also run the risk of a permanent loss of some customers.

Thus the proper comparison is not between an industrial coalition against a single multi-plant employer and selective striking of separate railroad companies. Rather it lies between a coalition against all companies in a given industry and one directed against a single employer alone. Perhaps, then, to paraphrase Karl Marx, to the multi-plant industrial employers the railroad case presents "the image of their own future," just as England was supposed to do for the other less developed industrial countries of the 19th century. With dialectical inevitability the movement of bargaining history may well be from the plant locus of negotiations to the entire company, and finally from the entire company to the entire industry. And once the goal of multi-employer bargaining is attained, then divide-and-conquer tactics—that is, selective striking—become the next order of business. And if industrywide bargaining of this type becomes widespread, then we would have a change of quantity becoming a change of quality, again in Marxian dialectical fashion. Can the system of organizational *laissez-faire* that we call free collective bargaining survive this kind of evolution? I defer this question until later. Meanwhile I want to refer briefly to the judicial reasoning by which selective railroad strikes were upheld.

Between 1969 and 1971, a manning dispute existed between the carriers and four railroad unions. The issue involved "national handling" in that it embraced the regional associations that bargain jointly for some 170 carriers. National handling, as Herbert R. Northrup has pointed out in an outstanding recent paper, is a requirement sought successfully by the railroads themselves in the thirties to overcome their vulnerability to whipsawing tactics under the earlier more decentralized bargaining systems.[7] In the case at hand, three of the unions settled, but the UTU held out. After bargaining had gone to an impasse and the procedures of the Railway Labor Act had been exhausted, the union began a series of strikes against selected properties. The carriers responded by seeking injunctions. In the *Delaware and Hudson* case they were successful, but met reversal in the Court of Appeals. In *Burlington Northern,* the lower court denied their request.[8]

Both cases rest on the same line of reasoning. First, the courts held, where a dispute begins under national handling, both parties remain obligated to keep negotiations at that level, and to settle on a multi-carrier basis. On the precedent in *Atlantic Coast Line,* both "practical appropriateness" and "historical experience" so dictate.[9]

Second, so long as the union seeks only to bring pressure to bear upon the whole carrier group on behalf of a joint settlement, and not to coerce the individual struck properties into making separate settlements, it is legally free to employ its basic right to strike in a selective manner. Essentially this is a matter of good faith. It cannot be decided beforehand, as the lower court attempted to do in *Delaware and Hudson.* Therefore an anticipatory injunction was inappropriate. Furthermore, the Appellate Court chose to believe the UTU President, Charles Luna, when he declared that his purpose in striking selectively was only to bring pressure to bear toward a national settlement, and not to extract separate agreements for the struck properties.

Third, the carriers are not without weapons in their own defense. They can impose their own work rules unilaterally, and they can resort to a nationwide lockout if they wish.

By these findings, the Appellate Court rejected the contentions of the carriers: that they are extremely vulnerable to whipsawing because they are weak financially and because they cannot produce for inventory; that the unions respect each other's picket lines and can easily close the roads down; that the railroad strikers can draw unemployment compensation paid for entirely by the company; and that the majority cannot reasonably be expected to yield to a pattern achieved on one property alone, under conditions of extreme inequality lying against the employer.

There can be little doubt that these rulings strengthen the position of the unions against the carriers. To combat whipsawing, the latter must risk a total shutdown at costs they can no longer easily absorb. They also risk ensuing congressional intervention, with politically dictated settlements that, if the Railroad Signalmen's case is typical, are likely to increase their burdens even further.[10] I also share Northrup's view that in addition to representing the most complete form of government control of collective bargaining now present in the country, the Railway Labor Act discourages voluntary settlements, rewards intransigent behavior, and perpetuates obsolete rules and work practices.[11] If this is typical of full-scale government intervention, then its extension indeed bodes ill for the survival of collective bargaining itself.

Yet, at the same time, I have to say that as these selective strikes eventually worked out, they yielded an almost unheard-of novelty in the dismal record of the railroad industry: a dispute that was allowed to run its full course without government intervention to bail out the intransigent party, but instead with a voluntarily negotiated settlement that includes some built-in provisions for resolving surviving issues. Compared with experience since 1941 under the Emergency Board procedures and subsequent interventions, this consummation is indeed as welcome as it was unexpected.

III. Inflation and Relative Bargaining Power

We have arrived now at the point where we ought to stand back and take stock before looking further into the question of changes in relative bargaining power in the economy. First, I contend that the right way to view the coalition movement is as an attempt to introduce the bargaining systems of basic steel and automobiles to a group of large companies that by chance rather than design emerged three decades or so ago with localized and fragmented rather than centralized and consolidated bargaining arrangements. The number of these concerns and their relative importance for aggregate production and manpower are not large. But if their systems eventually can be centralized, this will contribute significantly to the problems now confronting our general policy of relatively unhampered collective bargaining. Under that policy, some strong national unions have already emerged. If the efforts of coalition succeed, these organizations will grow even stronger. With this increase in strength, their political influence will also expand.

This leads me to my second point. The wave of inflation that set in early in 1965 has already seriously tilted the balance of bargaining power against management and toward the unions. In general impact, it has released the considerable potential of collective bargaining as an independent source of inflation of its own. It is in this context that the New Economic Policy of August 15 should be interpreted.

NEP is an incomes policy for the United States. In fact it is the second one attempted in peace time, the first having been introduced in 1962 and killed by the airline strike settlements of 1966.[12] Both versions involve guidelines. Both include prices along with wages. Both are attempts to restrain the use of market power by sellers, in particular the power of unions to raise wage costs through collective bargaining. And, finally, neither version contemplates any direct attack upon the sources of this market power. Rather, both of them aim only at restraint in the exercise of that power.

The only way that one can rationalize the 90-day wage-price freeze together with the subsequent creation of the Pay Board and Price Commission is to assume that the country now suffers from sellers' inflation, in particular, wage-push by the trade unions. In turn this implies a shift in relative bargaining power that for now at least cannot be adequately controlled by the indirect method of fiscal and monetary restraint alone.

General inflation contributes to excessive increases in wages through collective bargaining because it reduces the costs of larger demands to the unions at the same time that it lowers the costs of larger settlements to the employers. On the union side, the threat of ensuing layoffs is lowered; it is easier for men to quit and to get another job quickly; and rank-and-file militancy is increased by a rising cost-of-living, and, initially at least, higher profits. To management, it is more costly to take a strike and an excessive quit rate than it is to settle largely on the union's terms and then to recoup through higher prices without fear of reduced sales. In this way inflationary expectations develop for both sides, finding recurrent expression in ever larger wage settlements and price scales. Once started, the process becomes extremely difficult to check by the indirect method of fiscal and monetary restraint, not because the method will not work but because political considerations forbid its exercise to the possibly drastic degree required. Before August 15, 1971, this approach was in fact working slowly in the right direction. However, the fatal combination of some continuing inflation with relatively high continuing unemployment was more than the community seemed prepared to accept for much longer. In short, the old policy had lost popular support.

The current inflation had its inception in the beginning of 1965, when plenty of slack existed in the economy, both in plant capacity and in manpower. As both the money supply and public spending were rapidly expanded, the wage and price levels entered their sustained rise and inflationary expectations began to be built up. By this time the economy was undergoing an inflation based upon excess demand. As we can expect with excess demand, profits were strongly inflated as well. But by 1970 the period of excess demand had been passed and excess resources had reappeared. At the same time, corporate profits had been declining sharply since 1968. Although fiscal and monetary restraint were now the order of the day, general price inflation continued, interest rates soared, and the cost of wage settlements continued to rise. Thus we entered the period of "stagflation," that is, an inflation without excess demand in which there exists a substantial margin of unused resources and little or no growth in real output. The situation is rather like that of 1957-60. It has also been experienced recurrently in Great Britain ever since World War II.

At this point, the question of relative bargaining power comes up once more and some observations are in order. Cost-push inflation is primarily wage-push inflation. Its cause cannot be product-market monopoly because final price mark-ups have not been widening as this notion requires. Quite the contrary. Mark-ups must have been shrinking, because profits have been falling for over three years although output has been slowly rising. Thus we have to look specifically at wage costs as the source of the trouble.

What has been happening is that increases in the costs of compensation in 1970 alone, for example, were averaging 7 percent in the private sector; output per manhour (labor productivity) was advancing on average by only 1.0 percent; and unit labor costs accordingly were edging upward by about 6.0 percent. In short, these higher costs were being passed through to prices at mark-ups that themselves were slowly contracting. Finally, for the collective bargaining sector in 1970 the mean annual rates of increase for union wage settlements were running at over 10 percent throughout all industry, at between 15 and 21 percent in construction, and at over 8 percent in manufacturing. That is why the present situation can be attributed to wage-push inflation.

Now the mechanism by which the union sector of the economy serves as the pace-setter for wage-push inflation over the system is complex and cannot be examined here.[13] At the same time, it must be emphasized that this peculiar kind of inflation cannot emerge without an initiating impulse from excessive expansion of money. Nor can it continue indefinitely without renewed monetary expansion. Money, in short, remains the root of the inflation problem. Here again the mechanism is complex and cannot be considered. For present purposes, all that need be said is that inflations begin with the mismanagement of money by governments. Let the process persist and the inflationary expectations will become general. If, now, monetary restraint is introduced to check the inflation, it will take considerable time to become effective—all the more so if the inflation has been running for several years, as this one has. Meanwhile, during this lag before monetary slack is taken up, the accumulated force of wage-push begins asserting itself with increasing vengeance, prolonging the general rise of prices well after money restraint has taken over. This is the situation in which the NEP system of direct control has been introduced.

Just as the freeze can have brief effectiveness for dampening inflationary expectations, the control apparatus of Phase II can contribute to the same end for a short period. But the success of the Pay Board, for which we all hope, will depend upon that Board's ability to influence specific settlements. For, as Gottfried Haberler has pointed out, it is these individual settlements and not the wage level as a whole that are the controllable policy variable. Furthermore, the Board's success will also depend upon the continuing support of fiscal and monetary restraint. Without such restraint, we would find ourselves in a period of suppressed inflation, which is the worst of all economic worlds.[14]

Whatever one's view of the effectiveness of peacetime direct controls with sanctions, their introduction is a symptom of a loss of faith in the ability of relatively unregulated labor and commodity markets to produce wages and prices compatible with non-inflationary full employment. Thus the central question of the hour is: Will these controls ultimately disappear, or will they be extended and made permanent? To this I have no answer, only a closing comment.

The theme of this paper is changes in relative bargaining power and their significance for the survival of collective bargaining in the 1970's.[15] Collective bargaining has emerged as an institution over the years as part of what Clark Kerr once called the "system of liberal pluralism," or what Theodore Lowi more recently has termed "interest-group liberalism." [16]

However described, pluralism views modern society as a collection of independent groups—in our case, unions and employing companies—no one of which is dominant and all of which function under a government of limited powers. For the labor market, the basic premise is organizational *laissez-faire*. That is, the state sets the rules of the game. The parties are then left free to make their own private bargains. Above all, the key underlying assumption is that this bargaining struggle will produce a socially and politically acceptable economic equilibrium, compatible with sustained growth and non-inflationary full employment.

It is this system of self-equilibrating countervailing power that is now threatened by the several tendencies we have been considering. Are we about to enter an age of what we may call the socialism of interest-groups, or will we return eventually to the economy of private bargains in due course? That is the central economic issue for today.

NOTES

1. George H. Hildebrand, "Cloudy Future for Coalition Bargaining," *Harvard Business Review*, Vol. 46 (November-December 1968), pp. 114-128. My colleague, Professor Frederic Freilicher, has been most helpful in discussions of coalition bargaining and selective striking.

2. AFL-CIO Joint Negotiating Committee for Phelps Dodge v. Phelps Dodge Corp., 184 N.L.R.B. No. 106, 74 L.R.R.M. 1705 (1970). *See also* the Report of the Trial Examiner in Kennecott Copper Corp. v. United Steelworkers of America, 176 N.L.R.B. No. 13, 71 L.R.R.M. 1188 (1969).

3. Standard Oil Co. of Ohio, 137 N.L.R.B. 68 (1962).

4. American Radiator & Standard Sanitary Corp., 155 N.L.R.B. 69 (1965).

5. Libbey-Owens-Ford Glass Co. v. United Glass and Ceramic Workers of North America, 169 N.L.R.B. 2 (1968). *See also* Libbey-Owens-Ford Co. v. McCulloch, 67 L.R.R.M. 2712 (1968); and McCulloch v. Libbey-Owens-Ford Glass Co., 68 L.R.R.M. 2447 (1968).

6. Libbey-Owens-Ford Glass Co. v. United Glass and Ceramic Workers of North America, 189 N.L.R.B. No. 139, 76 L.R.R.M. 1806 (1971).

7. Herbert R. Northrup, "The Railway Labor Act: A Critical Reappraisal," Industrial and Labor Relations Review, Vol. 25 (October 1971), p. 9. This article is reprinted in Part IV (A) of this volume.

8. Delaware & Hudson Railway v. United Transportation Union, 76 L.R.R.M. 2898 (1971); United Transp. Union v. Burlington Northern, Inc., 76 L.R.R.M. 2838 (1971).

9. Brotherhood of Railroad Trainmen v. Atlantic Coast Line Railroad Co., 66 LRRM 2115 (1967).

10. The Signalmen were offered and rejected a pattern accepted by other unions, and instead went on a brief strike in May 1971. Congress intervened statutorily to end the strike; in doing so, it imposed a 13.5 percent retroactive wage increase upon the carriers, while doing nothing whatever about proposed legislation to improve the handling of emergency disputes. Thus the union gained a 13.5 percent increase as a reward for its irresponsible act. (Northrup, as cited, p. 14.)

11. *Ibid.*, pp. 29-31.

12. The previous policy carried no sanctions other than "moral suasion."

13. See George H. Hildebrand, "Structural Unemployment and Cost-Push Inflation in the United States," in George Horwich, ed., *Monetary Process and Policy: A Symposium* (Homewood, Ill.: Richard D. Irwin, 1967), pp. 15-29.

14. Gottfried Haberler, *Incomes Policies and Inflation: An Analysis of Basic Principles* (Washington: American Enterprise Institute, 1971), p. 24.

15. Unions and managements as such of course can survive without collective bargaining in a new environment of direct government controls, where political influence and bargaining would take over.

16. Clark Kerr, "Industrial Relations and the Liberal Pluralists," *Proceedings of Seventh Annual Meeting of Industrial Relations Research Association* (1954), pp. 2-17; Theodore Lowi, *The End of Liberalism: Ideology, Policy, and the Crisis of Public Authority* (New York: W. W. Norton, 1969).

PART II

COLLECTIVE BARGAINING AND REGULATORY MECHANISMS

The Viability of NLRB Regulation in the Future

John H. Fanning †

In the lexicon of administrative law, as in the title of these remarks, the National Labor Relations Board is frequently described as a "regulatory agency." This is somewhat misleading. The Board does not regulate, at least in the traditional sense. It decides specific cases that someone else initiates and enforcement comes from the courts, not the Board. When Congress decided in the mid-1930's that collective bargaining ought to be encouraged, it set up an agency with two major functions: (1) to conduct elections among employees under certain statutory standards for the purpose of selecting or rejecting a bargaining representative; and (2) to entertain and adjudicate charges that certain unfair labor practices have been committed.

This has been the Board's work for 36 years, and the viability of the Board now and in the future must be evaluated by how it has responded to the problems presented to it, whether it be the controversy and opposition of 1935 when the NLRB was an experiment, or the increasing maturity and high sophistication of labor-management affairs in 1971 or the unpredictability of 1980. We stand between labor and management and that insures that we have not been and cannot become an agency so encrusted with tradition that we will stop moving with the times.

The impact of the Board on labor-management relations derives not only from the substance of its decided cases; equally important are the efficiency and creativity of procedures designed to meet the dynamic needs of a new industrial world. Over the years, Congress has recognized the changing needs of a vital NLRB. In 1947, Taft-Hartley not only added the wholly new category of union unfair labor practices, but also changed significantly the internal structure of the Board, and set up the office of the independent General Counsel. In 1959, the Landrum-

---

† John H. Fanning, Esq. has been a Member of the National Labor Relations Board since 1957.

Griffin amendments made further substantive changes in the Act the Board administers, and also established the rights of union members in their unions, which are not, generally, within our province.

So that is one answer to the viability of Board regulation. As major changes in society have occurred, and the balance of forces in labor-management relations has changed, Congress has dealt with the problems it perceived by enacting remedial legislation.

But even though that is so, legislation does not settle all issues, or, if you like, every law, particularly in a field as controversial as labor relations, presents a new set of problems. The solution of those problems, the attempt to divine, from legislative history, what Congress would have done about some new wrinkle, the adaptation of legislation to conditions that keep changing, all these things are what the Board does, and has been doing, and my thesis, if that is not too pretentious a word, is that the best way to judge how the Board is going to fare in the years ahead is to consider what it has done up to now in some areas.

The 36 years of the Board's life have been far from uneventful. The Board began in the days of the greatest depression in history, when many sober observers thought the structure of the economy was in danger of collapse. We have fought World War II, and in Korea and Vietnam. We have seen the birth of the atomic age, the rise of automation, and the profound effect of the human rights revolution. Through all this, six Presidents of the United States have made their appointments to the Board. And while this is a government of laws and not of men, it is not possible to believe that these Board members have not come to their tasks with a varying awareness of the problems of the world that has been reflected in their reactions to the problems they faced on the Board.

To put it a little differently, the Board is not an ivory tower. True, we do not see the client, and we are not in the bargaining room. But the very nature of our process insures that the cases that come to us represent the sore spots, or perhaps, the growing points, in the labor-management relations structure. Just as happy marriages are not seen in the divorce courts, we do not see the peaceful situations where everything is working well. Ninety percent of the new cases which come to us every year are disposed of amicably at the local level by our field staff under existing Board precedents, guidelines and persuasion. And I suppose the fact that employees, their unions, and employers are coming to us in such large numbers—and continuing to increase at the rate of 5 percent per year—is some evidence that a lot of people think the Board is a viable and effective institution.

There are hundreds of thousands of issues that are resolved by the parties under contracts negotiated under our system and containing appropriate grievance procedures for the resolution of most of the disagreements arising between the labor-management signatories. More than 100,000 collective bargaining contracts a year are entered into in some part because we exist. This is also part of the viability picture.

Before considering specific representation and unfair labor practice doctrines, I want to touch on something basic to all cases —jurisdiction. The Board's jurisdiction is as broad as the commerce power. But the Board has never exercised that power to the utmost. Budgetary limitations make it necessary for us to choose. In the exercise of that choice, we have set dollar standards, which have changed as the times changed, although Congress has now limited our power to do that [1]—another instance of how Congress and the Board interact to establish policy. The Board has also chosen not to assert jurisdiction over certain classes of enterprise. However, that too can change in response to changes in society. Thus, when the Board decides to assert its powers over private hospitals and nursing homes,[2] non-profit colleges and universities,[3] and the sport of professional baseball,[4] it is making available to all those sectors of society the remedies of the Act, and providing a channel for the peaceful and orderly settlement of possible conflict.

Now, let me start with representation cases, a field sometimes treated like a poor relation. And yet, although representation cases may not seem to offer the intellectual challenge of some unfair labor practice issues, they are of crucial importance. The Board conducts about 8,000 elections every year, and most are run without incident because of our success in establishing, over the years, a proper environment for them. We have conducted more than 200,000 elections during our existence in which more than 26,000,000 voters cast a peaceful vote for or against representation. What a far cry from 1937 when there were more than 2,700 strikes for organizing purposes alone. Today four out of every five elections are conducted on an amicable basis by agreement of the employer and the union. Some evidence of viability, I would submit.

A basic question always has been when can an election be held at all, and for those cases where there is a bargaining relationship already established, our contract bar doctrines are central. If you read the text of the Wagner Act, you will not find any mention of contract bar. The Board is told only that it shall conduct an election if it finds that a question concerning representation exists. Faced with reconciling the equally important values of stability and change, the Board evolved contract bar as a way of effectuating the policies of the Act.

In the decade of the 1960's, the Board, in dealing with unit issues, realized that the criteria it had been applying were unduly restrictive. Accordingly, it stopped looking for perfection and sought instead to encourage collective bargaining by permitting the establishment of units that might not, perhaps, be the best possible, but which nonetheless afforded the possibility of effective collective bargaining. This flexible response led to the establishment of new and smaller units in cases involving insurance companies,[5] department stores,[6] and retail chains,[7] among others. Subsequent observation has indicated the Board was justified in rethinking its unit principles. Effective collective bargaining can take place in smaller units.

Similarly, the Board re-examined its craft-severance doctrines in the *Mallinckrodt* case.[8] This doctrine is another example of how Congress and the Board interact, since Section 9(b)(2) of Taft-Hartley, in dealing with craft severance, was a congressional reaction to the Board's *American Can*[9] decision, in early Wagner Act days. Thereafter, the Board took its first crack at interpreting Section 9(b)(2) in *National Tube*,[10] and tried again, with a different result, in *American Potash*,[11] and then reached *Mallinckrodt*, which is not necessarily the end of the road. Again, my point is not to consider which of these decisions is right. They all have elements of truth. The point, rather, is the Board's willingness to consider change and to effectuate it, when conditions warrant doing so. This, I think, is good and the real essence of the administrative or quasi-judicial process by which the Board conducts its business and discharges its statutory responsibilities.

So, too, in the conduct of election campaigns, the Board, becoming aware of the problem of communication in today's frequently dispersed industrial society, adopted its *Excelsior* rule,[12] requiring the employer to file with the regional director a list containing the names and addresses of all employees who are eligible voters in a particular election, which list is then made available to all parties.

Let me turn now to unfair labor practices. It has been said that the discriminatory discharge is the violation that goes to the heart of the Act, and there still are more violations of this nature than any other type of unfair labor practice. In fiscal year 1970, for example, about 3,500 employees received offers of reinstatement and some $5,000,000 in back pay pursuant to Board action. Although one may deplore the fact that after 36 years the statute still is violated so frequently with respect to such a fundamental right, these figures demonstrate to me the continuing human need for the Board as a guarantor to employees of the right to bargain collectively at that critical point in their lives when they may be seeking to exercise that right for the first time. And it is important, in these days of computerization, that there be a place where a man can be sure that he will be treated as an individual. No man thinks of himself as merely a statistic, and it is an essential of a viable legal system that justice should not only be done, but be seen to be done.

The unlawful refusal to bargain is an equally significant unfair labor practice. In the present state of labor-management relations, I think the developments in Board doctrine concerning refusals to bargain are especially suited to demonstrate the Board's ability to cope with change.[13]

The Act says only that it is a violation to refuse to bargain with the representative of the employees, and Senator Walsh's remark that we take the parties to the bargaining room and do not look at what happens there has often been quoted. But a long series of Board and court decisions has taken us far from there, and I want to consider a few of the more recent major steps in this area.

A bargaining relation has three major sections: how it is established, what is to be bargained about, how long it lasts. There have been interesting changes in all of them. In *Aiello*,[14] the Board held that a majority union, which participates in an election with knowledge of the employer's unlawful refusal to extend recognition and bargain, and loses that election, is precluded from filing Section 8(a)(5) charges based on the employer's pre-election misconduct.

In *Bernel*,[15] a later Board reversed that somewhat technical doctrine. The effect of *Bernel* was to produce a series of cases in which the Board was called upon to determine the reliability of the authorization cards forming the basis for the union's demand for bargaining rights—did the cards truly reflect a desire for union representation—as well as the motivation behind the employer's rejection of the union demand—did he in good faith doubt the union's majority status, or was his rejection of the bargaining demand a rejection of the collective bargaining principle, or a means of undermining the union's majority status. The Board grappled with these problems in many cases,[16] with varying results in the Court of Appeals, until some of the problems were resolved in *Gissel.*[17]

Some courts have had doubts about the authority of the Board to rely on authorization cards, in view of the Taft-Hartley withdrawal of Board authority to certify on a card check. The Supreme Court, although agreeing that an election would be the preferred way to determine representation rights—and the Board is of the same opinion—approved the use of cards and the Board's statement of its position on the validity of cards as set out in the *Levi Strauss* [18] case.

Perhaps the most important issue in *Gissel* is when is a bargaining order appropriate. The Court, noting that the Board had practically abandoned good-faith doubt as a test, dealt with the problem in terms of the severity of the interference with the election process and the amenability of those unfair labor practices to remedy by a conventional Board order. If the Board found that the unfair labor practices could be remedied, no bargaining order. If the Board found that on balance the possibility of a fair election rerun was slight, and the cards were a better indication of employee sentiment, then a bargaining order should issue.[19]

The teaching of *Gissel* on this issue has not been entirely clear, or easy to put into practice, and the Board's reaction to it has met with a mixed reaction in the Courts of Appeals. This problem is one that will be with us for a while, and may well reach the Supreme Court for further explication.

The basic bargainable matters appear in Section 8(d), added by Taft-Hartley, which speaks of wages, hours, and other terms and conditions of employment. In *Borg-Warner,*[20] the Supreme Court set out the fundamental distinction between mandatory subjects of bargaining, as to which a party may insist on its position to the point of impasse, and non-mandatory subjects, agreement on which cannot be made essential to the execution of a contract. It is obvious that these are all general terms.

Their meaning is not fixed and immutable, but has to be re-shaped constantly in the light of a changing economy and so-ciety. For example, as early as 1948, the Board decided that pension plans were a mandatory subject.[21] In 1969, society and the economy had changed to such an extent that the Board could decide that retired employees are employees within the meaning of the Act for the purposes of collective bargaining about changes in their retirement benefits, that bargaining about such changes is in any event within the contemplation of the statute because of the interest that active employees have in it, and that these benefits come within the statutory definition of bargainable matters.[22] This issue was argued before the Supreme Court in October and we should have our answer this term. [A decision was rendered on December 7, 1971 in the case of *Pittsburgh Plate Glass Co., Chem. Div.* v. *NLRB* in which the Supreme Court overruled the NLRB decision discussed above.]

The major development in bargainability is clearly *Fibreboard*.[23] There the Supreme Court held that the contracting out of unit work was well within the literal meaning of "terms and conditions of employment," and that therefore contracting out is a mandatory subject of collective bargaining. The Court did not purport to cover all forms of subcontracting, a term that has, as it noted, many meanings.

There has been criticism of *Fibreboard* on the ground, among others, that it interferes with management's right to manage, prevents employers from moving quickly to meet business con-tingencies, and requires the parties to engage in a futile exercise. I think that these dire predictions have not been fulfilled in the Board's subsequent decisions.[24] Possibly more objective evidence is found in a relatively recent study of subcontracting published by the Bureau of Labor Statistics of the Department of labor.[25] Taken in its entirety, that report demonstrates the ability of the parties in advance to establish ground rules for meeting the problem of subcontracting and also the practicability and utility of such negotiation. It eliminates many uncertainties on both sides and increases the stability of the labor-management rela-tionship.

It is important to note that *Fibreboard* requires bargaining not only about the decision to subcontract, but also about the effect of the decision on the unit employees. This is limited, how-ever, to those situations in which the subcontracting involves a change in prior practice or will result in a significant impairment of job tenure, employment security, or reasonably anticipated work opportunities for employees. In this connection, difficult problems have arisen as to the duty to bargain about a decision to close or sell a plant,[26] and I am certain there will be more for the Board to demonstrate its viability.

One of the matters that parties may bargain about is a grievance and arbitration procedure, something that has given rise to many problems at the Board, last explicated in the recent *Collyer* decision.[27] I cite *Collyer* not to discuss the merits of the decision. It may be right or wrong for the Board to decide to defer to arbitration. Obviously, since I dissented, I do not agree with the position of my colleagues, at least as I interpret it. But the important point here is that the Board has reacted and developed its doctrines in response to changes in the climate and structure of labor-management relations. There are cases before Taft-Hartley in which the Board has adverted to the possibility of the parties settling their disputes themselves.[28] But there was not much arbitration then. By the time the Board decided *Spielberg*,[29] in which it indicated the conditions under which it would accept an arbitration award as disposing of a dispute, the process was growing. With the stimulus of the *Steelworkers* trilogy,[30] arbitration achieved ultimate acceptance. That being so, the Board has a problem in deciding how to fit it into the scheme of things, bearing in mind that the statute still says that the power of the Board to remedy unfair labor practices is not to be affected by any other means of adjustment. Just what the accommodation should be is something that reasonable men may differ about—I am not to be taken as suggesting that my colleagues are unreasonable. Again, I repeat that the relevant point is that the Board is coping with new problems by rethinking previous patterns. Along the way there may be errors, but the willingness to rethink includes, of course, the willingness to correct errors.

From an arbitration clause comes another case—*Burns*[31]— which arose from the Supreme Court's decision in *Wiley*,[32] in which it was held that when a successor took over a business whose employees had been covered by a contract that included an arbitration clause, the obligation to arbitrate survived the termination of the contract, and devolved upon the successor even though he had not signed the contract. The Court reasoned that the right of the employer to rearrange his business or even eliminate himself from its operation must be balanced by protecting the employees from a sudden change in the employment relationship.

Wiley arose in the context of a suit to compel arbitration, and it could be argued, and was, that the Court was willing to bind a non-signer because of the strong policy considerations favoring arbitration. When the argument was made that *Wiley* required a successor employer to take over his predecessor's contract in its entirety, the Courts of Appeals split in their decisions.[33]

The Board decided the issue in *Burns* and held that an employer who is a successor is obligated to assume the labor contracts executed by his predecessor, and a successor employer can insist upon the union's adherence to the contract it executed with the predecessor employer. It is interesting to note that the courts of appeals have split in their reception of this development.[34] This issue also is pending before the Supreme Court and should be decided this term.

Many problems arise in this area. Obviously, who is a successor? And in what circumstances would it be inequitable to hold a successor to a prior contract? The recent *Emerald Maintenance* [35] case, which arose at an Air Force base, may be a portent of things to come.

There remains one more issue in connection with refusal to bargain. What is an effective remedy for a violation? Normally, a Board order is prospective only, and the employees have been, from the time of the unlawful refusal to bargain to ultimate compliance, denied the benefits of union representation, especially a contract providing for higher wages and fringe benefits. In *Ex-Cell-O*,[36] the Board decided that to make such an award would in effect be writing a contract for the parties. In view of the recent Supreme Court decision in *H. K. Porter*,[37] holding that the Board did not have the power, in any circumstances, to impose a contract clause that had not been agreed to, the Board held it could not grant this remedy, whatever its merits might be. So, as the Court noted, if Congress feels the Board should have this power, it is up to Congress to do something about it. The Board is very much aware of the need for more adequate remedies and is constantly striving to improve its remedies where the statute permits it, keeping in mind that the statute is remedial, not punitive.[38]

The cases I have discussed are not intended to be an exhaustive listing of the way in which the Board has adapted itself and its rulings to change. Because I have focused on refusal to bargain under Section 8(a)(5), there has been no discussion of union unfair labor practices; the great body of law under the secondary boycott provisions of the Act, the developing theory of fair representation, the union fine cases, coalition bargaining, the manner in which the Board has handled jurisdictional disputes—some 4,000 of which have been disposed of by Agency action since the Supreme Court decision in the *Columbia Broadcasting System* [39] case in 1961—all these are to be with us in the 1970's, and I suggest that the Board, having shown an ability to cope with complicated concepts and changing conditions, will be able to deal with these too, and others that may arise, if it has the time to do so.

This brings me to a consideration of the administrative viability of the Board—basically how efficient we are, or can be, in disposing of our workload. This issue is brought into sharp focus when you consider that in the ten-year period of 1960 through 1969 the Board was required to issue a little more than 6,000 initial decisions in contested unfair labor practice cases. In the same ten-year period, the Board was required to issue more than 6,200 decisions in representation cases. This, I think, is a significant record. At least equally important (and many would argue even more important) than cases resulting in formal decisions, however, are those which are adjusted amicably. These are the cases which never reach the Board in Washington for decision because the issues are settled by agreement of the parties under the guidance of the Agency's field representatives who have determined that the cases are meritorious. In the same ten-year period, the Agency was able to secure settlements in over 97,000 unfair labor practice and representation cases. Remedial action without litigation was secured in some 35,000 unfair labor practice cases and elections settled representation disputes in some 58,000 cases. An estimated additional 4,000 cases were withdrawn because the employer had recognized the union without an election. This must have facilitated collective bargaining and, in that part of our business, I am satisfied we are quite viable and expect to continue so.

But suppose that we had been unable to effectuate these settlements in just 10 percent of the cases and that another 3,500 unfair labor practice cases had reached the Board and required formal decision, or that another 6,000 representation cases had reached the Board for formal decision. Would we have been able to handle these cases and to give them the consideration they deserve? The median elapsed time in fiscal year 1970 from the filing of a charge to the issuance of a Board decision was 323 days. In 1950, it was 479 days. We have cut processing time by approximately 150 days in 20 years, despite the tremendous increase in workload to which I have alluded. And we have been able to increase the number of formal decisions issued by the Board in unfair labor practice cases to 840 in the last fiscal year, a new high. These accomplishments are a source of some gratification. But we cannot forget that the litigants in an unfair labor practice case still must wait almost 11 months for a Board decision in the median case.

In the complex economy in which we live today, labor-management disputes are rarely completely confined to the parties directly involved. They unquestionably ripple outward affecting uncounted and uncountable citizens and organizations in our society. It is vital, not only to the parties but to the public, that there be a forum to resolve these problems. It is even more important that that forum be able to operate on an efficient basis commensurate with its needs. We live in a fast-moving world. And unquestionably speeding up our decisional processes is more important than ever if we are going to keep up with the tempo of the 1970's, and an economy of 79,000,000 jobs.

In view of our constantly rising caseload, and I see no likely end to this, I think the problem of Board administration is likely to be the number one viability problem of the decade of the 70's. If it is solved, the entire administration of the statute will be improved, the processes of collective bargaining will be facilitated, the profit will be taken out of unfair labor practices, the incentive to violate the statute will be very much reduced, and our remedies will be more fully remedial. I say all of these things will be accomplished because time is of the essence in labor-management relations—decisional time so that the parties may then proceed after the Board has taken its action to make their own accommodations. Various concepts have been under consideration from time to time over the past decade. I cannot discuss all of them today, although I probably have commented on most of them during the past several years.[40]

In brief, I have supported a certiorari type review procedure in unfair labor practice cases which would permit the Board to delegate any of its functions, including those in unfair labor practice cases, to its Trial Examiners, with the Board retaining a discretionary right of review in the nature of a certiorari proceeding with two Members possessing the power to grant Board review. In practical terms, this would give greater finality to Trial Examiners' decisions subject to this right of review which is similar to that presently exercised by the Board in representation cases under the Landrum-Griffin authorized 1961 delegation to Regional Directors, the result of which has been to reduce processing time in representation cases to an average of about 43 days, at the present time, a drop of more than half the time required before the delegation. The existing system of judicial review would be retained regardless of whether the Board grantd or denied review in a particular case. The only changes would be internal to the Board. I also have urged making Board orders self-enforcing after a given period of time, say 30 to 45 days.

We have estimated that between 100 and 140 days could be saved under these new concepts, depending on whether a request for review was granted or denied by the Board and we believe that some of the game playing which now goes on to buy time would be eliminated. You must remember that the Board also is required to issue some 300 to 400 decisions each year in representation cases. These are cases referred to the Board by the Regional Directors for initial decision, or cases in which the Board has granted appellate review of Regional Director decisions. And, about 1,000 Regional Director decisions are appealed to the Board per year for review by it. Every day saved is thus important.

In summation, I believe that over the years the Labor Board has done a viable and commendable job of interpreting a controversial and difficult statute. Our success in the courts and the success of collective bargaining generally testify to that. I believe the quality of our decisions will withstand the judgment of time and the wear and tear of the bargaining table. Last year, for example, the Board was sustained completely in 74.1 percent of its decisions which were appealed to the Circuit Courts of Appeals. It was sustained with modification in another 12.4 percent. Its record of judicial enforcement has been consistently good, although I will admit that last year was a banner one. And so I have no fears regarding the decisional viability of the Board in the future.

I do have some concern with respect to our administrative viability. Hard work and efficiency can cope with an increasing workload only to a limited extent. If the Board continues to be the popular forum which it now is, some dramatic breakthrough in the handling of our business is going to be necessary. This may have to come in the form of legislative assistance which, I believe, is essential if we are to administer the statute as contemplated by Congress.

NOTES

1. See Section 14(c)(1) of the Act.

2. Butte Medical Properties, 168 N.L.R.B. 266 (1967); University Nursing Home, Inc., 168 N.L.R.B. 263 (1967).

3. Cornell University and Syracuse University, 183 N.L.R.B. No. 41 (1970).

4. The American League of Professional Baseball Clubs, 180 N.L.R.B. No. 30 (1970).

5. Quaker City Life Insurance Co., 134 N.L.R.B. 960 (1961).

6. Stern's Paramus, 150 N.L.R.B. 799 (1965); Arnold Constable Corp., 150 N.L.R.B. 788 (1965); Lord and Taylor, 150 N.L.R.B. 812 (1965).

7. Sav-On Drugs, Inc., 138 N.L.R.B. 1032 (1962).

8. Mallinckrodt Chemical Works, 162 N.L.R.B. 387 (1966).

9. American Can Co., 13 N.L.R.B. 1252 (1939).

10. National Tube Co., 76 N.L.R.B. 1199 (1948).

11. American Potash & Chemical Corp., 107 N.L.R.B. 1418 (1954).

12. Excelsior Underwear, Inc., 156 N.L.R.B. 1237 (1966).

13. This is not to suggest that there have not been significant developments under Section 8(a)(3). The line of cases that includes NLRB v. Erie Resistor Corp., 373 U.S. 221 (1963); NLRB v. Great Dane Trailers, 388 U.S. 26 (1967); NLRB v. Fleetwood Trailer Co., 389 U.S. 375 (1967); resulting in the Board's decision in The Laidlaw Corp., 171 N.L.R.B. No. 175 (1968), *enforced,* 414 F.2d 99 (C.A. 7) (1969), which considerably expanded the reinstatement rights of economic strikers, is clearly of major importance. So too is the basic change in the law of lockouts. *See, e.g.,* American Ship Building Co. v. NLRB, 380 U.S. 300 (1965); NLRB v. Brown, 380 U.S. 278 (1965).

14. Louis Aiello (Aiello Dairy Farms), 110 N.L.R.B. 1365 (1954).

15. Bernel Foam Products Co., 146 N.L.R.B. 1277 (1964).

16. These cases were decided under the principles enunciated in Joy Silk Mills, Inc., 185 F.2d 732 (C.A.D.C.) (1950) *cert. den.,* 341 U.S. 914 (1951), *as modified in* John P. Serpa, Inc., 155 N.L.R.B. 99 (1965), and Aaron Brothers Co. of California, 158 N.L.R.B. 1077 (1966).

17. NLRB v. Gissel Packing Co., 395 U.S. 575 (1969).

18. Levi Strauss, 172 NLRB No. 57 (1968). Note that none of the cases included in Gissel involved ambiguous, dual-purpose cards; the Supreme Court therefore expressed no opinion on how such cards are to be handled. I am inclined to think that the Board's earlier cases made clear to unions the need for explicit and unambiguous cards, and that that problem will no longer plague us.

19. Although this discussion assumes that at one point there was a valid union majority, the Court of Appeals for the Fourth Circuit has stated that in a case marked by sufficiently outrageous unfair labor practices, a bargaining order would be an appropriate remedy even if the union had never achieved a majority. NLRB v. Logan Packing Co., 386 F.2d 562 (1967). The Supreme Court appears to have left the point open in Gissel.

20. NLRB v. Wooster Div. of Borg-Warner Corp., 356 U.S. 342 (1958).

21. Inland Steel Co. v. NLRB, 170 F.2d 247 (C.A. 7) (1948), *enforcing* 77 N.L.R.B. 1 (1948).

22. Pittsburgh Plate Glass Co., Chemical Div., 177 N.L.R.B. No. 114, *enforcement denied*, 427 F.2d 936 (C.A. 6) (1970), *cert. granted*, February 22, 1971. (See Supreme Court ruling of December 7, 1971).

23. Fibreboard Paper Products Corp. The Board's second decision in this case, 138 N.L.R.B. 550 (1962), was affirmed at 379 U.S. 203 (1968).

24. *See, e.g.*, Westinghouse Electric Corp. (Mansfield Plant), 150 N.L.R.B. 1574; General Motors Corp., Buick-Oldsmobile-Pontiac Assembly Div., 149 N.L.R.B. 396 (1964), Supp. Dec. and Order, 158 N.L.R.B. 229 (1966), *reversed*, 381 F.2d 265 (C.A.D.C., 1967).

25. Bulletin No. 1425-8, April 1969.

26. *Compare* Ozark Trailers, 161 N.L.R.B. 561 (1966), *with* General Motors Corp., GMC Truck & Coach Div., 191 N.L.R.B. No. 149, 77 L.R.R.M. 1537 (1971). There appears to be no question about the duty to bargain about the effects of such a decision.

27. Collyer Insulated Wire, A Gulf And Western Systems Co., 192 N.L.R.B. No. 150, 77 L.R.R.M. 1931 (1971), Members Fanning and Jenkins dissenting.

28. Timken Roller Bearing Co., 70 N.L.R.B. 500 (1946).

29. Spielberg Manufacturing Co., 112 N.L.R.B. 1080 (1955).

30. United Steelworkers v. American Mfg. Co., 363 U.S. 564; United Steelworkers v. Warrior & Gulf Nav. Co., 363 U.S. 574; United Steelworkers v. Enterprise Wheel & Car Corp., 363 U.S. 593. All in 1960.

31. The William J. Burns International Detective Agency, Inc., 182 N.L.R.B. No. 50 (1970), *enforcement denied in relevant part*, 441 F.2d 911 (C.A. 2) (1971).

32. John Wiley & Sons, Inc. v. Livingston, 376 U.S. 543 (1964).

33. Wackenhut Corporation v. Plant Guards, 332 F.2d 954 (C.A. 9) (1964). *Compare* Steelworkers v. Reliance Universal, Inc., 335 F.2d 891 (C.A. 3) (1964).

34. *Compare* Burns, *supra*, *with* Ranch-Way, Inc., 183 N.L.R.B. No. 116 (1970), *enforced*, 445 F.2d 625 (1971).

35. Emerald Maintenance, Inc., 188 N.L.R.B. No. 139, 76 L.R.R.M. 1437 (1971).

36. Ex-Cell-O Corporation, 185 N.L.R.B. No. 20, 74 L.R.R.M. 1740 (1970).

37. H. K. Porter Company, Inc. v. NLRB, 397 U.S. 99 (1970).

38. *See* Fanning, "New and Novel Remedies for Unfair Labor Practices," 3 Ga. L. Rev. 256 (1969).

39. N.L.R.B. v. Radio and Television Broadcast Engineers (CBS), 364 U.S. 573 (1961).

40. "Legal Remedies Under the NLRA"—A paper presented to the Industrial Relations Research Association at its 23rd Annual Winter Meeting, December 29, 1970; "Significant NLRB Decisions in the 60's— And What They May Portend for the 70's"—A paper presented to the Labor Law Section of the Minnesota Bar Association, December 4, 1970. "Can We Make the NLRB Work More Effectively?"—A paper presented to the Twenty-third Annual Conference on Labor, New York University Institute of Labor Relations, May 25, 1970; "Current Issues Facing the NLRB—Evolving Law and Effective Remedies"—A paper presented to the Fifth Annual Labor Law Institute sponsored by Boston Bar Association and Boston University School of Law, March 7, 1970; "New and Novel Remedies for Unfair Labor Practices," *supra* note 38; "Procedural Reform—First Step Toward a More Effective National Labor Policy," 21 The Record of the Association of the Bar of the City of New York (1966).

The Need for New and Coherent Regulatory Mechanisms

Charles J. Morris[†]

The thesis of this paper is described by its title. It should be self-evident—but unfortunately it is not—that there is an urgent need for new and coherent regulatory mechanisms in the field of private sector labor relations, for it is a truism that labor law enforcement in the United States has become unduly complex and insufficiently reliable. Administration of the numerous federal labor statutes [1] is spread among a multitude of commissions, boards, courts and other bodies, and the jurisdictional lines which separate the various agencies and tribunals, and the areas of labor relations assigned to each of them generally overlap and often conflict.

I. The Case for Reform

Dissatisfaction with the administration of American labor law is, of course, a familiar story. It is accurate to report that almost all of the expert witnesses who have testified at recent Congressional hearings[2] which have focused on bits and pieces of the labor system have been critical of at least parts of the system and have complained about the manner in which existing enforcement mechanisms are now operating. True, there has been little, if any, agreement among the various interest groups as to what is primarily wrong and as to what should be done to alleviate the deep-seated problems. The most vocal criticisms of the way in which the procedures now function have come from both unions and management. Of course, their chief complaints are not the same.

A. Defects in NLRB Procedures.

1. *Delay and inadequacy of remedies.* Union spokesmen have tended to criticize the National Labor Relations Board primarily

---

† Charles J. Morris is Professor of Law, Southern Methodist University.

for its inability to process cases more quickly and to provide adequate and effective remedies.[3] These union spokesmen, often joined by distinguished labor law professors[4] and Labor Board personnel,[5] have supported such devices as giving the NLRB certiorari-type review over trial examiner's decisions and making NLRB orders self-enforcing. Such proposals, in my view, are at best only patch-work. It is doubtful that these proposals will pass Congress in the foreseeable future, but even if they were to pass, the source of the trouble would still remain; for as we shall see, the basic problem lies in the very structure of the system—in its dispersal of administrative authority and in its lack of concentrated judicial power.[6]

2. *Political swings in policy decisions.* Management spokesmen have been as critical if not more critical of the NLRB as have union spokesmen. But management criticism has most often centered on dissatisfaction with Labor Board decisions— the view being that the Board's policy decisions are attributable to the political complexion of the Board's membership.[7] Indeed, it is easily demonstrable that over the years, coincident with changes in political administrations, significant policy shifts have occurred in conjunction with changes in Board membership.[8]

There is considerable justification for the complaints which both unions and management have been voicing. It is true that the NLRB is inherently incapable of processing serious unfair labor practice cases with sufficient speed,[9] and it is a fact that the Board's remedial processes tend to be ineffectual. It is also true that the Board's policy decisions have tended to swing like a pendulum from one political administration to the next with stare decisis and predictability of decisions suffering accordingly.

There are many other serious procedural defects peculiar to the National Labor Relations Act. Most, if not all, of the shortcomings which I shall note here are also contributory factors to the Board's relative ineffectiveness and to its low level of acceptability.[10] It is my opinion that these defects are traceable to the basic structure of the Act's procedural mechanism and therefore are correctable only by radically altering that mechanism.

3. *Institutional unwieldiness.* Let us begin with one of the Board's most obvious defects: the institutional unwieldiness of the NLRB as an organization.[11] Unfortunately, wasteful duplication of effort seems to be inherent in the system. The time allotted for the presentation of this paper does not permit a

detailed recounting of how an NLRB case is handled from charge to enforcement. I can only remind you that the process contains much repetitious review and too much decision-making by anonymous and relatively invisible legal assistants. And the process is slow. Just how slow was revealed by figures which previous General Counsel Arnold Ordman supplied to the Thompson Committee last spring.[12] His charts indicated that for fiscal year 1970 the median elapsed time for the handling of a Section 8(a)(3) discharge—certainly not the most complicated of unfair labor practice cases—was the following: From filing to complaint, 55 days; from complaint to close of hearing, 61 days; from close of hearing to trial examiner's decision, 81 days; from trial examiner's decision to Board decision, 116 days; from Board decision to referral for enforcement, 44 days; from enforcement referral to filing of petition in the Circuit Court of Appeals, 243 days; and from filing of enforcement petition to the Circuit Court of Appeals opinion, 255 days. The total median days elapsed from filing of charge to issuance of a Circuit Court enforcement order was an incredible 855 days, or two years and four months.

4. *Absence of pre-trial discovery.* Another factor contributing to delay is the absence of pre-trial discovery. Its availability would shorten the time required for hearings and probably lead to fairer trials and settlements.[13] This has been the experience under the Federal Rules of Civil Procedure, and there is nothing peculiar to the law under the National Labor Relations Act which would suggest a contrary result.

5. *Unavailability of adequate equitable remedies.* Perhaps the most serious problem area in the Board's enforcement system is the unavailability of quick and certain equitable relief, in other words, temporary restraining orders and temporary injunctions, where and when needed and directly enforceable by the power of contempt. These are judicial remedies, and there is no direct means under the Constitution for an administrative agency to provide such remedies without an awkward reliance on judicial assistance. The absence of traditional judicial remedies has certainly encouraged violations of the Act. It is shocking that after 36 years, the largest segment of the Board's unfair labor practice business (in fact 68 percent) is still the discriminatory discharge.[14] The Board's performance has been so ineffectual that a prominent union attorney from the South, testifying recently before a Congressional committee, uttered this near heresy: ". . .

I have some tendency to believe that we need simply to abolish the National Labor Relations Board. . . . [I]t has come perilously close to being almost a fraud on the [unorganized] workers in our area." [15]

More meaningful remedies are required. And this is true for all types of unfair labor practices. For example, under the present practice when an order to bargain is finally issued in a refusal to bargain case, often after several years of frustrating litigation, the notice posted on the wall may seem hardly worth the effort. [16]

The tribunal which hears unfair labor practice cases should have authority to tailor-make equitable remedies early enough to preserve the vital positions of the parties. And this tribunal should also have sufficient remedial authority to provide certainty of enforcement. If these factors prevail, essential conditions for voluntary acceptance of the requirements of the Act will have been established, for if the mandates of the National Labor Relations Act are ever enforced with certainty and uniformity, the parties may stop playing games with the rights and obligations that the Act is supposed to guarantee.

6. *Unreviewable Power of the General Counsel.* Another serious procedural problem, one which many critics have tended to overlook or defend, [17] is the General Counsel's unreviewable power to determine whether a complaint should issue. Experienced labor law practitioners can usually cite numerous examples of meritorious cases which came to an early demise because the Regional Office refused to issue a complaint. Of course, no one really knows how many meritorious cases have been denied a hearing, for no one has yet undertaken the gargantuan empirical study required for a verified answer to that question. However, statistics in the Board's Annual Reports suggest that the number of meritorious cases for which complaints were denied may not be insignificant. But numbers alone may not be important if there are issues of Constitutional due process at stake.

The Annual Reports [18] show that approximately 85 percent of all unfair labor practice cases are disposed of prior to the complaint stage. Of the total cases filed, about two-thirds are found by the Regional Offices to be without merit and hence are dismissed or withdrawn. About 15 percent are settled by the General Counsel before complaint, therefore without the necessity of the charging party approving the settlement. Who is to say that the unreviewable decision of the General Counsel's office is always correct? Such decisions are often effectively made by lower echelon investigators and staff attorneys, who operate without the benefit of such elementary discovery devices as written interrogatories and oral depositions.

This problem of unreviewable discretion, whereby the charging party is never entitled to an evidentiary hearing and is never entitled to utilize discovery procedures himself, does raise, in my opinion, a substantial question of due process.[19] I hasten to make clear, however, that the appropriate response to the question is not to destroy the office of General Counsel, but rather to provide a viable legal alternative to the General Counsel's refusal to prosecute. The office of General Counsel, or one similar to it, is a most essential element in the statutory scheme if legal promises are ever to become realities for the groups intended to be protected. In fact, the office is so important that its jurisdiction should actually be extended—a point which I shall develop later.

7. *Conflict with the Arbitration Process.* Another conflict area, and the one which has been around the longest, involves the relation of NLRB action to the arbitration process.[20] In such cases, the Board may or may not choose to defer to arbitration, for the Board's power to make determinations in unfair labor practice cases is not affected by any other means of adjustment, including arbitration.[21] There is growing recognition, however, that the Board should exercise more restraint than it has previously shown in the issuance and processing of complaints that might be handled through the parties' own grievance and arbitration procedures. That seems to be the teaching of the Board's recent decision in *Collyer Insulated Wire.*[22] But even if the Board now chooses to adjust its receptivity to arbitration, such an effort at accommodation can be only palliatory because the Board has no direct control over the arbitration process and no responsibility for review under Section 301.

A more fundamental revision in procedure is required. Since arbitration of grievances concerning the application or interpretation of an existing collective bargaining agreement is favored by the national labor policy, as the Supreme Court most recently reminded us in *Boys Market,*[23] it would be desirable, and less destructive of established collective bargaining, for the tribunal which has jurisdiction in an unfair labor practice case involving arbitration and/or the interpretation of provisions in a collective bargaining contract also to have jurisdiction over any related Section 301 issue, including review of arbitration to the extent that judicial review is available.[24]

8. *Conflicts with Other Statutes and Other Tribunals.* Board jurisdiction is too often in conflict with other tribunals and other laws. Because unfair labor practice cases increasingly involve questions relating to enforcement and interpretation of collective bargaining contracts, situations which require an accommodation of arbitration awards and court decisions under both Section 301 of Taft-Hartley and Title VII of the 1964 Civil Rights Act have become commonplace. This conflict with Section 301 jurisdiction is but an additional dimension to the general conflict between Board action and the arbitration process which we have just noted.

It is deplorable that considerable amounts of time, money, and legal talent must be expended on the jurisdictional issues in these cases;[25] and yet, notwithstanding such efforts, the selection of appropriate forum is at best a Hobson's choice. At worst, it may be the wrong choice: An aggrieved party might obtain only an incomplete remedy, or even no remedy at all because he has chosen the wrong forum.

There are many types of cases which contain these incompatible elements of conflicting jurisdiction among separate forums. Unfortunately, no single forum can adjudicate all the issues or provide all of the relief. Elsewhere,[26] I have examined in detail several of these critical conflict areas, particularly in cases concerning union violations of the duty of fair representation,[27] cases concerning discrimination against minority employees, and cases concerning successorship in collective bargaining. Because of time limitations, but also because the problems are fairly well known and are documented elsewhere, I shall only note here, with as much emphasis as I can project, that these areas of conflict do exist, that they are so serious, and that they present formidable obstacles to the realization of the statutory objectives.

John Fanning has already mentioned the problem in the *Burns Detective Agency*[28] case. The Supreme Court, which has granted certiorari in *Burns,*[29] will soon grapple with the problem of collective bargaining successorship, where jurisdiction must somehow be divided, Solomon-like, among the NLRB, the arbitrator, and the courts.

A recent Sixth Circuit case, *Tipler v. duPont,*[30] illustrates the intolerable situation which prevails in discrimination cases involving Title VII. The court's opinion demonstrated that the present system cannot satisfactorily accommodate the doctrine of res judicata. The case involved an action for reinstatement and damages brought by a discharged employee claiming racial discrimination in violation of the 1964 Civil Rights Act. Previously, the employer had successfully defended against an unfair labor practice charge by the same employee regarding the same facts. Subsequently, the employer was hailed before the Equal Employment Opportunity Commission (EEOC) and then before the federal district court on the Title VII charge. Affirming the district court, the circuit court denied the employer's plea of res judicata and collateral estoppel, pointing out that although the NLRA and Title VII are not totally dissimilar "their differences significantly overshadow their similarities." [31] The appellate court had no other meaningful choice, considering the divided jurisdiction between the Board and the courts. Its decision meant re-trying the old facts under a new theory—an unsound practice which would have been obviated had the doctrine of res judicata been available.[32] This example is but one more situation, and not an unusual one, where the objectives of two separate laws could have been reconciled and better served if a single tribunal had jurisdiction to hear and determine claims arising under both laws.

The problem is getting worse, not better. In mid-November, 1971, the Board decided the remanded *Farmers' Cooperative* [33] case, finding that the employees were not discriminated against on account of their race or national origin. Under *Tipler,* this finding is, of course, not binding under Title VII. It would have been binding, however, if the same tribunal that had jurisdiction to decide unfair labor practices under the NLRA also had jurisdiction to decide cases under Title VII.

B. *Procedural Inadequacies among Other Agencies and Tribunals*

We have already noted some of the overlap between the National Labor Relations Board and other tribunals. It would indeed be a mistake to direct our analysis and efforts at reform only toward the NLRB. Private sector labor relations are also governed by other federal laws.

1. *Section 301.* At the present stage in our labor relations history, probably the most important statutory provision is Section 301 of the Taft-Hartley Act. All students of labor law are

aware that as a result of the Supreme Court's *Lincoln Mills*[34] decision in 1957 this Section became the fountainhead for development of a federal common law of the collective bargaining agreement. It was this common law which produced the *Steelworker Trilogy*,[35] which recognized and elevated the role of private arbitration to its high status as the primary mechanism for the settlement of labor disputes under collective agreements. And in *Boys Market*[36] it was this common law which adapted the strike injunction to a role in support of arbitration, notwithstanding the proscription of the *Norris-LaGuardia Act*.[37]

There is certainly a need for uniformity in the interpretation and enforcement of Section 301. I believe that this can best be achieved by channeling such cases into a judicial tribunal capable of establishing consistent rules of statutory application and uniform standards of procedure. And, as was previously noted in connection with unfair labor practice jurisdiction, it is important that such a tribunal also have jurisdiction to enforce other labor laws, so that by joinder of issues all related matters in dispute between the parties can be disposed of in a single action.

2. *Title VII of the 1964 Civil Rights Act.* I shall not take the time to elaborate the case for improved enforcement of Title VII. This has been the subject of Congressional hearings, and several bills now pending in the Congress are directed to the wholly inadequate enforcement system which now prevails.[38] I shall, however, note one area of conflict which is fast developing: the degree of accommodation which should be accorded grievance arbitrations when related actions are filed with the Equal Employment Opportunity Commission and the federal courts under Title VII.

Such a case was *Dewey v. Reynolds Metal Co.*[39] Dewey had been an employee who was discharged for refusing either to work on Sunday or to provide a replacement who would work on that day. He based his refusal on religious beliefs. A grievance was submitted to contractual arbitration, and the arbitrator found that Dewey's discharge had been justified under the collective bargaining agreement. Subsequently, Dewey requested the United States Office of Federal Contract Compliance (OFCC) to review his discharge and to find that it was based on religious discrimination. The OFCC found no basis for that charge, whereupon Dewey turned to the EEOC and submitted a charge with that agency claiming the discharge had been motivated by religious discrimination. The EEOC determined that there was reasonable cause to believe that the company had engaged in unlawful employment practices in violation of Title VII and authorized the filing of suit in federal district court. The district court ruled in Dewey's favor, ordering reinstatement with back pay and enjoining the company from requiring him to work on Sunday. The Sixth Circuit reversed, holding, *inter alia,* that by pursuing the grievance procedure under the agreement Dewey had made an election of remedies which thereby precluded his bringing an action in court. The court of appeals declared: "Where the grievances are based on an alleged civil rights violation, and the parties consent to arbitration by a mutually agreeable arbitrator . . . the arbitrator has a right to finally determine them." [40]

The Fifth Circuit in *Hutchings v. U.S. Industries, Inc.*[41] arrived at the opposite conclusion, holding that "[a]n arbitration award, whether adverse or favorable to the employee, is not per se conclusive of the determination of Title VII rights by the federal courts." Although the Supreme Court granted certiorari in *Dewey,* the conflict between contract arbitration and EEOC procedures remains unresolved, for the Court split four-to-four, affirming without opinion the Sixth Circuit decision. In early November 1971, the Sixth Circuit distinguished *Dewey,* holding in *Newman v. Avco Corp.*[42] that a discharged black employee's unsuccessful resort to contractual arbitration did not bar his subsequent action in a Title VII case. Although federal district courts already have jurisdiction under both Title VII and Section 301, a single judicial body charged with specialized jurisdiction over the major areas of labor relations would conceivably provide earlier resolution for the type of problem that the *Dewey, Hutchings,* and *Newman* cases illustrate.

The shortcomings in Title VII enforcement procedures are, indeed, serious. In particular, reliance on private litigation, except perhaps in pattern-of-practice cases, has meant that enforcement for some employees is difficult and for others it is non-existent.[43] Strong pressures are being exerted in Congress to improve these enforcement procedures;[44] however, the approach which seems to be most widely favored, giving the EEOC cease and desist power, would, if passed, trade one set of problems for another. If Congress should restructure the EEOC along the lines of the National Labor Relations Board nothing will have been learned from history. Even worse, setting up another independent agency, with jurisdiction overlapping that of the NLRB and the lower courts in such areas as contract enforcement and fair representation, would compound further an already chaotic jurisdictional system. With one more agency of narrow jurisdiction in operation, the state of affairs would be analogous to the six blind men touching and describing an elephant. The subject matter of employee relations would be even further fragmented into seemingly unrelated parts labeled *unfair labor practices, unfair employment practices, breaches of the duty of fair representation, contract grievances,* and *miscellaneous judicial actions for damages and injunctive relief.* A unitary system of enforcement which would interrelate these parts, and thereby identify and vitalize the elephant-like subject matter of the laws which regulate employee relations, would be a wiser course for EEOC reform to take.[45]

3. *Pension Plans.* Another area of developing and conflicting jurisdiction concerns employment pension plans. Such plans have long been subject to the mandatory bargaining obligation of Section 8(a)(5) of the NLRA.[46] However, such plans are primarily subject to the requirements of Section 302 of the Taft-Hartley Act. Substantial areas of jurisdictional conflict exist.[47] One such area concerns whether retired persons are "employees" for whom the employer must bargain collectively with the union about retirement benefits. The Supreme Court will shortly decide a case which contains that issue.[48] [The Supreme Court did, in fact, rule on this issue on December 7, 1971 in support of the Company's position.] The interrelation of the several statutes concerning employee pensions—not to mention the lingering impact of state law on this field [49]—suggests the advantage which might accrue if cases involving employee pension plans were concentrated in a single tribunal having jurisdiction broad enough to adjudicate all the related issues.

4. *Railway Labor Act Deficiencies.* The Railway Labor Act [50] is another statute which stands in need of reform. One of the infirmities from which that Act suffers is that its enforcement depends primarily upon local federal district courts even though limited areas are by law carved out for separate determination by the National Mediation Board,[51] by the various adjustment boards,[52] and by the Civil Aeronautics Board.[53] Just as the Tower bill [54] would give enforcement of the substantive provisions of the NLRA to the regular federal district courts, the RLA already confers similar jurisdiction on these trial courts, and the result is not a happy one.[55]

Another serious defect in the enforcement of the RLA is the absence of an officer comparable to the NLRB's General Counsel charged with prosecuting cases arising under the substantive provisions of the statute. Such an officer is especially needed to enforce individual employee rights, including rights involving breach of a union's duty of fair representation.[56]

Other deficiencies that relate to the administration of the RLA include the following: The National Mediation Board (NMB) is reluctant, or unable, to establish more realistic bargaining units, especially in the airline industry.[57] The hearing procedures, or absence of procedures in many instances, in NMB representation cases are less satisfactory than those which the NLRB maintains in representation cases under its jurisdiction.[58] Serious conflicts exist among various RLA tribunals in the determination of inter-union jurisdictional disputes. The mingling within the same agency of the NMB's mediatory role with its quasi-adjudicatory role, which it exercises in representation cases, hinders fulfillment of both roles. The cumbersome and fairly inflexible procedures which have been developed under the RLA contribute to the stifling of collective bargaining under that statute.[59]

It has become commonplace to criticize labor relations under the Railway Labor Act. Various reform proposals have been advanced.[60] However, the most serious problems under the existing statute stem more from inflexible and unwieldy administrative devices created by or developed under the statute than from any shortcomings in the substantive duties which the Act imposes. Therefore, when one considers the traditional attachment of both management and unions to the RLA, despite its shortcomings, it becomes apparent that procedural reform should be easier to achieve than outright repeal. But if it would be a mistake to create a new NLRA to enforce Title VII, it would be an even greater mistake to confer on the present NLRB Taft-Hartley Act coverage over railroads and airlines. There is nothing in the NLRB's record of coping with its present jurisdiction that would indicate a capacity for handling the sticky mess of collective bargaining problems which are common to the railroads and the airlines.

II. A Unitary System

The need for change within each of the major areas of labor law jurisdiction—not just one area—is great enough to suggest that enforcement as to each of these related statutory areas should be entrusted to a coherent and coordinated system. The devising of an appropriate unitary plan requires a delicate blending of judicial and administrative authority. Care must be taken to avoid Constitutional pitfalls in the task of separating judicial function from legislative and executive function. Fortunately, the Supreme Court in its 1962 decision in *Glidden v. Zdanok*,[61] which concerned the specialized United States Court of Customs and Patent Appeals, provided a strong foundation for the basic plan which is here advanced. It confirmed the constitutionality of a specialized court created under Article III, the judiciary clause, of the Constitution. Furthermore, the precedent of referees in bankruptcy acting as judicial officers[62] endowed with extensive judicial authority is analogous to the roles which commissioners will be expected to fulfill in the labor court which is proposed as part of the unitary system. I am entirely convinced that it is feasible to proceed along the lines suggested in this paper without running afoul of the Constitution. I can be more positive than that by stating that the proposed system will actually be more attuned to the division of powers assigned to the three great branches of the federal government than the present system. And it will also provide a greater measure of due process to the aggrieved parties.

Two years ago, I advanced the proposition of a program of procedural reform in labor law which had as its core a specialized Article III court.[63] That program, characterized as a "working hypothesis," was designed primarily for the administration of the Taft-Hartley Act and the Railway Labor Act, although the possibility of extending it to other related statutes, including Title VII of the 1964 Civil Rights Act, was noted.[64] Further study and reflection about that program have reconfirmed my view that development of a unitary system is the most logical way to achieve substantial improvement in both compliance and enforcement under the federal labor laws.[65] Moreover, further experience with Title VII, as indicated by the Congressional efforts to strengthen the procedural arms of the EEOC, demonstrates that it would be desirable to treat Title VII ills together with the older and more familiar ailments that have plagued the administration of the Taft-Hartley Act.

A case could be made for inclusion of enforcement procedures for other labor statutes such as the Labor-Management Reporting and Disclosure Act of 1959 (the Landrum-Griffin Act), the various wage and hour laws, the Age Discrimination in Employment Act of 1967, and the Veterans' Reemployment Act. However, the unitary system here proposed is designed initially for administration of the Taft-Hartley Act, the Railway Labor Act, and Title VII of the 1964 Civil Rights Act. The advisability of including additional statutes would be predicated on the relatedness of the subject matter of their coverage and on the premise that a unitary judicial system could provide a specialized forum ideally suited by experience and outlook to handle enforcement problems arising under interrelated laws. Their inclusion, however, might well await demonstration of successful administration of the three primary statutes within the proposed unitary system.[66]

The system which is proposed here recognizes that administration of public laws, that are designed primarily to protect employees, requires administrative action. Hence, certain administrative machinery should be retained, though modified. An administrative board can determine questions concerning representation (e.g., deciding appropriate bargaining units or conducting elections) better than a court. And an administrative general counsel, or public prosecutor, should be available to furnish investigatory and prosecutory services. But a court is needed to provide a judicial forum and a strong judicial process. These are the administrative and judicial elements which, in combination, comprise the unitary system.

Stated briefly, the system would consist of a constitutional court with jurisdiction over the enforcement of the substantive rights and duties contained in the Labor-Management Relations Act, the Railway Labor Act, and Title VII of the 1964 Civil Rights Act. As I have noted, additional jurisdiction could be added later. The court might appropriately be called the United States Labor Court. Complementing this judicial structure would be a revised administrative structure. With regard to the three named statutes, a merger of both personnel and function of the existing agencies would produce two new agencies and a new office for investigation and prosecution:

1) The representation functions of the National Labor Relations Board and the National Mediation Board would be combined for handling within a single board, which could be called the National Labor Representation Board—a new NLRB.

2) The mediation functions of both the National Mediation Board and the Federal Mediation and Conciliation Service would

be merged into a single mediation agency, which might be called the National Mediation Service—the NMS.

3) The General Counsel of the NLRB would be retained, but the scope of his jurisdiction would be expanded to include authority to investigate, issue complaints, and prosecute actions under the Railway Labor Act and Title VII as well as under the NLRA. This additional authority would not require merger of function or personnel for any agency under the Railway Labor Act, though a merger of the Equal Employment Opportunity Commission and its regional offices with the office of the NLRB General Counsel and the regional offices of the National Labor Relations Board would be required. The new office would also assume the pattern-of-practice function of the Justice Department in Title VII cases. By virtue of his expanded jurisdiction, the holder of this new office should perhaps be called the General Labor Counsel—a more accurate identification of the broad functions of the proposed new position.

III. Components of the Unitary System

A. *The United States Labor Court*

1. *The Three Primary Labor Statutes.* The jurisdiction of this Article III court would cover the enforcement of rights and duties under the three primary labor statutes, the Labor-Management Relations Act, the Railway Labor Act, and Title VII of the 1964 Civil Rights Act, but it could also cover other statutes.

Jurisdiction under the LMRA would include not only unfair labor practices under Section 8 of the NLRA [67] but also Sections 208,[68] 209,[69] and 210 [70] (the provisions relating to fact-finding and injunctions in national emergency disputes), Section 301 [71] (the provision for judicial enforcement of labor agreements), Section 302 [72] (the section relating to restrictions on payments to employee representatives), and Section 303 [73] (the secondary boycott damage suit provisions). Jurisdiction under the Railway Labor Act would be essentially the same as that now exercised by the regular United States District Courts. In like manner, jurisdiction under Title VII would also be transferred from the regular federal district courts to the United States Labor Court.

2. *Judges.* Inasmuch as the new court would be organized under Article III of the Constitution, its judges would have life

tenure and would be appointed with the advice and consent of the Senate. These appointments could pose a serious problem of political imbalance if made all at the same time or if all or most of them were made by one President.[74] Such an imbalance might be avoided if the appointments were spread over three presidential terms. These incremental increases in the number of judges would also be matched by corresponding incremental increases in the court's jurisdiction. A timetable that might achieve considerable political balance in the initial appointments, and also provide for a gradual transfer of jurisdiction from the tribunals of original jurisdiction while the court gains in both size and experience, is here suggested.

A court of thirteen judges is proposed. The number is arbitrary. It is based on sheer speculation as to how many judges would be needed; and the need would be contingent on how the court is organized, the extent to which it makes use of commissioners, and the amount of litigation which would be either generated or discouraged by the new system. The full complement of thirteen judges would not be attained for a period of from six to nine years, depending on the date of the enabling legislation in relation to the incumbent President's term of office. Only five of the judges would be appointed immediately. The next four judges would be appointed during the first year of the next presidential term, and the last four judges would be appointed during the first year of the following presidential term. The appointments—all subject to close senatorial scrutiny—would thus be made by two or three different Presidents. Since appointments would be national in scope, the political pressures at work would be oriented to the national rather than to the state or sectional level. This process could produce a bench of highly qualified judges from varying experiences and backgrounds.[75] Should the need for more judges later arise, Congress could of course authorize the appointment of additional judges.

3. *Acquisition of Jurisdiction. First Jurisdictional Stage.* The full statutory jurisdiction of the court would be acquired over the same six to nine year period during which judicial appointments are made. There are various combinations of statutory increments which could effect a reasonably smooth transfer of jurisdiction to the new court. One such plan is here offered. Immediate jurisdiction would be conferred over the principal statutory areas over which the United States district courts al-

ready have jurisdiction; *i.e.,* over Title VII actions, over enforcement of Railway Labor Act provisions, over actions under Section 301 of the LMRA, over the issuance of temporary injunctive relief under Sections 10(j)[76] and 10(l)[77] of the NLRA, and over enforcement of Sections 302 and 303 of the LMRA.

Pendent Jurisdiction. Notwithstanding these limits, the court could exercise pendent jurisdiction over any action which would ultimately be included in its regular jurisdiction.[78] The court, of course, would have complete discretion as to whether it would assert jurisdiction over the unfair labor practice charge, to avoid abuse by a party who might seek to extend jurisdiction through joinder of an unfair labor practice charge with a frivolous or minor claim under the court's direct and immediate jurisdiction. It is intended that during this initial jurisdictional period in the court's operations the National Labor Relations Board would continue to be the principal forum to decide unfair labor practice cases. Certain types of cases, however, would be especially appropriate for the exercise of pendent jurisdiction. For example, an unfair labor practice charge alleging that a union breached its duty of fair representation in failing to process a discharge grievance, thereby violating Sections 8(b)(1)(A), 8(b)(2), and 8(b)(3) of the NLRA, could and should be joined with a possible Section 301 action against the employer and/or a judicial action against the union. This should be done where a breach of fair representation is claimed and where the validity of the 301 claim depends, in whole or in part, upon a finding that the employer has violated the collective agreement. Pendent jurisdiction likewise would be appropriate in a Title VII case where possible unfair labor practices could also arise from the same fact situation.

Second Jurisdictional Stage. The court's second jurisdictional stage is reached with the appointment of four more judges. Statutory jurisdiction would then be expanded to cover the following sections of the NLRA: Section 8(a)(1) (relating to interference by employers with protected employee rights); Section 8(b)(1) (relating to union interference with protected employee rights); Section 8(a)(2) (relating to employer domination and support of labor organizations); Section 8(a)(3) (relating to discrimination in employment practiced by employers); Section 8(b)(2) (relating to union induced employment discrimination); Section 8(a)(4) (relating to protection of employees who file charges or testify under the Act); and Section 8(b)(5) (relating to excessive union initiation fees). These unfair labor practice sections primarily concern the individual rights of employees.

Third Jurisdictional Stage. The court's third and final jurisdictional stage [79] is reached when the last four judges are appointed. The court would then acquire coverage over the remaining provisions of the NLRA, which relate generally to the forms of unlawful activity that unions and employers might direct against each other rather than against employees. These include the unfair labor practices which are immediately concerned with operation of the collective bargaining process and use of economic weapons: Sections 8(a)(5) and 8(b)(3) (defining the duty to bargain collectively); Section 8(b)(4) (relating to secondary activity and jurisdictional disputes); Section 8(e) (proscribing "hot-cargo" agreements); Section 8(b)(7) (relating to picketing for organization and recognition); and Section 8(b) (6) (relating to "featherbedding").

None of the lines dividing the three suggested jurisdictional increments should be drawn too sharply, for the typical NLRB complaint case covers several unfair labor practice sections. During the court's early years it may be difficult to determine with precision whether some cases should be filed with the lame duck NLRB [80] or with the United States Labor Court. Guideline regulations would have to be devised.

4. *Organizational Structure and Method of Operation. Commissioners.* The court's method of operation should be organized for maximum efficiency consistent with judicial due process. It is contemplated that the court would make substantial use of commissioners who would act as hearing officers in most of the contested cases. Incumbent NLRB trial examiners would undoubtedly be eligible for selection as commissioners.

To a large extent the jurisdiction and duties of the commissioners would resemble that of referees in bankruptcy.[81] They would be invested, subject always to review by a judge of the United States Labor Court, with jurisdiction to hear cases, make findings, and issue orders. Like referees in bankruptcy, they would be appointed by the court and would serve as judicial officers.[82] Their appointments would probably be for terms of 6 or more years. A final order issued by a commissioner would be a final determination of the rights of the parties involved in the controversy, unless timely challenged by a petition for review to a judge of the court. Most, though not necessarily all, cases would be heard initially by commissioners. The court, subject to statutory requirements and guidelines, would determine its own organizational structure and method of operation.[83]

It may be assumed that the court's headquarters would be in Washington, D.C.; however, it should have authority to sit anywhere in the United States or its territories. Terms of court, with one or more judges and several commissioners sitting, would be held regularly in major metropolitan areas. The court would be empowered to sit and function through commissioners, as a single judge, in panels, or en banc. Either single judges or commissioners might act on pleas for temporary injunctive relief. Single judges would probably be assigned to jury trials in the limited classes of cases where a party would be entitled to a jury. In addition to the court's permanent judges, other federal judges would sit from time to time to aid in handling the docket. During the court's early years, before it acquires its full complement of permanent judges, it may be especially necessary to make regular and extensive use of judges borrowed from other federal benches. This practice of borrowing judges is not uncommon in the federal judiciary.

The congressional objective in the establishment of the court's structure should be to allow the court sufficient operational flexibility to achieve the most effective and efficient employment of both judges and commissioners, giving recognition of course to essential differences in their positions within the judicial system. Advisory councils of the labor bar would naturally be called upon to make recommendations for establishing rules of procedure and methods of operation. Inevitably, however, some trial and error will be essential in the development of an effectual plan of operation.

5. *Role of the General Labor Counsel. Unfair Labor Practice Charges: Public and/or Private Enforcement.* A key element in the proposed unitary system is that actions in the United States Labor Court could be initiated either by the General Labor Counsel (GLC) or by a private party. In most cases, however, the private party would have to give the GLC the first opportunity to bring the action. Initiating an action under the NLRA would be similar to the present practice. Under the new plan, when a charge is filed with the GLC it would be the responsibility of his office (acting as now through regional offices) to conduct an investigation; his office would then either dismiss the charge or file a complaint with the United States Labor Court, assuming no settlement had been effected. In the event of dis-

missal, the charging party could file and process his own case in court which is unlike the present procedure where the charging party has no recourse after the General Counsel refuses to issue a complaint.[84] Under the suggested plan, the GLC would have the right to intervene in any such action filed by a private party. This same procedure would be applicable to Railway Labor Act and Title VII actions.

Directly Filed Private Suits. All other actions of the type which may now be brought directly in federal district court, such as actions to enforce arbitration under Section 301 and actions for damages under Section 303, could be filed directly by the private plaintiff in the United States Labor Court. The GLC would have a right of intervention even in these actions if determination of the issue might affect the interpretation or enforcement of a law for which the GLC has prosecuting responsibility.

6. *Plenary Judicial Power. Orders and Remedies.* It is contemplated that within its jurisdictional coverage the new court would possess essentially the same authority, both legal and equitable, as any United States district court in the issuance of appropriate legal process, orders, and judgments. For example, the device of dismissal of a complaint for failure to state a claim upon which relief can be granted would be available to the court. Likewise, summary judgments,[85] temporary restraining orders, injunctions, and contempt orders, to name only a few varieties of orders, would also be available. The court's ability to tailor-make and effectively supervise its remedial orders sharply contrasts with the NLRB's lack of authority to exercise such remedial action. No changes with regard to the Norris-La Guardia Act[86] should be necessary, other than to effect a transfer of jurisdiction from the district courts and the courts of appeal so that the new court could issue injunctions now authorized by statute. The court would thus have injunctive authority under Sections 10(j) and 10(l) of the Taft-Hartley Act, after minor procedural adjustments are made to reflect the restructuring of the administrative-judicial relationship within the unitary plan. Substantial power already exists under the Railway Labor Act,[87] and under Section 301 of LMRA, to injoin strikes relating to arbitrable grievances under collective bargaining contracts.[88] Such jurisdiction would automatically be transferred.

Review of Arbitration and Adjustment Boards. Legislative changes in judicial authority to review adjustment board awards under the Railway Labor Act [89] and arbitration procedures and awards under Section 301 [90] are not contemplated. The present private and quasi-public systems for settling contractual disputes would not be superseded. Indeed, it is expected that these systems would be strengthened by the unitary approach. It is anticipated that the United States Labor Court's broad jurisdiction over both the collective bargaining process and the collective bargaining contract would stimulate the development of new and flexible remedies. For example, in an unfair labor practice proceeding under the NLRA the court would be able to require submission of an arbitral matter to an arbitrator while retaining jurisdiction for purposes of enforcing and/or reviewing the resulting arbitration award. The court could also refer or remand a question concerning representation to the new NLRB (National Labor Representation Board) for its determination when appropriate. The detailed mechanics of such referral and remand procedures will have to be worked out. It is intended for the court to have ample authority to fashion remedies which would more satisfactorily achieve the Congressional intent inherent in the three primary statutes than is now possible under the present system with its divided and inadequate powers.

Appellate Review. Much of the court's jurisdiction would cover matters which initially will have been submitted to subordinate tribunals—to arbitration, to an adjustment board, or to the NLRB for determining a question concerning representation. However, the court would possess original jurisdiction over such matters in a judicial sense, just as it would possess original jurisdiction over all other matters under its statutory coverage. Thus the courts of appeals would review representation or arbitration matters only in the context of appeals from orders of the United States Labor Court. This would represent no change in the scope of appellate review. All of the orders of the new court would be self-enforcing. A party to an action in the United States Labor Court would be entitled to appeal judgments and other appealable orders to a circuit court of appeals in essentially the same manner as an appeal is now taken from an order of a United States district court. No change is contemplated in appellate jurisdiction. It is intended that the present jurisdiction of the courts of appeals for each of the circuits be maintained. The continued scattering of appellate review among the eleven United States courts of appeals is calculated to produce a healthy cross-fertilization of judicial attitudes. This should counterbalance any tendency toward over-specialized expertise which might otherwise develop within a single court of original labor jurisdiction. Final reconciliation of differences among the circuits would naturally be the responsibility of the Supreme Court through the exercise of its power of certiorari.

B. *The General Labor Counsel*

1. *Functions.* The statutes under consideration were designed primarily to guarantee employee rights and protections. A federal administrative officer should be available to investigate charges of violations and to prosecute complaints under these laws. To leave their enforcement entirely to private litigation would be to overlook the public's interest in maintaining the labor relations system which was intended by Congress. Furthermore, private enforcement would mean no enforcement for substantial numbers of employees, especially those who are least able to protect themselves. And in private litigation too often the advantage lies with the party who can afford to hire the best legal talent, either the employer or the union, but rarely the employee. The need for a public prosecutor in many areas involving the public interest has long been recognized: Since its inception, the National Labor Relations Act has had a general Counsel; and the Fair Labor Standards Act has had a Wage and Hour Administrator who performs a comparable service. It is also commonplace for law enforcement to depend on both private litigation and governmental prosecution. This has been the pattern under the anti-trust laws [91] and, more recently, the pattern in school desegregation cases.[92] Under Title VII, the EEOC is authorized to investigate and conciliate; but judicial enforcement must depend on private suits,[93] except in pattern-of-practice cases where the Justice Department may bring the action.[94] Under the RLA, enforcement depends almost entirely on private litigation, although the scheme of that Act also provides for criminal penalties which theoretically could be enforced by the Justice Department.[95]

The proposed unitary system would create a new federal officer, here called the General Labor Counsel (GLC). He would have a threefold responsibility: To investigate charges of violations under the NLRA, the RLA, and Title VII; to attempt to achieve voluntary settlements of such charges; and to prosecute unsettled complaints which he deems meritorious. His role in the presentation of cases in the United States Labor Court, including his right of intervention in actions brought by private plaintiffs, has already been noted.[96] The GLC would of course handle appellate cases in the various courts of appeals. He would also join with the Solicitor General in the presentation of cases submitted for review in the United States Supreme Court.

2. *Organization and Personnel.* Under the proposed plan, there would be a merger of the personnel and function of the NLRB General Counsel (including the NLRB regional offices) and the Equal Employment Opportunity Commission (including its regional offices). Personnel might also be drawn from employees of the National Mediation Board since its representation function, particularly the holding of elections under the Railway Labor Act, would be taken over by the new National Labor Representation Board. It is anticipated that the regional offices of the GLC would assist the new NLRB in processing representation cases in much the same manner as present NLRB practice, where regional personnel, especially the regional directors, handle representation cases pursuant to delegation of authority from the National Labor Relations Board.[97] The basic structure and function of the NLRB regional offices would thus be preserved, though expanded in personnel and function to cover the additional duties under the RLA and Title VII.

The success of the GLC function is essential to the validity of the proposed unitary plan. The office of the GLC would be so designed as to have considerable administrative flexibility in the carrying out of the day-to-day operations under these laws. The GLC will look to the United States Labor Court—an arm of the judicial branch of the government—for adjudication and enforcement of contested cases. And it will be the responsibility of the GLC, pursuant to the orders of that court, to assist in achieving compliance with the court's orders and remedies.

C. *The National Labor Representation Board*

1. *Functions.* The National Labor Representation Board (also called the NLRB) would be expected to determine questions concerning representation under both the NLRA and the RLA. The representation functions of the present National Labor Relations Board and National Mediation Board would thus be merged. The new board should be equipped to operate representation and election procedures under both statutes with a reasonable degree of

uniformity even though the statutory language concerning representation—Section 2, Ninth, of the RLA and Section 9 of the NLRA—is different. Both allow for wide agency discretion in the determination of "appropriate bargaining unit" or "craft or class." There is no apparent legal reason why election procedures under both statutes could not be made substantially identical, provided the new NLRB should choose to make them so. Or the procedures might be different if this board were to find sufficient reason for making distinctions. This board should certainly be qualified to recognize basic differences affecting representation among various industries, or to apply differences which are spelled out in the respective statutes. The exercise of informed judgment and discretion are familiar functions in administrative law.[98]

2. *Delegation of Duties.* A single board should be able to operate with greater uniformity and improved efficiency as a result of the merger of personnel and certain functions of the present NLRB and NMB. As previously noted, the new NLRB would presumably also delegate to the new GLC and to personnel in his regional offices certain duties relating to the determination of union representation. The regional offices would thus continue to exercise responsibility in the field for both "C" (complaint) cases and "R" (representation) cases.

D. *The National Mediation Service*

1. *Consolidation of Mediation Agencies.* The unitary plan also carries over to the mediation process. The National Mediation Board, which performs various mediation duties under the Railway Labor Act,[99] would be merged with the Federal Mediation and Conciliation Service as to their corresponding duties and personnel. The new service, which is intended to be an independent agency, might be called the National Mediation Service (NMS). It would perform all of the mediation functions provided for by the Labor-Management Relations Act and the Railway Labor Act. It would also continue to assist parties to collective bargaining contracts in the selection of neutrals to serve on adjustment boards and as arbitrators.

2. *Strengthening the Role of Mediation.* The proposed change could strengthen the government's role in mediation. The voluntary nature of mediation and the absence of sanctions may well be its real strength.[100] The federal mediator has nothing to sell

but his good offices which consist primarily of his personal ability to persuade, to listen, and to suggest.[101] Whatever qualities he brings to the bargaining table, mediation services are often a catalyst in the process of making collective bargaining work. Although mediation procedures and the conditions under which mediation is invoked differ markedly under the LMRA and the RLA, the personalized nature of the job of mediating is similar under both statutes. A merger of the mediation functions of the FMCS and the NMB would provide an opportunity for both groups of mediators to share valuable experiences and techniques. A single agency would also provide a more centralized and uniform direction to the service. The new service would be of special benefit to collective bargaining on the railroads and the airlines—for the first time the mediation function would be separated from the quasi-adjudicatory function which the NMB also performs.[102] If mediators can confine their efforts to mediation, which the NMB as an agency presently cannot do under the RLA, their roles as neutrals might yield greater success in assisting the parties in reaching agreement.

IV. Conclusion

American labor law has come of age. It has arrived at a stage in its legal development where the nature of the need for change invites—though of course does not guarantee—an attitude of statesmanship among the various interest groups who participate regularly in the labor law process, i.e. unions, management organizations, minority groups, and public interest spokesmen.[103] Their common objective should be a joint effort [104] to achieve meaningful improvement in the administration and enforcement of existing labor laws in the private sector. I am mindful of the great odds against the formation of any program of togetherness among these diverse groups. However, within the procedural package presented here, there is perhaps enough mutual advantage to surmount innate suspicion, at least temporarily.

Let us not be afraid of the concept of a labor court. It should be obvious to us, as it is to many foreign observers, that the NLRB in the exercise of its unfair labor practice jurisdiction is in reality a court. But it is a court whose options for remedial action are severely limited. And this limitation is an Achilles heel. The debate about a labor court is thus not *whether* a court but *what kind* of a court.

This paper is a plea for realistic examination of the procedural fragmentation which characterizes the administration of federal labor law. It is a plea to use the administrative process wisely, to use it as a vital supplement to judicial action, but not as a substitute for it. It is a plea for bold development of a new court system which could tie together and enforce this nation's complex set of labor laws that operate in the private sector.[105]

I believe this to be the direction in which procedural reform, if it is to be true reform, should inexorably move. The country needs a simpler and more effective system, and the unitary system here invisioned is designed for simplicity of operation. If such a unitary system were successful, legal promises could become social realities. Absolute success would indeed be utopian, but any movement toward more effective administration would further the noble objectives of the federal labor laws.

NOTES

1. Consumer Credit Protection Act, Title III, 15 U.S.C. §§ 1671-77 (1970); Labor Management Relations Act, 29 U.S.C. §§ 141-67, 171-97, 185, 187 (1964); National Labor Relations Act, 29 U.S.C. §§ 151-68 (1964); Fair Labor Standards Act, 29 U.S.C. §§ 201-19 (1964); Equal Pay Act, 29 U.S.C. § 206(d) (1964); Portal-to-Portal Act, 29 U.S.C. §§ 251-62 (1964); Welfare and Pension Plans Disclosure Act, 29 U.S.C. §§ 301-09 (1964); Labor-Management Reporting and Disclosure Act, 29 U.S.C. §§ 401-531 (1964); Age Discrimination in Employment Act of 1957, 29 U.S.C. §§ 621-34 (Supp. V, 1970); Miller Act, 40 U.S.C. §§ 270(a)-270(d) (1964); Davis-Bacon Act, 40 U.S.C. § 276(a) (1964); Contract Work Hours Standards Act, 40 U.S.C. §§ 327-32 (1964); Walsh-Healey Public Contracts Act, 41 U.S.C. §§ 35-45 (1964); McNamara-O'Hara Service Contract Act, 41 U.S.C. §§ 351-57 (1964); Civil Rights Act of 1866, 42 U.S.C. § 1981 (1964); Civil Rights Act of 1964, Title VII, 42 U.S.C. §§ 2000e through 2000e-15 (1964); Hours of Service Act, 45 U.S.C. §§ 61-65 (1964); Railway Labor Act, 45 U.S.C. §§ 151-63, 181-88 (1964); Universal Military Training and Service Act, 50 U.S.C. §§ 451-73, at § 459 (reemployment rights) (1964).

2. "Amendments to Expedite the Remedies of the National Labor Relations Act," *Hearings on H.R. 7152 Before the Special Subcomm. on Labor of the House Comm. on Education and Labor*, 92d Cong., 1st Sess., 1-633 (Committee Print, 1971) [hereinafter cited 1971 Hearings].

3. *See, e.g.*, 1971 Hearings, *supra* note 2 at 148, 156, 185, 209, 219, 231, 239, and 391. *See also* Harris, *The Choice Before Us: Labor Board, Court, or District Court*, Southwestern Legal Foundation (1971), Labor Law Developments, 17th Annual Institute 331, 332-34 (1971).

4. 1971 Hearings, *supra* note 2 at 14, 469. *See also* Bartosic, *Labor Law Reform—The NLRB and a Labor Court*, 4 Ga. L. Rev. 647 (1970) [hereinafter cited as Bartosic].

5. 1971 Hearings, *supra* note 2 at 57. *See also* statements and testimony at 282, 299, 419, and 506. *Compare* Advisory Panel on Labor-Management Relations Law (Senate Comm. on Lab. and Public Welfare), Report on Organization and Procedure of the National Labor Relations Board, S. Doc. No. 81, 86th Cong. 2d Sess., 2 (1960); Subcomm. of the House Comm. on Educ. and Lab., Report on the NLRB, 87th Cong., 2d Sess., 2 (1961).

6. *See* Morris, *Procedural Reform in Labor Law—A Preliminary Paper*, 35 J. Air L. & Com. 536 (1969); also in Southwestern Legal Foundation (1971) Labor Law Developments—17th Annual Institute 351 (1971) [hereinafter cited as Morris].

7. *See, e.g.*, "Statement of Leonard Janofsky on behalf of the United States Chamber of Commerce," *Hearings on Congressional Oversight of Administrative Agencies (NLRB) Before the Subcomm. of Powers (Senate Comm. on the Judiciary)*, 90th Cong., 2d Sess., pt. 1 at 356 (1968). He observed: "What alarms the business community is that the NLRB restructures the Federal labor law to coincide with the political and socioeconomic predilections respecting industrial relations of those individual members who happen to constitute a majority of the Board at any particular time."

8. Examples of "Eisenhower" Board decisions which changed "Truman" Board decision include the following: McAllister Transfer, 110 N.L.R.B. 1769 (1954); B.V.D., 110 N.L.R.B. 1412 (1954); Terry Poultry Co., 109 N.L.R.B. 1097 (1954); Washington Coca-Cola Bottling Wks., 107 N.L.R.B. 299 (1953). Examples of pivotal "Kennedy" Board decisions include the following: Bernal Foam Products Co., 146 N.L.R.B. 1277 (1964), *overruling* Aiello Dairy Farms, 110 N.L.R.B. 1365 (1954) (which had overruled an earlier Board decision in M. H. Davidson Co., 94 N.L.R.B. 142 (1951)); Town & Country Mfg. Co., 136 N.L.R.B. 1022 (1962), *overruling* Brown-Dunkin Co., 125 N.L.R.B. 1379 (1959); Fibreboard Paper Products Corp., 130 N.L.R.B. 1558, *modified*, 138 N.L.R.B. 550, *enforced*, 322 F.2d 411 (D.C. Cir. 1963), *aff'd* 379 U.S. 203 (1964); Smitley, d/b/a Crown Cafeteria, 130 N.L.R.B. 1183, *aff'd* 327 F.2d 351 (9th Cir. 1964). The decision of the current Board in General Motors Corp., 77 L.R.R.M. 1537 (1971) may be indicative of a shifting of interest narrowing its predecessor Board's decision in Ozark Trailers, Inc., 161 N.L.R.B. 561 (1966). *See* C. Morris, The Developing Labor Law 418-22 (BNA, 1971) [hereinafter cited Developing Labor Law]. *See also* Collyer Insulated Wire, 192 N.L.R.B. No. 50 (1971).

9. *See* "Statement of Arnold Ordman, N.L.R.B. General Counsel [including charts compiled by NLRB Div. Admin. Data Processing Sect. (May 24, 1971)]," 1971 Hearings, *supra* note 2 at 299-389.

10. The low level of acceptability of NLRB authority is reflected in the high incidence of appellate review, which is illustrated by a comparison of NLRB appeals with those from all other federal agencies. Almost half (46.7 percent) of all cases of Court of Appeals review of administrative orders in 1969 were NLRB cases. The NLRB had three times as many appeals as the Tax Court, three times as many as the Immigration and Naturalization Service, more than four times as many as the Federal Power Commission, and more than four times as many as all the rest of the agencies combined.

11. *See* Murphy, *The National Labor Relations Board—An Appraisal*, Southwestern Legal Foundation, (1968) Labor Law Developments— 17th Annual Institute 113, 139 (1968).

12. *Supra* note 9.

13. "Discovery frequently provides evidence that would not otherwise be available to the parties and thereby makes for a fairer trial or settlement." Advisory Comm. Statement Concerning Amendments of the Federal Discovery Rules, 48 F.R.D. 487, 489 (1970), citing M. Rosenberg, Field Survey Of Federal Pretrial Discovery (1969). *Cf.* Jones, *Blind Man's Buff and the Now-Problems of Apocrypha, Inc. and Local 711— Discovery Procedures in Collective Bargaining Disputes*, 116 U. Pa. L. Rev. 571-610 (1968).

14. *See* "Statement of Arnold Ordman, NLRB General Counsel," *supra* note 2 at 312.

15. "Statement of Jerome A. Cooper, Attorney, Birmingham, Ala.," *supra* note 2 at 253.

16. *E.g.*, "Statement of Irving Abramson, General Counsel for Int'l Union of Elec., Radio and Mach. Wkrs. AFL-CIO-CLC," *supra* note 2 at 225. "Nothing so convincingly demonstrates the ineffectiveness of the collec-

tive bargaining obligation as reading opinions of the courts of appeals in the contempt cases, noting the date the union was certified, the date the court decided the contempt case, the reference to the loss of union majority, and the failure of the adjudication to do more than once again order the employer to bargain (citations omitted). . . . Legal scholars have repeatedly pointed to the ineffectiveness against a recalcitrant employer of the refusal to bargain obligation because of the absence of an effective remedy (citations omitted)."

17. Professor Bartosic, *supra* note 4 at 655, states that the alleged abuses have never been demonstrated. He may be correct if by "demonstrated" he has reference to a controlled study of the thousands of cases that have been dismissed or otherwise disposed of informally. It is hoped that such an empirical study will some day be conducted, though the task will be formidable. In the meantime, one must rely on personal observation and experience, which for this author (who actively practiced before the NLRB for 18 years) leads to the conclusion that a substantial number of meritorious cases have been dismissed by the General Counsel's office. Many such dismissals have been for lack of evidence, although the material facts establishing the unfair labor practice were usually suspected but not pursued. Since the charging party is generally required to produce evidence making out a prima facie case, and since discovery is not available, numerous meritorious cases which vigorous prosecution could save are never allowed to surface.

18. 35 [1970 F.Y.] N.L.R.B. Ann. Rep. 166-67 at Appendix A—Table 7 (1971). *See also* "Statement of Arnold Ordman, NLRB General Counsel," *supra* note 2 at 301-02, 310, 341-42.

19. On the nonreviewability of the General Counsel's discretion (court without jurisdiction either to order issuance or to set aside refusal to issue complaint), *see e.g.*: Dunn v. Retail Clerks Int'l Ass'n, AFL-CIO, Local 1529, 307 F.2d 285 (6th Cir. 1962); Retail Stores Emp. Union Local 954 v. Rothman, 298 F.2d 330 (D.C. Cir. 1962); Bandlow v. Rothman, 278 F.2d 866 (D.C. Cir.), *cert. denied*, 364 U.S. 909 (1960); So. Cal. Dist. Council Laborers v. Ordman, 318 F. Supp. 633 (C.D. Calif. 1970).

    Once a complaint issues, however, the charging party is entitled to an evidentiary hearing on his objections to an informal settlement between the regional director and the respondent. *See* Leeds & Northrup Co. v. N.L.R.B., 357 F.2d 527 (3d Cir. 1966). *See generally* Developing Labor Law, *supra* note 8, at 834-35.

    But cf. Beverly v. Lone Star Lead Const. Corp., 437 F.2d 1136 (5th Cir. 1971); Fekete v. United States Steel Corp., 424 F.2d 331 (3d Cir. 1970). Claimant, after first filing charges with Equal Employment Opportunity Commission under Title VII of the 1964 Civil Rights Act, may maintain separate civil suit to judicially: 1) Determine question of alleged employment discrimination even if EEOC found no reasonable cause to charge employer violation; or 2) Compel involuntary compliance with the law even if EEOC failed to get employer to voluntarily comply. There is no presumption against judicial review and in favor of administrative absolution unless that purpose is fairly discernible in the statutory scheme. Congress simply did not intend for EEOC to preempt the ultimate rights of the claimant. *See also* Goldberg v. Kelley, 397 U.S. 254, 261-71 (1970). The Court held: Duly qualified welfare recipient is entitled to evidentiary hearing before terminating

Title IV Social Security Act benefits which are considered a matter of statutory entitlement. Procedural due process requires: 1) Timely and adequate notice detailing the reasons for termination; 2) An effective opportunity to defend—confront adverse witnesses and present own arguments and oral evidence; and 3) Right to counsel. Moreover, the decision-maker must: 1) be impartial, not having participated before in the determination under review; and 2) state the reasons for his determination and indicate the evidence relied on. The Court went on to state its policy grounds: "The interest of the eligible recipient in the uninterrupted receipt of public assistance, which provides him with essential food, clothing, housing, and medical care, coupled with the State's interest that his payment not be erroneously terminated, clearly outweighs the State's competing concern to prevent any increase in its fiscal and administrative burdens."

20. Developing Labor Law, *supra* note 8, at 480-514.

21. National Labor Relations Act, § 10(a), 29 U.S.C. § 160(a) (1964). *See* N.L.R.B. v. Strong, d/b/a Strong Roofing Co., 393 U.S. 357 (1969); Cary v. Westinghouse, 375 U.S. 261 (1964). *See also* Woodlawn Farm Dairy Co., 162 N.L.R.B. 48 (1966); Great Lakes Carbon Corp., 152 N.L.R.B. 988 (1965), *enforced*, 360 F.2d 19 (4th Cir. 1966).

22. 192 N.L.R.B. No. 50 (1971).

23. Boys Mkts., Inc. v. Retail Clerks, Local 770, 398 U.S. 235 (1970).

24. *See* United Steelworkers v. Enterprise Wheel & Car Corp., 363 U.S. 593 (1960); United Steelworkers v. Warrior & Gulf Navigation Co., 363 U.S. 574 (1960); United Steelworkers v. American Mfg. Co., 363 U.S. 564 (1960).

25. *See* Bok, *Reflections On The Distinctive Character of American Labor Laws*, 84 Harv. L. Rev. 1394, 1462-63 (1971). The author takes issue with "the highly decentralized, adversary environment" of labor law practice, "the traditional preference for elaborate procedures, multiple opportunities for review, and highly particularized decisionmaking" and a mentality "motivated by individual, short term interests [which] encourages the search to find loopholes and exceptions or create tactical delays." All of this is productive of litigation, and adds to the legal burdens. He questions "the efficiency of the system" and asks "whether all of its forms and elaborations are worth the cost they entail." Dean Bok calls "for new methods of research . . . not favored by legal scholars" to "confront such issues and develop new ways of analyzing them. Students of regulation must point to inefficiencies in the process and suggest simpler or more effective substitutes."

26. *See* Morris, *supra* note 6.

27. *E.g.*, Automotive Plating Corp., 170 N.L.R.B. No. 121, 67 L.R.R.M. 1609 (1968).

28. Wm. J. Burns Detective Agency, Inc. v. N.L.R.B., 441 F.2d 911 (2d Cir. 1971), *modifying* 182 N.L.R.B. No. 50, 74 L.R.R.M. 1098 (1970).

29. *Cert. granted*, 40 U.S.L.W. 3142 (1971).

30. 443 F.2d 125 (6th Cir. 1971).

31. *Id.* at 128.

32. *See* C. Wright & A. Miller, 5 Federal Practice And Procedure § 1270 at 289-303 (1969); J. Moore & T. Currier, 1B Moore's Federal Practice §§ 0.405-0.422 at 621-3455 (2d ed 1965); W. Barron, A. Holtzoff, & C. Wright, 3 Federal Practice And Procedure § 1246 at 208-12 [1970 Supp. at 143-44] (1958).

33. Farmers' Cooperative Compress, 169 N.L.R.B. No. 3, 78 L.R.R.M. 1465 (1971).

34. Textile Workers Union v. Lincoln Mills, 353 U.S. 448 (1957).

35. *Supra* note 24.

36. 398 U.S. 235 (1970).

37. 29 U.S.C. §§ 101-15 (1964).

38. *E.g.*, Erelebron Bill, H.R. 6760, 92d Cong., 1st Sess. (1971); Hawkins Bill, H.R. 1746, 92d Cong., 1st Sess. (1971). *See also* Comment, *Employment Discrimination and Title VII of the Civil Rights Act of 1964,* 84 Harv. L. Rev. 1109 (1971).

39. 429 F.2d 324, *rehearing denied,* 2 F.E.P. Cases 869 (6th Cir. 1970). *See* Blumrosen, *Labor Arbitration, EEOC Conciliation, and Discrimination in Employment,* 24 Arb. J. (n.s.) 88 (1969). Peck, *Remedies For Racial Discrimination in Employment: A Comparative Evaluation of Forums,* 46 Wash. L. Rev. 455 (1971).

40. 429 F.2d at 332.

41. 428 F.2d 303 (5th Cir. 1970).

42. —— F.2d ——, 3 F.E.P. Cases 1137 (6th Cir. 1971).

43. *E.g.*, the experience of one district EEOC office (Dallas, Texas) to date indicates the following case disposition percentages (working estimates): Of the "total number of charges filed" (TNCF), approximately 50 percent show "reasonable cause" the law has been violated after an investigation of the facts. Of this number, approximately 50 percent (25 percent TNCF) are successfully conciliated to the complete satisfaction of the respondent employer and the employee charging party. For the remainder (25 percent TNCF), there is no completely satisfactory conciliation—15 to 25 percent (4 to 6 percent TNCF) of this group go to court; 75 to 85 percent (19 to 21 percent TNCF) of this group go without any remedy, although in this number are some instances where the employer has partially complied with the EEOC requested remedy. Interview (KERA-TV Channel 13 "Newsreel") with Mr. Gene R. Renslow, Dallas District Director of Equal Employment Opportunity Commission, in Dallas, Texas, September 18, 1971.

44. *Supra* note 38.

45. *See* Morris, *supra* note 6. *See also* Northrup, *Will Greater EEOC Powers Expand Minority Employment* (in Proceedings of Industrial Relations Research Association, 1971) 22 Lab. L.J. 513 (1971); reprinted in this volume, Part IV B.

46. *E.g.*, Inland Steel Co. v. N.L.R.B., 77 N.L.R.B. 1, 21 L.R.R.M. 1316, *enforced* 170 F.2d 247 (7th Cir. 1948), *cert denied,* 336 U.S. 960 (1949).

47. *See* Goetz, *Current Problems in Application of Federal Labor Law to Welfare and Pension Plans,* in Southwestern Legal Foundation, [1970] Labor Law Developments—16th Annual Institute 107-41, 130, 139 (1970); Goetz, *Developing Federal Labor Law of Welfare and Pension Plans,* 55 Cornell L. Rev. 911-39, 931, 937-38 (1970). "Where the welfare or pension plan is a jointly administered Taft-Hartley trust . . . employer contributions to a fund [can be enforced] by the union as promisee, but more commonly [are] enforced by the trustees of the fund as third-party beneficiaries. Actions to enforce such contributions . . . clearly are suits for violation of a contract between a union and employer within the ambit of section 301. Suit may therefore be brought either in Federal or state court. . . . [W]here an insurance policy, pension plan, or trust agreement is referred to in the labor agreement, or is designed to implement an agreement reached through bargaining, suit based on rights under such separate documents could properly be considered a suit under section 301 to which federal law would apply. [B]ut the fact that a union could have demanded bargaining about a plan does not seem to be a sufficient basis for applying section 301, [especially if the union] is not a party to the annuity contract [or] the collective bargaining agreement makes no reference to it [or] the annuity plan had only been discussed very indirectly in negotiations."

48. Pittsburgh Plate Glass Co., Chem. Div. v. N.L.R.B., 177 N.L.R.B. No. 114, 71 L.R.R.M. 1433 (1969), *enforcement denied,* 427 F.2d 936 (6th Cir. 1970), *cert. granted* 401 U.S. 907 (1971). [See Supreme Court ruling of December 7, 1971.]

49. *See* Goetz, *supra* note 47.

50. 45 U.S.C. §§ 151-63, 181-88 (1964).

51. Railway Labor Act §§ 4, 5, 10, 45 U.S.C. §§ 154, 155, 160 (1964).

52. Railway Labor Act, §§ 3, 204, 45 U.S.C. §§ 153, 184 (1964).

53. Federal Aviation Act of 1958 § 401(k)(4), 49 U.S.C. § 1371(k)(4) (1964). *See generally* Comment, *CAB and Labor Jurisdiction,* 33 J. Air L. & Com. 334 (1967).

54. S. 3671, 91st Cong., 2d Sess. (1970).

55. *See* Morris, *supra* note 6, at 546, 552. The absence of a single decisional authority other than the Supreme Court has also contributed to the confusion regarding the respectvie roles of courts and boards in the resolution of disputes based on statutory violations. *See* also Chicago & N.W. Ry. Co. v. United Transportation Union, 402 U.S. 570 (1971).

56. *See* Morris, *supra* note 6, at 553.

57. *Id.* at 551. *See also* Harlan, *Developments Past and Future in the NMB's Determination of "Craft or Class,"* 35 J. Air L. & Com. 394 (1969); Heisler, *Inconsistencies of the National Mediation Board in Its Interpretation and Definition of the Terms: Craft or Class,* 35 J. Air. L. & Com. 408-13 (1969).

58. *See* Morris, *supra* note 6, at 551. *See also* Curtin, *The Representation Rights of Employees and Carriers: A Neglected Area Under the Railway Labor Act,* 35 J. Air. L. & Com. 468 (1969); Goulard, *The Employee's "Free and Clear Choice,"* 35 J. Air L. & Com. 420 (1969).

59. *See* Morris, *supra* note 6, at 552.

60. *See, e.g.* Redenius, *Airlines: The Railway Labor Act or the Labor Management Relations Act?*, 20 Lab. L. J. 293-303 (1969); *Symposium on Air Transportation Relations*, 35 J. Air. L. & Com. 313-530, 338-57, 414-19, 433-37, 450-67, 493-97, 497-505, 513-20 (1969), esp. Aaron, "Comments on Papers Presented at the Symposium on Air Transport Labor Relations" at 513-20. "With varying degrees of intensity, the speakers have expressed dissatisfaction with the application of the Railway Labor Act to airlines. . . . Suggested remedial measures have ranged from modest proposals for more research into existing practices to bold recommendations for a complete reorganization of labor law administration, including creation of a labor court. . . . My own view, repeatedly stated for some time past, is that the Railway Labor Act has outlived its usefulness and should be repealed."

61. 370 U.S. 530 (1962). The Court there gave effect to a congressional declaration that the Court of Customs and Patent Appeals was a "court established under Article III." The Supreme Court stated that "Congress has never been compelled to vest the entire jurisdiction provided for in Article III upon inferior courts of its creation." This holding was reaffirmed in Brenner v. Mason, 383 U.S. 519 (1966). The Court specifically declared that because the Court of Customs and Patent Appeals was an Article III court, its order was "judicial" in character and "final and binding in the usual sense." *See also* Application of Fischer, 360 F.2d 230 (CCPA, 1960); Cephas, Jr. v. Busch, 47 F.R.D. 371 (E.D. Pa. 1969). *Cf.* So. Carolina v. Katzenbach, 383 U.S. 301, 335 (1966).

62. *See* note 82 *infra*.

63. *See* Morris, *supra* note 6, at 560-62. Though the label "labor court" means different things to different people, let us not be frightened by the tyranny of labels. The labor court which I recommended was neither a legislative court to be substituted for the National Labor Relations Board nor an Americanized version of any of the several European labor courts which exist primarily to settle "rights" disputes. For a discussion of European labor courts, *see* Labor Courts And Grievance Settlement In Western Europe (B. Aaron ed. 1971); Aaron, *Labor Courts: Western European Models and Their Significance for the United States*, 16 U.C.L.A. L. Rev. 847-82 (1969); Fleming, *The Labor Court Idea*, 65 Mich. L. Rev. 1551 (1967).

64. *See* Morris, *supra* note 6, at 560 n.154.

65. Consider the recent comment of NLRB Chairman Miller before the Thompson Committee: "Thus far in our history we have seen fit to let each of these policies be administered and adjudicated by independently isolated administrative and judicial bodies. This has a potential . . . of creating multiplicity of litigation even to the point of harassment of respondents. . . . [I]f the Congress is seriously to consider action designed to produce a truly modern and effective labor judiciary, might it . . . be time now to establish some kind of consolidated or coordinated labor judiciary, both in order to achieve a consistent and unified administration of Federal policy and in order to avoid multiplicity of litigation over complaints growing out of the same conduct by a single alleged offender. . . . [W]e should be looking to develop a labor judiciary adequate not only to overcome our immediate problems, but adequate also to the total needs of our time." *Supra* note 2 at 294-95.

66. *See* Morris, *supra* note 6, at 568-73. Inclusion of these other statutes might be advisable for the additional reason that the regular federal district courts are overcrowded and transfer of jurisdiction of cases under these statutes to a specialized court would relieve some of the congestion. Conditions relating to these other statutes, standing alone, would not at this time justify establishment of a specialized labor court; but in view of the critical enforcement problems which do exist under the primary labor statutes, some consideration should be given to establishing a court system with broad coverage over substantially all federal labor statutes.

67. 29 U.S.C. § 158(a) & (b) (1964).

68. 29 U.S.C. § 178 (1964).

69. 29 U.S.C. § 179 (1964).

70. 29 U.S.C. § 180 (1964).

71. 29 U.S.C. § 185 (1964).

72. 29 U.S.C. § 186 (1964).

73. 29 U.S.C. § 187 (1964).

74. The problem brings to mind President Adams' famous "midnight appointments" to pack the judiciary with Federalists prior to Jefferson and the Republicans taking office. The lame duck Federalist Congress had passed the Judiciary Act of 1801 creating sixteen new circuit courts, and Adams immediately filled the posts. Forty-two justices of the peace were also named for the District of Columbia. One of those named was William Marbury. It was the refusal of James Madison, the new Secretary of State under Jefferson, to deliver the commission confirming Marbury's appointment that led to the landmark decision of Marbury v. Madison, 1 U.S. (1 Cranch) 368 (1803). *See* S. Morison, The Oxford History Of The American People 362-63 (1965).

75. N.L.R.B. Chairman Miller, testifying recently before the Thompson Committee, said "[A]ny reconstituted labor judiciary, to be truly effective, must not only be impartial but also *appear* to be impartial and the parties who appear before it must have faith and confidence in its impartiality." *See supra* note 2, at 291.

76. 29 U.S.C. § 160(j) (1964).

77. 29 U.S.C. § 160(l) (1964).

78. United Mine Workers of Am. v. Gibbs, 383 U.S. 715 (1966); Lomax v. Armstrong Cork Co., 433 F.2d 1277, 1281 (5th Cir. 1970); Lewis v. Pennington, 257 F. Supp. 815, 864 (E.D. Tenn. 1966).

79. *See* Morris, *supra* note 6, at 565.

80. *Id.*

81. 11 U.S.C. §§ 66 and 67.

82. Collier on Bankruptcy (14th Ed.) ¶¶ 22.05, 38.02; Weidhorn v. Levy, 253 U.S. 268 (1920); Mueller v. Nugent, 184 U.S. 1 (1902).

83. *Compare* United States Court of Claims, 28 U.S.C. § 1492, which also uses a commissioner system. *See* 28 U.S.C. §§ 792, 2503 (1970); U.S. Ct Cl. Rules 52-27.

84. *Compare* Civil Rights Act of 1964, Title VII § 706(k), 42 U.S.C. § 2000e-5(k) (1970), under which reasonable attorney's fees are allowed by the court in its discretion as part of the costs of suit to an individual plaintiff who prevails in his enforcement of the Act. Private suits are allowed only after the aggrieved party as complainant files charges with the Equal Employment Opportunity Commission, and the EEOC within the statutory time period is unable to obtain voluntary compliance. Irvin v. Mohawk Rubber Co., 308 F. Supp. 152, 161-62 (E.D. Ark. 1970); Dobbins v. Local 212, Intern. Broth. of Elec. Workers, AFL-CIO, 292 F. Supp. 413, 450 (S.D. Ohio 1968); Quarles v. Philip Morris, Inc., 279 F. Supp. 505, 521 (E.D. Va. 1968). Under the proposed unitary system, a similar procedure, including the allowance of attorney fees, should be available after the claimant has exhausted his remedy through the GLC and thereafter successfully processes his own action in the labor court.

85. Granting summary judgment, like the device of dismissal for failure to state a claim upon which relief can be granted [*see* Fed. R. Civ. P. 12(b)(6)], should be especially useful in disposing of frivolous claims.

86. 47 Stat. 70, 29 U.S.C. § 101 *et seq.* (1964).

87. Bhd. of Ry. Trainmen v. Chicago River & Indiana R. Co., 353 U.S. 30 (1957).

88. Boys Mkts., Inc. v. Retail Clerks, Local 770, 398 U.S. 235 (1970).

89. § 3(p) & (q), 45 U.S.C. § 153(p) & (q) (1964). *See* Gunther v. San Diego & Arizona Eastern Ry., 382 U.S. 257 (1965); Int'l Ass'n of Machinists v. Central Airlines, 372 U.S. 682 (1963); Air Line Pilots Ass'n v. Northwest Airlines, 415 F.2d 493 (8th Cir. 1969); Bhd. of R.R. Trainmen v. Central of Georgia Ry. Co., 415 F.2d 404 (5th Cir. 1969).

90. *See* John Wiley & Sons v. Livingston, 376 U.S. 543 (1964); United Steelworkers v. Enterprise Wheel & Car Corp., 363 U.S. 593 (1960); United Steelworkers v. Warrior & Gulf Navigation Co., 363 U.S. 574 (1960); United Steelworkers v. American Mfg. Co., 363 U.S. 564 (1960).

91. Sherman Antitrust Act, 26 Stat. 209, *as amended*, 15 U.S.C. §§ 4, 9 (1964); Clayton Antitrust Act, 38 Stat. 730, *as amended*, 15 U.S.C. §§ 15, 26 (1964).

92. Civil Rights Act of 1964, Title IV, 42 U.S.C. §§ 2000c-6 & 2000c-8 (1970). *See also* Civil Rights Act of 1968, Title VIII, 42 U.S.C. §§ 3610, 3612, 3613 (1970) (fair housing enforcement by HEW, Justice Department, or private party).

93. *E.g.*, Miller v. Int'l Paper Co., 408 F.2d 283 (5th Cir. 1969); Oatis v. Crown Zellerbach Corp., 398 F.2d 496 (5th Cir. 1968). *Cf.* Newman v. Piggie Park Enterprises, Inc., 390 U.S. 400-03 (1968). The Court, concerning private civil suits to enforce Title II, said: "It was evident that enforcement would prove difficult and the nation would have to rely in part upon private litigation as a means of securing broad compliance with the law." The individual plaintiff sues ". . . not only for himself alone but also as a 'private attorney general,' vindicating a policy that Congress considered of the highest priority" and "one who succeeds . . . should ordinarily recover attorney's fee . . . unless special circumstances would render such an award unjust."

94. Civil Rights Act of 1964, 42 U.S.C. §§ 2000e-5(a) & 2000e-6(a) (1970).

95. Railway Labor Act § 2 (Tenth), 45 U.S.C. § 152 (Tenth) (1964).

96. *See* text accompanying and following note 84 *supra*.

97. National Labor Relations Act § 3(b), 29 U.S.C. § 153(b) (1964).

98. *See, e.g.*, Bhd. of R. & S. S. Clerks v. Ass'n for Benefit of Non-Contract Employees, 380 U.S. 650, 668-70 (1965); Switchmen's Union of N. Am. v. Nat'l Mediation Bd., 320 U.S. 297 (1943). *See also* K. Davis, [1970 Supp.] Administrative Law Treatise §§ 28.02 at 941-42, 28.16 at 964-90, 30.05 at 1025-30 (1971); L. Jaffee, Judicial Control Of Administrative Action 359-63, 555-64, 575-79, 586-89 (1965).

99. Railway Labor Act §§ 4, 5, 45 U.S.C. §§ 154, 155 (1964).

100. *See generally* W. Simkin, Mediation And The Dynamics Of Collective Bargaining (Wash. D.C.: BNA, 1971).

101. It must be conceded that these mild attributes have on occasion been reinforced by "arm twisting" and "jaw-boning" emanating from the White House.

102. *See* Gamser, *The Role of Mediation in Airline Labor Disputes*, 35 J. Air L. & Com. 505-12 (1969).

103. N.L.R.B. Chairman Miller, testifying recently before the Thompson Committee, commented: "[T]he problems go wider and deeper than I think the testimony before you thus far has directly indicated. . . . [W]e need some new, creative thinking in order to develop proposals which are both sound and also as acceptable as possible to the sometimes divergent views of the several segments of the industrial relations community and of the variety of views represented in Congress. . . . [I hope there will develop] a joint labor-management initiative which would result in a mutually acceptable approach which could then be articulated in draft legislation for the consideration of the Congress." 1971 Hearings, *supra* note 2 at 295.

104. Joint legislative action has not been the norm in the passage of federal labor laws. *See* Developing Labor Law, *supra* note 8, at 1-110. However, the railroads and railroad unions on several notable occasions have jointly sponsored legislation. *See* dissenting opinion, Frankfurter J., in Railway Employees Dep't v. Hanson, 351 U.S. 225, 240 (1965) regarding the passage of the 1926 RLA; Bhd. of R. R. Trainmen v. Chicago River & I.R.R. Co., 353 U.S. 30, 37 (1957) regarding the passage of the 1934 RLA.

105. This paper has been confined to private sector labor relations, but the jurisdiction of the proposed labor court could also be extended to federal labor laws applicable to public employees.

Collective Bargaining and the Rule of Law

Francis A. O'Connell †

The conjunction, expressed in the title of this paper, of the concepts of collective bargaining and the rule of law would no doubt have horrified some of the earlier practitioners of each, but is taken rather for granted by those who (like myself) are latter-day practitioners of both. Indeed, the plain fact is that collective bargaining, like the entire field of labor relations, has been growing steadily more technical and legalistic over the past 25 years.[1]

The Meaning of "The Rule of Law"

And so to speak of collective bargaining in the same breath as the law is not so anomalous as might once have been thought. What, however, is the import, in this context, of adding the phrase "the *rule* of law"? As used in this paper, that phrase will have reference to one or the other of the following concepts:

(1) The existence of an objective standard of conduct, which has been promulgated by society for its own governance and to which all members of society are required to conform. This sense of the rule of law involves primarily the Legislature and the Executive and, therefore, the much-debated phrase "law and order" is relevant.[2] I shall be dealing briefly with that aspect of the law, and the problems which are posed for law*makers*, as well as law *enforcers*, not to mention the public at large.

(2) In another sense—perhaps the more traditional one—the phrase "the rule of law" involves primarily the Judiciary —in its role as the guardian of rights—this stewardship

† Francis A. O'Connell is Vice President, Employee Relations, Olin Corporation. The author wishes to acknowledge the valuable and indispensable assistance rendered by his associates, Arthur W. Dulemba and William B. Dickinson.

being carried out by faithful adherence to the body of rules, of statutes, of precedents, of customs, which are the substance and essence of the law itself. It is this aspect of the "rule of law" which makes ours "a government of laws and not of men." By that is meant that the individual's fate rests *not* on a particular magistrate —guided or driven by whim, weakness or bias, or induced by background, philosophy, or inclination. Instead, his fate rests on the *law itself*, as an objective standard. The personal views and preconceptions of the magistrate are accordingly to be suppressed (as thoroughly as human fallibility permits) and subordinated to the "letter of the law" in the formulation of his decision. In short, under our system, the rule of law means that the judge *interprets* the law; he does not write it. And he comes to the task of interpretation as free as honest human intellection can make him free of his personal politics, his personal philosophy, or his personal views as to what the law *ought* to be. I shall in this meaning of the "rule of law" give some attention to the impact of individual philosophy upon the development and application of the law and the stability of the rule of law.

The Judge and the Rule of Law

The rule of law has a noble lineage in our constitutional history. Indeed, it *is* in large part our constitutional history, commencing (in a sense, although not entirely) with the granite interpositions and interpretations of Chief Justice Marshall in *Marbury* v. *Madison* [3] and others. Instead of a tedious exegesis of that fairly obvious proposition, let me return to the encapsuled statement of it: That ours is a government of laws and not of men. Like all inspirational generalities, this one has its flaws—at least when slavishly applied. For, as I heard the present Chairman of the National Labor Relations Board remark, not long after he took office, it would be foolish to assume that one arrives at judicial or quasi-judicial office unaccompanied, unshaped, uninfluenced by the congeries of experience which transpired, for him, on his way to that position. And, in saying so, Chairman Miller ranged himself alongside the quintessential jurist, Mr. Justice Cardozo, who had reflected deeply on this phenomenon almost half a century earlier. [4]

We are all, in this sense, the total of our experience, and bring to our latest task that mind and that philosophy—that mental mode—which was gradually developed as we went along in our professional careers. It would be fatuous, for example, to assume that Arthur Goldberg ceased to reason, *au fond*, as Arthur Goldberg, Labor Lawyer, when he became Mr. Justice Goldberg. Indeed, his deep belief in, and dedication to, the principle of collective bargaining was plainly in evidence in his opinions in the *Pennington* [5] and *Jewel Tea* [6] cases, for example, and just as clearly influenced other members of the Court in those cases.[7] Holmes, Brandeis and Cardozo—to name three of the acknowledged giants in the Supreme Court pantheon—also foreshadowed earlier the lines along which they would travel as Justices.

I have even heard it persuasively argued that the career of the late Mr. Justice Black on the Supreme Court did not constitute nearly the philosophical tergiversation which many observers and admirers—legal and lay—had seen it to be. Nor is this less to his credit. It simply teaches us that *real* change in human beings is a rare event, and "development" and "modification" are more accurate descriptions of what takes place over time.

The conventional wisdom has it that men rise to the stature of the Supreme Court and, almost without fail, superbly justify their presence there. But we are not satisfied with that. As incorrigible romantics, we persist in believing that the majestic judicial philosophy was *always* there, albeit inchoate. Stripped of its romanticism, however, it must be said that, on the whole, the proposition holds. And its core is integrity, governing and shaping the accrued experience and developed wisdom of the individual. In approaching the judicial task, the true judge consciously attempts to divest himself of those assumptions and predilections which so often serve so many of us daily, in lieu of judgment, and he approaches even the familiar context, if not *de novo*, at least in a spirit of objectivity. In the philosopher's terms, the *essence* remains, but those *accidents* which cloud or cripple the judgmental faculty are stripped from it when the judge approaches his judicial task.

The National Labor Relations Board and the Rule of Law

Perhaps because their station is less lofty, their appointments generally fraught with politics, and the matters with which they deal inevitably and exceptionally imbued with the heat of partisanship, the members of the National Labor Relations Board, through the years, seem to have been peculiarly unable to rise to that distance above the fray which is the desideratum for a judge. That thesis could readily be sustained by a detailed review of the Board's decisional lines over the 36-year span of the Board's existence—especially the shifts in decisional doctrine which followed shifts in the political complexion of the Board, as well as the varying degrees of activism which have characterized the Board's approach to its mission, from time to time. But such a review is impractical in this paper and, in any event, I believe, not necessary to the making of the point that our experience with the National Labor Relations Board has been rather persistently an experience in "government of *men*" rather than of laws. The decisions of the Board have too often represented an undue intrusion of the philosophy of the man upon the interpretation and application of the law by the judge. By way of demonstrating that proposition, let us examine briefly several policies and lines of decision followed by the Board during the past decade and the *philosophy* which informed many of the decisions of the Board during those years.

First, with respect to the underlying philosophy: The perceptible philosophy of the Board has tended to be that, from a socio-economic standpoint, unionization is a desirable state for the American worker—that, at all times, under all circumstances, unionization is vastly to be preferred to its opposite, the state of non-unionization. It was, in other words, a philosophic Good.

It is easy to understand how one who started from that premise could persuade himself that the Congress shared those views and had, indeed, implemented them in the National Labor Relations Act. Thus we find the Board, notwithstanding the language of the law, behaving as though in the National Labor Relations Act, Congress intended not only to protect the right to organize—which it did—but affirmatively to *foster* and *encourage unionization*, as such, which it did not. By the simple device of ignoring the context of the word "encouraging" in the Wagner Act's preamble, the Board was able to see its legislative mandate as the *encouragement* of *unionization*. Its own defense of its actions often seemed to rest on this rationale: We are only "encouraging the practice and procedure of collective bargaining" when we promote unionization, for how can there be collective bargaining without it? And the answer, of course, is that there cannot be; but a further response is that the Congress did not intend the *encouragement* to take place until there was first achieved (if at all) a state of unionization, and it finally was forced to make that point explicit in the Taft-Hartley amendments in 1947. But the Board of recent years seemed never really to have understood or accepted the distinction between *protecting* unionization and *promoting* or *encouraging* it, notwithstanding Congress' clear assertion in the Taft-Hartley Act of the right not to unionize.

The corollary of the proposition that unionization is a Good is, of course, that non-unionization, or anything which tends to avert or even delay unionization, is a Bad. And from those twin philosophical roots sprang the decisions abridging employer freedom of speech in unionization campaigns and insisting upon "laboratory conditions" for employee elections; [10] constructing bargaining units which maximized the union's chances of prevailing in an election; [11] demonstrating a marked disposition, wherever possible, to circumvent the Act's election processes in favor of installing the union immediately by ordering the employer to bargain forthwith; [12] and even attempting to compel an employer to agree to a specific union proposal. [13]

A second keystone of the philosophy which I have been describing holds that the enhancement of the union's role in and through the bargaining process is not only desirable, but so essential that it, too, must have been the will of Congress, notwithstanding the absolute absence of evidence to that effect. And thus we found the Board, beginning in 1962, vastly expanding the area and subject matter of mandatory bargaining [14] until it embraced virtually the entire managerial decision-making process—even those basic "survival" decisions which, as Mr. Justice Stewart put it, disagreeing with this quasi-judicial activism, "lie at the core of entrepreneurial control." [15] But with the bargaining of such sweeping demands and the ever increasing power to make it effective, we come upon this corollary: If unionism is good, strong unionism is better; and thus whatever enhances or unshackles the power of unions still further is likewise beneficent. And so the Board has been as myopic concerning the true and illicit objective of the union power tactic known as "coalition bargaining" [16] as it has been lynx-eyed for the transgressions of employers. [17]

I conclude with reference to several areas of the law in which the Board appears quite clearly to have ignored or overridden the intent of the Congress:

(1) Decisions involving secondary boycotts—in which the Board ignored or distorted the intention of Congress to prohibit such conduct and strained to permit unions to exercise their power and work their will through this illicit tactic.[18]

(2) Decisions involving so-called "work preservation"—in which that concept (basic and traditional to organized labor, but nowhere finding sanction in the National Labor Relations Act) was imported bodily into the law by the National Labor Relations Board.[19]

The cited case and others of its genre are interesting for several reasons. First, it is an especially bold illustration of "legislating" by the adjudicating agency. Second, the case is a striking example of the inadequacy of our present law with respect to anti-competitive practices by *unions*—a gap which is further examined below. Finally, the case provides a useful insight into the manipulation of the quasi-judicial process to serve a particular point of view. Motivated by its perception of the desirability of increases in union power, the Board deliberately ignored the clearly indicated intent of the Congress and pursued a contrary course.

In the *National Woodwork* case, the Board held that employees of a building contractor did not violate either the "hot cargo" or the secondary boycott provisions of the Act when (in what would appear to be a classic violation of both) the union refused to permit its members to hang doors which had been precut and prefitted and shipped to the job site by another manufacturer. (Ordinarily, the work of cutting and hanging doors would have been performed on the job site by the carpenters employed by the contractor.)

The refusal-to-handle was based on a contract provision that no member of the Union would be required to handle precut or prefit materials—a provision which would seem quite plainly to run afoul of the proscription in Section 8(e) of the Act against "any contract . . . whereby such employer ceases or refrains or agrees to cease or refrain from handling, using . . . any of the products of any other employer . . . ."[20] Nevertheless, the Board held that neither the contract nor the conduct transgressed Section 8(e) or the "secondary boycott" provisions of Section 8(b)(4),[21] finding first that the contract provision was legitimate, because it was aimed at "preserving their unit work," and, therefore, that conduct in support of that assertedly legitimate contractual provision was likewise legitimate. As will be readily perceived, the entire rationale rests on the *presumed* legitimacy of the "work preservation" principle, which was nowhere permitted or sanctioned by the Congress and which, in fact, is the root of many of the evils which the Congress was seeking to eliminate.

Although the *National Woodwork* decision was ultimately affirmed by a divided Supreme Court,[22] a strongly worded dissent was entered by Justice Stewart, who was joined by Justices Black, Douglas and Clark. In the view of the dissenting members, a clear violation of both the hot cargo and secondary boycott provisions of the Act was established, and, they charged, by deciding to the contrary, "the Court has substituted its own notions of sound labor policy for the word of Congress."[23]

(3) Decisions permitting boycotts of products—another area which Congress thought it had marked "out-of-bounds," but which the Board legalized by such verbal and mental gymnastics as finding that a radio station, with whom a union was having a dispute, was a "producer" of the products advertised over its airwaves. With *that* hurdle overcome, the Board was able to find the union thoroughly within its rights in boycotting the products of those companies who refused to obey its demand to cease patronizing the station.[24]

(4) Decisions permitting organizational or recognitional (so-called "blackmail") picketing—a tactic by which a union, avoiding the channels which the law provides for establishing its right to represent, attempts to force an employer to recognize it or force his employees to join up, or both. This is another area at which the Congress struck in the 1959 amendments to the Act, but which the Board has blandly (and often in the teeth of evidence to the contrary) found to be merely a permissible publiciz-

ing by a union of its allegation that the employer does
not observe "union standards." [25]

It is submitted that the point is established in the foregoing
that, during the years and in the decisions in which the philosophy which I have described was implemented, labor relations in
the United States was being improperly subjected to a "government of men, not of laws." There was conspicuously lacking
that subordination of personal philosophy to the spirit and intent
of enacted law which is required of the judge. This undermining
of the rule of law, moreover, appears to be a propensity to which
quasi-judicial tribunals, especially the Board, are particularly sus-
ceptible, because their decisions on policy and other matters involving "expertise" seem to be uniquely—perhaps excessively and
dangerously—immune to judicial review. For it is in precisely
those areas that the man is most likely to overshadow the law.[26]

The Resulting Imbalance of Power

When the law is canted in one direction and in favor of one
group over a sufficient period of time, there develops an unintended shifting of the balance in favor of that group. In a
democracy, rooted as it is in a series of delicate balances, imbalance is a serious flaw. When such an imbalance is in the
economic sphere, the result is realignment of the system and,
usually, an untoward share of the fruits flowing toward the
favored group at the expense of the others. That is what has
happened as the rule of law in labor-management relations has
gradually but steadily given way to a sort of "rule of *political*
law," and the proper and rightful power of labor has gradually
but steadily become excessive.

Our history is replete with examples of legislation brought
about as a result of the creation or development of forces which
contain a potential for harm to society. Labor and management
represent such forces, as they repeatedly demonstrate. (And,
for purposes of this point, management may be deemed to include the government as an employer.) More often than not,
the conversion of the *potential* for harm into the actuality—the
practical demonstration—has taken place before society acts to
protect itself, as society ultimately did in other spheres by the
enactment of the Sherman Act; the establishment of regulatory
bodies such as the Interstate Commerce Commission, the Federal Trade Commission and so forth; and the recent legislation

reflecting mounting concern for air, water, and other aspects of our environment.

The Need for Legislative Correction

Legislation to correct the imbalance of power and other developing flaws in the collective bargaining process will introduce no alien element into the collective bargaining sphere; equalization of power has always been the objective, and collective bargaining is already awash in legalism. The remedy now, therefore, can only be to *correct* bad law and the imbalances of power legislatively or administratively created. Some day, perhaps, there will come a second or third phase in which we can do with no law (or less of it) than labor-management relations are burdened with now, but for the time being, law and collective bargaining *are* inextricably mingled by the need for that corrective action.

We come now to specifics. In what respects, if any, is the rule of law either absent from or overridden in collective bargaining? Although there are admittedly a number of different *aspects* to this question, there are few *answers* which do not find a root in some variation of "might makes right." That is to say that, just as in other social areas where law is lacking or diminished in importance or impact, force tends to hold sway. In the context at hand the force is economic and, by and large, it belongs to organized labor. Curiously enough, however, the very ability of labor to substitute force for law is *itself* a product of the law. Indeed, many of the sources of labor's power to frustrate the intent of enacted law and (often simultaneously) to demonstrate the desperate need for additional law are found to lie in what Dean Pound saw as the "legal immunities" [27] enjoyed by organized labor for which there is no justification in law, economics, politics or sociology.

The Antitrust Problem

There is ambivalence in our system of federal labor law, resulting from an overlapping of areas touched by the National Labor Relations Act and the antitrust laws, and yet a failure by either of them really to regulate conduct which clearly calls for legislative regulation. In the area of antitrust policy, in particular, the Congress has been especially ambivalent. In consequence, the courts have been left with inadequate guidance when confronted with cases in which activities of a union are clearly incompatible with the policy which informs our antitrust laws. Too little attention has been paid to this anomaly, and a brief review of the legislation and the decisions which have led to the present lacuna will help to make clear the proposals which follow.

The rule-of-law problem, in respect of labor's virtually unfettered ability to restrain trade and stifle or interfere with competition, is a curious one. In a sense, it can be said to involve at once too *much* law and too *little*. There is too much law in the sense that activities of labor unions in the area generally considered to be within the purview of our national policy with respect to competition and restraint of trade are purportedly regulated under *both* the antitrust laws and the National Labor Relations Act. In point of fact, however, under *neither* law are certain activities touched which clearly and significantly impinge upon the antitrust area. These practices constitute conduct which would unhesitatingly be labeled "anti-competitive" if it occurred in the business sphere—for example, refusals (enforced by the strike power) to accept new technology; strikes or threats of strikes to enforce a traditional "right" to particular work; and boycotts of products. In consequence of the legislative-juridical process described below, these activities escape prohibition or regulation under either the antitrust laws or the National Labor Relations Act.

This is not to say that there is not a clear expression of a Congressional intent to subject unions to such regulation. Notwithstanding the so-called "labor exemption" included in the Clayton Act,[28] union activities are by no means wholly insulated from the application of the antitrust laws. As the Supreme Court cautiously noted in the *Apex Hosiery* case, unions and their activities are within the purview of the Sherman Act "to some extent and in some circumstances . . . ."[29] As the Court demonstrated in that case, however, and in a series of decisions over the next five years, there was very little that unions could do in restraining trade which the Court would find offensive, unless the unions absorbed "guilt by association" by joining with businessmen in the pursuit of anti-competitive activities which were, and had long been, illegal for the latter.[30]

The rather shocking scope of the *carte blanche* which the Court of those days was prepared to issue to organized labor—and the use and exploitation of which, as labor grew more and more powerful, has been the source of so much mischief—was summed up by Mr. Justice Frankfurter in the *Hutcheson* case this way:

> So long as a union acts in its self interest and does not combine with non-labor groups, the licit and illicit under Sec. 20 [of the Clayton Act] are not to be distinguished by any judgment regarding the wisdom or unwisdom, the rightness or wrongness, the selfishness or unselfishness of the end of which the particular union activities are the means.[31]

It is submitted that, if ever an immunity of that sweep had been justified by a socio-economic need to build up a labor strength equivalent to management's, the time for reconsideration of that immunity has long since arrived, even as the objective of enhancing labor's relative power has long since been achieved and even over-achieved.[32]

The same process of re-examination, while we are at it, should extend to another hoary dogma, traceable to the *Apex* case,[33] to the effect that it is our national policy to "take wages out of competition." Here again, recent events have sharply demonstrated that wages *cannot* be taken out of competition any more than the cost of materials (or the competitive practices which influence their price) can be disregarded. Indeed, wages are increasingly found to be the *crucial* element in competition. When, as demonstrated by innumerable union negotiations during recent years, wages can be propelled upward by union power, *regardless* of market forces—where the rate of the wage increase secured bears no relationship whatsoever to the rate of productivity increase, either actual, assumed or predicted—then the wage ingredient can become not only competitively critical, but quite capable of bringing the enterprise down.

The recognition of the need for a broad re-examination of the "labor exemption" is picking up momentum and support. In a piece written for the Op-Ed page of the *New York Times,* John F. Wharton, of the New York Bar, a long-time observer of the labor-economic scene, noted the fact that the shift in the economic balance of power over the years had reached a point where it permitted unions to achieve and enforce their desires at the expense of the rest of the economic community, and he thereupon made this proposal:

> I suggest that a solution could be obtained if the situation were viewed as a problem in monopoly. It is an established thesis of this country that monopolies of goods require government control; even union members agree with this. Hence, they might see that there

is no reason why a monopoly of manpower, which is what a union is, should not also be subjected to some sort of control. The purpose of those laws is to try to stimulate increasing production and distribution of needed useful goods and services—for example, houses, electric power, technical skills. To the extent that a manpower monopoly derogates from this purpose, it should be curbed, but this would not mean the destruction of union power. With the proper controls worked out, a way might be open for a solution that would permit capital and labor "to git together without its being Good Night fer the rest of us." [34]

There are two points worth making in connection with Mr. Wharton's idea: (1) The need for treating "Capital" and "Labor" alike, whether in freedom or restraint (which, incidentally, was a burning issue at the time of the passage of the Sherman Act!); [35] (2) the "freeze" of August-November, 1971, and the current "Phase 2" demonstrate once again that the workers' wage and the price of the product are inextricably linked, and that both must be dealt with, or neither. Moreover, the wage stabilization effort itself constitutes, in a sense, an acknowledgement of the monopoly power of labor,[36] as well as of the heavy impact of wages upon the health of the economy and their role in "cost-push" inflation.

It therefore would seem reasonable to suggest that, at a minimum, Congressional review of the position of labor under the antitrust laws is highly appropriate and even urgent, especially in the light of the assertions heard more frequently that "Big Labor" and "Big Business" together embody the capacity of ruining the economy, if they pursue single-mindedly their respective selfish interests and exert their full economic muscle in the course of that pursuit.

The Overlap into NLRA and Its Ineffectuality in Antitrust

The need for the proposed legislative review is made more keen by the fact that the other half of the "rule of law" in the antitrust area (i.e., the National Labor Relations Act) has been quite ineffectual. Unions are, to be sure, regulated under the provisions of the National Labor Relations Act with respect to certain anti-competitive activities of the sort referred to above, although antitrust terminology is not used.[37] Interestingly enough, and perhaps providing a clue to the Congressional attitude toward the sweeping immunities bestowed by the Supreme Court in the 1940's, the anti-competitive union tactics and practices (e.g., product boycotts, jurisdictional strikes, secondary boycotts) *proscribed* in amendments to the National Labor Relations Act which were enacted subsequently to the *Hutcheson* decision were all activities which probably would have been *permissible* under the 1940-1945 decisions of the Court.

However that may be, the fact is that the conduct thus aimed at by the Congress has *not* been curbed. On the contrary, as noted earlier, the National Labor Relations Board has been prone to view with a tolerant eye the secondary boycott, the product boycott, and various "work preservation" activities, being heavily influenced by conventional union philosophy and sloganeering concerning the right of unions to protect, by any means at hand, their "jurisdiction" or "traditional work." Indeed, the Board has often seemed to be following to its extreme the "hands off" doctrine laid down by Mr. Justice Frankfurter in the *Hutcheson* case and to make no effort to distinguish the "licit from the illicit," so long as the union activity in question was demonstrably "traditional" and "self-interested"—a rather frightening test. As Dean Pound bluntly put it: "In such matters as procedure in violation of antitrust laws, restraint of trade and interference with commerce, security of private property, and the right to work they [the NLRB] protect labor organizations and labor leaders *against* the public," rather than protecting the public.[38]

The Rationale for the Antitrust Approach

Both the urgent need and the inherent equity of applying the rule of law to anti-competitive activity from whatever source can be illustrated very simply: If, in the business sphere, one were to substitute, in each of the classic union "work preservation" situations, the word "market" or "product" for the word "work," and were thereby to permit business to think in terms of protecting a "traditional market" (as a barrier to competition) and "market preservation" (as an objective justifying the suppression or exclusion of competition) and "market jurisdiction" (as a right permitting agreement among competitors to allocate markets), any first-year law student would spot the most flagrant and elemental violations of both the letter and the spirit of the antitrust laws; and any economist, of whatever school, would blanch. Yet, despite a national policy which cherishes competition to the highest degree, we have persistently overlooked the devastating effects upon competition of union activities which, these days, are permitted to and engaged in by economic giants who are fully as powerful in their sphere as most corporations are (or ever were) in theirs. The inequity of such a double standard is obvious; its continued viability—or, more precisely, the viability of an economy which tolerates it—is certainly open to question. And it is simply the posing of that urgent question which is here intended.

The Present Anomaly of a Double Standard

The circumstances which gave rise to the double standard for the respective anti-competitive activities of labor and management is easily understood. One need not take issue with the early protectionist view of labor, which enabled it to increase membership more than 500 percent [39] during the past four decades, to raise a question as to whether those protectionist policies are appropriate today. One need not be unsympathetic to labor to note its vast progress from the days when its foremost leader languished in jail, in the early years of this century, to the present when its leader (Mr. Meany) clearly held in the palm of his hand the fate of the nation's fight against inflation—and, earlier, a single union, the United Automobile Workers, was credited with having, by its crippling strike of General Motors, disrupted the economic "game plan" with which the Administration had hoped to save the economy without controls.

So the question "whence the double standard?" is easily answered. The question "why . . . today?" is more difficult. When business outgrew the need for the protectionist coddling in which our society had indulged, when it was deemed in the national interest to do so—when business became huge and powerful enough to *harm,* as well as to *help,* society—the antitrust laws were passed; and they continue to be refined and applied to this day.

Labor, as suggested above, has likewise long since outgrown its swaddling clothes, and so one might reasonably expect it now to be treated as an economic adult, with a drawing back from the over-permissive protectiveness of the *Hutcheson* era. In short, it is time for labor (to paraphrase an old English judge [40]) to be put in "the humiliating position of being on an equality with the rest of the King's subjects"!

Yet, so far are we from that goal—so much are we still in the anachronistically protective and permissive mood of *Hutcheson*—that only a few years ago we find the Supreme Court, speaking through Mr. Justice White in the *Jewel Tea* case, say-ing, with respect to the "labor exemption" from the antitrust laws: "That exemption for union-employer agreements is very much a matter of accommodating the coverage of the Sherman Act to the policy of the labor laws." [41] I suggest that the *reverse* of that proposition is a more valid objective today. As we have seen, a great deal of the "policy of the labor laws" is formulated by decisions of the National Labor Relations Board, which has been extraordinarily permissive with respect to the very matter of collective bargaining and its scope, which was at issue in the *Jewel Tea* case.

Justice White went on to comment in that case on the kind of union activity which would *not* be immune to antitrust law, citing, by way of example, an effort by the union to bargain over the company's prices.[42] Yet Justice White found tolerable a union demand reenforced by the strike power to compel the com-pany to agree upon the precise hours during which it would be open for business—a matter which, on its face, would seem to go to the heart of the company's ability to compete. Mr. Justice White condoned the union's invasion of this area on the ground that it "falls within the protection of the national labor policy and is *therefore* exempt from the Sherman Act." [43]

The proposition implied in Mr. Justice White's opinion is that where and when the antitrust laws and the labor laws overlap or collide, the antitrust laws must yield and the labor laws pre-vail. The proposition advanced in this paper is to the contrary. There is no defensible basis for such a preferred status for "labor" law over any other kind. More to the point, perhaps there is no evidence of a *legislative* intent or policy that there be such a preference. And, finally, to the extent that a preferred position for "labor law" results in a preferred position for labor *activities* which would otherwise be illegal, any policy to that end is in urgent need of critical re-examination. To put it more specifically, is there—can there sensibly be—a policy which, under cover of the labor laws, permits frontal assaults upon that very competition which it is also (and far more clearly) our avowed national policy to promote and protect? [44]

More than five years ago, a Committee of the American Bar Association's Section of Labor Relations Law (of which I had the honor to be a member) joined a number of other expert observers and commentators in urging that Congressional atten-tion to the overlap and conflict between so-called national labor policy and the national policy with respect to antitrust and competition was long overdue.[45] That recommendation, which was sound then, is still sound—and more urgent.

Labor's Ability to Suspend Economic Law

We turn now to another area of "might makes right," wherein the "rule of *economic* law" is assaulted by the massed power of organized labor, in the following respects, among others:

(1) Unions demand and (backed up by the strike power) obtain wage increases at a rate far above the rate of increase in productivity. In fact, a notable feature of collective bargaining in the recent past has been the virtual substitution of the Consumer Price Index for the productivity indices as a measure of the appropriate increase in wages.

(2) Unions have been demanding and obtaining large wage increases at a time when unemployment has been high and rising.

That the strike threat is an important element, either active or potential, in labor's success in the foregoing areas requires special consideration. Its role in the achievement of objectives which—however well they may serve the interests of the labor group involved—may run counter to the overall national interest gives rise to significant social, economic and legislative questions concerning the strike privilege. (As noted below, there is not, strictly speaking, any *right* to strike.) Does the strike power give one side an undue advantage at the bargaining table or in the resulting dispute? Is that advantage in the public interest (i.e., in the interest of the 180 million citizens who are not in unions)? Is it in the interest of the approximately 60 million workers, not in unions, at whose expense the union gains may be achieved? Is it even in the interest of other segments of organized labor who may stand to lose precisely that portion of *their* "fair share" which goes to make up the excess in the settlement won by virtue of the superior economic power of the striking union?

These questions go to the core of key economic issues; and the question of the absolute legitimacy of the strike weapon itself is sharpened by the fact that the classic feature of the strike— the factor which is relied on to make collective bargaining work

—is mutuality of "economic pain" during the strike, or the mutual fear of it. Today, the advent of unemployment compensation for strikers, as well as public assistance (food stamps, welfare, etc.), coupled with union pressures on lending institutions for credit and moratoria on installment payments, have operated to eliminate much of the "economic pain" to the striker. The result is an adverse and subversive impact on collective bargaining, in that the absence of the factor of economic pain not only prolongs strikes, but it encourages them in the first place and tends to result in strikes in support of unrealistic demands. Where such demands are monetary and, through the use of the strike weapon, they are pressed successfully, it is at the expense of some other segment of the economy, as noted above. In addition, as already indicated, a key underpinning of collective bargaining (the *mutual* fear or fact of *mutual* economic pain—the pressure that forces the accommodation that *is* collective bargaining) is substantially removed; and it is questionable whether collective bargaining as a system can succeed or survive without it. At the very least, it is submitted, the strike which is embarked upon and continued in the secure knowledge that it will not be painful or costly, except to the employer, has ceased to be a fair contest between relatively equally matched economic adversaries and has become instead an exercise in extortion.

Proposals for Legislative Reform

One hopes that, for the reader as for the writer, contemplation of all of these factors leads to a conviction that a re-examination and overhaul of our labor policy and our labor laws is already long overdue. Having come this far this boldly, I cannot evade the task of proposing a course, even if the limitations of a paper such as this do not permit charting it in detail.

As already indicated, the major areas for reform legislation are the National Labor Relations Act and the antitrust laws. There are others, such as the abuse of welfare programs to sustain strikes, the perversion of unemployment insurance to the same end. And there is an area of great delicacy, because it is an emotional and propaganda mine field: the strike and the injunction. Precisely because it is so sensitive, I turn to it first in offering ideas for legislative reform to cure the ills which I have been describing.

Norris-LaGuardia Act

The Norris-LaGuardia Anti-Injunction Act of 1932[46] was aimed at protecting labor from the devastating and destructive effects of court injunctions aimed at breaking strikes and (in many cases) unions. That it was an essential part of the protectionist era in American labor relations (perhaps *the* most essential part, given the time and the context of its enactment) is undeniable. Compared to its impact in its time even the New Deal labor legislation which came later is almost dwarfed. The absolute sweep of its provisions and of the immunity which (as spelled out later in the *Hutcheson* case) it confers is, however, highly dubious in light of labor's vast power today; and probably it will prove ultimately destructive. In order to approach with any objectivity at all the possible revision of Norris-LaGuardia, it is necessary to re-examine the status of the strike itself.

Re-Examination of the "Right" to Strike

A great deal of the emotionalism surrounding injunctions in labor disputes springs from an erroneous notion—not confined to labor but probably fairly widespread among the public—that the "right to strike" is either God-given and inherent, or (at the very least) it is protected in the Bill of Rights or elsewhere in the Constitution. None of these things, of course, is true. If this paper succeeds no further in this area than to introduce this truth to those who may not now be aware of it, especially members of the public, it will have done a considerable service.

In point of fact, *there is no "right to strike"* in any absolute sense, and we were reminded of this by the decision in the recent *Postal Clerks* case, in which the union attacked head-on the prohibition in Federal law against strikes by government employees. A three-judge Constitutional Court, whose decision was affirmed without opinion by the Supreme Court, rejected the Postal Clerks' assertion that the right to strike is a "fundamental right protected by the Constitution." The Court (echoing Justice Brandeis) replied that "the right to strike cannot be considered a 'fundamental' right" and that "there is no Constitutional right to strike." [47]

The Court made clear a fact which has been largely obscured by labor's incessant assertion of the sanctity of the "right" to strike, namely, that there is no such "right" save as society permits it by legislation; that, indeed, the basic common law doctrine that a strike is an illegal combination to injure another would still exist, but for such statutory provisions conferring or protecting the right to strike as are found in the National Labor Relations Act, the Norris-LaGuardia Act and the Clayton Act. The fact that the "right" to strike is non-existent, save as it is conferred as a privilege by society through its legislators, is highly significant today. The privilege which society confers, it can revoke. And the circumstances for revocation are simple: the privilege (or the manner of its use) is no longer in the public interest. It is as simple as that (as predatory businessmen came to learn long ago). While it may well be that the strike ought not to be stripped entirely of its legislative immunity, it is important to any rational consideration of this issue that it be recognized that neither does it have the sanctity of Holy Writ; nor is it among the "unalienable rights" referred to in the Declaration of Independence; nor is it among the liberties protected by the first ten Amendments to the Constitution, or elsewhere in the Constitution itself. If we can get past those erroneous notions, and the emotion which they generate, we can consider whether and to what extent the strike power can and ought to be controlled in the interest of the very society which extended that privilege in the first place.

It is proposed that:

(1) The Norris-LaGuardia Act and the relevant provisions of the National Labor Relations Act be amended so as to give effect to the decision in the *Boys Markets* case, permitting injunctions against strikes in breach of union agreements.[48] More than that—but still minimally—Norris-LaGuardia should be reframed to permit injunctions against any type of conduct which is either illegal or in breach of contract, without such clouds or conditions as have grown up or still persist as a result of the particular facts and the language used by the Supreme Court in *Boys Markets*.[49]

(2) The virtually absolute ban on injunctions against strikes should be moderated so as at least to *permit* courts of equity in certain cases to weigh the rights and interests of the striking union and its members, on the one hand, against the damage caused by the strike to the employer, the community and other innocent third parties, and to determine, on the basis of the totality of the situation, whether the power to strike ought equitably be permitted to be exercised in that situation.

This is, indeed, no more than the application to labor disputes of a centuries-old Common Law doctrine, which calls for the "balancing of conveniences" when one disputant seeks to enjoin the action of another.

The rationale for both of these approaches is the same: the "right to strike" is a privilege extended by society in its socio-economic interest and any such privilege is revocable by society (in the case of unions, just as in the case of predatory business interests) whenever the exercise of the privilege harms, rather than helps, the society which extends it. I suggest, in passing, that such regulation and moderation as I propose might very well save the strike from the possibly *fatal* effects of a wave of public hostility, signs of which are already apparent and which could crest at any time as the result of any strike which sufficiently outrages public opinion by its display of apparently unbridled union power. History teaches that reaction to the abuse of power is almost always excessive, rarely discriminating, and frequently total, as regards the offending power.

National Labor Relations Act

With respect to the National Labor Relations Act and the imbalances and distortions which have arisen under it, there are a number of areas in which the law requires amendment, if the "Rule of Law" in labor-management relations subject to the Act is to be meaningful. One objective is to expunge from the law the decisional manifestations, heretofore described, which arose out of the steady application to decision-making of the outdated philosophy of "labor as underdog." This has not been the case for some time.

Then there is the need for correction of those decisions which have improperly and unduly enhanced labor's economic power in the labor-management relationship generally, and in the collective bargaining arena in particular. Included here would be legislation *truly* accomplishing the prohibition of secondary boycotts, "work preservation" actions of various types, "hot cargo" clauses and the like. These union activities are all, in one way or another, notably anti-competitive, and no acceptable reason can now be advanced for continuing to exempt unions from the rules which govern the rest of the business community. Finally, there are those doctrinal errors which tend to subordinate the will and the wishes of the individual to the union as an institution.

There have been introduced during this Congress a number of bills designed to correct the decisional distortions of the intent of Congress in the National Labor Relations Act.[50]   A greater service to the cause of labor-management relations than hearings and action on these bills can hardly be imagined.

With respect to the antitrust laws, I suggest that the present sloppy legislative arrangement between the antitrust laws and the National Labor Relations Act be tidied up. In addition, the Congress (which frequently joins in the clamor that "Big Business" and "Big Labor" have too much power) should address itself to putting the two under equal restraint, insofar as antitrust policy is concerned. Those exercises of market power which eliminate competition or make it difficult, or which suspend or interfere with the operation of market laws, should be as illegal for labor as they are for business. I suggest simply that the time for effectuating that self-evident proposition has arrived. I forbear to adduce specific proposals in this paper, since acceptance of the proposition that the "antitrust approach" is a proper one is substantial progress in the right direction; and it is, perhaps better that the debate, if any, over this question be conducted, at first, in generalities. It should be made utterly clear, however, that (although some amendment to the Sherman and Clayton Acts will be necessary) no assault is intended upon the rights of unions to *exist* and function as labor organizations without being, *ipso facto*, held to be conspiracies or combinations in restraint of trade. In other words, the union's right to exist is equated with the corporation's. It is the *conduct*, not the form of the organization, which should be the object of the law.

With that aside, it is proposed merely that any conduct which (using the same standards applicable to business organizations) diminishes or threatens competition or offers the possibility of illicit restraint of trade be treated the same in the case of labor organizations as in the case of business corporations. And if the cry goes up that this opens the way to another "Danbury Hatters" case,[51] the answer is that it is not intended to and it need not. A simple solution would lie in the incorporation of unions, and perhaps this is the time and the occasion for it.

As has been made abundantly clear, the thrust of this paper is toward legislative reform—restoration of the rule of law by legislation. However, no paper with any pretense of scholarship and objectivity could treat of the rule of law and collective bargaining without at least acknowledging (and condemning) a situation which is best summed up in the aphorism "Justice delayed is justice denied."

It would be blind and foolish to ignore the fact that, just as there are unions with whom the wildcat strike is an instrument of polity, so with unfair labor practices and some employers. Nothing said or implied at any point in this paper is intended to overlook, condone or defend the conduct of those employers who deliberately and wantonly trample on the rights of workers and then rely on the inhert delays of legal procedure to so defer the time of reckoning that the remedy never quite mends the breach. I condemn that cynical sort of behavior as every bit as contemptible as any of the other conduct discussed herein which makes a mockery of the rule of law.

Respect for Law

Returning, by way of conclusion, to the legislative problem: given the proper legislative reform, have we solved the problem of return to the rule of law? I think not. Indeed, I would be remiss, I think, if I should fail to discuss a problem which has increasingly preoccupied me in recent years. It is particularly apropos both in light of the proposals heretofore made for "more law" and in light of another which I shall discuss in a moment.

It seems to me self-evident that nothing is more necessary to the restoration of the rule of law than the restoration of *respect* for law. And respect for law has declined alarmingly during the past decade. It is idle to talk of equity, public interest or restoring balances, if the attitude of the individual is simply that he need not obey a law or an order or a decision which he does not like or considers improper. We thus return to "rule of law" in the sense of "law and order" and I submit that a concerted effort to rehabilitate respect for the law is the duty of all responsible citizens and a *sine qua non* of the achievement of *any* further progress by *any*body.

Compulsory Arbitration

Let me dramatize the dangerous potential of the current decline in respect for the law by discussing, briefly, the much-vexed subject of compulsory arbitration. This is a solution which my friend A. H. Raskin has been advocating for a long time, it being his profound conviction that the strike is an outmoded and atavistic tool for the settlement of labor-management disputes. What Mr. Raskin advocates is that, when labor and management demonstrate (as they do with such regrettable frequency), that they are unable to submerge their quarrels in the public interest and are reckless of the damage which their battles do to the public, then, in its own interest, society must step in and take back some of that decision-making sovereignty which it had extended to business and labor at earlier times. More specifically, Raskin recommends that arbitration of contract disputes be imposed by law—at least in those industries where strikes have a tendency to hurt the innocent bystander far more (or, at least, every bit as much as) they hurt the parties themselves.[52] Industry has long inveighed against this alternative, although lately (reflecting the gross imbalance of power in the transportation industry) spokesmen for transportation interests have been loud in their recommendations that compulsory arbitration come to that segment of the economy. Congress would be well advised to reflect upon the combination of circumstances which thus causes a significant segment of American industry to abandon a position so staunchly and traditionally held by virtually all industry. The answer is simply that the arbitrator ceases to be a threat to industrial sovereignty when it becomes obvious that one will almost certainly obtain more (or lose less) *through him* than through a test of strength with one's collective bargaining adversary. That, in a word, seems to be the situation in which the transportation industry sees itself.

But the plight of transportation deserves a little further examination. The procedures under the Railway Labor Act rested in part upon an assumption—virtually a presumption—that, when a public board recommended terms of settlement, neither party to a dispute would dare to incur or be able to withstand the public disfavor with which failure to accept would be met. I have no doubt that there was a halcyon time when this might have been true. It is no more—at least, not for unions. Long ago, unions began demonstrating in the transportation industry that either such a force of public opinion was non-existent—or, if it did exist, it never quite got itself together—or, if it got itself together, it just did not matter! Accordingly, unions in that industry have tended of late years to ignore the recommendations of Presidential boards and have simply used those recommendations as new plateaus for bargaining. Management, on the other hand, reacts as the framers originally expected both sides to act. It feels inhibited from rejecting the recommendations and thereby incurring the disfavor of "public opinion." So the transportation industry sees the "non-compulsory" recommendations technique as being essentially both compulsory and unilateral in its pressure. In consequence, the industry feels (and quite properly in my judgment) that the "recommendation" technique is no longer viable.

But this matter of the non-acceptance of recommendations or awards leads to a much more ominous question. The debate continues to rage over compulsory arbitration, even in connection with the Administration's Bill to handle critical disputes in the transportation industry.[53] But I suggest that that debate may already be moot; for, if there is a serious possibility that the arbitration award will not be obeyed and that a strike in defiance of it will begin or continue, then we have a failure of the very objective that compulsory arbitration is aimed at. And that is precisely the possibility which looms out of the current decline in respect for law, in all its aspects—as embodied in contracts, awards or judicial decrees. The spectre of a massive confrontation between the government and its citizens—of the possibility of massive defiance of court orders, for example—can only comfort those hostile to our system and anxious for its discredit.

Our experience already alarmingly demonstrates that this danger is far from theoretical here. It is supplemented by the Australian experience, the able presentation of which by Professor Kingsley Laffer, as a part of this symposium, would make any further discussion of that by me both superfluous and presumptuous. I am not sure of the state of "the rule of law" in Australia; but I suggest that, if it is *not* on the general decline there, and they are nonetheless having unhappy experiences with the non-acceptance of arbitration awards, it simply indicates how much must be done in the way of moderating labor's power to have its way before we can even consider less destructive means of settling labor-management disputes.

Conclusion

By way of conclusion, it is observed that neither the proposals in this paper—nor, indeed, collective bargaining itself or any other area or aspect of our freedoms—are likely to survive and succeed, if the rule of law cannot survive and succeed. Accordingly, this paper makes an earnest plea for a revival of *respect* for law—on all sides, at all levels of our society—so that the *rule* of law can once again become a meaningful concept and regain its preeminent role as both source and guardian of our **freedoms**.

NOTES

1. Dr. George W. Taylor, of the Wharton School, saw the possibilities for this—particularly for excessive refinement and technicality in the area of the duty to bargain—and, accordingly, when the Wagner Act was being considered, he urged the omission of Section 8(5), and the "duty-to-bargain" provision. Taylor, "Collective Bargaining in Transition," in The Structure of Collective Bargaining 343 (A. Weber ed. 1961). He saw no reason to alter his thinking as time wore on, and he likewise opposed the Taft-Hartley attempt to define the duty to bargain. *Id.* at 347-48. Subsequently, he, along with an impressive panel of fellow-experts in the field, urged the repeal of Section 8(a)(5) on the ground that it had become so over-refined as to be unworkable. The Public Interest in Collective Bargaining 81-82 (Comm. for Economic Development 1961). The same view, somewhat surprisingly, has been advanced by Professor Gomberg (in *Government Participation in Union Regulation and Collective Bargaining*, 13 Lab. L. J. 941, 946-47 (1962)) and, not so surprisingly, by Dr. Herbert Northrup (in Compulsory Arbitration and Government Intervention in Labor Disputes 103-05 (Labor Policy Ass'n 1966)).

2. Any word of support (or nostalgia) for "law and order" tends, these days, to bring forth the assertion—deemed by some, it appears, to be somehow a rejoinder or refutation—that the time has come to put "human" rights above "property" rights. It seems to me that this bespeaks a conflict or a displacement where there is none and need be none. The right to own and hold property, safe from invasion, damage or theft by another, *is* a human right. The right to defend one's home against unlawful entry *is* a human right, ranking, indeed, immediately after the right to protect life itself. Finally, I suggest that even "law" and "order" are not *two* things, but different aspects of one. Law guarantees order. Indeed, law (viewed as embodying both the making of the rule and its observance or enforcement) —law in *that* sense—*is* order. Its absence is chaos—a fact not lost upon those few who, having chaos—at least in this society—as their objective, most loudly decry and deride law and order.

3. 5 U.S. (1 Cranch) 137 (1803).

4. B. Cardozo, The Nature of the Judicial Process 167-76 (Yale U. Press 1971).

5. United Mine Workers v. Pennington, 381 U.S. 657, 697 (1965) (Goldberg, Harlan & Stewart, JJ., dissenting from majority opinion but concurring in the judgment), 59 L.R.R.M. 2369, 2385.

6. Local 189, Meat Cutters v. Jewel Tea Co., 381 U.S. 676, 697 (1965) (Goldberg, Harlan & Stewart, JJ., concurring), 59 L.R.R.M. 2376, 2385.

7. *See, e.g.,* the excerpts from the opinion of Mr. Justice White in *Jewel Tea,* in text at 91 *ff.*

8. The contrast in context between "encouraging," on the one hand, and "protecting," on the other, is clearly seen in Section 1 (Findings and Policies) of the Wagner Act, as reenacted in the Taft-Hartley Act:

> It is declared to be the policy of the United States to eliminate the causes of certain substantial obstructions to the free flow of commerce and to mitigate and eliminate these obstructions when they have occurred by *encouraging* the practice and procedure of collective bargaining and by *protecting* the exercise by workers of full freedom of association, self-organization, and designation of representatives of their own choosing, for the purpose of negotiating the terms and conditions of their employment or other mutual aid or protection. Labor Management Relations Act § 101, 29 U.S.C. § 151 (1964) (emphasis added).

9. Section 7 of the National Labor Relations Act, as amended by the Taft-Hartley Act, provides:

> Employees shall have the right to self-organization, to form, join, or assist labor organizations, to bargain collectively through representatives of their own choosing, and to engage in other concerted activities for the purpose of collective bargaining or other mutual aid or protection, and shall also have the *right to refrain* from any or all of such activities except to the extent that such right may be affected by an agreement requiring membership in a labor organization as a condition of employment as authorized in section 158(a)(3) of this title. Labor Management Relations Act § 101, 29 U.S.C. § 157 (1964) (emphasis added).

Obviously, the "right to refrain" is seriously compromised when the weight of the relevant government agency is cast in the opposite direction.

10. In its ability to find an implied or inferred threat in employers' statements, the Board demonstrated, in effect, a working presumption that *any* employer statement opposing unionization will have a coercive effect on his employees. *See, e.g.,* Dal-Tex Optical Co., 137 N.L.R.B. 1782 (1962), 50 L.R.R.M. 1489; Lord Baltimore Press, 142 N.L.R.B. 328 (1963), 53 L.R.R.M. 1019; Trane Co., 137 N.L.R.B. 1506 (1962), 50 L.R.R.M. 1434; Raytheon Co., 160 N.L.R.B. 1603 (1966), 63 L.R.R.M. 1180; Thomas Products Co., 167 N.L.R.B. 878 (1967), 66 L.R.R.M. 1147. It is interesting to note that, in its obsession with "laboratory conditions" for employee elections (by which the Board usually meant conditions under which employees were untouched by employer expressions of opinion, though not necessarily free of the union's), the Board was demanding a far purer atmosphere than is required or exists in our political elections.

11. Section 9(c)(5) of the Act provides that in determining whether a unit is appropriate "the extent to which the employees have organized shall not be controlling." Despite this explicit Congressional hostility toward "extent of organization" as a criterion, the Board frequently assigned decisive weight to that factor. Both in Quaker City Life Insurance Co., 134 N.L.R.B. 90 (1961), 49 L.R.R.M. 1281 and in Sav-On Drugs, Inc., 138 N.L.R.B. 1032 (1962), 51 L.R.R.M. 1152, the Board abandoned long-established precedent which had denied requests for fragmented units. *See also,* Stern's Paramus, 150 N.L.R.B. 799 (1965), 58 L.R.R.M. 1081.

12. *E.g.,* Snow & Sons, 134 N.L.R.B. 709 (1961), 49 L.R.R.M. 1228; Bernel Foam Products Co., 146 N.L.R.B. 1435 (1964), 56 L.R.R.M. 1039; Northwest Engineering Co., 158 N.L.R.B. 624 (1966), 62 L.R.R.M. 1089.

13. H. K. Porter Co., 153 N.L.R.B. 1370 (1965), 59 L.R.R.M. 1462. The Board was rebuffed in this effort by the Supreme Court. H. K. Porter Co. v. N.L.R.B., 397 U.S. 99 (1970), 73 L.R.R.M. 2561.

14. Town & Country Mfg. Co., 136 N.L.R.B. 1022 (1962), 49 L.R.R.M. 1918; Fibreboard Paper Products Corp., 138 N.L.R.B. 550, 51 L.R.R.M. 1101.

15. Fibreboard Paper Products Corp. v. NLRB, 379 U.S. 203, 217 (1964) (Stewart, Douglas & Harlan, JJ., concurring), 57 L.R.R.M. 2609, 2617. *Accord,* NLRB v. Adams Dairy, Inc., 350 F.2d 108 (8th Cir. 1965), 60 L.R.R.M. 2084, *cert. denied,* 382 U.S. 1011 (1966), 61 L.R.R.M. 2191; NLRB v. Royal Plating & Polishing Co., 350 F.2d 191 (3rd Cir. 1965), 60 L.R.R.M. 2033.

16. General Electric Co., 173 N.L.R.B. 253 (1968), 69 L.R.R.M. 1305.

17. General Electric Co., 150 N.L.R.B. 192 (1964), 57 L.R.R.M. 1491

18. *E.g.,* United Steelworkers of America and Local 6991 (Auburndale Freezer Corp.), 177 N.L.R.B. No. 108 (1969), *rev'd sub nom.,* Auburndale Freezer Corp. v. N.L.R.B., 434 F.2d 1219 (5th Cir. 1970), 75 L.R.R.M. 2752, 2755; Local 861, IBEW (Plauche Electric, Inc.), 135 N.L.R.B. 250 1962), 49 L.R.R.M. 1446; Local 3, IBEW (New Power Wire and Electric Corp.), 144 N.L.R.B. 1089 (1963), 54 L.R.R.M. 1178.

19. United Brotherhood of Carpenters and Joiners (National Woodwork Manufacturers Ass'n), 149 N.L.R.B. 646 (1964), 57 L.R.R.M. 1341.

20. 29 U.S.C. § 158(e) (1964).

21. 29 U.S.C. § 159(b)(4) (1964).

22. National Woodwork Manufacturers Ass'n v. NLRB, 386 U.S. 612 (1967), 64 L.R.R.M. 2801.

23. *Id.* at 653.

24. American Federation of Radio and Television Artists (Great Western Broadcasting Corp.), 150 N.L.R.B. 467 (1964), 58 L.R.R.M. 1019.

25. *E.g.,* Local 741, Plumbers and Pipefitters Union (Keith Riggs Plumbing and Heating Contractor), 137 N.L.R.B. 1125 (1962), 50 L.R.R.M. 1313.

26. As Arthur Krock recently put it, "[J]ustice from a judge depends on his degree of mental and moral integrity, as well as on his legal capacity and the cold detachment which subordinates his doctrinal and political leanings to the clear letter of the law." Krock, *Those Crucial Court Vacancies,* N.Y. Times, Oct. 19, 1971, at 43, col. 1. The application of that standard to the NLRB and its failure to maintain it, are all too obvious, reflecting no doubt the fact that members of the Board are appointed politically and for short terms.

27. R. Pound, Legal Immunities of Labor Unions (American Enterprise Ass'n 1957).

28. 15 U.S.C. §§ 17, 26; 29 U.S.C. § 52 (1964).

29. Apex Hosiery Co. v. Leader, 310 U.S. 469, 510 (1940), 6 L.R.R.M. 647, 651, and the Court was still acknowledging that fact (and wrestling with the problem of degree or extent) twenty-five years later in *Pennington* and *Jewel Tea,* notes 5 and 6 *supra.*

30. Allen Bradley Co. v. Local 3, IBEW, 325 U.S. 797 (1945), 16 L.R.R.M. 798.

31. U.S. v. Hutcheson, 312 U.S. 219, 232 (1941), (footnote omitted), 7 L.R.R.M. 267, 269.

32. It should be made emphatically clear that what is being dealt with here may not be dismissed as one more venture in what is sometimes referred to as "the discredited Antitrust approach" to the problem of labor's power. What that remark deprecates is probably best summed up in the Neanderthal demand (heard less and less frequently of late) to "put the damned unions under the Antitrust laws!" That approach (if so misinformed and misguided an attitude can be dignified by that term) was indeed an assault on unions—on their very right to exist and to function; and it was properly discredited. It was a destructive, blunderbuss approach.

It is not what is advocated here. What is proposed here might be called, by way of metaphoric contrast, a *rifle* approach. It has the objective of zeroing in on specific targets, the validity of which cannot be gainsaid by any objective observer who is willing to concede that the free market system is a proper way of life for us and that competition is its life blood. If that be so—and it is, as a matter of national policy—then whatever is antagonistic to it needs to be looked to and remedied. And the broad-ranging "labor exemption" is precisely that.

33. Apex Hosiery Co., note 29 *supra*, at 501-04.

34. Wharton, *Unions Are Monopolies*, N.Y. Times, Sept. 6, 1971, at 19, col. 1.

35. 21 Cong. Rec. 2468-2729 (1890), *passim*.

36. See, *e.g.*, Letter from Milton Friedman, N.Y. Times, Nov. 24, 1971, at 34, col. 3.

37. See, *e.g.*, §§ 8(b)(4) and 8(e) of the Taft-Hartley Act, 29 U.S.C. §§ 158(b)(4), 158(e) (1964).

38. Pound, *supra* note 27, at 44.

39. *See* U.S. Department of Labor, Bureau of Labor Statistics, Bulletin No. 1666, Handbook of Labor Statistics 338-39 (1970).

40. Pound, *supra* note 27, at 1.

41. 381 U.S. at 690, 59 L.R.R.M. at 2381. The untenable priority of "labor policy" over "antitrust policy" persists to this writing. *See, e.g.*, Intercontinental Container Transport Corp. v. N. Y. Shipping Ass'n, Inc., and ILA, 426 F. 2d 884 (2d Cir. 1970), 74 L.R.R.M. 2530, discussed in ABA Committee Reports, Section on Labor Relations Law 11-13 (1971). The case involved a stringent "work preservation" agreement concerning containerized shipments, which had been forced upon the Shipping Association by the union. The plaintiff was an "outsider" prevented by that agreement from competing in the Port of New York. Its effort to obtain, under the Sherman Act, an injunction and treble damages failed, solely on the grounds that the injury it sustained was the result of a union's acting in its own self-interest in the monopolization of its "traditional work." Accordingly, the action was insulated from Antitrust law. It is precisely this "Divine Right" theory of labor—at once offensive to democracy, economics and good sense—which this paper asserts we can no longer afford.

42. *But see* the Brief for Appellee at 22, in Fibreboard Paper Products v. NLRB, note 16 *supra*, in which Solicitor General Cox acknowledged that the Board's interpretation of the bargaining obligation imposed by the Act could extend to a requirement that the employer bargain over his prices.

43. 381 U.S. at 690, 59 L.R.R.M. at 2381.

44. The question raised here is neither novel nor new. "There is a definite clash between the ideal of a competitive economy which underlies the Sherman Act and the essentially anti-competitive philosophy that characterizes the National Labor Relations Act." Mishkin, *The Supreme Court, 1964 Term,* 79 Harv. L. Rev. 56, 181 (1965). It has simply become more urgent as the ability of unions to stifle economic laws and deeply affect the course of the economy has become more and more obvious, as noted below.

45. ABA Committee Reports, Section of Labor Relations Law 61 (1966).

46. 29 U.S.C. §§ 101-15 (1964).

47. United Federation of Postal Clerks v. Blount, 325 F.Supp. 879, 883 (D.D.C. 1971), *aff'd without opinion,* 40 U.S.L.W. 3160 (Oct. 12, 1971). Also, *see* Dorchy v. Kansas, 272 U.S. 306, 311 (1926), in which Justice Brandeis wrote: "Neither the common law, nor the 14th Amendment, confers the absolute right to strike." *Accord,* UAW v. Wisconsin ERB, 336 U.S. 245 (1949).

48. Boys Markets, Inc. v. Retail Clerks, Local 770, 398 U.S. 235 (1970), 72 L.R.R.M. 2527.

49. *E.g.,* General Cable Corp. v. IBEW, Local No. 1644, —— F. ——, (W.D. Md. 1971), 77 L.R.R.M. 3053; Rochester Telephone Corp. v. Communications Workers, ——F. ——, (W.D. N.Y. 1971), 78 L.R.R.M. 2213.

50. S. 1055, H.R. 7787; S. 1613, H.R. 9038; S. 1780, H.R. 9320; S. 1903, H.R. 9458; S. 2169, H.R. 11072; S. 1844, H.R. 9148; S. 1873, H.R. 9149; S. 1659, H.R. 10437; S. 2053, H.R. 8359; S. 2168, H.R. 8358; S. 552, S. 1320, H.R. 5807.

51. Loewe v. Lawlor, 208 U.S. 274 (1908); Lawlor v. Loewe, 235 U.S. 522 (1915).

52. Raskin, *Automation Has Made Strikes Senseless,* N.Y. Times, Oct. 31, 1965, § 6 (Magazine), at 45.

53. H.R. 3586, 92d Cong., 1st Sess. (1971).

Injunctive Powers under the
National Labor Relations Act

John E. Abodeely[†]

Throughout the history of the labor movement in the United States one of the most controversial issues has been the use of the injunction in labor disputes. Adopting the theory of conspiracy, early court decisions used it to stifle union organization.[1] In 1932, Congress sought to control the abuses by enacting section 4 of the Norris-La Guardia Act: "No court of the United States shall have jurisdiction to issue any restraining order or temporary or permanent injunction in any case involving or growing out of any labor dispute. . . ."[2]

As in many other areas of law, the swing of the pendulum reached extremes on both ends of the spectrum. The almost blanket prohibition against the use of the injunction was to deprive the National Labor Relations Board and the courts of an effective remedy in the search for industrial stability.

Attempting to return the pendulum to a middle position, Congress, as part of the Taft-Hartley Amendments of 1947, provided the NLRB with a limited right (and obligation) to such injunctions in unfair labor practices.[3] There are three distinct proceedings by which the Board may obtain judicial aid in enforcing the amended Act: (1) prior to the issuance of a complaint, the Board has authority under section 10(1) to petition the federal district court for injunctive relief against certain alleged unfair labor practices; (2) after the issuance of a complaint, the Board may under section 10(j) petition the district court for injunctive relief against any alleged unfair labor practice; and (3) after a final decision and order, the Board has authority, under section 10(e), to petition the circuit court of appeals for enforcement of its order.[4]

The NLRB's broad authority to seek injunctions in unfair labor practice cases and the lack of Congressionally mandated

---

[†] John E. Abodeely is former Director of the Labor Policy Section of the Industrial Research Unit, Wharton School, University of Pennsylvania.

standards for its use provides a potentially powerful weapon in the agency's arsenal. In fact, one author has commented that "it would not be unreasonable to view this section [10(j)] as the potential source of a new labor remedy—the Board repeatedly exercising its discretion to petition the district courts for injunctive relief and the courts acting independently to reach the merits of the unfair labor practice charges." [5] Fortunately, this has not been the case. In fiscal year 1969, the Board was involved in a total of 210 section 10(l) proceedings and only 19 section 10(j) cases, significantly small numbers in view of the agency's overall case load.[6] Notwithstanding these figures, section 10(j) and (l) conjunctions constitute a significant area of labor law. Pointing to the long delays in NLRB proceedings, some authorities have advocated the increased use of injunctions.[7] Admittedly, the problem of delay exists. The question, however, is whether the injunction provides a realistic and effective solution or whether, in fact, it contains the seeds of greater industrial disharmony.

An analysis of section 10(j) and (l) injunctions must begin with the specific Congressional mandates and the legislative history surrounding them. After reviewing the role of the NLRB in such proceedings, the scope and function of judiciary will be examined. Such an approach, it is believed, will lead us closer to a determination of the proper utilization of the injunction in national labor policy.

Sections 10(j) and (l): Their Mechanics and Legislative History

Pursuant to the National Labor Relations Act and the rules and regulations promulgated by the NLRB, there has developed a specific procedural process for adjudicating an unfair labor practice case. Regional offices, acting as agents for the General Counsel's office, proceed upon the filing of a formal charge by investigating the alleged violation. The charge may be either voluntarily withdrawn by the charging party or dismissed by the Regional Office if the facts so warrant. Alternatively, if the jurisdictional requirements are met and if there is reasonable cause to believe that the Act has been violated, a formal complaint against the charged party will be issued. If the parties are unable to settle the dispute voluntarily, a hearing is held before a trial examiner. Based on his findings of fact and conclusions of law, the examiner may either sustain or dismiss the complaint in whole or in part. Within a given period of time after the examiner's findings are filed with the Board in Washington, the parties may file briefs, exceptions and requests for oral argument. The full Board or a three-man panel will review the evidence and either sustain, reverse or modify the trial examiner's decision. An appeal may be taken before the appropriate federal circuit court and certiorari may be sought before the Supreme Court.[8]

The procedure currently used by the NLRB initially proved effective in maintaining and preserving the interests of the parties and the guarantees of the Act. Unfortunately, as the Board's caseload increased, the time delay between the filing of the formal complaint and the agency's final decision also continued to grow. Estimating this delay to be nearly one year, Chairman Miller and his colleagues have expressed deep concern over the problem of shortening this period and preserving the efficacy of the Act.[9] Congress, as far back as 1947, recognized the potential of the time delay problem and sought to solve it by promulgating sections 10(j) and (l) of the amended Act.

Section 10(j)

During the 1947 debates surrounding the proposed amendments to the National Labor Relations Act (Wagner Act) of 1935, both the House and the Senate recognized the need to make available injunctive relief in appropriate cases. The approaches of the two chambers, however, were markedly different. Section 12 of the House bill provided the federal courts with independent jurisdiction over cases involving concerted violations. Adopting the position that by allowing private parties to enforce violations of the law the public interest would be best protected, the House version of the bill would have allowed private individuals to initiate injunctive actions as a matter of right.[10]

The Senate, however, rejected this philosophy and provided the NLRB with exclusive discretion to seek injunctive relief. To the majority of Senators, section 10(j)—as it was finally enacted—was intended to permit injunctive relief only to preserve the public interest and not to create a private course of action.[11] To align the House version with that of the Senate, a joint committee recommended adoption of the final version of 10(j):

> The Board shall have power, upon issuance of a complaint as provided in subsection (b) charging that any person has engaged in or is engaging in an unfair labor practice, to petition any United States district court within any district wherein the unfair labor practice in question is alleged to have occurred or wherein such person resides or transacts business, for appropriate temporary relief of restraining order. Upon the filing of any such petition the court shall cause notice thereof to be served upon such person, and thereupon shall have jurisdiction to grant to the Board such temporary relief or restraining order as it deems just and proper.

The legislative conflict over the private and public aspects of section 10(j) were subsequently alleviated by a 1948 decision of the Fourth Circuit Court of Appeals. In *Amazon Cotton Mills,*[12] the court reviewed the legislative history and concluded that except in unusual cases only the Board could seek an injunction against an unfair labor practice. No private party, be it employer or union, was so authorized in the ordinary unfair labor practice case. Subsequent courts, relying on the Fourth Circuit Court's decision, extended the rule to prohibit any private party from instituting civil contempt proceedings for an alleged violation of an injunction.[13]

Shortly after its enactment, the discretionary injunction provision came under attack as being violative of the anti-injunction clause of the Norris-La Guardia Act. It was argued that section 10(j) failed expressly to negate the application of other laws, as did its companion section 10(l). This latter provision specified that the district court may grant such relief as it deems just and proper "notwithstanding any other provision of law." Relying on the obvious Congressional intent behind section 10(j), the courts have uniformly held that the "notwithstanding" clause of section 10(l) is mere surplusage and does not imply a different test of authority under 10(j), which contains no such phrase.[14]

The broad grant of power in section 10(j) contains no limitations upon the NLRB's discretion to seek injunctive relief in unfair labor practice cases. After a complaint is issued, the Board may seek an injunction in any type of unfair labor practice except those enumerated in section 10(l), wherein the agency must seek to enjoin the alleged conduct. In its petition before the federal district court, the Board need only allege: (1) the filing of an unfair labor practice; (2) the issuance of a complaint on the charge; (3) the facts supporting the charge; and (4) the likelihood that the unfair labor practice will continue unless restrained.[15]

Despite this broad delegation of authority, the Board has been reluctant to exercise its 10(j) discretion. Such injunctions are sought only rarely, generally in emergency situations involving some degree of alleged public harm.[16] Furthermore, 10(j) cases usually involve situations where the "violations are clear and flagrant, and where immediate relief seems necessary because a subsequent Board order and decree would be inadequate to remedy the injury." [17] In comparing sections 10(j) and (l), it would appear that the NLRB's decision-making process under the former section is quite similar to the Congressional determinations made in the latter section. In 10(l), Congress specifically determined that the effect of certain unfair labor practices upon the public, the private parties and the Board's adjudicative process was so detrimental that an injunction should be sought in all such cases. The NLRB's decision to seek an injunction under 10(j) should likewise consider the potential effect of the alleged unfair labor practice upon the public, the private parties and its own procedures. That these factors are generally considered is revealed by the NLRB's own statement of the criteria used in determining the appropriateness of a 10(j) action:

1. the clarity of the alleged violation;
2. the likelihood of a business dispute's resulting in an extraordinary public impact;
3. the presence of special remedy problems that would not be solved by a final Board order absent interim relief;
4. flagrant disregard for the Board's procedures;
5. the continuous or repetitious nature of the alleged violation;
6. the threat of the alleged violation to the public order;
7. the timeliness of the request for relief.[18]

A secondary reason for the limited use of section 10(j) injunctions may be the burdensome procedures utilized in obtaining the necessary authorization. Under this section, application for injunctive relief is under the control of the Board, whereas, under section 10(l) the General Counsel has the primary responsibility. Examining the Board's procedure in 10(j) cases, one commentator has noted that

> In practice, the Board in Washington authorizes in advance each and every application for Section 10(j) relief filed in court. This does not mean that the Board sees every request made for Section 10(j) relief; it does mean, however, that an application for 10(j) relief is in court without its approval. This cumbersome statutory

procedure for authorizing the filing of Section 10(j) injunction suits contributes to the limited use of that device and, accordingly, to the difficulty with which the remedy is obtainable.[19]

Regardless of the cause, it is certain that up to the present time the section 10(j) injunction proceeding has not been frequently used.[20] Superficially, the statutory mandate seems sufficiently broad to cover those situations requiring injunctive relief. Yet, the NLRB has hesitated to exercise its discretion and, when it has, the courts have generally been reluctant to grant the requested injunction. In contrast to this, however, the mandatory injunction proceedings of section 10(l) have had a somewhat more fruitful history.

Section 10(l)

The legislative history surrounding the development of section 10(l) reveals a strong Congressional awareness of the time lapse between the initial violation and the final adjudication. Moreover, "the congressional reports indicate that the section 10(l) injunction was conceived as a public remedy to help eliminate obstructions to the free flow of commerce due to labor disputes which continued pending final Board adjudication." [21] Notwithstanding this need to protect the public interest, there is implicit in the specific enumeration of certain unfair labor practices in section 10(l) the Congressional attempt to protect the interests of private parties and the efficacy of the Act's guarantees. Congress was aware that the substantial harm imposed upon both the public and the private parties by an illegal secondary boycott could not be remedied by a traditional cease and desist order issued nearly a year after the violation had occurred. The solution was to authorize the Board to obtain an injunction against the alleged violation pending final adjudication by the NLRB. Going even further than this, however, Congress mandated that in certain unfair labor practice cases, the harm to the public, the private parties and the Board was so substantial that the regional attorney must in all such cases seek an injunction. Thus it provided in section 10(l) that

> Whenever it is charged that any person has engaged in an unfair labor practice within the meaning of paragraph (4) (A), (B), or (C) of section 8(b) or section 8(c) or section 8(b)(7), the preliminary investigation of such charge shall be made forthwith and given priority over all other cases ---. If, after such investigation, the officer or regional attorney to whom the matter may be

referred has reasonable cause to believe such charge is true and that a complaint should issue, he shall, on behalf of the Board, petition any United States district court. . . . Upon the filing of any such petition the district court shall have jurisdiction to grant such injunctive relief or temporary restraining order as it deems just and proper, notwithstanding any other provision of law. . . .[22]

A comparison of section 10(l) with 10(j) reveals a number of similar prerequisites in obtaining injunctive relief. The requirements of a *prima facie* case under either section are a showing of the factual jurisdictional requirements and the presentation of any credible evidence which, if uncontradicted, would warrant the granting of the requested relief in light of the Act's policies and the interests of the parties involved. The Board is not required to present all its evidence nor is it required to prove the unfair labor practices complained of in order to authorize relief.[23] Moreover, it is not necessary to prove the existence of each element of the unfair practice but only to show that there is reasonable cause to believe that the elements exist.[24]

Another similarity between the two sections is the power of the federal district court to issue a temporary restraining order pending the issuance of an injunction. Section 10(l), however, also authorizes an *ex parte* restraining order, but only when the petition alleges "that substantial and irreparable injury to the charging party will be unavoidable and such temporary restraining order shall be effective for no longer than five days and will become void at the expiration of such period."

The differences between the optional and mandatory injunctive relief proceedings are also worthy of note. In addition to specifying the unfair practices covered, section 10(l) allows the regional officer or attorney to institute proceedings even before a formal complaint has been filed. Thus, before the regional officer may petition for 10(l) relief he must merely show that there has been an unfair labor practice charge, that a preliminary hearing has been conducted and that there exists reasonable cause to believe that the charge is true and that a complaint should issue.[25] As to the preliminary investigation, the district courts have generally held that this hearing is a prerequisite to the maintenance of a mandatory suit under 10(l).[26] In *Sperry v. Operating Engineers*,[27] the court somewhat lessened the requirement by holding that the jurisdiction of the federal district court does not depend upon a showing that the Board's regional attorney conducted a sufficient preliminary investigation. The court reasoned that the NLRA does not spell out the extent of the preliminary investigation nor does it require a formal hearing. It merely requires, for evidentiary purposes, an investigation capable of producing in the mind of the regional attorney a reasonable cause to believe that the charges are true.

The "reasonable cause to believe" requirement of section 10(l) has been liberally interpreted by most federal courts. All available evidence, including the deposition of the regional director,[28] will be examined to determine if there is reasonable cause to believe that the unfair labor practice charge is true.[29] This evidence need not be such as to support a finding that the unfair practice had actually been committed, but rather that it is reasonable to believe that this has occurred.[30]

The similarities and differences between sections 10(j) and (l) are more procedural than substantive. Although not underestimating the importance of the mechanics of the law, it is submitted that the potential worth of injunctive relief will be determined by the standards adopted by the courts. Again with the objective of determining the proper role of section 10(j) and (l) proceedings in national labor policy, the scope and function of the district courts' rulings will next be examined.

The Judicial Function

The injunctive powers provided in sections 10(j) and (l) of the Act may well constitute an integral ingredient in the mixture of remedies needed to preserve the efficacy of the NLRB's orders. The time delay between the filing of the unfair labor practice and the Board's final adjudication may be so substantial as to undermine the guarantees of the Act, absent some sort of interim relief. On the other hand, the granting of an injunction designed to preserve the status quo may so damage the rights of the charged party as to nullify any subsequent Board adjudication as to the parties' innocence. Furthermore, a premature or incorrect use of an injunction could serve to frustrate the freedom from interferences so essential for successful collective bargaining.

The two-sidedness of the injunctive sword requires both the NLRB and the courts to conduct a delicate balancing process when deciding whether to seek and grant an injunction. The statute itself provides little help in developing feasible and just standards. Under both sections, an injunction may be granted when it is "just and proper"—a term engendering much debate and confusion. The federal district courts have generally provided disparate treatment for 10(j) and (l) proceedings. Furthermore, the various federal circuits have come into conflict over the appropriate standard in 10(j) cases. The disparate treatment between 10(j) and (l) proceedings, the conflict in 10(j) cases and a proposed solution are next to be considered.

Judicial Standards Under Section 10(l)

The mandatory injunction proceeding under section 10(l) of the NLRA is a Congressionally established procedure and is thus distinguishable from the normal equity proceeding. According to generally accepted procedural rules, courts need only follow the standards enumerated in the statute and are not required to follow the general principles of equity.[31] Accordingly, the district court will grant a requested 10(l) injunction when the regional director has satisfied the minimal requirements of the statute in his petition.[32] More specifically, the judicial function in 10(l) proceedings entails an initial determination that there exists reasonable cause to believe that an unfair labor practice has occurred and then a "balancing of the equities" to decide that relief which is "just and proper." [33] Thus, it is this last criteria which is the only statutory limitation on the exercise of judicial discretion.[34] Correspondingly, the scope of an appeal to a circuit court is limited to whether the finding of reasonable cause was erroneous and whether the form of relief granted showed a proper exercise of discretion.[35]

An examination of many of the court decisions dealing with the section 10(l) injunction revealed that they were based on whether or not the facts under applicable legal principles did or did not suffice to support a "reasonable cause to believe" that the statute had been violated. Thus, their precedence value is limited to facts rather than to law. Additionally, the judicial findings of fact are not binding upon the Board in the subsequent unfair labor practice proceeding since the court's decision under 10(l) does not reach the merits of the charge.[36] This latter determination is within the exclusive jurisdiction of the NLRB.

The discretion given to the district court in section 10(l) proceedings, although only limited by the statutory standards of just and proper, may be influenced by the general principles of equity.[37] Thus, in *Elliott v. Meat Cutters*,[38] the court denied relief on the equity principle that an injunction will not issue where no benefit will be derived therefrom. A court may also exercise its discretion to deny injunctive relief where it would not protect the public welfare or the free flow of commerce and where it would not encourage free and private collective bargaining.[39] Furthermore, one district court has held that in deciding what is just and proper the *ex parte* temporary restraining order provision, requiring a showing of substantial and irreparable injury, should serve as a guide.[40]

These and other such decisions have provided the courts with standards, other than the statutory requirement of just and proper, which aid in the process of balancing conflicting interests. Generally, the courts are guided by a balancing of the public interest on one side and the harm to the parties on the other side. Thus, for example, the court in *Le Baron v. Los Angeles Building and Construction Trades*[41] granted an injunction against a striking union where the effect would be to deprive union members of at most two jobs and where the strike was substantially interfering with essential services to the public. Nevertheless, it is most important to remember that section 10(1) is a mandatory injunction proceeding where there occurs certain, specified unfair labor practices. The legislative history clearly indicates a definite Congressional determination that where these unfair practices occur there exists a high potential of substantial harm to the public. In 10(1) situations, Congress has exercised its legislative powers by weighing the harm to the public against the potentially deleterious effects of the injunction on the charged party and has balanced the scales in favor of the former. Therefore, after determining "reasonable cause to believe," it is the role of the court in 10(1) proceedings to implement Congressional policy by issuing an injunction which is "just and proper" in that it protects the public interest—predetermined by Congress to be paramount—while at the same time lessening the harm to the charged party.[42] As will be discussed below, it is the absence of a predetermined public interest in section 10(j) proceedings that rightfully accounts for disparate judicial standards.

A recent issue confronted by the Supreme Court and two circuit courts concerned the status to be attributed to the charging party in a section 10(1) proceeding. In the two cases, both brought by Sears, Roebuck and Company, the question presented was whether the charging party was entitled to the status of a full party litigant in the district court injunctive proceeding, and if not, was the party entitled to intervene as of right in that proceeding. The Eighth and Tenth Circuit Courts of Appeals answered both questions in the negative.[43] On appeal from the Tenth Circuit Court's decision, the Supreme Court found the issue moot and refused to rule on the merits of the case.[44]

The most recent of the decisions, that of the Court of Appeals for the Eighth Circuit, provides an incisive analysis of the status of a charging party under section 10(1). The case began with a charge filed by Sears alleging that a local of the International Brotherhood of Teamsters was conducting an illegal secondary boycott. After determining that a complaint should issue, the regional director filed for injunctive relief pursuant to section 10(1). In the proceedings before the district court, Sears sought to appear as a full party litigant or, alternatively, to intervene as a party. The court denied both requests but did grant a limited appearance—the right to be present, to introduce evidence and to be kept informed. Subsequently, the regional director and the respondent union reached a settlement stipulation, over the objection of Sears, in lieu of the injunctive proceeding.

On appeal to the circuit court, Sears argued that although the legislative history supported the rule that only the Board may *initiate* an injunction suit, a charging party was entitled to full litigant status after the suit was instituted. The court, relying on both precedent and legislative history, disagreed:

> We think the attempt to interpret § 10(1) so as to accord charging parties full party status in a § 10(1) proceeding fails because of lack of legislative support. While there exist cogent reasons why charging parties should be accorded full party status, these reasons should be addressed to Congress, the policy making branch of the government. In enacting § 10(1), Congress created a narrow exception to the Norris-La Guardia Act in allowing injunctions to be issued in labor disputes. While the role of private parties in this facet of the labor law field was considered, such parties were not given the right to privately seek injunctive relief nor were they designated as or given the status of full party litigants. The interpretation argued by appellants twists the plain meaning of the statute as written and is at odds with the overall scheme of injunctive relief embodied in the National Labor Relations Act and the Norris-La Guardia Act.[45]

The court went on to reason that since the charging party was not entitled directly to a full party litigant status, he could not be allowed to obtain this status indirectly by the process of intervention.

The decision of the Eighth Circuit Court of Appeals in *Sears* appears to comply with both the legislative history of section 10(1) and the proper scope of the injunctive proceedings. The legislature intended the interim injunctive relief to be a remedy designed to protect the public interest and not to promote private rights. As the court noted, the Senate report commenting on the proposed section 10(1) stated

> Hence we have provided that the Board, acting in the public interest and not in vindication of purely private rights, may seek injunctive relief in the case of all types of unfair labor practices and that it shall also seek such relief in the case of strikes and boycotts defined as unfair labor practices.[46]

Furthermore, the allowable use of an injunction in a labor dispute should be considered as a narrowly defined exception to the anti-injunction provision of the Norris-LaGuardia Act. As provided in 10(1), the injunction must, and should, be sought where there is reasonable cause to believe that one of the specified unfair practices has occurred. A "just and proper" injunction, although sufficiently broad to protect the public interest, should be restrictively drawn to minimize the potentially harmful effects on the charged party. At the same time, the rights of the charging party are preserved in that the normal Board procedures remain available and that the court may grant an injunction notwithstanding an attempted settlement between the regional director and the charged party.[47] The courts should not extend the use of the section 10(1) injunction beyond the minimal level necessary to protect the law and the public.

Judicial Standards Under Section 10(j)

Pursuant to the mandates of section 10(j), the district court is obligated to determine whether the acts charged are, as a matter of law, unfair labor practices and whether the records show reasonable probability that such acts were in fact committed. Where both questions are answered affirmatively, the court has authorization to grant such injunctive relief as it deems "just and proper."[48] As with section 10(1), the district courts have generally followed the principle that where its jurisdiction over an injunctive proceeding is derived solely by reason of a statute, the traditional principles of equity are not prerequisites to the granting of relief.[49] Once again, the only Congressional limitation on the exercise of the court's judicial discretion is the "just and proper" standard.

Disregarding the breadth of their discretion, the district courts have generally imposed a stricter standard in granting injunctive relief under section 10(j). The courts have reasoned that such relief is not to be lightly granted and that it is intended to be remedial rather than punitive. Under the discretionary injunction proceeding, the court has greater freedom of discretion in weighing the public interest against those of the private parties. Thus, where the evidence tends to establish deliberate, willful or at least sporadic acts which constitute an unfair labor practice and when there is no evidence of intent to avoid like conduct in the future, injunctive relief is just and proper.[50] One court, for example, listed the following criteria in determining the appropriateness of the requested relief: (1) a complaint has issued from the Board charging an unfair labor practice; (2) there is reasonable cause to believe that the charged party is engaging in the unfair labor practice affecting interstate commerce; (3) the party will continue such practices unless restrained; and (4) there is imminent danger of such practices resulting in irreparable injury to the nation, to the policies of the Act, and to the employers and employees involved.[51]

Although it may be alleged that the standards applied under section 10(j) are more restrictive than those under 10(l), currently no definitive ruling exists on the appropriate criteria to be applied. A number of the federal circuit courts are in conflict as to the appropriate role of the district court in 10(j) cases. Recent decisions coming from the Second, Eighth and Tenth Circuits provide insight into this conflict in that the standards adopted by the courts range from the restrictive to the liberal.

In *McLeod v. General Electric Co.*,[52] the Second Circuit Court of Appeals rendered a restrictive interpretation of section 10(j). The case arose out of a dispute between the General Electric Company and the International Union of Electrical Workers over the composition of the union's bargaining committee. In an attempt to enhance its economic bargaining strength, the union adopted a "coalition bargaining" strategy[53] and invited representatives of seven other unions to sit in its negotiating committee. Refusing to be subjected to coalition bargaining tactics, the company discontinued negotiating until all non-IUE members were removed from the negotiating committee. The union responded by charging the company with a violation of section 8(a)(5) by its having refused to bargain in good faith. Two

days after the complaint was issued, the General Counsel of the
NLRB, at the behest of the union, requested the district court
to issue an injunction against General Electric under section
10(j) of the Act.

On August 18, 1966, District Court Judge Marvin Frankel
granted the Board's petition and ordered the company to bargain with a committee of the union's choosing.[54] After finding
reasonable cause to believe that General Electric had committed
the unfair labor practice charged, the court reviewed the evidence to determine if the Board had abused its discretion in
seeking 10(j) relief. Admitting that the use of the injunction
in labor disputes was an extraordinary remedy reserved for special situations, Judge Frankel rejected the view that an injunction should only issue when the charged violation is "flagrant." [55]
He reasoned that the company's plea to balance the equities was
misplaced because Congress had conducted this weighing process
when it provided the Board with broad discretion to seek 10(j)
relief. The standard of "just and proper," the court concluded,
when viewed in light of the NLRB's wide discretion meant that
the district court should deny injunctive relief only when there
exists no valid reasoning for circumventing the Board's normal
adjudicative process. The facts of the instant case warranted
the issuance of an injunction since a strike at General Electric
would have substantial impact on the national defense and
economy.

On appeal before the Second Circuit Court the decision was
reversed and the injunction vacated.[56] Noting that an injunction
is a most extraordinary remedy, the Circuit Court rejected Judge
Frankel's conclusion that the single standard of public impact
was alone sufficient to justify 10(j) relief. Offering its own interpretation of "just and proper," the Court stated:

> It is black letter law that the issuance of an injunction is an
> extraordinary remedy indeed. This is especially true in the labor
> field.
>
> . . . .
>
> We are not convinced that the facts in the present case reveal
> those special circumstances which must be present before a court
> will intervene and issue an injunction prior to the Board's hearing
> and decision. *The Board has not demonstrated that an injunction
> is necessary to preserve the status quo or to prevent any irreparable
> harm.* Moreover, the basic legal question underlying its conduct—
> the very same question presented in the *American Radiator* case,
> 155 NLRB No. 69 (1965) in which the Board did not see fit to seek

an injunction—is a very difficult one to resolve and one which no court has considered. It would be more in keeping with the scheme intended by Congress to have this case, particularly because of its unusual characteristics, follow the path of Board hearing and decision on the unfair labor practice charges, rather than to short-circuit the established administrative design. The Board cannot abdicate one of the prime purposes for which it was created and thus deprive the Court of the expertise which would be available to it in reviewing the Board's holding in an enforcement proceeding.[57]

In thus ruling, the Circuit Court not only exposed a non-restrictive standard in 10(j) proceedings, but it also noted that the issuance of an injunction in the instant case would effectively give to the union the final relief which it hoped to gain by a successful Board determination. On application to the Supreme Court, Justice Harlan granted a stay of the Second Circuit Court's dissolution of the injunction.[58] Subsequent to the filing of the NLRB's petition for certiorari, General Electric and the IUE agreed upon a new three-year contract. In a somewhat unusual step, the Supreme Court granted certiorari but remanded the case back to the district court to determine if the new labor agreement had mooted the need for interim relief.[59] The result was to leave standing the decision of the Court of Appeals, within the jurisdiction of the Second Circuit, as to the appropriate standards under section 10(j).

In *Minnesota Mining & Manufacturing Co. v. Meter,*[60] the Eighth Circuit Court of Appeals evolved a different approach to section 10(j). As in *General Electric,* the dispute arose out of attempts by the union to bring "strangers" into the bargaining room as part of its coalition bargaining strategy. The 3M Company refused to negotiate under such circumstances and was charged by the union with having violated section 8(a)(5). Pursuant to the section 10(j) petition filed by the General Counsel, the district court granted a temporary injunction ordering the company to bargain with the mixed union committee. In determining the propriety of injunctive relief, the district court offered a three-pronged approach. The issuance of an injunction, it was reasoned, would be proper where there existed a serious threat upon the public interest grave enough to justify swifter corrective action than the Board could mete; or where there was a high potential that the charging party would suffer irreparable harm; or, finally, where there existed a definite necessity to maintain the status quo pending final Board action. Reviewing the facts, the district court found sufficient evidence to conclude that all three of the standards had been satisfied.

On appeal to the Eighth Circuit Court of Appeals, 3M argued that injunctive relief was not just and proper under the circumstances of the instant case. In reversing the decision of the lower court, the Circuit Court indicated that it did not quarrel with the finding of reasonable cause to believe that the Act had been violated. Nevertheless, the court was unable to find sufficient evidence to meet the standards applicable in 10(j) proceedings. Directing itself to each of the three standards, the Circuit Court offered the following analysis:

> The district judge in part predicated his order upon a finding that the situation created by 3M's refusal to bargain posed a serious threat " 'upon the public interest . . . grave enough to justify swifter corrective action . . .' than the Board can mete." The problem with the district court's finding, however, is that the record is devoid of any evidence which would support it. The Board has utterly failed to present any factual data which would remotely suggest that the public interest is or may be affected by the alleged unfair labor practices.

> Moreover, we find the district court's determination that the OCAW and its affiliated Locals will suffer irreparable harm unless relief is granted equally untenable in light of the record before us. The court based its finding of irreparable harm on the rationale that if it was ultimately determined that the Union had a right to the presence of temporary union representatives at its negotiating sessions, it would have been deprived of a clearly determined legal right, for which compensatory damages would have proved an inadequate redress. . . . In view of the past history of acceptable contracts negotiated between 3M and the OCAW, we find it highly unlikely that the OCAW will sustain any injury in its bargaining position if it retains the present composition of its negotiating committee pending a determination on the merits of this labor dispute.

The district court also determined that injunctive relief was necessary to maintain the status quo. It concluded that by reason of the long history of amicable collective bargaining there existed a harmonious relationship between the parties and that:

> "it might well be determined that the status quo which the court is called upon to preserve is that peaceable, desirable, continuing relationship and status which has lasted for so many years and that failure to grant the injunction for that for which there is reasonable cause to believe the union has a legal right, may disrupt the status quo in this sense."

No authority is cited to support the court's concept of status quo. We agree with 3M that the status quo consists of the bargaining position of the parties prior to the attempt by the OCAW to include representatives of other labor organizations as a part of its negotiating committee.[61]

Although the Court of Appeals dissolved the injunction issued by the district court, it did not disagree with the standards utilized by the court in the 10(j) proceeding. These standards appear to be more liberal than those advocated by the Second Circuit Court of Appeals in *General Electric*. Yet both courts referred to the traditional equity principles—irreparable injury and status quo—the *3M* decision would have treated public impact as alone sufficient to warrant injunctive relief. This result has led one commentator to ". . . assume that faced with the *General Electric* fact pattern, where public impact had indeed been documented by the Board, the Eighth Circuit would have approved the issuance of section 10(j) relief." [62]

The most liberal test for determining just and proper relief under section 10(j) was evolved by the Tenth Circuit Court of Appeals in *Angle v. Sacks*.[63] The case involved a charge of a section 8(a)(3) violation when the company discharged six of twenty production and maintenance employees allegedly to impede a union organization movement. In affirming the granting of a section 10(j) injunction, the Court of Appeals rejected the theory that "just and proper" implies an "emergency situation" where the labor dispute may have a widespread impact upon the general public. Rather, the court reasoned, section 10(j) relief should be granted where the injunction would serve to protect the policies and purposes of the National Labor Relations Act.[64] In the instant case, the court affirmed the use of injunctive relief since there was "a reasonable apprehension that the efficacy of the Board's final order [could] be nullified, or the administrative procedures [would] be rendered meaningless. . . ." [65]

In adopting a test of "frustration of the statute," the Court in *Angle* paved the road for an almost unlimited use of a section 10(j) injunction. In nearly every case where there exists reasonable cause to believe that an unfair practice has been committed, there may also exist reasonable cause to believe that the policies of the Act have been frustrated. In *Angle*, for example, the court concluded that a discriminatory discharge before a certification election would frustrate the Act. It would seem, however, that the court overlooked the fact that the normal Board processes would adequately serve to protect the interests of the discharged employees. Should a violation of the Act be found, the employees would not only be reinstated but would be given back pay with 6 percent interest. As to the potential effects of the discharges on the certification election, here again the normal Board procedures are capable of remedying the problem. The use of a rerun election or a mandatory bargaining order based upon the authorization cards[66] would more than adequately protect the union's interests. Finally, the court failed to consider the irreparable harm which the injunction would inflict upon the employer should the Board find the company's actions to have been justified. In addition to the wages paid out and the potentially harmful effects on employee relations, the injunction would have forced an abdication of management's right to manage. Such a result becomes unduly harsh when viewed in light of the fact that the company was not allowed to contest the merits of the case against it.

The proper scope and function of the judiciary in section 10(j) proceedings must be realized by examining the legislative history behind and the policies of the NLRA, as well as the interests and needs of employers, employees and unions. It is submitted that such an examination favors the adoption of a restrictive standard in the granting of 10(j) injunctions. Congress created this limited exception to the Norris-LaGuardia Act as a means of protecting the public interest and not as a promotion of private rights. The courts should not readily circumvent the normal adjudicative process performed by the NLRB. Furthermore, unlike the mandatory injunction provisions of section 10(l), section 10(j) does not contain a Congressional determination that there exists a high potential of substantial harm to the public. The section being discretionary means that the Board and the courts must perform the same balancing of interests test that Congress performed in 10(l). When conducting this balancing process, the courts should realize that an injunction may not only cause irreparable harm to the charged party, but it may severely interfere with the free system of collective bargaining.

Conclusion

The role of the injunction in the American labor movement has had an impressive history. It was used to stifle the growth of unionization and to suppress employee freedom of choice. As the nation and its people matured, Congress sought to curtail the use of the injunction in labor disputes. Sections 10(j) and (1) of the National Labor Relations Act represent an attempt to balance the public interest against the sanctity of free collective bargaining. To date, this balancing process generally has been successful.

As society becomes more complex, so do the problems involved in labor relations. The NLRB continually faces new problems to which there are no easy solutions. Major among these is the increasing time delay in the Board's administrative procedures. Some authorities advocate a more liberalized use of injunctive relief as an "easy answer." An examination of the policies of the Act and of the needs of the parties, however, reveals potential dangers in grasping too readily for this "easy" solution. Irreparable damage to the charged party and a destruction of free collective bargaining are high prices to pay for the possibility of shortening NLRB delay. History has taught us to be cautious of the injunction in labor disputes. As we encounter new labor relations problems, let us hope that the lessons of the past lead us to wiser solutions for the future.

NOTES

1. One of the first American labor cases was the Philadelphia Cordwainers' case decided in 1806. *See* Gregory, Labor and the Law 22 (2d rev. ed., 1961).

2. 29 U.S.C.A. § 101 *et seq.* (1932).

3. This article is not intended to cover the use of injunctions against strikes in lockouts which threaten the national health or safety. *See* Labor-Management Relations Act, 29 U.S.C.A. § 141 *et seq.*

4. Jaffee v. Newspaper & Mail Deliverers' Union, 97 F. Supp. 443 (1951). During fiscal year 1969, the NLRB was involved in only three section 10(e) proceedings. The judicial standards governing the use of this injunction will therefore not be considered. For a recent case dealing with section 10(e), *see* UAW v. N.L.R.B., 449 F.2d 1046 (1971).

5. Note, *Temporary Injunctions under Section 10(j) of the Taft-Hartley Act,* 44 N.Y.U.L. Rev. 181 (1969).

6. 34 NLRB Annual Report 238 (1969).

7. Asher, "Discussion," Proceedings of the Twenty-Third Annual Winter Meeting of the Industrial Relations Research Association 273, 275 (1970).

8. For a more detailed review of NLRB procedure, see Morris ed., The Developing Labor Law (1971).

9. "Something Old, Something New" remarks of Chairman Edward Miller, reported in the *Daily Labor Report*, No. 15, January 22, 1971; "Some Reflections on Remedies under the NLRA" remarks of Member John Fanning, reported in the *Daily Labor Report*, No. 12, January 19, 1971. See Member Fanning's article in this volume.

10. H.R. 3020, 80th Cong., 1st Sess. § 12(b) (1947).

11. S. Rep. No. 105, 80th Cong., 1st Sess. 8 (1947).

12. Amazon Cotton Mills, 167 F.2d 183 (4th Cir. 1948).

13. NLRB v. Retail Clerks, 243 F.2d 777 (9th Cir. 1956). The federal courts have also upheld the constitutionality of the NLRB's delegation to the General Counsel of the authority to seek a section 10(j) injunction—Evans v. Typographical Union, 76 F. Supp. 881 (1948)—and of the General Counsel's incidental authority to institute contempt proceedings for violations of such injunctions—Evans v. Typographical Union, 81 F. Supp. 675 (1948).

14. Fusco v. Kaase Baking Co., 205 F. Supp. 459 (1962); Douds v. Teamsters Local 294, 75 F. Supp. 414 (1948).

15. In its petition to the district court, the Board must also allege that the court has jurisdiction and that the persons sought to be restrained are subject to the National Labor Relations Act.

16. NLRB Release No. R-4, September 23, 1947.

17. The Developing Labor Law, *supra* note 8, at 845-46.

18. Note, *Temporary Injunctions under Section 10(j) of the Taft-Hartley Act*, *supra* note 5, at 192. Fusco v. Kaase Baking Co., 205 F. Supp. 465, 478 (1962).

19. The Developing Labor Law, *supra* note 8, at 850.

20. McCulloch, *New Problems in the Administration of the Labor-Management Relations Act: the Taft-Hartley Injunction*, 16 Sw. L. J. 82 (1962).

21. Note, *Temporary Injunctions under Section 10(j) of the Taft-Hartley Act*, *supra* note 5, at 190.

22. Section 10(l) does contain the exception that no restraining order shall be applied for under section 8(b)(7) if a charge against the employer under section 8(a)(2) has been filed and, after the preliminary investigation, the regional attorney has reasonable cause to believe that such charge is true and that a complaint should issue.

23. Douds v. Teamsters Local 294, 75 F. Supp. 414 (1948).

24. Styles v. Electrical Workers Local 760, 80 F. Supp. 119 (1948).

25. Le Baron v. Los Angeles Bldg. & Construction Trades Council, 84 F. Supp. 629 (1949).

26. Madden v. Machinists, Automobile Mechanics Lodge 701, 46 LLRM 2572 (1960); Le Baron v. Kern County Farm Labor Union, 80 F. Supp. 151 (1948).

27. Sperry v. Operating Engineers Local 6-6A-6B, 36 L.C. 65036 (1958).

28. Madden v. Teamsters Local 753, 229 F. Supp. 490 (1964).

29. McLeod v. Bookbinders Local 119, 220 F. Supp. 133 (1963).

30. Hull v. Teamsters Local 24, 148 F. Supp. 145 (1957).

31. Hecht Co. v. Bowles, 321 U.S. 321, 331 (1944).

32. Douds v. Wine, Liquor & Distilling Workers, 75 F. Supp. 184 (1947).

33. San Francisco & Oakland Newspaper Guild v. Kennedy, 412 F.2d 542 (9th Cir. 1969); Penello v. American Federation of Television & Radio Artists, 291 F. Supp. 409 (1968).

34. Sperry v. Teamsters Local 659, 149 F. Supp. 243 (1956).

35. Schauffler v. Teamsters Local 107, 230 F.2d 7 (3rd Cir. 1956).

36. NLRB v. Teamsters Local 74, 181 F.2d 126 (6th Cir. 1950).

37. Cosentino v. Longshoremen, 126 F. Supp. 420 (1954).

38. 91 F. Supp. 690 (1950); *appeal dismissed*, 189 F.2d 965 (8th Cir. 1951).

39. Douds v. Wine, Liquor & Distilling Workers, 75 F. Supp. 447 (1948).

40. Douds v. Wine Liquor & Distilling Workers, 75 F. Supp. 184 (1947).

41. 84 F. Supp. 629 (1949).

42. See Brown v. Lithographers Local 17, 180 F. Supp. 294 (1960).

43. Solien v. Teamsters Local 610 and Sears, Roebuck & Co., 440 F.2d 124 (8th Cir. 1971); Sears, Roebuck & Co. v. Carpet Layers Local 419, 410 F.2d 1148 (10th Cir. 1970).

44. Sears, Roebuck & Co. v. Carpet Layers Local 419, 397 U.S. 655 (1970).

45. Solien v. Teamsters Local 610 and Sears, Roebuck & Co., 440 F.2d 124 (8th Cir. 1971).

46. S. Rep. No. 105, 80th Cong., 1st Sess. at 8.

47. Retail Clerks Union v. Food Employers Council, Inc., 351 F.2d 525 (9th Cir. 1965).

48. McLeod v. Sewer Construction Workers, 292 F.2d 358 (2nd Cir. 1961).

49. Douds v. Anheuser-Busch, 99 F. Supp. 479 (1951).

50. Johnston v. Hackney & Sons, 300 F. Supp. 373 (1969).

51. Madden v. Mine Workers, 79 F. Supp. 616 (1948).

52. McLeod v. General Electric Co., 366 F.2d 847 (2nd Cir. 1966).

53. Chernish, Coalition Bargaining, University of Pennsylvania Press (1968).

54. McLeod v. General Electric Co., 257 F. Supp. 690 (1966).

55. *Id.* at 708.

56. McLeod v. General Electric Co., 366 F.2d 847 (2nd Cir. 1966).

57. *Id.* at 850 (emphasis added).

58. McLeod v. General Electric Co., 87 S. Ct. 5 (1967).

59. McLeod v. General Electric Co., 385 U.S. 533 (1967).

60. 385 F.2d 265 (8th Cir. 1967), *reversing* 273 F. Supp. 659 (1967).

61. 385 F.2d at 272.

62. Note, *Temporary Injunctions under Section 10(j) of the Taft-Hartley Act, supra* note 5, at 193.

63. 353 F.2d 655 (10th Cir. 1967).

64. *Id.* at 659.

65. *Id.* at 660.

66. *See* McFarland and Bishop, Union Authorization Cards and the NLRB, University of Pennsylvania Press (1969).

PART III

ALTERNATIVES TO STRIKES

Collective Bargaining Where Strikes Are Not Tolerated

Benjamin Aaron †

I. Introduction

The title of this paper (which I did not choose) expresses an assumption, formerly accepted by most people as a matter of course, but vigorously challenged in recent years. The assumption is that strikes are not and should not be tolerated in some areas of our economy. The title also raises a question, at least by implication: is collective bargaining possible when strikes are not permitted? If the answer to this question is negative, we must consider what system we are prepared to use in place of collective bargaining; if the answer is affirmative, we must indicate existing or possible procedures that can serve as adequate substitutes for the strike.

This paper is addressed to both the assumption and the questions implicit in the title. Of necessity, it will refer to developments in the public, as well as the private, sector of the economy. It will concentrate primarily on those activities in which it is alleged that strikes create economic and political "emergencies" of varying scope and severity. To the extent deemed useful, references will occasionally be made to law and practice in other countries.

II. The Rationale of the Strike [1]

There is no constitutional right to strike.[2] All strikes result in economic loss to someone, and many impose, directly or indirectly, inconvenience or hardship on various segments of the public. Why, then, has protection of the right to strike been given such a high priority in our national system of values? The answer is to be found, I suppose, in our historic dedication to the principles of free competition, with a minimum of govern-

---

† Benjamin Aaron is Professor of Law and Director, Institute of Industrial Relations, University of California, Los Angeles.

ment intervention, and in our recognition that, in the words of the Norris-LaGuardia Act, "the individual unorganized worker is commonly helpless to exercise actual liberty of contract and to protect his freedom of labor, and thereby to obtain acceptable terms and conditions of employment." [3] From this it naturally follows that workers should be allowed to organize without interference by their employers and to engage in "concerted activities for the purpose of collective bargaining or other mutual aid or protection," [4] including strikes. Justice Holmes referred to the conflict of interests between the employer and his employees as a form of competition, which he termed "the free struggle for life." [5] Long before that principle was embodied in the federal legislation of the 1930's, Holmes expressed it in one of his most famous dissenting opinions:

> One of the eternal conflicts out of which life is made up is that between the effort of every man to get the most he can for his services, and that of society, disguised under the name of capital, to get his services for the least possible return. Combination on the one side is patent and powerful. Combination on the other is the necessary and desirable counterpart, if the battle is to be carried on in a fair and equal way.[6]

The principle of collective bargaining, now deeply imbedded in our national labor policy, presupposes private collective agreements reached without government intervention. And the strike, in George W. Taylor's useful phrase, provides the "motive power for agreement." Thus, it makes sense to allow the bargaining partners, within certain limitations, freely to engage in their competitive struggle, so long as the weapons of strike and lockout are employed against each other for the purpose of reaching an agreement. Incidental inconvenience or even damage to neutral third parties is tolerated because the worth of the system is deemed substantially to outweigh these costs.

III. The Rationale of Restrictions on the Right to Strike

A. *"Emergency" Disputes in the Private Sector*

The most commonly expressed reason for restricting the right to strike in the private sector has been succinctly stated by Taylor as follows:

> With the widespread extension of employee organization . . . it has become increasingly apparent that, important though the strike

> may be as a support for collective bargaining, some work stoppages cannot . . . perform their collective-bargaining function of bringing the parties to terms because if work stoppages ran their course the whole social structure would break down.[7]

In short, the immediate parties to the dispute may be able to hold out longer than the public at large.

We speak of such strikes as creating "emergencies," a term that is not free from ambiguity. Under the Labor-Management Relations (Taft-Hartley) Act, 1947 (LMRA), an emergency is

> a threatened or actual strike or lock-out affecting an entire industry or a substantial part thereof engaged in . . . [interstate] commerce or . . . in the production of goods for commerce, [which] will, if permitted to occur or to continue, imperil the national health or safety. . . .[8]

Although, for practical purposes, this definition has been expanded to include any strike denominated an emergency by the President,[9] it has so far not been applied to so-called local emergencies, such as a strike by sanitation workers in a large city.[10]

An emergency under the Railway Labor Act (RLA) is one that "threaten[s] substantially to interrupt interstate commerce to a degree such as to deprive any section of the country of essential transportation service." [11] Because of the past tendency in the railroad industry to reserve important collective bargaining issues for "national handling," the threat of strikes that would deprive all sections of the country of essential transportation service has been a real and frequent one. It remains to be seen whether this pattern of converting local disputes into national ones and thereby creating an "emergency" will be significantly affected by the recent decision of the Court of Appeals for the District of Columbia permitting a limited resort by rail unions to selective strikes.[12]

The definition of an "emergency" in the LMRA cannot be said to represent a national consensus, except in the sense that any act of Congress is claimed to be an expression of the national will. In the opinion of most scholars, if purely economic criteria are used, few cases have met or will meet the test.[13] It is also generally conceded, however, that the determination of an emergency is basically a political act, "and is as much a reflection of the incumbent President's temperament and style as of the actual or potential economic impact of the dispute." [14]

Moreover, extrinsic circumstances, such as war, may compel the treatment of any strike as an emergency, regardless of its economic impact. Thus, in World War II, any violation by a union of its no-strike pledge was considered as a kind of emergency, if for no other reason than its possible contagious effect.

B. *"Political" Disputes*

It is well established in our law that although strikes for "economic" purposes or to protest against an employer's unfair labor practices are protected activities, strikes for "political" purposes are not. It is also generally conceded that the state has a right to defend itself against overt threats to destroy it; the real problem is to distinguish between such threats and legitimate protest. In the United States the issue is academic, however, because our unions have traditionally worked within the accepted political and economic system, rather than against it; purely political strikes, including the general strike, are virtually unknown in this country. Apart from the criminal statutes against obstructing the mail, interfering with the war effort, and the like, we have not found it necessary to enact specific laws against political strikes in the private sector. They would simply be treated as unprotected activities and not as bona fide labor disputes; participants in such strikes could be disciplined or dismissed, and the strikes themselves could be enjoined.

As other countries have already found, however, we may discover that the problem of distinguishing between a "political" and an "economic" strike is insoluable. To consider a current possibility, suppose that during "Phase II" of the economic stabilization program a union strikes for a wage increase that exceeds the allowable limits: is this a "political" or an "economic" strike? Obviously, it is both, and applying one label or the other will not contribute much to the problem of devising an appropriate policy to deal with such a strike.

C. *Disputes in Government Employment*

In this country government employment—federal, state, county, and municipal—is generally referred to as the "public sector." The term is misleading for a number of reasons, not the least of which is that some government agencies and their employees carry out largely proprietary functions,[15] whereas many so-called "public" utilities are privately owned. Another reason is that one of the common bases for distinguishing government employment from private employment is the allegedly greater amount of "public interest" invested in the former. Yet, few would deny that the "public interest" is more vitally affected by a major strike in private industry than by a minor strike by public employees. For example, the public is far more concerned over a lengthy walkout by dock workers, than over one by clerks in state-operated liquor stores.

Nevertheless, our law applies a double standard in the case of strikes by employees in private industry and by those employed by government; with few exceptions, the latter are absolutely denied the legal right to strike.[16] The basic reasons for this double standard were succinctly stated recently in the per curiam opinion of the three-judge federal district court in the *Postal Clerks* case:

> Given the fact that there is no constitutional right to strike, it is not irrational for the Government to condition employment on a promise not to withhold labor collectively, and to prohibit strikes by those in public employment, whether because of the prerogatives of the sovereign, some sense of higher obligation associated with public service, to assure the continuing functioning of the Government without interruption, to protect public health and safety or for other reasons.[17]

The theory thus expressed is hardly peculiar to this country; it is known in many others. A few examples will suffice. The Swedish scholar, Stig Jägerskiöld, writes,

> For many years it was said in Sweden, as well as in other northern countries, that a full labor law system could not properly be applied within the field of public administration. It was argued that the introduction of the collective agreement in public service [and, *a fortiori*, the right to strike] would be contrary to the concept of state sovereignty and would unduly restrict the power of decision which the authorities must be able to exercise. It could eventually give rise to obligations of public officials toward their associations that would bind them improperly and impair their loyalty to the state or the local government.[18]

Speaking of the German *Beamter* (for whom it is impossible to find a closer description than the admittedly inexact term, "civil servant"), Professor William H. McPherson remarks:

> Considering his relationship of service and loyalty to the state, it is quite "inconceivable" that he might strike against the state. The incongruity of such action was felt to be so clear that it was

considered unnecessary and inappropriate to spell out a strike prohibition in the public law. This is still the prevailing view although
a few labor law specialists have recently challenged it. . . .[19]

Beamte, however, are to be sharply distinguished from public
service employees, whose status is different and whose right to
strike after reaching a deadlock in negotiations is "unquestioned." [20]

In France, prior to 1946, civil servants *(fonctionnaires)* and
public service employees *(salariés des services publics)* were denied the right to organize in trade unions, bargain collectively,
or strike. According to Professor Frederic Meyers,

> the Conseil d'Etat [the supreme judicial body in the hierarchy
> of administrative courts] seemed to read into the right of organi-
> zation the right to strike which, it held, was "incompatible with
> the essential continuity of national life." [21]

As we shall see, however, in each of these foreign countries,
as well as in Canada, the attitude toward strikes by public employees has changed, in some instances quite drastically, in recent years. This fact should be sufficient justification for a re-
examination of our own policies, even if the result is only to re-
assure ourselves of their essential validity within the context of
our economic and political structure.

IV. Substitutes for the Strike

A. *"Emergency" Disputes*

The procedures provided by the LMRA and the RLA for the
settlement of "emergency" disputes have been the subject of
widespread analysis and criticism, and a variety of suggestions
have been offered for their improvement.[22] The LMRA procedures have been attacked less savagely than those prescribed by
the RLA, but the basic complaints of most of the critics of both
statutes turn out, really, to be directed at the collective bargaining practices in those industries in which "emergency" disputes are likely to arise, rather than at the statutory procedures
themselves. Thus, although most of the procedural steps under
the LMRA are rather silly and counter-productive, the emergency
provisions have been used relatively little because collective bargaining works reasonably well in most industries covered by that
statute. The RLA procedure, on the other hand, although con-

siderably more sensible, has been the subject of increasing public irritation and ridicule because it has not solved problems resulting mainly, although not entirely, from inept and irresponsible collective bargaining in the railroad industry.

Under these circumstances, the search for new procedures to deal with the phenomena of "emergency" disputes, like all quests for magical formulas, cannot succeed in solving the underlying problem. The present Administration's highly touted "final-offer selection" proposal [23] is no exception to the foregoing judgment. As a tool to be used occasionally, preferably by agreement between the parties, it could be very useful, particularly during a period of wage and price restraints; as a mandatory procedure to be applied uniformly as a substitute for strikes in the railroad, airline, maritime, longshoring and trucking industries, which the Administration's bill proposes, it would, like the more conventional procedure of compulsory arbitration which it closely resembles,[24] probably create more problems than it could solve. If consistently applied for a sufficient period of time, it might well replace collective bargaining in those industries, and probably others, with an entirely different system of government regulation. Perhaps the time has come seriously to consider the possibility of making such a fundamental change in our national labor policy, but that decision should be made deliberately, and not be permitted simply to emerge gradually as an unintended consequence of our efforts to deal with a different and less important problem.

As yet, however, there is no convincing evidence that collective bargaining has broken down so consistently and completely that it should be replaced by an entirely different regulatory system. It is probably true that most strikes in the transportation industries are, or soon tend to become, "emergencies," because their effects on the public are direct, immediate, and harmful. Yet to deal with that problem by absolutely forbidding all strikes in those industries would be a singularly unimaginative solution, even assuming that it might work, which is doubtful. The position taken in this paper is that efforts to improve the present situation should concentrate on the collective bargaining systems in those industries tending to generate "emergencies," rather than on statutory substitutes for the strike, the most useful of which—mediation, fact-finding, and voluntary arbitration—are already well known. Unless and until this approach is tried and found to be unworkable, we need not, at least in respect of the private sector, reach the question whether a system of collective bargaining can exist when the right to strike is denied absolutely.

In this connection the Swedish experience is instructive. As is well known, collective bargaining in the private sector in Sweden is under the virtual control of two large organizations: the Swedish Employers' Confederation (SAF) and the Swedish Confederation of Trade Unions (LO). Although the Government has traditionally limited its intervention in major disputes to the threat of enacting ad hoc legislation, the collective bargaining partners have mutually assumed a responsibility of preventing the need for any governmental interference. In 1938 they executed the justly famous "Basic Agreement," a remarkable document which sets forth the parties' views of their interrelated rights and responsibilities. The following excerpt conveys something of the flavor of their joint declaration:

> Although the organizations are . . . consciously aiming at a peaceful solution of labour market problems, disagreement . . . cannot always be avoided. The economic losses resulting from a contest in such a situation are in themselves regrettable, but they cannot be regarded as sufficiently important to justify a replacement of the present freedom of collective bargaining by compulsory state control of the differences of interest in the labour market. Nor from other points of view can the State be justified—apart from the sphere of social welfare legislation proper—in forcing upon Swedish employers and workers a regulation of working conditions, either in general or in specific instances. So long as organizations in the labour market are prepared also to take note of the general public interest involved in their activities, the measures reasonably called for in the interest of industrial peace should most naturally and appropriately rest with the organizations themselves.[25]

To implement this agreement the parties established the Labour Market Board *(Arbetsmarknadsnämnden)*, consisting of three representatives each of SAF and LO, whose responsibilities include preventing labor disputes from disturbing essential public services, "in so far as possible," by taking up jointly "for prompt consideration any situation in a dispute where protection of any public interest is called for by either of the two organizations or by a public authority or by any other similar body representing the public interest in question." [26] The agreement also binds each party immediately to implement any decision reached by a majority of the Labor Market Board in a public interest dispute.

This system has worked remarkably well in the private sector, and the Swedish Government has never found it necessary to intervene directly in labor disputes. The situation in respect of public employees will be discussed below.

Of course, Sweden is not the United States; the widely different economic, political, and social conditions prevailing in the two countries, and particularly the centralized system of collective bargaining that exists in Sweden, preclude any possibility of "importing" the Swedish model to the United States. Yet the Swedish experience reminds us once again of the proposal in this country that strike-prone industries be urged to develop their own agreements for handling disputes having a direct, immediate, and harmful impact on the public interest.[27] It is one that has received insufficient attention, probably because it is undramatic, lacks the illusory magical qualities of a new statutory procedure, and requires much hard work and the use of some imagination by the labor and management leaders in the industries involved.

The standard objection to this approach is that the industries immediately concerned, of which the railroads are the most frequently cited example, lack both the will and the ability to develop new and more effective ways of limiting the harmful impact on the public of their disputes. If collective bargaining functioned even fairly well, it is argued, the existing RLA procedures for dispute settlement would be quite sufficient. Railroads may be a very special case, however; similar evidence is lacking for the airline, maritime, longshoring, and trucking industries. Strikes that tie up all shipping on any of our coasts are undoubedly serious, but they have not occurred with great frequency. The dreaded nationwide strike in trucking and air transport have so far failed to materialize. In any case, as the late William H. Davis, a very wise man, once remarked, in a genuine emergency that everyone recognizes as an immediate and serious threat to the national health and safety, the President will always do what is necessary to preserve the nation; and if in so doing he exceeds his authority, the Supreme Court will, in due course, declare that he acted unconstitutionally, thereby preserving the Constitution. Moreover, Congress always has the power to deal with individual disputes by enacting ad hoc legislation.

It may be that this expressed faith in the possible redemption of collective bargaining in those industries in which it now functions in an unacceptable manner will prove to have been ill-founded, and that despite the increasingly frequent Presidential and Congressional interventions and the continuing demands upon labor and management voluntarily to improve their internal dispute settlement procedures, private collective bargaining will not be equal to the task of protecting the public against serious harm. In that event it is likely that both the right to strike and the collective bargaining system itself may have to be scrapped.

Some have suggested that what is needed is a specialized labor court or courts to decide those issues that collective bargaining cannot resolve without subjecting the nation to the agony of trial by economic combat. Should we reach that stage, however, collective bargaining as we now know it will be dead. One is reminded of the apocalyptic warning sounded by the late Judge Learned Hand in his discussion of judicial review; [28] if we substitute the words, "collective bargaining system," for the word, "society," his statement carries the same somber message for our present national labor policy:

> [T]his much I think I do know—that a [collective bargaining system] so riven that the spirit of moderation is gone, no court *can* save; that a [collective bargaining system] where that spirit flourishes, no court *need* save; that a [collective bargaining system] which evades its responsibilities by thrusting upon the courts the nurture of that spirit, that spirit in the end will perish.

B. *"Political" Disputes*

As previously indicated, it is idle to consider substitutes for the political strike, as such, primarily because declared political strikes are simply not a problem in the private economy of the United States. The substitute for such strikes already exists: lawful political action. Like most other citizens, union members have at least limited access to their elected representatives at all levels of government; unlike most other citizens, union members are represented, in the large, by a powerful union lobby, which is constantly increasing its political influence. Subject to the possibility previously suggested,[29] so long as this situation continues, local and national unions can be expected to work within the system and not seek to undermine or destroy it by political strikes.

It is in the sphere of public employment, however, that the distinction between "economic" and "political" strikes tends to disappear; for, as we have seen, any concerted activity by government employees against their employer is widely perceived as a challenge to the sovereign authority of the state.

In all probability, the phenomenon of strikes by public employees will increase in both frequency and seriousness relative to strikes in the private sector. Thus, the questions whether any strikes in government employment can be tolerated and, if not, whether effective collective bargaining is possible under those circumstances, assume a critical importance.

C. *Disputes in Government Employment* [30]

The rising demand of public employees for the right to strike is based on two major contentions: first, that effective collective bargaining is impossible without that right, and second, that strikes in many areas of public employment are potentially far less serious to the public welfare than are many strikes in the private sector which are protected by law. The second argument has led to the development of a compromise position, namely, that strikes by public employees in "nonessential" services should be permitted. This principle has been recognized by implication in the public employee labor relations acts of Hawaii and Pennsylvania.[31]

The arguments for both the unrestricted and the limited right of public employees to strike have found an increasing amount of support not only among public employees themselves, but also among scholars and experts in the field. Probably most persons in each of these groups now would support the following statement by Professor Jack Stieber:

> The "sovereignty doctrine" which holds that a strike of public employees, whatever their occupation or the nature of their activity, is an attack upon the state and a challenge to government authority will no longer suffice. [Former] Secretary of Labor Wirtz put it succinctly when he said: "This doctrine is wrong in theory; what's more, it won't work." [32]

The other countries previously mentioned, in varying degrees, have reached the same conclusion. Swedish legislation governing the right of "public officials" to organize, bargain collectively, and engage in concerted activities, including strikes, dates from 1965.[33] Under present law, the peace obligation imposed by the 1928 Act Concerning Collective Agreements applies to collective agreements between public officials and public administration agencies. Disputes over the interpretation and application of such agreements may be submitted to the Labor Court for final determination. Even a threat to stop work or a notice of intention to stop work during the life of the agreement has been held to violate the peace obligation and to render the offending organization liable in damages.[34]

Prior to 1965, strikes by Swedish public officials were held to be violations of the Penal Code and punishable by fine, dismissal, or imprisonment. But the public officials found different ways to exert pressure, such as boycotts of vacancies, mass resignations, and the like. Jägerskiöld notes that such offensive actions "have been used to a far greater extent than would be presumed if only existing legal rules prohibiting strikes were considered." He continues:

> The steps taken in recent years by the Norwegian, Swedish, and Finnish governments to permit coercive measures are thus not so radical as they might at first seem. In these countries it was thought that to elaborate a legal system in which strikes and lockouts have their well-defined place may be advantageous.[35]

Although the right to strike has now been granted to public officials during bargaining for collective agreements, it may not be used to exert pressure in matters about which no agreement can be concluded. An equally limited right to lock out is accorded the public administration agencies. Under the terms of the 1965 basic agreement on negotiating procedures between the state and the main organizations of state officials, offensive action must be postponed if either party, claiming that a dispute "is calculated unduly to disturb important social functions," refers the matter to a bipartite Public Service Council. If the Council concurs in the view that offensive action would unduly disturb important social functions, it "request[s] those concerned to avoid, limit or end the dispute." [36]

In West Germany the solid consensus that civil servants *(Beamte)*, unlike employees in the public service, do not have the right to strike began to erode in 1970. Although a 1922 decision to that effect by the Federal Constitutional Court is still the controlling precedent, two of three legal opinions on the point commissioned by three different unions argued in favor of a limited right to strike for civil servants,[37] not unlike that provided for government employees in the Hawaii and Pennsylvania statutes previously mentioned.[38] McPherson concludes that "it can no longer be said . . . that the complete illegality of a civil servant strike is almost universally recognized [in West Germany]. It can only be said that it is generally recognized, but increasingly questioned." [39]

The French constitution of 1946 declared that "the right to strike may be exercised within the ambit defined by statutory law." Servants of the state were not exempted from this guarantee. Until 1963, the only employees expressly forbidden by statute to strike were the police, the judiciary, and certain employees of penitentiaries. The government was permitted to adopt reasonable administrative regulations governing strikes by its own employees, however, and public servants "possessed of a part of the public authority and whose presence is indispensable to the life of the nation" were forbidden to strike. Violators of this rule were subject to be "requisitioned" (a procedure analogous to being drafted into military service) for the duration of the strike. Public employees lacking the authority described, but whose interruption of service might endanger public property or safety or the continuance of activities essential to the life of the nation, were explicitly made subject to requisition in the event of a strike.[40]

In 1963 a statute specifically regulating the right of public employees to strike was enacted. It covers persons directly employed by the national government, employees of nationalized industries operating under statute, and those working for certain other enterprises performing a public function. The two major restrictions on the right to strike are a minimum five-day notice requirement by one or more of the "most representative" union organizations, and a flat prohibition of so-called "revolving strikes" *(grèves tournantes)*. The required notice, according to Meyers, "is not primarily to permit further negotiation or mediation—it is too short for that—but to permit preparations for safeguarding health and property and the necessary minimum of service to essential users, or to permit users to prepare." [41]

Of the various countries mentioned in this essay, Canada offers perhaps the most interesting and useful comparison, because its federal system and industrial organization are most nearly like our own. Ontario is the most representative of Canada's ten provinces, being also the most populous and the most heterogeneous. According to Professor Harry W. Arthurs, Ontario is neither the most conservative nor the most innovative of the provinces; but more importantly, "Ontario and federal legislation encompass examples of each of the five main models of public employee collective bargaining systems found in Canada:" [42] private sector, public-private, formal public, informal public, and professional. Each merits a brief reference.

Private sector model. In Ontario municipal employees have been bargaining collectively with their public employers for a quarter-century or more. They have all the rights of employees in the private sector, including the right to strike. Under the terms of the Labor Relations Act,[43] however, conciliation procedures provided by the Act must be exhausted before any strike is permitted. In 1966 and 1968 there were strikes in Toronto by "outside" workers, including garbagemen and operators of the sewage and water supply systems. Arthurs' account of what occurred is instructive:

> Although these strikes potentially posed a serious threat to the community, . . . in fact no danger ensued. In 1966 key functions were maintained in the sewage and water plants by supervisors, in 1968 by union-arranged emergency crews. In 1966 cold weather prevented the spoilage of garbage, while in 1968 polyethylene bags were distributed to homeowners, who either retained the garbage for the one week duration of the strike or deposited it in pre-designated dumps in city parks.[44]

The Ontario government has found it necessary to intervene only once; in 1965 it enacted ad hoc legislation to require compulsory arbitration to forestall a threatened strike by municipal hydroelectric employees.[45]

Public-private model. In 1967 the federal government of Canada adopted the Public Service Staff Relations Act,[46] which established for employees of the Canadian federal government a complete system of collective bargaining, paralleling in all essential respects, including the right to strike, the system prevailing in the private sector. A novel provision of the statute relates to the resolution of negotiation impasses; following certification, the bargaining agent must indicate which of two alternatives it will choose in the event such an impasse is reached: arbitration or conciliation. The former necessarily results in a final and binding award, but the latter, if unsuccessful, does not preclude a subsequent strike. If the union chooses the latter alternative, certain "designated" employees within the bargaining unit are forbidden to strike if their jobs "consist in whole or in part of duties, the performance of which at any particular time or after any specified period of time is or will be necessary in the interest of the safety or security of the public" (Section 79). The employer must establish the list of "designated" employees within twenty days after notice to bargain has been served by either party. Disputes over the propriety of any particular designation are submitted to the tripartite Public Service Staff Relations Board (PSSRB). Somewhat surprisingly, there has been relatively little disagreement over designations, probably, as Arthurs observes, because government agencies have not used the device promiscuously in order to undermine the statutory right to strike.[47]

If arbitration is chosen by the union as the means of resolving bargaining impasses, the dispute is submitted to the Arbitration Tribunal created by the statute, which also sets rather broad guidelines which the Tribunal is to follow in reaching its decision. The Tribunal is staffed by men of high competence, leading Arthurs to remark that arbitration "is not likely to be feared by either side as involving risks of irresponsible or ill-informed third-party decision-making." [48]

How has the system worked so far? Arthurs reports:

> As of March 3, 1970, all 114 bargaining units had elected between arbitration and conciliation-strike. Only 14 units, containing approximately 37,000 employees, have turned their back on arbitration, and all but some 10,000 of these employees are the militant postal workers [who struck for seventeen days in July, 1965]. The balance of almost 160,000 employees in 100 bargaining units have voluntarily relinquished the right to strike—surely evidence of their desire to avoid disruption of public services, if at all possible.[49]

Formal public service model. The municipal police forces of Ontario are governed by the Police Act.[50] Police employment disputes are settled by compulsory arbitration, and no stoppage of work is permitted. Arthurs characterizes the police employer-employee relationships as "authoritarian and paramilitary rather than bilateral and democratic," but notes that "these distinctive characteristics of police personnel policies are rapidly being brought into question." [51]

Space does not permit a summary of the recent developments in collective bargaining between municipal police and local police commissions or councils in Ontario. Arthurs' judgment is that the present system for the resolution of disputes and the effective adjudication of controversies has achieved "a reasonable measure of fair dealing" between the police and their employers.[52] He notes that P. C. Brown, the president of the International Conference of Police Associations (ICPA), with which most American police organizations are affiliated, is a Canadian. In a recent speech Brown said in part:

> Strange as it may seem, the Canadian police officers have had and will have a greater effect on American forces. . . .
> Under our newly rejuvenated ICPA, we hope to provide the guidance and assistance that will provide for adoption of model legislation, similar to the Police Act of Ontario, for all Canadian and American police officers.[53]

Informal public sector model. Public service employees of Ontario have the right to organize and to obtain adjudication of grievances through a formal procedure initially established by the Public Service Act of 1962.[54] As is typical of Canadian labor legislation generally, the statute neither expressly prohibits nor expressly permits strikes; but the terminal step in interests disputes is final and binding arbitration by a tripartite board appointed by the provincial cabinet. Both the government and the Civil Service Association of Ontario, Inc. (CSAO), which represents the main body of public service employees in Ontario and which enjoys a special status under the statute vis-à-vis other employee organizations, have expressed satisfaction with this arrangement. At the same time, the CSAO, which is becoming increasingly militant, has insisted that there must be no direct prohibition of the right to strike. The ambiguity of CSAO's position is noted by Arthurs:

> This statement [that there should be no direct prohibition of the right to strike] seems to suggest that the employees consider that if legislation is silent in regard to this matter, they now have the right to strike as an ultimate recourse. If this is indeed true, the provisions making compulsory arbitration final and binding might be rendered meaningless.[55]

Professional model. "Collective bargaining in Ontario's school system," writes Arthurs,

> presents a paradox: although educational policy and administration are undergoing profound, perhaps revolutionary changes, although education has ranked highest on the list of municipal and provincial spending priorities, Ontario teachers participate in collective bargaining through institutions which resemble medieval guilds.[56]

Under the Ontario Labor Relations Act,[57] teachers are expressly denied the right to organize, bargain, or strike; nevertheless, they have developed a workable collective bargaining system by virtue of the Teaching Profession Act,[58] which gives great powers to the Ontario Teachers Federation (OTF). For example, the statute requires that every teacher in Ontario must belong to the OTF, and also provides for compulsory checkoff of dues. The real power within the OTF rests with its principal affiliates— the Federation of Women Teacher Associations of Ontario (FWTAO); the Ontario Public School Men Teachers Federation (OPSMTF); and the Ontario Secondary School Teachers Federation (OSSTF)—which "bargain" with local school boards. Because no formal procedures for bargaining are included in the statute, the process, according to Arthurs, is "a melange of practice, precedent, convenience, and informal agreement." [59]

The use of formal procedures to resolve impasses is virtually unknown in this context, and the teachers have in the past resolutely rejected third-party intervention. The ice was broken for the first time in 1969, when the Metropolitan Toronto School Board and the Toronto Secondary School Teachers agreed upon the appointment of a mediator, with mutually satisfactory results. Lacking both the legal right and, apparently, the inclination to strike, the Ontario teachers use their power in dispute situations by applying various sanctions. What might be called an intermediate sanction—variously described as "pinklisting" or "graylisting"—consists of officially warning present and prospective teachers that if they should accept a teaching position within the area involved in the dispute, they might lose association privileges and protection. The ultimate sanction—the blacklist— is specifically provided for in a regulation made under the Teaching Profession Act, which declares that "a member [of the OTF] shall . . . refuse to accept employment with a board of trustees whose relations with the Federation are unsatisfactory." [60] Both forms of sanctions have proved effective, especially in tight labor markets for teachers.

In addition to blacklisting, the teachers sometimes resort to mass resignations. Teacher contracts permit either party to give written notice of termination on either August 31 or December 31 of any year. A mass resignation of teachers just before the fall or spring terms of school would, of course, close the schools and constitute a strike; but, so far, the OTF has opposed such tactics except at the expiration of a contract term.

V. Concluding Observations

A. *The Usefulness of Foreign Comparisons*

As previously mentioned, the methods and experiences of foreign countries in dealing with labor relations problems roughly similar to those in the United States are of limited utility in developing and improving our own collective bargaining systems. The laws and practices in Sweden, West Germany, and France are interesting and suggestive, however, because they demonstrate a movement toward the liberalization of relationships between governments and their employees which seems to represent a pronounced trend within the western democracies.

Quite clearly, the notion of government sovereignty in the area of labor relations in those countries is dead, as in the principle exemplified by President Roosevelt's statement in 1937 that a strike of public employees "manifests nothing less than an attempt . . . to prevent or obstruct the operations of government until their demands are satisfied . . . [and is] unthinkable and intolerable." [61]   Moreover, it is now accepted that there is no way to prevent illegal strikes. As Jägerskiöld observes in reference to wildcat strikes and "sickouts" by government employees in Sweden, "If these methods are used by many officials, and by those whose services are of great and immediate importance, even a public employer will probably have to give way. Very often the result will depend on the political situation." [62]

The Canadian experience, as reflected by the five models in Ontario briefly described above, is of special relevance, not only because of the closer similarity between Canada and the United States, but also because at least some of the Canadian experiments could be tried in this country. Of all the nations here considered, the United States lags furthest behind in the development of collective bargaining systems for government employees. Like Canada's, only more so, our federal system permits a wide degree of state experimentation in this area, which is the only major sector of industrial relations not yet preempted by federal laws. The Canadians have dared to experiment far more than we, and they have shown themselves to be more flexible and more imaginative than we. Their experiences can be of great value to us, if only we are prepared to study them carefully and to learn from them.

B.   *The Importance of Government Employment in the United States*

Government employment, particularly at state and local levels, has been growing steadily in the United States, and there are no indications that this secular trend will be reversed. The development of collective bargaining procedures for government employees is likewise moving forward, but much more sporadically. Meanwhile, the number of illegal strikes by government workers has sharply increased.[63] Whether it is possible to devise a collective bargaining system that denies the right of employees to strike but provides acceptable alternatives is almost certainly going to be decided in the government employment sector, not the private sector. What this means is that, contrary to the common assumption, public employment may provide the model for private employment, rather than the reverse. The crucial question is whether the nation will become so impatient and disillusioned with collective bargaining deficiencies in the private sector that it will abandon the present national labor policy before new methods of collective bargaining in public employment, which offer greater protection to third-party interests, can emerge as possible models for the private sector.

C.   *Should Government Employees Have the Right to Strike?*

The question whether government employees should have the *right* to strike really misses the main point; for whether or not they have the right, government employees are striking, and in increasing numbers. To concentrate on the right to strike is to overlook the underlying process, which is, of course, the nature of the employer-employee relationship. In this country, unlike the others cited for purposes of comparison, we still find widespread opposition by state and local government entities to any form of genuine collective bargaining with representatives of their employees. At the same time, the rising costs of government, the growing taxpayer rebellion, and the continued demands for greater government efficiency and accountability will put increased pressure on government employees to protect their own interests, and will give impetus to the trend toward more rapid organization and greater militancy. It seems unlikely that public managements can hold out much longer against collective bargaining by government employees; the question is whether they will have the willingness and the imagination to propose credible alternatives to the strike.

In this regard the public-private model represented by the Federal Public Service Staff Relations Act in Canada suggests some interesting possibilities. If adopted here, would it result in a rash of strikes by government employees? The Canadian experience to date suggests not, but everything depends upon the nature of the day-to-day administration of the public service. One would suppose that no system for resolving impasses over interests disputes would work in this country unless it also provided for the negotiation of collective bargaining agreements and for final and binding third-party adjudication of grievances.

Most strikes by government employees in the United States have occurred thus far in situations in which a genuine collective bargaining relationship did not exist. Once such a relationship is established, much of the pressure for strikes will be dissipated. On this point, Jägerskiöld's observations on four years of Swedish experience are instructive:

> [O]n the one side strikes have in fact proved to be a weapon of more doubtful importance in the public administration than was originally believed. The associations of the public employees have probably exaggerated their possibilities. As a rule, an association must have at its disposal very large sums of money in order to carry the strike to victory. For the most part, funds of that size are not available.[64]

Of course, the availability of the strike weapon does create risks for the government employer. In Sweden, says Jägerskiöld, "Probably the original idea on the employer's side was that the introduction of full bargaining rights would achieve a diminution of friction so that serious conflicts would seldom arise. In this respect, events proved otherwise." [65]

The trouble with allowing the right to strike only in "nonessential" government services is that the definition of essentiality is extremely difficult and rests primarily on philosophical rather than factual considerations.[66] At the extremes, there is not much controversy: police protection is generally considered essential, whereas numerous clerical functions in government agencies are conceded not to be essential. But the problem becomes more difficult as we move from the two poles toward the center. What about social workers and school teachers; what about clerks who prepare and mail welfare and social security checks?

The essential-nonessential dichotomy also raises the problem of contagion. Legal strikes by employees on one side of the line are apt to encourage illegal strikes by employees on the other side, especially if the latter group does not accept the basis for the distinction between it and the other.

Absent some mutually acceptable procedure that provides an alternative for the strike, therefore, it seems best to avoid a policy stating categorically that any group of public employees may or may not strike, and at the same time to make any strike subject to injunction by the regular courts if, but only if, the public authorities can demonstrate by credible evidence in open court that the strike would cause more harm to the public if allowed to continue than would be caused to the striking employees if it were halted. Procedural safeguards similar to those provided in Section 7 of the Norris-La Guardia Act [67] should be observed, but the courts should not be denied jurisdiction to enjoin strikes by government employees for proper cause shown.[68]

D. *Can Collective Bargaining Survive Where Strikes Are Not Tolerated?*

In the light of the foregoing analysis, the question whether collective bargaining can survive where strikes are not tolerated is reduced to comparatively simple dimensions, although some may think that the answer offered here merely begs the question. The answer is that if collective bargaining works well enough to produce alternatives to the strike mutually satisfactory to the parties, it will survive. If the alternatives, such as compulsory arbitration, are imposed by legislation, however, the result will be much more doubtful; for if the law is perceived by the employees to be oppressive or unfair, they will continue to strike or to resort to other illegal forms of job action.

As in the private sector, there is no "final solution" [69] to the problem of strikes in government employment. Whether the institution of collective bargaining can survive in the private sector and become firmly established in government employment will depend upon the continued vigor of "the spirit of moderation" of which Learned Hand spoke. For the spirit of moderation, of mutual accommodation and forebearance, is the very essence of collective bargaining, without which it, no more than our other cherished institutions, can long endure.

NOTES

1. The term, "strike," is used throughout to include lockout as well. As A. M. Ross and P. T. Hartman point out, "there are two parties to every dispute, in equal disagreement with each other. . . . Therefore the strike is really a bilateral suspension of work, although it is generally described as a unilateral act. . . ." *Changing Patterns of Industrial Conflict* (New York, 1960), p. 3.

2. United Fed'n of Postal Clerks v. Blount, 325 F. Supp. 879 (D.D.C. 1971), *aff'd*, 40 U.S.L.W. 3143 (1971), Dorchy v. Kansas, 272 U.S. 306 (1926).

3. 29 U.S.C. § 102.

4. *Id.*

5. Vegelahn v. Guntner, 167 Mass. 92, 107, 44 N.E. 1077, 1081 (1896) (dissenting opinion).

6. *Id.* at 108, 44 N.E. at 1081.

7. G. W. Taylor, *Government Regulation of Industrial Relations* (New York, 1948), p. 87.

8. 29 U.S.C. § 176.

9. See Aaron, *National Emergency Disputes: Is There a "Final Solution"?* 1970 Wis. L. Rev. 137, 140.

10. The states have limited powers to deal with local emergencies. Some seventeen state laws prescribe special procedures to be followed in strikes or threatened strikes involving public utilities; but all such laws are unconstitutional to the extent that they purport to affect public utilities in interstate commerce in a manner inconsistent with the LMRA. Division 1287, Amal. Ass'n of Street, Elec. Ry. & Motor Coach Employees v. Missouri, 374 U.S. 74 (1963); Amalgamated Ass'n of Street, Elec. Ry. & Motor Coach Employees v. WERB, 340 U.S. 383 (1951).

11. 45 U.S.C. § 160.

12. Delaware & Hudson Ry. v. United Transportation Union, 76 L.R.R.M. 2900 (D.C. Cir.), *cert. denied*, 91 S. Ct. 2209 (1971).

13. *See, e.g.,* Hildebrand, "An Economic Definition of the National Emergency Dispute," in I. Bernstein, H. L. Enarson, & R. W. Fleming (eds.), *Emergency Disputes and National Policy* (New York, 1955), p. 3; Bernstein, "The Economic Impact of Strikes in Key Industries," in *id.*, p. 24.

14. Aaron, *supra* note 9, at 141.

15. *See, e.g.,* International Bhd. of Elec. Workers v. Salt River Project, 78 Ariz. 30, 275 P.2d 393 (1954).

16. Of sixteen "vanguard" states which have enacted comprehensive statutes dealing with collective bargaining by government employees, twelve have specifically prohibited the right to strike, and all but three deny it by judicial decision. Seidman, *State Legislation on Collective Bargaining by Public Employees,* 22 Lab. L. J. 13, 18 (1971). The other states outlaw strikes by express statutory provision or judicial decision. Federal employees are, of course, forbidden to participate in a strike or to assert the right to strike, 5 U.S.C. §§ 7311, 3333 and 18 U.S.C. § 1918.

17. United Fed'n of Postal Clerks v. Blount, 325 F. Supp. 879, 883 (D.D.C. 1971).

18. S. Jägerskiöld, *Collective Bargaining Rights of State Officials in Sweden* (Ann Arbor, 1971), p. 21.

19. W. H. McPherson, *Public Employee Relations in West Germany* (Ann Arbor, 1971), p. 24.

20. *Id.* at 163.

21. F. Meyers, *The State and Government Employee Unions in France* (Ann Arbor, 1971), p. 18.

22. The literature is voluminous. Two particularly useful books are Bernstein, Enarson & Fleming, *supra* note 13, and D. E. Cullen, *National Emergency Strikes* (Ithaca, 1968). See also, *Final Recommendations by a Special Comm. of ABA on National Strikes in Transportation Industries*, Bureau of National Affairs, Inc., *Daily Lab. Rep.*, No. 23, Feb. 3, 1970, p. D-1; Aaron, *National Emergency Disputes: Some Current Proposals*, 22 Lab. L. J. 461 (1971); and Stevens, *Is Compulsory Arbitration Compatible with Bargaining?* 5 Ind. Rel. 38 (1966).

23. For a detailed description and analysis of this proposal, see Aaron, *supra* note 21, at 470-72.

24. *Id.*

25. Basic Agreement between the Swedish Employers' Confederation and the Confederation of Swedish Trade Unions (1938), as amended (1947), translated by W. N. Lansburgh, reprinted in F. Schmidt, *The Law of Labour Relations in Sweden* (Cambridge, Mass., 1962), p. 264.

26. *Id.* at 267.

27. See, e.g., *Final Recommendations by a Special Comm. of ABA, supra* note 21.

28. Hand, "The Contribution of an Independent Judiciary to Civilization," in I. Dilliard (ed.), *The Spirit of Liberty* (New York, 1953), p. 125.

29. See discussion under III-B, in text.

30. See generally, M. H. Moskow, J. J. Loewenberg, E. C. Koziara (eds.), *Collective Bargaining in Public Employment* (New York, 1970), especially the bibliography, pp. 307-25; *Symposium: Labor Relations in the Public Sector*, 67 Mich. L. Rev. 891-1082 (1969).

31. Section 12 of the Hawaii Collective Bargaining in Public Employment Act, Act 171, L. 1970, provides that, subject to a number of procedural requirements, covered employees may strike. Subsection (c) provides, however, that "[w]here the strike occurring, or is about to occur, endangers the public health or safety, the public employer concerned may petition the [tripartite public employee relations] board to make an investigation. If the board finds that there is imminent or present danger to the health and safety of the public, the board shall set requirements that must be complied with to avoid or remove any such imminent or present danger."
    Section 1101.1001 of the Pennsylvania Public Employee Relations Act, Pa. Stat., tit. 43, §§ 1101.1001-.2301 (1970), absolutely forbids strikes by guards of prison or mental hospitals or by employees "directly involved with and necessary to the functioning of the courts." Section 1101.1003 provides that, subject to certain procedural limitations, other employees may strike "unless or until such a strike creates a clear and present danger or threat to the health, safety or welfare of the public." In that event, public authorities may petition the courts for relief.

32. Stieber, "Collective Bargaining in the Public Sector," in L. Ulman (ed.), *Challenges to Collective Bargaining* (Englewood Cliffs, N.J., 1967), pp. 65, 81.

33. English translations of this legislation and of related collective bargaining agreements are included in Jägerskiöld, *supra* note 18, at 82-143.

34. *Id.* at 58.

35. *Id.* at 65.

36. *Id.* at 112, 116.

37. See W. Däubler, *Der Streik im öffentlichen Dienst* (Tübingen, 1970), prepared at the request of the Union for Public Services, Transport and Communications (ÖTV), arguing, *inter alia*, that the right of civil servants to strike is sanctioned by the European Convention on Human Rights and the European Social Charter, but conceding that even civil servant strikes are illegal under some circumstances, depending primarily on the essentiality of services; and T. Ramm, *Das Koalitions-und Streikrecht der Beamten* (Cologne, 1970), prepared at the request of the German Trade Union Federation (DGB), arguing that civil servants are subject to no more stringent strike restrictions than those imposed on public employees generally, and suggesting alternatives such as arbitration for strikes by persons performing services the interruption of which would infringe upon the rights of others or transgress the constitutional order or moral code. Both sources are cited and discussed in McPherson, *supra* note 19, at 164-65.

38. See note 31 *supra*.

39. McPherson, *supra* note 19, at 165.

40. Meyers, *supra* note 21, at 19-21.

41. *Id.* at 21, citing H. Sinay, *La Grève* (Paris, 1966).

42. H. W. Arthurs, *Collective Bargaining by Public Employees in Canada: Five Models* (Ann Arbor, 1971), p. 10.

43. R. S. O. 1960, c. 202.

44. Arthurs, *supra* note 42, at 18.

45. *Id.*

46. Stat. Can. 1966-67, c. 72.

47. "As of March 31, 1970, some 37,725 employees were included in units which had opted for the strike; of these only 2,700 were designated employees—about 7.5 percent." None of the 27,500 postal workers, who did opt for the strike, is a designated employee. This means that 25 percent of the remaining 10,000 employees are designated; but in only one instance among the fourteen units involved was there a dispute over this matter. Arthurs, *supra* note 42, at 34.

48. *Id.* at 39.

49. *Id.*

50. Rev. Stat. Ont. 1960, c. 298, as amended.

51. Arthurs, *supra* note 42, at 78.

52. *Id.* at 101.

53. Quoted in *id.* at 102.

54. Stat. Ont. 1961-62, c. 121, as amended.

55. Arthurs, *supra* note 42, at 123.

56. *Id.* at 131.

57. See note 43 *supra.*

58. Stat. Ont. 1960, c. 393.

59. Arthurs, *supra* note 42, at 140.

60. Ont. Reg. 63/55, S. 18(1)(c).

61. Quoted in Stieber, *supra* note 32, at 80.

62. Jägerskiöld, *supra* note 18, at 71.

63. In 1958 there were only 5 work stoppages in government service, involving only 980 employees and 4,170 man-idle days. In 1968 the number of work stoppages was 177; the number of involved employees, 177,000; and the number of man-idle days, 2,398,000. White, *Work Stoppages of Government Employees*, 92 Monthly Lab. Rev. 29, 34 (1969).

64. Jägerskiöld, *supra* note 18, at 71.

65. *Id.* at 72.

66. See Hildebrand, "Collective Bargaining in the Public Sector," in J. T. Dunlop & N. W. Chamberlain (eds.), *Frontiers of Collective Bargaining* (New York 1967), pp. 139-40.

67. 29 U.S.C. § 107. Before issuing an injunction, the court must find that unlawful acts have been threatened and will be continued unless restrained; that substantial and irreparable injury to plaintiff's property will follow; that as to each item of relief granted greater injury will be inflicted upon plaintiff by a denial of relief than will be inflicted upon defendants if relief is granted; that plaintiff has no adequate remedy at law; and that public officers charged with protecting plaintiff's property are unable or unwilling to furnish adequate protection.

68. This appears to be the present law in Michigan. See School Dist. v. Holland Educ. Ass'n, 380 Mich. 314, 157 N.W. 2d 206 (1968); Smith, *State and Local Advisory Reports on Public Employment Labor Legislation: A Comparative Analysis*, 67 Mich. L. Rev. 891, 912-13 (1969).

69. See Aaron, *supra* note 9.

Does Compulsory Arbitration Prevent Strikes?

The Australian Experience

Kingsley Laffer[†]

I. Industrial Disputes in Australia

The short answer to this question must of course be: No one can scarcely imagine any system of industrial relations working so smoothly that strikes were abolished completely, although some countries, e.g., the Netherlands and the Scandinavian countries, have come close to it at times. In fact, in Australia last year (1970), 1,367,400 [1] employees were involved in industrial disputes. This may be compared with a total of wage and salary earners in civilian employment at June 1970 (excluding employees in agriculture and private domestic service) of 4,479,900.[2] The number of working days lost from these disputes was 2,393,-700, which works out to 534 days lost for every 1,000 employees, or slightly over half a day per employee. The average duration of disputes was 1.75 days. During the first seven months of this year, 1971, working days lost already total 1,845,300, so last year's figure seems certain to be substantially exceeded this year. No, compulsory arbitration has not abolished strikes in Australia. Indeed our system at present is in a turmoil, as we shall see.

It must be said, however, that for a time it did look as though we might, if not eliminate strikes altogether, at least go a long way in this direction. Over the greater part of the century there had been a secular decline in the number of working days lost from industrial disputes, notwithstanding a large growth in the work force. If I may quote from an earlier study, "The down-

[†] Kingsley Laffer is Associate Professor of Industrial Relations and Editor, *Journal of Industrial Relations*, University of Sydney, Australia. The author would like to thank Mr. Philip Bentley of Macquarie University for some most helpful comments on a draft of this paper.

ward trend in Australia becomes clear if we take two broadly comparable sixteen year periods, 1913-1928 and 1939-1954. Over 1913-1928, the average number of man-days lost per year was 1,638,000: for 1939-1954 the average was 1,230,000: in the past eleven years, 1955-1965, the average annual loss was 702,-000. This fall in man days lost occurred notwithstanding an increase of 123.0 percent in the number of wage and salary earners between 1921 and 1961." [3] These hopes have, however, turned out to be illusory, at any rate from the vantage point of 1971. In recent years the industrial disputes trend has been fairly steadily upward, as the following table shows:

Australia, Industrial Disputes Experience, 1965-1971

Year	Number	Workers Involved	Working Days Lost
		(000)	(000)
1966	1,273	394.9	732.1
1967	1,340	483.3	705.3
1968	1,713	720.3	1,079.5
1969	2,014	1,285.2	1,958.0
1970	2,738	1,367.4	2,393.7
Seven months ended July 1971	1,473	932.5	1,845.3

Source: C.B.C.S., *Labour Report* and *Industrial Disputes* Bulletin. The statistician explains that "The statistics of industrial disputes refer only to disputes involving a stoppage of work of ten man-days or more. Workers involved include workers directly or indirectly involved in disputes. Workers indirectly involved are employees thrown out of work at the establishment when the stoppages occurred but not themselves parties to the disputes."

"Workers indirectly involved" are usually only a fraction of one percent of the total.

The low point for the post-war period was 1959 (or a few years earlier if coal strikes are excluded) when 365,000 working days were lost. Unquestionably the authority of our arbitration system in respect to dispute settlement is being severely challenged at the present time.

Two main issues arise in an analysis of the working of the system at present. These are: (a) the terms on which disputes are settled and (b) the methods by which disputes are settled.

II. The Terms on Which Disputes are Settled

In their settlement of disputes the Commonwealth and State arbitration systems together with other arbitral bodies have determined minimum wages and conditions for almost 90 percent of Australian employees. These wages and salaries are minima and have been added to by bargained supplements known as "over-award" payments. Overall, however, these have tended to be of modest dimensions. Professor Keith Hancock, commenting on a survey by the Commonwealth Statistician in 1965, puts them at only 8.7 percent of the total wage and salary bill.[4] Even if one were to regard this calculation as much too low, as giving too little weight to over-award elements in overtime and systems of payment by results, one would still have a figure of modest dimensions. Although arbitration determined only minimum wages, actual wages were fairly close to these by and large, suggesting that arbitration exercised some measure of control. In 1966 I sought to explain this as follows, "This control is obtained mainly by the persuasiveness of arbitration standards over the whole area of employer-trade union bargaining. The employer in negotiation keeps these standards continually in mind and contrives not to depart too far from them. The trade union knows that it can seldom achieve more than modest gains in relation to arbitration standards."[5]

The effect of these controls has been mainly on the structure of industry differentials, but has almost certainly affected the general level of wages as well. If we take 1967 as the last fairly "normal" year before the major upsurge in industrial disputes that began in 1968 and is still continuing, we find that average hourly earnings of full time, male non-managerial employees in private industry groups ranges from $1.36 in retail trade to $1.86 in mining and quarrying with a mean deviation of 9 cents or 6 percent around an average of $1.50.[6] This remarkably even income distribution by industry arises in large measure from the principles followed by arbitration bodies in determining wages[7] which have been very influential throughout the whole system and which by applying uniform principles to weak and strong groups of workers alike have operated to assist weaker groups and to check stronger groups.[8] The weakened influence of arbitration since then is illustrated by the development of a range of $1.60-$2.32 with a mean deviation of 14 cents or 76 percent around an average of $1.84, by October 1970. The influence of arbitration, however, though weakened, is still strong. This is so, notwithstanding that Australia now has a large number of directly negotiated agreements. (I avoid the term collective bargaining agreements, because of the essential difference from the latter, namely that our agreements are all negotiated under the shadow of the standards determined by arbitration.) Dianne Yerbury and J. E. Isaac give a number of examples of these.[9]

The effect of arbitration on the general level of wages is less clear-cut. This is because determinations such as those in "Total Wage" [10] cases based on the capacity to pay of the economy, which in effect lead to increases through virtually the whole wage and salary structure, are influenced, sometimes explicitly, by the current level of over-award payments. This clouds the direction of causality. It seems likely, however, that by imposing checks on the differentials secured by strong groups of workers, arbitration has modified the impact the leadership of these groups has had on wage levels generally, and has thus kept wage levels lower than they might otherwise have been. Arbitration has thus probably had some anti-inflationary effect. Australia's three main trading partners are Japan, the United Kingdom and the United States. Up to December 1967, consumer retail prices since 1963 had risen 24 percent in Japan by December 1967, 16 percent in the United Kingdom, and 10 percent in the United States, as compared with 14 percent in Australia.[11] As Australia had extremely low unemployment over this period, ranging between one and two percent of the labour force,[12] this record is quite good, even by comparison with the United States, with its lower rate of price increase.

Experience since 1968, when Australian prices have risen increasingly sharply, paradoxically also gives some support to the view that arbitration exercises a restraining influence. Over the ten year period 1957-1958—1967-1968, the consumer price index rose by 25.6 percent.[13] In 1968-1969, however, the rate of price increase was 2.9 percent, in 1970, 3.7 percent, and in 1971, 5.4 percent.[14] Between 1967 and March 1971, however, prices rose in Japan by 24.4 percent, in the U.K. by 23.9 percent, and in the U.S. by 19.5 percent, as compared with Australia, 13.2 percent.[15] Yet Australia in this period has had the mining boom, strong capital inflow, an increasingly favorable balance of payments and very full employment, as compared with the balance of payments uncertainties and unemployment problems of the U.K. and the U.S. Japan, we know, like Australia, has had an under-valued currency. Australia has not had particularly adept government policies over the period and it is highly probable that her lower rate of price increase, notwithstanding her extremely buoyant economy, is in some measure due to institutional restraints still arising from the arbitration system.

This restraint has, however, necessarily been a qualified one. Arbitrators have had to temper their decisions to the prevailing economic and industrial relations winds. Thus in the Total Wage case in 1970 the Commonwealth Arbitration system awarded a 6 percent wage and salary increase which in effect sought to give employees a share in the prosperity arising from the mineral boom.[16] "We have had to balance the probable economic effect of our decision against other considerations, mainly of equity, which would arise if we awarded less than we propose," said the Commission. Arbitration wage increases led indeed to an interchange between the Prime Minister and the President of the Commonwealth Arbitration Commission, Sir Richard Kirby,[17] and the Commonwealth Government has consistently put a large share of the blame for the current inflation on to the Commission. It is difficult, however, to see how the Commission could have acted very differently in the context of the mineral boom and the failure of the government itself to appreciate the Australian dollar when required and to carry out appropriate manpower, taxation, and other policies to help take some of the pressures off the industrial relations system. In an international context the Commission seems not to have done as badly as many believe.

Arbitration bodies, then, seem certainly to have exercised some control over industry differentials, assisting the weak and checking the strong, and it seems probable that they have had some control of the general level of wages and salaries as well. Whatever views may be held about this, however, many, particularly among economists, employers, and governments, see a greater potentiality here. No doubt these sections have at times exaggerated these potentialities, e.g., when they have naively assumed that arbitrators could immediately implement productivity-geared wage policies, without regard to the governmental, economic, and industrial relations context. It is even probable that economists have at times done more harm than good by the advice they have tendered. For example, the abolition of cost of living adjustments, which looks so well in economic models, has probably undermined the ordinary worker's security, and accentuated his alienation from arbitration thus intensifying resort to direct action with its sometimes inflationary effects. The introduction of the Total Wage procedure designed to give more control over wage levels also seems to have reduced the flexibility of the system and led to more direct action. But if one could envisage the Arbitration Commission dealing with economic matters in a broad inter-disciplinary way, taking account of sociological, trade union organizational, and other aspects, and steadily developing its expertise and techniques, with suitable parts being played by governments, personnel management, and the trade unions, also with adequate expertise, one might well wish to keep a significant place for it in the Australian industrial relations system.

The terms on which disputes are settled has then been a most important aspect of the work of Australian arbitration, that must be included in any assessment of it. The apparent weakening of its control is causing a good deal of concern.

III. The Methods by Which Disputes Are Settled

Without doubt there has in recent years been a drastic decline in the degree of acceptance of the authority of arbitration bodies both as an alternative to the strike and in their ancillary function as a setter of wage standards. "In parts of Australia, not least Sydney, we are approaching intolerably close to industrial anarchy," [18] commented the *Sydney Morning Herald* recently after a particularly bad day in Sydney during which train, postal, and television services among others, were seriously disrupted by strike activity. A question that arises is whether these events are a mere aberration in the long history of Australian arbitration, or whether we are experiencing the growing pains of a greatly changed industrial relations system.

One might support the former view by comparing the present situation with the inflationary effects of the wool boom of the late forties and early fifties. The wool boom passed and the economy moved back to a more stable state. Similarly costs at the present time are catching up with the mineral boom and in due course a more normal wage pressure may eventuate. It is also possible that the long-run secular decline in man-days lost from strikes will be resumed. The decline that occurred in both the United Kingdom and Australia was associated with development of the recognition of the trade unions, of machinery and procedures of collective bargaining in the U.K. and of compulsory arbitration in Australia to assist the accommodation of conflict, and of negotiating and similar skills. The cost of strikes to managements and unions induced them to participate in these developments. Moreover, the state itself took drastic action on occasion, as in the British general strike of 1926 and the New South Wales coal strike of 1949,[19] and trade union leaders in both countries came to feel that the state would intervene if strike activity became excessive and that they could not win such a conflict. Thus, as Knowles says, "The resistant, militant elements in the Unions, although they have always given life and enthusiasm to the movement, have proved less and less able to dominate it." [20] Perhaps history will repeat itself.

It seems likely indeed that some of these things will happen. There are straws in the wind already. At the national biennial conference of the Australian Council of Trade Unions in September 1971, the left-centre emerged dominant, both the extreme right and the extreme left being defeated on critical motions.[21] The young, aggressive and somewhat charismatic new President of the A.C.T.U. Mr. R. J. Hawke, is a social democrat who delieves that the trade unions would benefit greatly by the return of the Labour Party to power in the federal parliament. He therefore does not want public opinion to be alienated from Labour by excessive strike activity. He recently warned unionists in Sydney against incorrect rash strike action.[22]

It seems nevertheless very unlikely that we shall return to the old order of things. A large part of the historical development that occurred in the U.K. and in Australia was associated with the progressive expansion and growth of conciliation and other procedures to assist accommodation between managements and employees. Thus in Australia the Commonwealth and the various States have frequently amended their arbitration legislation to improve their accommodation and arbitration machinery. Both in the U.K. and in Australia the decline in man-days lost through industrial disputes was paradoxically associated with a large increase in the number of employees participating in these disputes, the explanation being a big decline in the duration of disputes. The tactical one-day protest stoppage replaced the strategic long strike.[23] There is reason to believe, however, that in Australia this long orientation towards improvements in the conciliation and arbitration machinery is coming to an end and that the emphasis will now be on the development of a new type of system. It is likely that we are nearing the end of a long, historical phase in our arbitration history.

To be sure one can readily find important areas where improvements in the machinery are desirable. Examples are the need for development of procedures for accommodation at the plant level, especially as regards interests disputes concerning over-award payments and the like, but also to some extent in regard to grievances. In our development of arbitration by awards largely on an industry and craft basis we have neglected relations at the plant and the analysis of the Donovan Commission regarding the U.K.[24] largely applies to us. These needs, however, only illustrate the important changes occurring in our industrial relations system, involving a shift in its centre of gravity in the direction of the plant, with consequent far-reaching implications for arbitration, management, and trade unionism.

In fact, two recent and apparently well worthwhile attempts to deal with the present industrial relations crisis by means of procedural improvements have been an almost complete failure. As a result of growing trade union opposition to the penalties against strikes available under Commonwealth awards, leading to the gaoling of Mr. Clarrie O'Shea, Victorian Secretary of the Australian Tramways and Motor Omnibus Employees' Federation, in May 1969,[25] the Commonwealth government introduced greatly improved procedures for applying penalties. These, being less legalistic and necessitating thorough conciliation, removed some of the extremely unsatisfactory factors of the previous legislation[26] but they proved to be of little significance. The trade union opposition to penalties was by this time so strong that probably they should not have been expected to work. Insofar as they have been brought into operation they have tended to involve conciliation to the utmost.

Another attempt at procedural improvement was announced by the Minister for Labour and National Service in May 1970.[27] Very sensible step-by-step procedures for avoiding and settling industrial disputes were agreed upon and published in a booklet issued jointly by the Department of Labour and National Service, the Australian Council of Trade Unions and the National Employers' Policy Committee. They also appear to have had little effect.

Events have indeed demonstrated the ambiguity of the term "conciliation." While conciliation can certainly act as "a lubricant, perhaps as a catalyst" it can readily "become a tactic of labor, management, or the government to force peace at an un-

toward price." [28] In recent years trade union demands for more
conciliation and for "meaningful negotiation," though sometimes
justified, have increasingly been in effect demands for capitulation. As Yerbury and Isaac point out, "The union's approach
on over-award payments is often not to negotiate at all, but to
demand, with immediate threat of the strike." [29] More claims
lead to more conciliation which results in more inflation. A distinction must be made between conciliation around the standards
set by arbitration and conciliation that feels forced to depart
substantially from these standards. It is the latter that is now
developing more and more, so that over a large part of our industrial relations system we have too much conciliation and
pressure to concede, not too little.

The Commonwealth Minister for Labour and National Service
is nevertheless putting his faith largely in improvements in the
arbitration machinery. He explained in July that "it was fifteen
years since substantial alterations were made to the Act" and
that "it was most important that it should be amended in the
light of the realities of present-day industrial relations." [30] A
number of minor anomalies in the Conciliation and Arbitration
Act now seem likely to be removed.[31] A continuation of the historical process of amending the arbitration legislation from time
to time does not now, however, seem in principle to be what is
wanted. From the standpoint of conciliation the arbitration
machinery is in some respects now working too well for its own
good. Rather should we recognize that we are experiencing the
birth of a new phase in our industrial relations system, and
develop our policies accordingly.

The development of a one-sidedness in conciliation has necessarily been associated with a decline in respect for the standards
of arbitration. Arbitration has traditionally determined wage
differentials on principles of "comparative justice" according to
which the relative wages paid depended on the degree of skill,
responsibility, training, and the like, and in so doing has tended
to assist weaker groups of workers and impose checks on the
strong. In a test case in 1966, the *General Motors* case, the
union sought to obtain special loadings based on the prosperity
of the company. The claim was, however, rejected. "First and
foremost it seems to us to be completely incompatible with the
doctrine of comparative wage justice (or equal pay for equal
work) and with the universal practice in the tribunals of this
country of uniform marginal rates throughout an industry,

which rests on the doctrine mentioned." [32]   Since then the Commonwealth Arbitration Commission has tried, through carrying out what it calls "Work Value" studies, to modify the long-established relativities perpetuated by the Comparative Justice Doctrine, while retaining the underlying principle. [33]

The development of direct bargaining between employers and unions has, however, increasingly produced relativities, based on market and bargaining factors, that are at variance with Comparative Justice differentials. Arbitrators often find themselves forced, using one escape device or another, to go along with this in their conciliation and arbitration. In this connection it is interesting to compare the decision in the *Oil Refineries* case, 1970, with the *General Motors* decision referred to above: "Although the Commission refused to accept union submissions to the effect that the industry's capacity to pay should be taken into account in determining the unions' claims, it awarded increases in wage rates and certain other concessions to the employees concerned, taking account in this regard of the offers and counter offers which had been made by the parties." In this case they felt that they could not realistically arbitrate in terms of their traditional principles but "must regard the arbitration as a prolongation or extension of the negotiations." [34]

IV. The Problem of Sanctions

The above discussion of the terms and methods of dispute settlement may be linked with current thought concerning the arbitration system through consideration of the question of penalties against strikes. The dynamic Mr. Hawke, who was elected President of the A.C.T.U. in September 1969, while wishing to retain the arbitration system, has a number of times indicated his belief in negotiated agreements, stressing the importance of the honoring of such agreements by the trade unions. Mr. Clyde Cameron, shadow Minister for Labour in the federal Labour Opposition has also for some time advocated "industrial agreements for the sharing of prosperity in return for industrial peace." [35]

A scheme along these lines for the development of a strong collective bargaining adjunct to Australian arbitration was accepted first by a Labour Party industrial committee,[36] and subsequently with modifications, by a federal conference of the Party.[37] The proposals provided for "the repeal of all penalties for strikes and lockouts against arbitral decisions of the Commission or a conciliation committee." But whereas the original

scheme provided for penalties to be obtained through civil action
if agreements were breached, this was deleted from the scheme
finally approved, which provided rather vaguely for the honoring of agreements, without explicit reference to sanctions. A
Memorandum of June 28th, however, signed by Mr. Cameron as
Chairman of the A.L.P. Executive Industrial Relations Policy
Committee, stated that it included "enforcement provisions similar to existing A.C.T.U. agreements." Mr. Cameron recently explained that the Labour Party would retain section 41 of the
Conciliation and Arbitration Act, which provides for penalties
up to $200 for organizations and up to $20 against members of
organizations that breach agreements.[38] This interpretation was
promptly repudiated by the members of the Parliamentary Labour Party. So, Mr. Cameron's agreements will contain no sanctions.[39]

If Labour obtains power as a result of the federal elections
to be held next year there will, however, certainly be amendments to the arbitration legislation that will provide for a very
substantial recognition of and support for direct bargaining between employers and unions. But even if Labour does not then
attain power (at the moment it appears to have something like
an even chance) it seems certain that the support for direct
bargaining from both the A.C.T.U. and a Party that commands
the support of nearly half the electorate, when added to current
trends, must be very influential.

We come now to some fascinating events, the eventual outcome of which is not yet clear. One aspect of compulsory arbitration in Australia is the very considerable provision, either by
legislation or procedures, for penalties against strikes and lockouts.[40] Now in December, 1967, as a result of its first Work
Value enquiry, the Commonwealth Arbitration Commission awarded substantial increases in wages to the more skilled workers in
the metal trades, at the same time giving a strong hint to employers that there might well be some substantial absorption of
over-award payments when these new wages were paid.[41] The
Minister for Labour and National Service made a statement that
in effect encouraged employers to insist on absorption [42] and in
the event employers generally took a hard line on absorption
while the unions resisted this. Many strikes occurred, the penal
provisions of Commonwealth arbitration were invoked and extensive fines were imposed, which the unions refused to pay and
have never paid. In this particular case, the Commonwealth

Arbitration Commission climbed down in an appeal and in effect accepted the non-absorption of over-award payments.[43] The authority of arbitration bodies declined sharply from this time on, though the events themselves should perhaps be seen as a catalyst rather than as a basic cause.

The Commonwealth government has, however, continued to maintain that penalties against strikes are an essential part of a compulsory arbitration system, and has therefore insisted that all unpaid fines, totalling $48,150 in April 1971, be paid. A large part of this amount which related mainly to the absorption disputes just discussed, was imposed before the new procedures regarding penalties, referred to earlier, were introduced, and there has been a strong suggestion that this part was negotiable. It seemed likely that the government was mainly concerned with persuading the unions to accept the principle of penalties, and would probably have been content provided that penalties imposed subsequently to the new procedures, except for some under legal challenge, were paid. It approached a meeting of the National Labour Advisory Council, consisting of representatives of government, employers and employees, in April, 1971, with a very hard line attitude on this question. Employers' organizations supported the policy of the government. The government's strong line was probably partly influenced by political considerations. After a serious crisis in the Liberal Party government Hon. W. McMahon has recently emerged as a new Prime Minister and many believed that he was thinking strongly in terms of an early election to strengthen his position, with industrial relations as a leading issue on which he might hope to obtain public support.

Mr. Hawke of the A.C.T.U. must have gone to the conference with considerable feeling of unease. The unions were strongly opposed to the penal provisions and he did not appear to have much room for maneuver in his negotiations with the government. Yet in an all-out struggle with the government, the unions would be certain to lose, with the likelihood of a severe weakening of his own position in the A.C.T.U., whatever the political consequences for the government. During the course of the conference, however, a bombshell was dropped by Mr. Hawke and by Mr. George Polites of the National Employers' Committee. They had met and reached agreement to arrange for discussions concerning the whole field of conciliation and arbitration. This cut the ground from under the feet of the government as it would not have looked very sensible for it to persist with its determination to force a showdown on the penalties issue while employers and unions were prepared to hold discussions that might have a constructive outcome.[44] One can only speculate as to what happened between Mr. Hawke and Mr. Polites. Possibly Mr. Hawke offered his strong support for something like the Cameron proposals discussed above, which included provision for penalties through civil action. Mr. Polites might have been less willing than the government to face the industrial upheaval that was likely to result if the government forced the penalties issue. He might also have felt that some variant of the Cameron proposals was more realistic in terms of the current industrial relations climate. He was, however, severely criticized by some employers for his action.

The Hawke-Polites discussion occurred in between the Labour Party Industrial Committee's acceptance of the Cameron scheme with its provision for civil sanctions and the federal Labor Party Conference's modification of them, which, following militant union pressure, omitted direct reference to sanctions. Mr. Hawke thus now has less to offer Mr. Polites than seemed likely at the time of their discussion. As Mr. Polites has always stated that sanctions are necessary he may well be disappointed at the turn of events. He has, however, now himself put forward proposals for negotiation of agreements not unlike those of Mr. Cameron.[45]

Further talks have since taken place between the Commonwealth government, employers, the A.C.T.U. and white collar unions, but they appear to have become bogged down and are expected to end shortly with no more than agreement on some useful but minor amendments to the arbitration legislation. Both the Commonwealth government and employers are reported to be insisting on sanctions, while the unions reiterate their opposition to them.[46] It is probable that the Commonwealth government will then embody its views in its own legislation which, though containing some minor useful features, is unlikely to seriously come to grips with current problems.

The New South Wales government, following a recent severe outbreak of strikes in N.S.W., is following a minor hard line of its own and is legislating to provide for secret ballots in striking unions and to tighten up procedures for deregistration of unions in essential services that strike illegally.[47] Though these measures may have some value in particular circumstances, in the present industrial relations climate they must be regarded largely as window-dressing.

V. The Future of Compulsory Arbitration

Thus the Australian industrial relations system is at present in rather a chaotic state and the authority of the arbitration system is currently very tarnished. This raises the question as to whether the latter can in the near future recover its place or whether we shall move to something much more like a collective bargaining system. As we have seen, most of the evidence appears to point in the latter direction.

Commonwealth government policy is, however, to restore the authority of the arbitration system. It rejects the Labour Party's proposals discussed above. The Minister for Labour and National Service recently stated that "Industrial relations could not be left solely to employer and employee bodies . . . the Government has vital interests to protect which could well be overlooked during negotiations between employers and unions." Of particular concern to the government were the "repercussions which the industrial relations developments can have on the economy, the general management of which is the Government's responsibility." [48] He reiterated the need for sanctions to give judicial backing to awards. In effect the government wants a continuance of the existing type of system, though with appropriate amendments to the arbitration machinery to make it work better and wants the trade unions to accept sanctions to give the system authority.

Now in one sense we can probably all agree that there will always be an arbitration system in Australia. Many countries have found the need for conciliation, investigation and arbitration machinery of various kinds and it is reasonably certain that our arbitration system will continue to perform functions such as these. Such procedures, however, would be little different from those used in various ways and degrees in collective bargaining systems, and if the arbitration system confined itself to these it would become but a pale shadow of its former self. The true significance of our compulsory arbitration system is that in settling disputes it has also largely determined wage standards. Unless it continues to do this it is not compulsory arbitration as we have known it.

Yerbury and Isaac,[49] however, argue that "in connection with national issues (the national minimum wage, national wage adjustments, standard hours of work, annual leave and long-service leave) we may expect tribunals to continue to determine these issues by arbitration largely because both employers and unions would want them to be so determined." This is one of the few points in this excellent article with which I find it difficult to agree. Mr. Cameron, also, notwithstanding the tremendous collective bargaining orientation of his proposals considers that the arbitration system could continue to fix minimum standards for wages, hours, leave and overtime.[50] But it is very doubtful that this is what employers and unions now want. Unions are at present very actively engaged in direct action over hours, leave and overtime in particular cases and appear to be no longer content to have these matters determined by arbitration. The President of the Metal Trades Industries Association (formerly the Metal Trade Employer's Association) recently "cast doubt on the future of the annual national wage case conducted by the Commonwealth Conciliation and Arbitration Commission." [51] The crux of the matter is that the more that is obtained by direct action the less there is available to be distributed in national awards. National awards in the above matters may continue but they are likely increasingly to become welfare minima rather than the egalitarian minima hitherto awarded, and any influence on the general level of wages will be slight. Arbitration would then be much more like Wage Councils and similar devices for assisting weaker groups in collective bargaining countries and quite different from the compulsory arbitration system we have had.

Everything depends no doubt on what happens in the direct negotiation area. It is at least conceivable that a new structure of differentials will be worked out by arbitration that will be more acceptable than the largely rejected comparative wage justice structure. At present the arbitration system, while trying to maintain some semblance of order, is being forced to deal fairly pragmatically with demands for relative wage increases. Can a new stable structure of differentials be reached that will replace the old Comparative Justice structure? The odds seem very much against this happening. It is not easy to see why the system of differentials should become stable; one would expect continual "leap-frogging" to occur as in many collective bargaining countries. Also such a structure of differentials, being pragmatically derived rather than based on any principle, would lack the authority that formerly attached to a principle such as Comparative Justice. Any stability reached in the differential structure would therefore seem to be very fragile. A major requirement is that the arbitration system should be able to develop a new principle or set of principles appropriate to the new situation, and be able by and large to get these accepted. But the present arbitration system, dominated by legal personnel, is not very well qualified to develop such new principles. In any case, it would be an almost impossible job for anyone, whatever their qualifications. Even so, the role of arbitration in the Australian system, and the traditional reliance on it, are important cultural factors that should not be underestimated. These may predispose all concerned to go back to the arbitration system if it can work out reasonable new approaches.

In this connection it is interesting to note that the formerly rather conservative and legalistic Metal Trades Industries Association is now advocating that wage determination be more realistic in the sense that over-award payments be brought within the framework of arbitration. The N.S.W. President recently announced, "The association has recently decided as a matter of policy that the usefulness of the Commission would be extended and its authority enhanced by its engaging in the process of conciliation and arbitration on actual rates of pay and conditions in individual industries and establishments. We do not believe in the principle of collective bargaining in lieu of arbitration. We believe rather that the greatest benefit can accrue by having negotiations conducted within the framework of the Commission, thereby having decisions arrived at and supported by the authority of the Commission." [52] The Commonwealth Public Service Board, which bargains with Commonwealth public service employees has for some time taken into account over-award payments in outside industry. [53] Thus there are some strong forces making for the development of a new differentials structure under the aegis of arbitration, though one suspects that arbitration has left it too late.

The differentials structure, however, is not the whole of the problem. The arbitration system, at the same time as it has assisted the trade unions by recognition and by determination of minimum standards has also assisted management in the preservation of some of its important prerogatives. Arbitration bodies have, for example, largely preserved for management its right to dismiss, deploy and promote labor and have generally refused to impose seniority criteria. [54] In 1970, 28.67 percent of all industrial disputes involving 12.02 percent of man-days lost were concerned with managerial policies. Over the period 1952-1966, 59.9 percent of disputes involving 41.5 percent of man-days lost were concerned with these issues.[55] It is certain that unions will continue to press in this area and a broader approach by arbitration tribunals seems essential if they are to recover their authority. While managements may not welcome any extensive intrusion of arbitration into this area, they will probably be forced to accept it. They may decide, of course, when it comes to the point, that they would rather handle many of these matters for themselves, i.e. through direct negotiation. Constitutional difficulties, which confine Commonwealth arbitration to interstate disputes may in any case sometimes make this essential.

Many causal factors in industrial disputes are, however, to be found more deeply embedded in organizations. Personnel departments may be inadequate and insufficient attention may have been given to the development of suitable socio-technical systems.[56] It is very difficult to envisage the arbitration system moving successfully into such fields, and even more difficult to imagine management accepting it. Yet it seems likely that there are strong links between the widespread protest movement in society and the upsurge in industrial disputes. Values are changing, especially among the young, and these changes are pressing on the adequacies of both governments and organizations. Firms with advanced industrial relations managements are aware of this and are carefully appraising their policies. But these are in a minority in Australia and they are understandably moving very slowly and cautiously. Solutions, when they are found, are much more likely to come from managements and perhaps also unions in some cases, than from arbitration. Thus the Commission on Industrial Relations in the U.K. studies the industrial relations systems of plants and makes recommendations on a wide variety of matters including the role of shop stewards, plant negotiating machinery, the functions of personnel management, and the like, and arbitration could undertake similar approaches in Australia. It is likely, however, that if such approaches went at all deeply into personnel management, they would be strongly resisted by employers.

Perhaps the essence of the matter is that Australian arbitration has been basically a paternalist system. It has sought to do good to management, the unions and the community, and has to a considerable extent succeeded in this. But just as paternalist managers in organizations tend to fail in the end through inability to understand and cope with the real issues in conflict with employees, so a paternalist arbitration system is now finding itself unable to come to grips with the deeper issues underlying industrial disputes. More sophisticated managements and unions seem increasingly likely to want to find their own solutions to the problems confronting them. This almost certainly means that the recent growth in direct negotiation will continue and that emphasis will continue to shift to personnel and industrial relations management at the plant level. The future of arbitration appears to depend a great deal on its ability to develop the orientation and expertise necessary for it to make a meaningful contribution in this area.

We may return briefly to some questions raised earlier. Will industrial relations in Australia settle down after costs have caught up with the mining boom, and will the long-term downward trend in strike activity, associated with recognition of unions and the development of the arbitration machinery, be resumed? The experience of the U.K. and the U.S.A. in recent years will of course warn us not to expect too much from a decline in the mining boom. Though these countries have nothing corresponding to this boom, they are nevertheless facing very similar industrial relations problems. Basically it would appear that we are now facing a new type of problem, or the very great magnification of an old one, the intensification of frustration, protest and unrest at the plant level. Our industrial relations system is now centered much more in the plant. Improvements in the arbitration machinery are not likely to help very much. Additional conciliation is more likely to produce greater inflation than proper attention to causal factors. Recognition of unions has gone almost as far as it can and what is wanted here is better accommodation between the policies of unions and the needs of rank and file members. The latter often have almost equally low opinions of managements, arbitration and their own unions.[57] New approaches to industrial relations are therefore essential and if the secular downward trend in strike activity is resumed it is likely to be for other than the historical reasons.

The Commonwealth government in its desire to have arbitration continue in its traditional role as arbitrator of the public interest shows virtually no awareness of these various issues.

It quite rightly stresses the economic significance of arbitration though it gives no indication as to how this is to be restored. Except for its insistence on provision for sanctions against strikes it has given no indication of having any viable policy. Sanctions themselves seem to be rather a frail reed on which to hang the future of the arbitration system. The A.C.T.U. is so strongly opposed to them that their imposition would almost certainly result in a major confrontation between government and unions. Though the government could be expected to win such a conflict this would do nothing to solve the basic problems of industrial relations at the plant level and would retard the constructive development of our industrial relations system for many years.

The proposals of Mr. Clyde Cameron, providing for the encouragement of agreements through direct negotiations between employers and unions, and an unfettered right to strike, with no penalties, in the negotiation of such agreements, certainly seem more realistic in terms of trade union attitudes. A vital question is that of the honoring of agreements. The A.C.T.U. policy emphasis on this and the value of such agreements to both employers and unions are favorable factors here. Mr. Cameron also looks to developments in trade union organization and amalgamation, more trade union research and increased trade union education as needed to make his system work satisfactorily. Plant pressures and unofficial strikes might, however, constitute a problem and it is doubtful whether Mr. Cameron has given sufficient attention to these aspects. Certainly a merit of his proposals is that he has considerable awareness of rank and file problems and he stresses the need for rank and file involvement in union policy-making, but important though this is, it is perhaps still at the machinery level, rather than orientated towards the deeper needs of rank and file workers. He did recognize that agreements might be broken and supported sanctions in such cases, but this very emphasis on sanctions perhaps indicated an orientation away from looking for causal factors. From the standpoint of rank and file workers agreements could easily mean the substitution of a new form of paternalism for that of arbitration. Strikes would also be likely to occur at the time of the making of the agreements as in the United States and little attention has so far been given to this aspect of the proposals. Mr. Cameron also wants more, say, for trade unions in what have hitherto been managerial prerogatives protected by arbitration. This could provide an opening for greater attention to rank and file needs but may often merely reflect union interpretation of those needs.

Mr. Cameron's proposals are weakest on the economic side. He sees arbitration as continuing to fix minimum standards for wages, hours, leave and overtime but we saw earlier that this would probably become increasingly of welfare rather than economic significance. Another likely role is that of arbitration of over-award rates between unions and "prosperous employers." [58] Essentially the industrial relations system is to be geared primarily to the settlement of industrial disputes. There is no indication that wage settlements are to be negotiated or arbitrated on any principles that will assist the gearing of wage determination to the requirements of the economy. This is the crucial difference between the new proposals and the type of arbitration system which the Commonwealth government and many employers are trying to retain. Thus the Cameron system may be expected to run into problems of preventing wage settlements being so large as to accentuate inflation, very similar to those being experienced in collective bargaining countries.

The answer being sought in many collective bargaining countries is experimentation with income policies. Mr. Cameron perhaps recognizes this when he says that control over prices, restrictive trade practices and excessive tariffs were elementary necessities if a cure was to be found for economic instability. [59] Mr. Hawke and other trade union leaders continually reiterate the need for price control. Thus the Cameron approach leads us into many of the same problems as are besetting collective bargaining countries and the need to seek similar solutions. Greater freedom to engage in industrial disputes and the denial of principle in wage determination lead to new complex measures, involving incomes policies to control the effects of the new found freedom. The arbitration system dealt with these issues much more simply. It provided "a high degree of freedom for both employers and trade unions, whilst still achieving a considerable measure of control." [60] Are not the Cameron proposals, despite the deep thought that has gone into them, the sincerity with which they are presented, and their attractiveness in many ways, really a false move? Should we not even at this late stage try to reform and save our arbitration system?

This hardly seems to be in the cards. The supporters of arbitration, from the Commonwealth government downwards, have virtually nothing worthwhile to put up. Two years ago, which even then was rather late in the day, one of the more percipient and successful arbitration judges, Mr. Justice Beattie, President of the Industrial Commission of New South Wales, said, "In my view the systems are better in settlement than in prevention . . . . The question is whether the development of the laws has kept pace with the changes which full employment has brought about . . . . The best industrial brains of government, employer organizations, trade unions, universities and industrial tribunals should be seeking solutions to these problems." [61] Nothing, however, was done, and of course it is always possible that the problems are insoluble. A concerted inter-disciplinary approach should, however, have been tried.

VI.   Conclusion

The short answer to the title question of this paper has already been given. No, compulsory arbitration in Australia has not prevented strikes. A longer answer is that it has tended to develop excessive emphasis on conciliation, it has failed to develop its principles of wage determination to meet the changing needs of a full employment economy, and most important of all it has failed to appreciate and adapt itself to the shift in the center of gravity of the industrial relations system in the direction of the plant level. It has pursued paternalistic approaches that are no longer accepted. As a result the time lost from strikes has tended to grow in recent years. There is intense controversy in Australia at present concerning the future of arbitration, but there seems to be no more than a bare possibility that it will re-establish itself. Meanwhile we are moving headlong in the direction of collective bargaining.

NOTES

1. Commonwealth Bureau of Census and Statistics, Bulletin, *Industrial Disputes*.

2. Commonwealth Bureau of Census and Statistics, *Quarterly Summary of Australian Statistics*.

3. Kingsley Laffer, "Compulsory Arbitration: A New Province for Law and Order," in Richard Preston, ed. *Contemporary Australia* (Duke University Commonwealth-Studies Center, 1969), pp. 159-160.

4. K. J. Hancock, "Earnings-Drift in Australia," *Journal of Industrial Relations*, July 1966, p. 136, reprinted in J. E. Isaac and G. W. Ford (eds.), *Australian Labour Economics, Readings* (Sun Books, Melbourne, 1967).

5. Kingsley Laffer, "Whither Arbitration?—Problems of Income Policies in Australia and Overseas," *Journal of Industrial Relations*, Vol. 10 (November 1968), p. 215.

6. Based on figures in Commonwealth Bureau of Census and Statistics, *Survey of Weekly Earnings and Hours*, October 1971.

7. See papers by Kingsley Laffer and J. E. Isaac, in Richard Preston, *op. cit.*, for accounts of these.

8. Harold Lydall in *The Structure of Earnings* largely rejects such institutional factors as compulsory arbitration (pp. 245-247) as determinants of the distribution of employment incomes, attributing this mainly to the degree of inequality in education and the proportion of male workers in agriculture. In arguing the supremacy of market forces he considers mainly differentials for skill, and one is disposed, with some qualification for cultural factors, to agree with him here. But bargaining power depends on many factors besides demand for and supply of skill, and differences of bargaining power are not minor imperfections, as he seems to assume, but a very significant aspect of the industrial relations scene. It is the inequalities in bargaining power in this sense that Australian compulsory arbitration has to a considerable extent controlled, by assisting the weak and by providing a focal point for employer resistance to the strong.

   It is also interesting to note that Lydall states the proportion of foreign born workers as increasing the dispersion of U.S. incomes at certain periods (pp. 220-225). Australia, however, with its large postwar immigration programme, has now a high proportion of foreign born workers, and yet has one of the least unequal distributions of income in the world (p. 156). It is one of the major achievements of arbitration to have assisted this by minimizing the exploitation of immigrants by employers. This has at the same time helped to secure official and very general trade union support for and acceptance of the immigration programme.

9. Dianne Yerbury and J. E. Isaac, "Recent Trends in Collective Bargaining," *International Labour Review*, Vol. 103 (May 1971).

10. Keith Sloane, "The National Wage Case, 1967," *Journal of Industrial Relations*, Vol. 9 (November 1967).

11. Commonwealth Bureau of Census and Statistics, *Monthly Review of Business Statistics*.

12. Commonwealth Bureau of Census and Statistics, *Labour Report;* R. V. Horn, *Labour Economics, Australia* (Cheshire, Melbourne, 1969), Ch. 7.

13. Based on figures from Commonwealth Bureau of Census and Statistics, *Monthly Review of Business Statistics.*

14. *Ibid.*

15. *Ibid.*

16. Department of Labour and National Service, *Industrial Information Bulletin,* Vol. 26 (January 1971), pp. 18-36.

17. See C. P. Mills, "A Review of Developments in Industrial Relations, 1970-1971," *Journal of Industrial Relations,* Vol. 13 (September 1971), pp. 229-230).

18. *Sydney Morning Herald,* 23rd July, 1971.

19. Kenneth F. Walter, *Australian Industrial Relations Systems* (Harvard 1970), pp. 309-310.

20. K.G.J.C. Knowles, *Strikes* (Blackwell, 1954), p. 61.

21. R. M. Martin, "The A.C.T.U. Congress of 1971" in the forthcoming issue of the *Journal of Industrial Relations,* December 1971.

22. *Sydney Morning Herald,* 28th September, 1971.

23. Knowles, *op. cit.,* Introduction.

24. Royal Commission on Trade Unions and Employers' Associations 1965-1968, *Report* (H.M.S.O. Cmnd., 3632) Ch. IV.

25. K. W. Hince, "Australian Trade Unionism, 1968-1969," *Journal of Industrial Relations,* Vol. 11 (November 1969), pp. 272-273.

26. See the statement by the then Minister for Labour and National Service, Mr. Billy Snedden, *Industrial Information Bulletin,* Vol. 25 (June 1970), pp. 1263-1267.

27. *Industrial Information Bulletin,* Vol. 25 (May 1970), "Procedures for Dealing with Industrial Disputes," after p. 1041.

28. Herbert R. Northrup, *Compulsory Arbitration and Government Intervention in Labor Disputes* (Labor Policy Association, 1966), pp. 161-162.

29. Dianne Yerbury and J. E. Isaac, "Recent Trends in Collective Bargaining in Australia," *International Labour Review,* Vol. 103 (May 1971), p. 451.

30. *Sydney Morning Herald,* 29th August 1971.

31. *Australian Financial Review,* 7th October, 1971.

32. *Australian Industrial Law Review,* 17th September, 1966.

33. See J. H. Portus, "Inter-Industry Wage Fixation Under the Commonwealth Act," *Journal of Industrial Relations,* November 1969.

34. *Australian Industrial Law Review,* 17th October, 1970.

35. *Australian Financial Review,* 2nd April, 1971.

36. *Australian Financial Review,* 19th April, 1971.

37. *Australian Financial Review*, 24th June, 1971, 28th June, 1971. P. Bentley, *Journal of Industrial Relations*, Vol. 13, No. 4 (forthcoming).

38. *Australian*, 4th October, 1971, *Sydney Morning Herald*, 13th October, 1971.

39. *Sydney Morning Herald*, 14th October, 1971.

40. See Kingsley Laffer, in Richard Preston, *op. cit.*, for a summary of these penal provisions. The main change since then is the modification of Commonwealth procedures referred to above.

41. See C. P. Mills, "Legislation and Decisions Affecting Industrial Relations," *Journal of Industrial Relations*, Vol. 10 (March 1968).

42. Department of Labour and National Service, *Industrial Information Bulletin*, December 1967, pp. 1892-1893.

43. C. P. Mills, "Legislation and Decisions Affecting Industrial Relations," *Journal of Industrial Relations*, Vol. 10 (July 1968).

44. *Australian Financial Review, Sydney Morning Herald*, 23rd April, 1971.

45. *Australian Financial Review*, 12th August, 1971.

46. *Australian Financial Review*, 7th October, 1971.

47. *Australian Financial Review*, 24th September, 1971, 30th Setpember, 1971, C. P. Mills, *Journal of Industrial Relations*, December 1971, (forthcoming).

48. *Sydney Morning Herald*, 8th June, 1971.

49. *Loc. cit.*, p. 448.

50. *Sydney Morning Herald*, 9th December, 1970.

51. *The Australian*, 7th October, 1971.

52. *Sydney Morning Herald*, 22nd June, 1971.

53. *Australian Financial Review*, 10th July, 1970.

54. F. T. deVyver, "The Weakening of Managerial Rights," *Business Horizons*, Vol. 2 (1959), pp. 38-48. See also the forthcoming article by Philip Bentley and Barry Hughes, "Australian Cyclical Strike Patterns," *Journal of Industrial Relations*, Vol. 13 (December 1971), for some current discussion.

55. D. W. Oxnam, *Journal of Industrial Relations*, Vol. 13 (June 1971), p. 135.

56. F. E. Emery and E. L. Trist, "Socio-technical Systems," in ed. F. E. Emery, *Systems Thinking* (Penguin Modern Management, Readings, 1969), pp. 281-296.

57. See N. F. Dufty, "The A.I.S. Kwinana Strike," *Journal of Industrial Relations*, Vol. 13 (June 1971).

58. *Australian Financial Review*, 2nd April, 1971.

59. *Australian Financial Review*, 2nd April, 1971. The policy obviously is not yet well worked out, however. Thus he advocated both relative wages geared partly to the "prosperity" of particular concerns and price control. From an incomes policy standpoint, however, there is little room for the former. The granting of preference in wage increases to sectors which achieve a high increase in labor productivity is, in practice, largely offset by the need of those sectors not thus favored to achieve a faster employment growth, so that their wages rise too, as well as by the resistance of conventional ideas of equity to this discrimination. (H. A. Turner and D. A. S. Jackson, *British Journal of Industrial Relations*, Vol. VII, March 1969). Thus all wages rise. The spread of wages from high productivity sectors to the rest of the economy that occurs all over the world (H. A. Turner and D. A. S. Jackson, *Economic Journal*, Vol. LXXX, December 1970) may under an incomes policy suggest price control in the high productivity sectors, and this is where attention might have to be mainly directed.

60. Kingsley Laffer, "Whither Arbitration?—Problems of Incomes Policies in Australia and Overseas," *Journal of Industrial Relations*, November 1968, p. 215.

61. *Sydney Morning Herald*, 8th November, 1969.

What Mediation Can and Cannot Do

J. Curtis Counts †

It is appropriate that, on the fiftieth anniversary of the Industrial Research Unit of the Wharton School, such a conference is held to explore the future of collective bargaining in the decade ahead. Looking into the crystal ball is a hazardous occupation at best, especially for the mediator who schools himself to deal with things as they are—the pragmatic approach. But an invitation to explore the future for bargaining and the role the mediator will play is too tempting to avoid. Perhaps, just as the football forecasters are forgiven from one week to the next, we who are called upon today to size up the bargaining future will be forgiven if our forecasts do not quite pan out when the 1970's dwindle into the 1980's.

In forecasting the bargaining future, we can look at some of the present trends for guidance. Place a representative portion of the problems holding the attention of our population alongside the problems which concern labor and management; the resemblance is impressive. Inflation policies, controls, unemployment, foreign trade competition, health care, effective use of manpower resources, drugs, safety, alcoholism, concern for the environment, conglomorates, racial equality, productivity—this is just a partial list.

Most of these subjects, and many more, are already being dealt with in some fashion or phase at bargaining tables across the land. It is most likely that at least part of the answers to these problems will be worked out in the bargaining process. We all recognize that bargaining has shown a high degree of adaptability and that subjects which at one period of time were absolutely taboo, are now matter-of-factly accepted as bargaining table routine. So it is very probably a safe bet that, in our forecast of the bargaining future, we can expect the scope of subject matter will continue to reflect the concern of labor and

---

† J. Curtis Counts is Director of the Federal Mediation and Conciliation Service.

management over current problems. That has been our past experience.

We can easily foresee, also, a continuing expansion of union organization and bargaining in the public sector. The degree of growth in this area is phenomenal. Approximately half the states have passed laws in the past two years dealing with public employees. In the Federal area, approximately 55 percent of all employees belong to labor organizations. In the quasi-federal Postal Service, 85 percent of the workers are union members. In the non-federal public sector, where there are some 8½ million in the work force, already 16 percent have been organized and, at that rate, the day is fast approaching when it will surpass the 21 percent organization in the private sector. So, I think a second safe bet is that bargaining activity in the public sector is with us to stay.

Another area for speculation is bargaining in agriculture. We have all followed the activities of Mr. Cesar Chavez in the West. There is a growing sentiment in Congress for repeal of the exemptions that have removed farm workers from the scope of many basic worker laws such as National Labor Relations Act, Unemployment Compensation and Social Security. I believe we are going to see more "action" in the areas of organization and bargaining in agriculture.

Next, we can study the changing nature of the work force and the projections drawn by the experts. Toward the end of this decade, the work force of the United States will be approaching one hundred million workers. It is already about 80 million. The educational level of the work force is rising and will have gone up significantly from its present high levels by the end of the decade. The trend toward greater numbers of white collar workers and comparatively fewer blue collar workers can be expected to continue.

Mediators by nature have to be optimistic. I believe that, as a group, they tend to feel that the bargaining process is gradually, year by year, growing more mature and effective! I grant you that this trend may, at times, be almost imperceptible and its existence may be thoroughly doubted and denied by a great many people, particularly those members of the public "caught in the middle" by strikes affecting their own jobs or welfare.

But the gradual increase in acceptance of the bargaining process and the role of labor organizations is definitely happening. Unions may not always be admired by management or the public, but they are fairly widely regarded as both useful and necessary. I handle a good deal of correspondence from citizens concerning particular labor disputes. A frequent opening line of these letters is "I'm not opposed to unions, but . . ."

If, by looking back a decade, we can detect a gradual increase in acceptance and more mature exercise of the bargaining process, it is a reasonable conclusion that still more acceptance and maturity is another factor foreseeable for the future. Maybe I should take some odds on this bet because it may not be as sure a thing as some of my earlier observations.

Perhaps a stimulus to greater bargaining maturity may be the new economic facts of life our country now faces. We are not so dominant in world trade and competition as we used to be. We are going to have to pay more attention than we did before to costs, competition, productivity and the national interest. These aspects are going to be felt in more and more bargaining situations as it becomes clearer that labor and management have a stake in maintaining an efficient, imaginative and successful enterprise.

The rise in bargaining table maturity, which I have cited, has been accompanied by a parallel rise in use of mediation. The caseload of the Federal Mediation and Conciliation Service (FMCS) has remained fairly constant over a period of years. One reason for this is that we tailor our workload to what our mediator staff can handle. I know that you are aware that the National Labor Relations Act directs us to avoid entering cases with minimal impact on interstate commerce. But while our caseload is fairly constant, our degree of active participation has increased. By "active" participation we mean cases in which the mediator actually sits in joint bargaining with the parties. Our non-active cases are those which range from simply monitoring a situation in which no "active" mediation is needed to those where constructive work is done to aid settlement by private sidebar talks, but without sitting down with both parties present.

The figures on joint session mediation have increased steadily over the years. In fiscal 1968, we had "active" mediation in 39.9 percent of all of our cases. In 1969, it was 42.3 percent; in 1970, it was 44.3 percent, and in the 1971 fiscal year it had grown to 45 percent.

The only way to interpret these statistics is that our mediators are "actively" mediating more and more cases. They are increasingly being accepted and utilized at the bargaining tables. This, in turn, means to us an indication of greater bargaining maturity and willingness to listen to the advice and recommendation of the trained neutral. If maturity is going to continue to increase, then use of mediation can be expected to increase as well during the decade under analysis.

The FMCS has launched a number of projects to ensure that our Agency will be capable of providing the maximum level of effective service to labor and management in the years just ahead. We are placing new and more practical emphasis on that phase of our mediation work which we call Preventive Activity. This consists of efforts undertaken during the term of labor contracts to improve existing bargaining relationships. The mediator, after spending a period of days or weeks with union and management representatives in a specific situation, is usually able to appraise the basic shortcomings of that relationship and can suggest, with the cooperation of the parties, a course of action seeking to remedy those shortcomings. Much of our Preventive Activity in the past has consisted of training foremen and supervisors in their proper relations to each other and in fair and effective daily administration of their contracts.

We are broadening our Preventive Activity goals to concentrate more specifically on the actual barriers to labor peace in bargaining relationships. We anticipate a clinical examination of deteriorated bargaining situations and a concentrated effort toward their correction. With improved relationships we are hopeful of encouraging more "early bird" negotiations in efforts to reach agreements well ahead of contract deadline crises. Such early negotiations are more likely to be undertaken and to succeed, if the bargainers for both sides have spent some time on improving their problem-solving capacity through the joint committee approach or some similar device.

In addition, the FMCS has just put into effect what we call our ARBIT system. This involves the computerization of our arbitrator referral program. As you know, the Service maintains a roster of qualified arbitrators. They are private citizens whose names are included on panels from which parties to labor and management agreements may choose neutrals to supply binding decisions in disputes.

Requests for such panels have risen tremendously over the years. In the most recent year the increase was over 20 percent. In order to handle this rising caseload, and to make provision for future increases, we have put all our arbitration data into a computer. An immediate benefit is that we will reduce the time it has taken to respond to requests for panels from three weeks to 24 hours. This should help, to some extent, correct the time lag from the inception of a grievance to its final determination which has been a frequent complaint of the users of arbitration.

The computer will be helpful in many other ways. We will be able to more equitably distribute the caseload among arbitrators and thus develop new arbitrator talent. We can spot unnecessary delay in arbitrator awards. We will know the labor-management situations in which an over-abundant grievance load may indicate the need for corrective mediation. We will be able to monitor arbitration trends and suggest possible improvements.

In preparing ourselves for the future, the Service is also doing its best, through workshops, seminars and regional training conferences, to give our mediator staff the opportunity to examine the problems that lie ahead for labor and management in the future years of this decade, and their possible solution. We have adopted re-training for mediators as a continuing, forward-looking policy. Incidentally, we are most fortunate that the most prominent leaders of labor and management generously cooperate in helping us in these training endeavors.

What will be the mediator's role in this decade and, to address myself to my particular topic, what can and cannot the mediator do to facilitate the bargaining process?

I believe the mediator will function in the years ahead much as he has done in the past, but that his contribution to the process will become increasingly more significant and effective. Just as parties will mature, so will mediators. We all learn as we go along.

The mediator will continue to suggest, advise and reason with the parties to help both management and labor reach the most mutually acceptable solution of their problems. The mediator will listen, review and analyze, help the parties communicate with each other, pose alternate approaches to settlement, provide data and information, apply judicious persuasion, suggest procedures and, over-all, seek solutions to both immediate and future problems while, if possible, developing a permanent improvement in the bargaining relationship.

The mediator cannot force parties to accept anything. He cannot compel agreement. He cannot require a change in attitude, although he, of course, will argue for a change or modification of viewpoint. Among other no-no's for the mediator, he cannot be partial to one side against the other, he cannot betray confidences, and he cannot be a policeman to enforce laws or policies.

The mediator is a constructive peacemaker who brings objectivity to disputed issues, and opens new roads to problem solving and decision making. He can spot potential pitfalls, such as lack of proper care and preparation in ratification procedures. On occasion and, if necessary, he can make a formal recommendation on a particular issue or issues that hold up a settlement and which the parties are unable to settle without an outsider's prod.

Since the mediator depends upon persuasion and skill for his effectiveness, it is his job to cultivate these talents. He must keep current with the abundant literature of the business. He must develop his personality and knowledge of the individuals around the bargaining tables. He must have a store of not-too-corny jokes. He must have a sense of humor and be tolerant of the weaknesses and shortcomings of others. He must be a good listener. He must have a highly developed sense of intuition and be willing to do a little gambling on an idea. But the old saying about the non-drinking horse being led to the trough applies pretty well to mediation. The mediator can lead the parties toward solution, but it is their job to embrace it.

Just as collective bargaining is an indispensible ingredient of our society, mediation is a time-tested tool in helping preserve and extend the bargaining system.

PART IV

SELECTED ISSUES IN
COLLECTIVE BARGAINING

A. Transportation

The Railway Labor Act:
A Critical Reappraisal

Herbert R. Northrup †

The Railway Labor Act provides the framework for the most comprehensive control of labor relations and labor disputes on the American scene. The present basic law, the Railway Labor Act of 1926, as amended in 1934 and in several subsequent years, is an outgrowth of legislative experimentation and government intervention which date back to the 1880's. In 1936 the air transport industry was brought under the Act, and in recent years, Congress has no less than four times felt it necessary to prescribe special legislative remedies to avert nationwide strikes.[1] The theses of this article are that the Act, by its very nature, was certain to preclude settlement through collective bargaining; that since the Act purported to assist, not to supplant collective bargaining, it was equally certain to fail; and finally that by writing the status quo into law and administering the law with an obvious bias to the status quo ante, the Act and its administartors have reinforced the forces opposed to change which abound in the industry's collective bargaining system. After a brief review of the Act's provisions, its various facets are discussed, concluding with comments on the Nixon Administration's proposals for change, some industry reactions thereto, and some observations on the impact of recent settlements.

The Law: Background and Summary

Dissatisfied with the governmental intervention system which followed government operation of the railroads during World

† Herbert R. Northrup is Professor of Industry and Director of the Industrial Research Unit, Wharton School of Finance and Commerce, University of Pennsylvania.
Reprinted with permission from *Industrial and Labor Relations Review*, Vol. 25, No. 1, October 1971. Copyright © 1971 by Cornell University. All rights reserved.

War I, railway management and unions agreed on a bill which embodied the collective bargaining system developed prior to the war and saw it adopted as the Railway Labor Act of 1926.[2] This act made it the duty of the parties to exert every reasonable effort to "make and maintain agreements concerning rates of pay [and] working conditions" and to attempt to adjust all differences by peaceful methods. A five-man non-partisan Board of Mediation was created to try mediation if the parties could not agree among themselves. The board was further instructed to urge voluntary arbitration if mediation proved unsuccessful. If arbitration was refused and the dispute was such as "substantially to interrupt interstate commerce," the Board of Mediation was instructed to notify the President, who could create special emergency boards to investigate and publish findings. During the pendency of these various proceedings and until thirty days after the report of the emergency board, neither party was to alter "the conditions out of which the dispute arose" except by mutual agreement. The parties, however, were under no legal obligation to accept the recommendations of the emergency board.

The Act of 1926 also provided that "boards of adjustment shall be created" by the parties for the purpose of handling disputes arising out of the interpretation of agreements. Such boards already established by the operating brotherhoods under the Transportation Act of 1920 continued in operation. In the case of the nonoperating groups, however, negotiations between the carriers and the unions broke down over whether the boards should be regional or local in scope. Some three hundred adjustment boards were established but many not until several years after 1926, and for many classes of employees, no boards were set up. Moreover, the adjustment machinery provided no means to break deadlocks, and since the boards were all bipartisan in character, deadlocks occurred with increasing frequency. By 1934 when the adjustment boards were abolished, some 2,500 disputes remained to be adjudicated.[3]

The Railway Labor Act of 1926 also provided (Section 2, Third):

> Representatives, for the purpose of this Act, shall be designated by the respective parties in such manner as may be provided in their corporate organization or unincorporated association, or by other means of collective action, without interference, influence or coercion exercised by either party over the self-organization, or designation of representatives by the other.

No specific machinery for determination of employee bargaining representatives was contained in this law, nor did it compel carriers to deal solely with the representative of the majority. The Act also contained no specific penalties for carriers which violated prohibitions against interference with the free choice of representatives by employees, as guaranteed by Section 2, Third. The Supreme Court, however, ruled that such interference was subject to the injunctive process.[4]

The 1934 Legislation

Whatever its merits, the 1926 Act was found defective by the railway unions [5] on several counts. They desired national adjustment boards with effective machinery for breaking deadlocks and for enforcing awards; specific penalties, in addition to the injunctive process, to prevent carriers' influence over the choice of employees' representatives; formal machinery by which bargaining agents could be selected; and drastic changes in the personnel of the Board of Mediation, which had fallen from their favor. All these objectives were achieved by the 1934 amendments to the Railway Labor Act, which were backed by the railway unions (assisted materially by the late Joseph B. Eastman, then Federal Co-ordinator of Transportation) and which were bitterly opposed by the carriers.

The amended Railway Labor Act maintains the basic structure of the 1926 legislation insofar as mediation, arbitration, and appointment of emergency boards are concerned. The main difference is that the five-man Board of Mediation was abolished and replaced by a three-man National Mediation Board (NMB).

The 1934 amendments established the National Railroad Adjustment Board (NRAB), which has jurisdiction over grievances and disputes arising out of the interpretation of agreements. The Adjustment Board is a bipartisan agency composed of thirty-four members, half of whom are selected and compensated by the carriers and half by unions "national in scope." (Thus, smaller organizations of workers have no representation on the Adjustment Board.) The Adjustment Board has four divisions, each of which has jurisdiction over certain crafts. If a division deadlocks, referees are appointed by the National Mediation Board or by the division, if it can agree on a selection.

The 1934 amendments also provided elaborate safeguards for the free choice of employee representatives by setting forth a

list of unfair labor practices similar to those contained in the
National Labor Relations (Wagner) Act. Enforcement is different from the Wagner Act in that violations are punishable by
criminal penalties and prosecution is under the jurisdiction of
the Department of Justice. These penalties, of course, supplement the employees' right to use the injunctive process.

Prior to 1951, union security and checkoff provisions were outlawed by the Railway Labor Act, but in that year Congress
amended the law to permit such agreements. Most of the industry then acceded to union demands to grant the union shop
and the checkoff.

In 1936, the air transport industry was brought under all
provisions of the Railway Labor Act except those pertaining to
the National Railroad Adjustment Board. That agency's jurisdiction is confined to the railway industry. Provision is made,
however, for a National Air Transport Board when the National
Mediation Board deems it desirable, but thus far there has been
no demand for the establishment of such an agency.

Analysis of Railway Labor Act

The Railway Labor Act is thus a comprehensive code of labor
legislation which (1) establishes definite provisions for conduct
of negotiations and provides for postponement of strikes or lockouts until a variety of government intervenor techniques have
occurred; (2) provides for compulsory arbitration of grievance
disputes before a national, publicly supported, bipartisan board;
(3) provides for a method of selecting bargaining representatives; (4) proscribes employer unfair labor practices; and (5)
applies the principles and practices of the Act (except for compulsory arbitration of grievances) which were developed in the
railroad industry to a new industry—air transportation. What
have been the results?

Section 2, First, of the Railway Labor Act establishes "the
duty of all carriers, their officers, agents and employees to exert
every reasonable effort to make and maintain agreements concerning rates of pay, rules, and working conditions and to settle
all disputes" peacefully. Ensuing paragraphs of the same section
set forth a procedure for collective bargaining which includes
(1) written request for a conference relating to a dispute served
by one party on the other; (2) written reply by the second party,
setting a time and place mutually agreeable for a conference;

(3) requirement that the conference be held within twenty days after the receipt of the original notice at a location "upon the line of the carrier," except that the time and place may be altered by mutual agreement; and (4) prohibition of unilateral changes in contracts except in the manner prescribed in the Act.

Thus the first basic element in the Railway Labor Act's disputes settlement is the obligation of the parties to make and to maintain collective agreements which, by custom, are written agreements. Corollary to this obligation is a second one: the duty to dispose of disputes quickly and peacefully.

The National Mediation Board, the Railway Labor Act's mediation agency, has placed much stress on the policy pronouncement and the procedure for collective bargaining embodied in the Act. The Board as well as many other authorities has argued that the Act's stated policy and procedure encourage collective bargaining and collective agreements which, it believes, are "primarily" responsible for the alleged (and not proved) "peaceful nature" of collective bargaining in the railroad industry.[6]

Undoubtedly, the Railway Labor Act encouraged the making of collective agreements, particularly in the earlier years of its existence, when collective bargaining was much less universally accepted. Few will deny, however, that the National Labor Relations Act, or indeed any other law which required employers to recognize unions, also resulted in a substantial increase in collective agreements. Is the strike record under the Railway Labor Act superior to that in many other industries because the Railway Labor Act makes it the duty of unions and employees to settle disputes peacefully, whereas the Wagner Act did not deal with labor-management disputes? One may well doubt that policy pronouncements have so compelling an influence.

Mediation

If the parties are unable to settle a dispute by collective bargaining, they may seek mediation by the National Mediation Board, or the NMB "may proffer its services in case any labor emergency is found by it to exist at any time." On the basis of statistics which show that mediation has settled far more cases than have other forms of intervention, the Mediation Board and many observers who have studied the Railway Labor Act have concluded that mediation is the most important and most effective method of intervention under the Act. One can assume that the NMB and its staff have enjoyed the respect and confidence of the parties in the railway industry and, to a lesser degree (as will be discussed), in air transport as well. The availability of a mediation service which enjoys good relations with the parties is surely an aid to peaceful settlement. To that extent the National Mediation Board and its employees have performed a real service in aiding industrial peace.

On the other hand, statistics of cases settled (and arguments based thereon) do not distinguish qualitatively among cases. A dispute involving all the standard unions and railroads and one involving three train dispatchers on a single road receive the same weight. Actually, very few nationwide railroad wage cases have been settled by mediation since 1936. In an industry like the railroads where national collective bargaining determines basic wage and rule issues, but much else is left to local determination, it would be surprising indeed if most cases requiring government intervention were not settled by mediation. Hence, the fact that mediation is used more than any other form of government intervention does not mean that it is either the most satisfactory or the most successful, but rather that it is the method most useful for minor controversies when the major issues have been disposed of.

One should not infer from this discussion that mediation is unimportant in railway labor disputes. Quite the contrary is true. Some cases conceivably might have erupted into stoppages if mediation had not been available. More important, the Mediation Board is able to "sit on" cases which could erupt into strikes but which are either cooled off by NMB inaction or held by the Board by tacit consent of carrier and union leadership so that they cannot be pushed to conclusion. This not only prevents quickie strikes but also buries frivolous but nonetheless potentially troublesome issues. On the other hand, mediation rarely is the final step in major national disputes.

One other aspect of the availability of a special mediation agency deserves mention. On several occasions in its annual reports the National Mediation Board has noted that it is too frequently requested to mediate without any genuine attempt at settlement having been made by the parties themselves.[7] This, as will be noted below, is partially, if not largely, the result of the parties getting ready for an emergency board instead of bargaining. It is also the result of the very availability of a special agency, the National Mediation Board, which the parties feel is there to serve them, assist them, or otherwise suit their purposes of strategy, rather than just to mediate.

Voluntary Arbitration

If the National Mediation Board is unable to settle a dispute by mediation, it must request the parties to arbitrate. Either or both may refuse to do so without penalty. However, if both agree, Sections 7, 8, and 9 provide a detailed procedure for establishment of an arbitration board and for conduct and enforcement of the arbitration. An award issued under this procedure is final and binding on the parties, as it is filed in the nearest federal district court and becomes a court order. It is enforceable as such unless overturned on one or more of the following three grounds: either the award or the proceedings were not in conformity with the requirements of the Act, the award did not conform nor confine itself to the stipulations of the agreement to arbitrate, or fraud or corruption affected the results of the arbitration.

Under the Railway Labor Act, voluntary arbitration boards may be composed of either three or six members, who are evenly divided among those chosen by unions, those chosen by carriers, and those representing the public. Public members are selected by the partisan members or by the National Mediation Board if the partisan members are unable to agree. Arbitration boards may be reconvened to interpret any section of an award on which the parties disagree.

Arbitration under the Railway Labor Act is not utilized with great frequency. During the period 1926-1934, a total of 538 disputes were settled by arbitration, but most were over contract interpretation or involved unsettled grievances. Since 1934, such disputes have been handled by the National Railroad Adjustment Board, as will be discussed later in this article.

In the period from 1934 to June 30, 1970, during which arbitration of disputes involving contract interpretation and arbitration of disputes arising from proposed contract changes were processed separately, only 305 cases of the latter type were submitted to arbitration boards, an average of less than nine per year for the railroad and air transport industries combined, with their multitude of carriers and unions.[8]

The reason for this lack of interest in voluntary arbitration appears to be the existence of other means of settlement. Minor disputes have been settled mainly either by the parties or by mediation. This is, of course, all to the good, since the responsibility for settlement is directly on the parties. On the other hand, major disputes (as well as many minor ones) have tended to go to emergency boards rather than to arbitration boards. The reason for this is rather obvious. As the late Sumner H. Slichter pointed out, "it is easier for the representatives on one side or the other to . . . refuse to arbitrate if an immediate result is not a strike or a lockout, but the appointment of an emergency board which has no authority to make a binding award." [9]

Emergency Boards: The Record to 1941

Between 1926 and 1934, when the Act was amended, only two minor strikes occurred, and only ten emergency boards were appointed. In at least one case a board's recommendation was disregarded by a carrier, but no strike occurred although the resulting grievances did cause a stoppage in 1936.

Five of the ten boards appointed during this period were created in the fiscal year 1933-1934. The fact that as many boards were appointed during the last year of the unamended Act as in the previous seven years is attributable to the social unrest of the period, the increased organizing activity begun then and the disputes resulting therefrom, and the greater willingness on the part of President Franklin D. Roosevelt, as compared to his predecessors, to appoint emergency boards.

Of the ten emergency boards appointed prior to July 1934, nine involved relatively minor cases concerning small segments of the railroad system, and only one involved a regional case of major importance. In both 1933 and 1934 the Federal Coordinator of Transportation, an office established in the early 1930's to reexamine all federal transportation policies, took over the handling of most important railway labor disputes. Nationwide negotiations between carriers and unions were mediated by the Federal Coordinator and frequently by the President himself. In a period of turmoil in industrial relations the major disputes were thus handled outside the framework of the Railway Labor Act.

In 1937 the railway unions negotiated a general wage increase with the carriers with the help of mediation by the National Mediation Board. The following year, as a result of the recession, the carriers made a demand for a 15 percent nationwide wage reduction. The case went to an emergency board, which recommended the demand be denied. The carriers acquiesced in the settlement. This was the last major dispute prior to 1941.

It was in the period 1933-1941 that the Railway Labor Act achieved its now thoroughly tarnished reputation as a "model law." This reputation was based on an alleged relationship between railway labor peace and the procedures of the Railway Labor Act, compared with strife in industry generally where this Act did not apply. A more sophisticated analysis would point to the absence of great organizing drives and new unionism on the railroads at a time when other industries were involved in the difficult task of adjusting to unionism for the first time. Moreover, as already noted, in the years 1933-1935, key railway disputes were handled by extralegal procedures. Finally, if the emergency board in the 1938 wage reduction case had recommended a reduction in wages, one may well speculate that union acquiescence would have been difficult to obtain. In short, prior to 1941 the Act was not tested by any decision or recommendation which the unions considered adverse.

Three other aspects of railroad labor relations are worth noting here. First, as a direct result of the 1934 amendments pertaining to representation, which will be discussed below, the standard nonoperating unions eliminated most of their mainly local independent rivals. Because the operating brotherhoods had been recognized on most railroads since the turn of the century, the amended Act had achieved by 1941 a key purpose of its sponsors—hegemony of the standard unions. Second, during the 1930's, at the insistence of the carriers, who felt they were being whipsawed, wage negotiations were made national in scope instead of regional, as had been the case for many years. Finally, the invidious racial discrimination which always had been an integral part of the railroad collective bargaining system not only continued unabated under the New Deal but also was actually aided by the agencies established under the 1934 amendments. Thus, two members of the National Mediation Board mediated and signed as witnesses the infamous Southeastern Carriers' Conference Agreement of 1941, which sought to eliminate Negroes from long-held firemen's jobs.[10] The discussion of representation matters and of the function of the National Railroad Adjustment Board will note further how railway labor agencies have acted to curtail rights of black workers.[11] The discriminatory policies of the unions during this period were sharpened by the great fall of employment, which curtailed jobs by 50 percent from the peak World War I figure of two million.

World War II to 1960

The tone of wartime labor relations on the railroads was set by the 1941 dispute, in which all the standard railway unions demanded substantial increases and an emergency board was appointed to hear the case on a national basis. The recommendations of the board did not meet the unions' desires. They appealed to President Roosevelt; he reassembled the board and, in effect, put pressure on the carriers and the board to grant further increases. They complied.

During the war and immediate postwar periods, similar developments were common. The 1943 diesel case, the nonoperating employee disputes of the same year, the 1943-1944 case involving operating employees, the *Illinois Central* case of 1945, and the 1946 and the 1947 wage cases were the most important of those which featured union repudiation of emergency board decisions, threatened or actual strikes, and usually government seizure, culminating on several occasions with more favorable terms to the unions than were recommended by the Boards. Further union repudiations of emergency board recommendations were involved in the *Pacific Electric*, and the *Chicago-Milwaukee* interurban cases. Some emergency boards were appointed from the National Railway Labor Panel, which was established during World War II so that emergency boards could be created without a union strike vote, but otherwise the procedure was consistent with the provisions of the Railway Labor Act.[12]

The climax came in 1946, when the Engineers and Trainmen struck all the nation's railroads after rejecting both an emergency board recommendation and a proposal of President Truman which, as had become the custom, modified upward the recommendations of the fact finders. The strike lasted for two days and ended on the President's terms as he was asking Congress for a drastic strike law to deal with the emergency.

In 1947, three unions—the firemen, conductors, and switchmen —precipitated a crisis by refusing an emergency board award. The engineers and conductors had already agreed to terms. Using his unexpired war powers, President Truman seized the railroads to prevent a strike but this time declined to add to the emergency board recommendations. After a time the unions capitulated and settled. Labor relations on the railroads continued in somewhat of an upheaval for the next several years, with strikes by the locomotive firemen over the extent and number of firemen (actually helpers) to be carried by diesel engines, and by the switchmen, trainmen, and others over the forty-hour week. In addition, numerous difficulties arose because of unsettled grievances pending before the National Railroad Adjustment Board.

During the latter part of the 1950's, the bigger cases were settled without great difficulty, although strikes resulting after recommendations of emergency boards had been rejected by unions continued to occur on some railroads. In this period unions could not count on favorable intervention from the White House. Moreover, union power was weakened by the steady erosion of the railroads' competitive position through loss of traffic. After rising to 1.6 million during World War II, employment on the railroads fell rapidly, reaching 885,300 in 1960, and dropping another 250,000 during the next decade. Jobs were eliminated not only by declining business but also by expanded mechanization, which affected every sector of the industry's employment. Under tremendous competitive and cost pressure, the carriers became more insistent on the elimination of obsolete work rules and featherbedding practices, and the weaknesses of the unions' case on these issues discouraged them from invoking the emergency board procedure.[13]

In a report involving a dispute between the larger railroads and the conductors' and trainmen's unions in 1955, an emergency board recommended a detailed study and review of the railroad industry's wage structure and working rules for the operating classifications, noting that none had been made since World War I. James P. Mitchell, Secretary of Labor in the Eisenhower Administration, succeeded in obtaining agreement between the railroads and the five operating unions to the setting up of a tripartite commission, which was done by an executive order of President Eisenhower just prior to the close of his administration. As with an emergency board, recommendations of the commission were not to be binding on the parties.

The Record of the 1960's

The Presidential Railroad Commission made an exhaustive study and issued its report after a year spent in hearing evidence, having special studies made, and observing the matters at issue. It recommended changes in existing practices, many favorable to employees, and the elimination of wasteful practices and unproductive jobs, including the use of "firemen" on yard and freight diesels.[14] The carriers accepted the recommendations, but the unions did not. President Kennedy withheld his support from the Railroad Commission's recommendations. Instead, he told the parties that the Commission report was a basis for further negotiations, and referred it back to them for collective bargaining. The unions interpreted this as a message to hold out for further concessions, such as they were used to obtaining in the Roosevelt-Truman eras after rejecting an emergency board report.

Kennedy's action was consistent with his handling of other disputes. For example, when the Order of Railroad Telegraphers struck the Chicago and North Western Railway, the issue was the union's demand for a veto over job abolishments. An emergency board had instead recommended liberalized unemployment, retraining, and severance payments which the carrier was willing to accept. The President demanded "sufficient concessions" from both sides to get an agreement. A few days later the parties agreed to arbitrate, giving the union "another bite at the apple," although the arbitrator, in effect, sustained the carrier's position. At the same press conference at which Kennedy declined to support the recommendations of a statutory board established pursuant to the Railway Labor Act, he threw the full weight of his office behind the recommendation of a panel which he had created (without legislative sanction) to handle a dispute in the aerospace industry and which had recommended a voting procedure in regard to the union shop—to the dismay of the companies and to the joy of the unions.[15]

The Kennedy policy of intervention in railway labor disputes in behalf of unions is further illustrated by the *Florida East Coast Railway* case. Here an emergency board requested by management was refused because the issue was whether the railroad should put into effect rates of pay agreed to by other railroads. After a strike was called, the Secretary of Labor set up a special extralegal inquiry board, which recommended reinstatement of the strikers and institution of national rates. When the company declined, an emergency board was appointed, which also failed to settle the strike. The issues since then have been in court litigation with operations (except passenger service) continuing with nonunion crews.

When the railway unions and the carriers did not solve the rules disputes analyzed by the Presidential Commission, Kennedy appointed a regular emergency board to rehear the issue. This board made recommendations embodying several concessions to the unions. Again the carriers accepted and the union rejected the recommendations.

There then followed a series of interventions by the Secretary of Labor, the President, the President's Labor-Management Advisory Committee, and several members of Congress, with a Supreme Court Justice in the wings. The unions continued to make and then postpone strike threats, while refusing any settlement. The carriers threatened, as a counter tactic, to put revised work rules into effect while advocating compulsory arbitration as the only solution. Finally, Congress enacted a law on August 23, 1963, providing for compulsory arbitration of the diesel firemen and crew-consist issues. No strike on this issue was permitted for two years after an award was issued. The remainder of the issues were required by the law to be held in status quo, pending negotiations by the parties, with the right to strike suspended on such issues till early 1964.

Board's Provision

The arbitration board provided for eventual elimination of the firemen—by a process of attrition—a more liberal procedure than had been proposed either by the Presidential Commission or by the emergency board. For the crew-consist issue, the award provided for a settlement for road service, but referred yard issues to local negotiation and eventual arbitration. Almost two years later, the arbitration board was still busy interpreting its award. The railroads did, however, make substantial reductions in the number of firemen.

The aspects of the dispute not settled by the Compulsory Arbitration Act of 1963 still were not settled by early 1964. To avert a strike, President Johnson called the parties to Washington and, with the aid of two special mediators, George W. Taylor and Theodore Kheel, obtained a settlement under which "the railroads failed to achieve any significant revision" of the other work rules they were attempting to change.[16] Since then the firemen have raised the issue again without success, but the trainmen by a series of threatened and actual single-carrier strikes, have won back some of the nonessential jobs lost in the 1963 arbitration.

Neither the trainmen's nor firemen's issues were settled until August 1971. Meanwhile the carriers strove to free themselves of expensive featherbedding and restrictive practices, and the unions fought to hold what they had in the face of continuing and pervasive losses in employment and membership.

The 1963 arbitration did achieve one notable result. Decimated by the decision, the Brotherhood of Locomotive Firemen and Enginemen gave up the ghost of separatism and joined the fast declining Order of Railway Conductors and the tiny Switchmen's Union of North America to merge into the Brotherhood of Railroad Trainmen, under the new name of the United Transportation Union. The Brotherhood of Locomotive Engineers remained independent.

Congressional intervention in the firemen's dispute set the standard for major disputes to mid-1971. The typical *de facto* procedure has been mechanical adherence to the Act's procedures until the emergency board recommendation is issued, followed automatically by the carrier's reluctant (or even dismayed) acceptance and union's rejection thereof. At this point, mediation outside the framework of the Act is commenced by the Secretary of Labor or his deputy, attempting to evolve a peace formula based on an additive to the emergency board report. If this fails, the administration goes to Congress for a special law. This has occurred four times since 1963, although in one case, the parties settled prior to the law's enactment.

The climax of this questionable procedure came in December 1970. Perhaps imbued with the Christmas spirit, or perhaps outraged because a Republican Administration had adopted the Kennedy-Johnson technique of a special-law-to-get-us-out-of-this-mess, the Democrat Congress enacted a stopgap law guaranteeing labor peace only for forty-five days but giving the offending unions a 13.5 percent wage increase, retroactive for 1970, without the *quid pro quo* of restrictive rule changes recommended by the emergency board. One did not need prophetic insights to forecast that this act of "sheer stupidity compounded with cowardice . . . short-sightedness and irresponsibility" [17] would be interpreted by the unions as an invitation to create further emergencies so that Congress could indulge them.

Indeed it was. The unions which struck in December did settle with the carriers without further disruptions, except for the United Transportation Union, whose dispute remained in litigation over the issue of selective strikes. But in May 1971, the

10,000 member Brotherhood of Railroad Signalmen shut down the nation's railroads for two days in a particularly uncalled-for-action. This union was offered the pattern won by other unions: 42 percent over forty-two months effective January 1, 1970. The large increase offered was a result not only of the inflationary times but also included the "buy out" of work rules. For the Signalmen, this was a bonus—they gave up nothing, but they struck anyway knowing that Congress was in a generous mood.

Congress did not disappoint the strikers. Rejecting the Nixon Administration's proposal to legislate an end to the strike and to get on with consideration of permanent changes in the Railway Labor Act, Congress voted the Signalmen a 13.5 percent increase retroactive to January 1, 1970, put a moratorium on the strike until October 1, 1971, and indicated no action on overall legislation, despite the warning of the Secretary of Labor, James D. Hodgson, that such rewards for irresponsibility insured further disruptive escapades.

After the Signalmen had been thus rewarded by Congress, the dispute involving the United Transportation Union came to the fore. On June 7, 1971, the U.S. Supreme Court declined to review a decision by the Court of Appeals, District of Columbia, which held that a union could engage in selective strikes after a national bargaining impasse was reached and that carriers also could initiate unilateral action (*Delaware & Hudson Railway Co.* v. *United Transportation Union*, U.S. C.A., D.C., March 31, 1971; cert. den., June 7, 1971.) The UTU had adamantly refused to accept the recommendations of Emergency Board No. 178 which, as sweetened by later negotiations, gave railroad workers a 42 percent wage increase over forty-two months in return for union agreement to give up a number of featherbed restrictions, including allowing use of radio communications without having to pay additional premiums to UTU employees; eliminating the requirement for changing crews each time a train enters another "seniority district," based on a day's pay for a run of only 100 miles; permitting freight train crews to deliver their train to another railroad (on arrival at a terminal) instead of requiring a separate yard crew to make this move; and allowing yard crews to serve *all* shippers within four miles of switching limits. Crews were bypassing pre-1951 industrial plants within the four-mile area, requiring two crews to do the work of one.

These recommendations and the Board's proposal that the parties establish a standing tripartite arbitration board to resolve grievances arising out of rule changes were accepted on May 13, 1971 by the Brotherhood of Locomotive Engineers, the only other surviving operating union. They also were part of an agreement entered into on July 15, 1971 by all railroad unions and the New Jersey Central as a last-ditch means of attempting to save this bankrupt line. Nevertheless, on July 16, 1971 the UTU struck the Southern and Union Pacific and then over a period of two weeks added eight more lines to the struck list.

The carriers responded with a new and effective tactic. Except for the Chicago and North Western (which was in a cash emergency as a result of dissipating its resources in a vain attempt to become a successful conglomerate) which made a separate agreement with the UTU, and except for a few small carriers not involved, the carriers unilaterally effectuated the work-rule changes and also eliminated several others. Under orders from the UTU, nonstriking employees did not protest. In addition, the carriers invoked their mutual aid program which paid substantial amounts to struck carriers. For example, the Southern was entitled to payments of $635,000 per day, which reduced its daily losses to $150,000.

On August 2, after ten carriers were struck, the UTU reached agreement with a committee of carrier presidents. It agreed to the rule changes and to the special arbitration board. Instead of making immediate rule changes, the carriers agreed to work these out with the UTU on each road within ninety days and to submit any unresolved issues to the new board. Of major interest is the reference of the rule resolution to the local level and the bypassing of the National Railroad Adjustment Board in favor of a special tribunal. The agreement did provide that any UTU member who lost pay because of the carriers' unilateral imposition of work-rule changes during the strike could seek reimbursement by filing a formal complaint under existing contract procedures, but the nearly 25,000 members laid off as a result of the rule changes instituted unilaterally by the carriers were not automatically entitled to reimbursement. The carriers also somewhat sweetened the dismissal pay recommendation of Emergency Board No. 178. By letting a dispute run its course, government may have helped to produce a lasting, needed settlement, and one which could dampen the enthusiasm for both intervention and strikes. Moreover, for future reference, the carriers now have irrefutable data on the savings potential available through the elimination of restrictive rules.

Emergency Boards: Analysis of Results

From the time the Railway Labor Act was amended in 1934 to June 30, 1970, emergency boards were appointed to hear 176 cases (of which about 35 were airline cases), and 58 additional boards were selected from the National Railway Labor Panel. These boards considered cases involving nearly all the nation's railroads, as well as cases involving one issue on a small, localized carrier. The record indicates three conclusions: the appointment of emergency boards has become commonplace; recommendations of emergency boards at critical times have been handled with political expediency; and the procedure has severely inhibited collective bargaining.

1. The thinking which went into the creation of the Railway Labor Act assumed that emergency boards would be appointed only in rare instances of genuine emergency. In other cases where disputes were not settled by collective bargaining or mediation, it was felt that arbitration would be utilized.[18] William M. Leiserson, for many years chairman of the National Mediation Board, emphasized this thinking when he declared that emergency boards were merely an extension of arbitration, with public opinion the force to secure compliance.[19] The union view is that such boards provide "a basis for negotiation." [20]

Actually, to term emergency boards "arbitration" boards is as much a misnomer as to term them "fact-finding" boards, because public opinion usually is not as effective as proponents of this view believe. It is correct that one reason why public opinion has not turned the emergency board procedure into an effective, binding-award-making mechanism is that far too many boards have been appointed, but it is not practical to assume that any strict limit can be kept on the number of emergency boards which are to be appointed. As long as the emergency board procedure is available, one side or the other will create the "emergencies" if the possibility of gaining a better settlement exists. When that occurs, the pressure on the President or whoever must appoint such boards (from well-meaning citizens and newspaper headlines to prevent the "emergency" plus added pressure from labor or industry to aid the emergency creator) usually results in the appointment of a board, the establishment of a precedent, and an ever-increasing number of "emergencies" and boards.

2. Great opportunities to make the Railway Labor Act's emergency procedure work have been lightly jettisoned. When President Roosevelt, first in 1941 and then repeatedly throughout the war years, assisted the railroad unions to gain additional benefits over and above emergency board recommendations, he set the tone for over a decade of railway labor relations. President Kennedy's failure to support the impressive findings of the Presidential Railroad Commission and his lack of endorsement of the recommendations of other emergency boards reactivated and accelerated the "platform" approach to emergency board procedure, that is, use of the board recommendations as a starting point for future benefits.

This, of course, is not surprising if viewed in the context of political power, instead of industrial relations. The Railway Labor Act, and especially the 1934 and 1951 amendments, stand as testimony to the ability of the railway unions to achieve goals via the political route when the procedures of the Act fail to accommplish desired ends. The Santa Claus-like performance of Congress more recently shows that despite great losses of membership, railway union political power remains potent. It remains to be seen whether the lesson that intervention creates more strife, particularly if it benefits the party creating the emergency, has been learned as a result of the recent rash of strikes and settlements.

3. Preparing for an emergency board proceeding and bargaining collectively are quite different approaches to the tasks of either winning gains or achieving agreement. If one is doing the former, it is often wiser to ask for more than expected, in both number and size of demands, in the hope that the emergency board will recommend the maximum possible. Why bargain away anything when it might be granted? This is what has happened in the railway industry. The parties usually go through the procedure of the Act with little or no intention of yielding on anything until the emergency board stage is reached and then too often not until after the emergency board recommendations are issued. Repeatedly, neutrals appointed to emergency boards have been flabbergasted by this procedure. In 1948 a board noted that it

was asked to find the answers to all these quibbles in a mass of evidence which covered 230 pages of exhibits and 150 pages in the record . . . within a two week period as 1 little piece of a job which included the disposition of 36 other issues on the basis of well over 12,000 pages of testimony and exhibits.[21]

Fourteen years later, a board, after reporting that the carriers and unions in a major case "conferred with each other but four times in as many months" and then subjected the Board to 2,649 pages of transcript and fifty exhibits, commented, "It bespeaks a traditional failure to meet problems and an unwillingness to grapple with them without invoking the aid of outsiders. . . ." [22]

More recently a board noting again the great accumulation of record, exhibits, and reiteration of testimony by witnesses who always seem to testify, commented

This Board had the distinct impression that this was, to a great extent a repeat performance of an even longer run than "My Fair Lady," with each side knowing exactly what the other side would present and to what each witness would testify.

The parties appear to regard the Board as an audience to an elaborate ritual—something like the Japanese Kabuchi Theater.

Attempts by previous Boards and by our own Board to break through this ritual were quite unsuccessful.[23]

The absence of bargaining before an emergency board is appointed not only insures the creation of a large number of such boards and therefore aids in making public opinion an ineffectual enforcement measure but also produces a real emergency (if such can occur) *after* the emergency board has reported and one of the parties has declined to accept the recommendations. This usually brings the Mediation Board back into the situation; or the Secretary of Labor or Congress or the President or all three enter the picture, putting pressure on the carrier either to accept the emergency board recommendations or grant more in order to induce the union to accept peaceful settlement. In such cases the emergency procedure may even create the emergency: if the procedure were not in existence, the parties would have to settle the dispute themselves, as they do in most other industries.

In this respect, emergency board procedure is less in the public interest than is compulsory arbitration. Both inhibit collective bargaining, but compulsory arbitration at least affords a substitute method of settlement, whereas the railroad emergency board procedure (or other so-called "fact-finding" arrangements) does not but merely invites further intervention to settle the problem. Before a final assessment of the Railway Labor Act procedure is made, however, other aspects of the law must be analyzed.

National Railroad Adjustment Board

The great majority of collective bargaining contracts—probably more than 95 percent—provide that disputes arising over contract interpretation are to be determined by arbitration. Contracts also usually provide for a means of appointing arbitrators if the parties cannot agree on a selection. Only in the railway industry has Congress provided for compulsory arbitration of such disputes and established an agency, the National Railroad Adjustment Board, "the only administrative tribunal, federal or state, which has ever been set up in this country for the purpose of rendering judicially enforceable decisions in controversies arising out of the interpretation of contracts." [24] The NRAB was created by the 1934 amendments to the Railway Labor Act. It marked the return to the settlement of grievances on a national basis, which had prevailed during World War I and which the railroads had refused to continue in the interim period. The NRAB consists of thirty-four members, one half chosen by the carriers and one half by unions "national in scope" and free from carrier domination. It has four divisions and is actually four separate boards rather than a single agency.

Although in some cases other unions have more members or more contracts, only the standard unions (mostly AFL-CIO affiliated, plus a few older independents) have been designated "national in scope" or otherwise permitted to participate in the selection of employee representatives. This has proved a decided advantage to these unions in competitive organizing situations.[25]

When a division of the NRAB cannot agree on a case, a referee is appointed either by the division or, if it cannot agree, by the National Mediation Board.[26] If they so desire, carriers and unions can set up system regional boards, or special boards to hear their cases, instead of referring them to the NRAB. This has been done in a number of instances, sometimes because of the long wait for a decision from the NRAB, on other occasions because of the desire of a nonstandard union to select its own employee representatives. An amendment to the Act in

1966 authorized the establishment of special boards of adjustment at the request of either party in an attempt to reduce the
huge backlog of cases, especially in the First Division.[27] Unfortunately, any progress made was more than offset by a flood of
cases sent to the supplemental boards and by a procedural dispute between the United Transportation Union and the Brotherhood of Locomotive Engineers over representation on the First
Division, which prevented any awards from being issued between January 1969 and April 1970. Congress stepped into the
dispute by reducing membership on the First Division from ten
to eight and dividing the four labor representatives equally between the disputing unions.[28]

Procedure of the NRAB

Cases may be submitted to the NRAB by one or both parties
to a dispute, but the bulk are submitted by the standard unions.[29]
Neither notice nor a right of hearing is given to any individual
or organization which might be affected other than the carrier
or union involved, although awards of the NRAB have been enjoined or otherwise collaterally attacked on many occasions because of this lack of elementary due process.[30] The fact that the
divisions operate in secrecy without stenographic records, re-
porters, or other outsiders present, accentuates the problem of
due process. Historically, the awards have been brief and unin-
structive; more recently, perhaps as a result of much criticism,
they have tended to be more informative. Nevertheless, it is
very difficult to understand their meaning and precedent impact
in many cases. Yet the divisions rely heavily on precedent, frequently with little or no regard to local or system variations.

Although reluctant to accept cases not submitted by standard
unions, the divisions have not hesitated, when it served the interests of these unions, to receive cases where their jurisdiction
has been questionable[31] or counterproductive socially. Included
in the last category are a number of cases where jobs held by
Negroes (who were denied membership in a railroad union)
have been declared to be the "property" of the union's white
membership without notice to or right to be heard being afforded to the affected black workers, or indeed without logic or
decency in the decision.[32]

Originally, judicial review of NRAB decisions was permitted
only when the refusal of the losing party to put the award into

effect stimulated the winning party to institute enforcement proceedings by suit in federal court. For years the operating unions frustrated this process by an agreement among themselves not to take such cases to court but to threaten a strike. In addition, strike threats aimed at bypassing the NRAB altogether became increasingly common. The net effect was to invoke the Railway Labor Act's disputes procedure and, often, emergency board proceedings. In some years, such cases were the leading cause of emergency boards being created, thus nullifying the distinction between "major" and "minor" disputes.[33]

Court proceedings and the 1966 amendments have now checked extralegal enforcement. If a case is before the NRAB, the courts will enjoin a strike and require the unions to rely solely on NRAB procedures.[34] If the NRAB has issued a decision, the courts will enjoin a strike aimed at enforcing an award, making judicial review a real instead of an empty route.[35] In addition, the 1966 amendments made all awards of the NRAB "final and binding" and "conclusive on the parties." Court review is now open to both parties but is limited in scope.[36]

A judicial and procedural problem arising out of the willingness of the courts to limit direct union action in minor disputes (that is those subject to the NRAB) is the requirement that the courts determine whether a dispute is minor—and hence enjoinable—in litigation. Risher has found considerable differences among judges and courts in this classification problem and much maneuvering on the part of labor and management to turn the case to the type which the party favors.[37] Needless to say, this concentration on legalistic forms and pretensions does little to solve problems, improve relationships, or increase the potential for peaceful settlement.

Case Load and Issues

The case load of the NRAB remains awesome. Some seventy thousand cases have been docketed since 1934. Originally, the First Division accounted for 80 percent of the docketed cases, but now the Third Division carries the biggest load. This change did not occur because grievance filing among operating employees has been reduced; rather it is the result of a plethora of special and supplementary boards which have received an increasing share of the First Division's "business." In fact, the number of cases involving operating employees has risen. The additional boards seemingly have generated additional cases.[38]

The number of cases involved and the length of time required to decide them, particularly for operating employees, is totally unprecedented and unique in American industrial relations practice. There are several reasons for this.

In the early days when precedents were established, unions clearly won the advantage, both in terms of numbers of claims sustained [39] and the nature of the decisions, which Slichter termed "among the strangest in the annals of industrial relations." [40] The unions were able to install the principle that each and every bit of work is "owned" by a craft or class of employees and that any deviation therefrom is at the carriers' risk. No matter how long a carrier had engaged in a practice of doing something differently, that carrier was liable—sometimes as far back as the 1920's—for deviating from a practice deemed correct by a referee and five union representatives who made up a majority of the First Division. Thus, through the Adjustment Board the unions nationally were able to apply restrictive rules which obtained on one railroad, despite the wide variety of different conditions and history of bargaining which prevailed on many railroads.

The carriers, however, refused to concede precedent, while the unions attempted to expand precedent as widely as possible. Moreover, to the outsider, the new referee, or even the parties, the awards seem written with such "telegraphic brevity" [41] that what was and was not meant by an award is often difficult to determine, let alone apply as precedent.

In recent years the carriers have succeeded in reversing the First Division box score and now win most cases, partly because they already have lost on the basic issues, and the interpretations sought by the unions are simply beyond credibility; and partly because the carriers are now better and more thoroughly represented. This has not, however, reduced the grievance flow or backlog. It appears that union representatives still process cases they are certain to lose but find it easier to "send to Chicago" than to settle and thereby possibly alienate some constituents.

The changing box score of the First Division and the court rulings which estopped extralegal enforcement of awards have lessened the railway brotherhoods' opposition to regional and system boards of adjustment to relieve the First Division's case load and paved the way for the 1966 amendments. Unfortunately, as noted, the many supplemental boards which have been appointed have not lessened the problem. The backlog is still so great that about seven years would be needed to clear it up *without* docketing any new cases.

What is needed, of course, is not more boards but rather a desire to work out problems, not pass them on to others for decision. No industry faces more severe problems than those with which railway employers and unions must grapple. The carriers require relief from the oppressive work rules, which often have been expanded and reinforced by NRAB awards, if they are to achieve solvency and meet the competition of rival carriers. The unions, with a membership decimated by unemployment and dominated by old men desirous of working out their lives as nearly as possible in the manner to which they have grown accustomed, stand firm against change and hope for more favorable governmental intervention to maintain the status quo. Both are so inured to governmental solutions that the need to step up to their problems is rarely given serious mutual consideration. The failure to settle grievances where most of them should be settled (at the local level) is just one aspect of a total situation.

Public versus Private Financing of Arbitration

In the final analysis, the single most significant factor which (when all else fails) forces unions and companies to settle their disputes over contract interpretation is absent from the railroads. Only in this industry does the taxpayer support grievance settlement. "An arbitration rate of one per year for every 220 employees would bankrupt most local unions and would be a serious financial burden to most international unions and employers at the usual cost of private arbitration." [42] NRAB procedures cost local unions nothing and cost national unions and carriers only the salaries of their representatives on the divisions. All other costs are met by the taxpayers, who year after year pay out in excess of $800,000 to maintain the NRAB and its referees. This amounts to nearly $500 for each award issued by a division. Taxpayers are charged additional amounts to maintain the system (regional and supplementary boards) which (like Xerox machines) seem to create their own demand. The marginal cost to the unions of submitting cases to the NRAB is zero.

As the Presidential Railroad Commission stated, "There is no reason for the public to continue to support from public funds" [43] grievance settlement in this industry any more than in any other. The "unique" National Railroad Adjustment Board requires many reforms, but none would be as important as withdrawing taxpayer support and compelling the parties to finance their own industrial relations system, as do labor and management in every other industry in the United States.

Representation Disputes

Section 2, Ninth, of the amended Railway Labor Act requires the National Mediation Board to investigate representation disputes and to determine, by secret ballot or other means, which organization or individual, if any, represents a "craft" or "class." By requiring that the bargaining unit be a craft or class, Congress limited the discretion of the Mediation Board to define the bargaining unit (and the freedom of employees to organize on other bases). Outside of specifying that the principle of majority rule should hold, Congress left the procedure and methods for determining bargaining agents, as well as the definition of "craft" or "class," to the Mediation Board.

As of June 30, 1970, the Mediation Board had decided 4,145 representation disputes. Recently, about 60 of these have occurred per year, with a substantial number involving the airline industry. The NMB has been very careful to define craft or class to match the jurisdictional claims of the standard unions. In addition, the Board has insisted that no craft or class smaller than an entire carrier can be recognized. The net effect has been to assist the standard unions to eliminate and/or to resist raiding attempts from nonstandard organizations.[44] This policy has been defended by the Board on the ground that it encourages stability and therefore labor peace. The policy is understandable in view of the Board's prime concern, as a mediation agency, with the maintenance of peaceful collective bargaining. This favoritism of one group of unions over another is, as previously noted, a feature of the Railway Labor Act and much of its administration. It is, nonetheless, questionable public policy to anoint a group against competition, for it ill serves employees who deserve full freedom of association. The basic mistake was to give a mediation agency the judicial function of bargaining unit determination, for the two are fundamentally administratively incompatible.

An even more basic question is why Congress should have institutionalized what is certainly now a very unsatisfactory status quo ante by confining the unit to a craft or class. The declining employment in the industry and the changing character of jobs have left neither crafts or unions in the same status as in 1934. Confinement of the bargaining unit to a craft or class, plus adherence to union jurisdictional claims as a basis of determining crafts or class, tends to retard solutions to problems which must be solved.

Some Questions of Procedure

The Mediation Board at first acted very informally and actually published no rules of procedure until forced to do so by the Administrative Procedures Act of 1946. In this early period the Board tended to certify unions on the basis of card authorizations obtained by the unions themselves. Its members and staff were, on occasion, not too careful in observing reasonable rules of conduct in other respects or in protecting the rights of nonunion employees, nonstandard unions, and especially Negro railroad employees. The bargaining unit determinations of the NMB in numerous cases consigned Negro employees to units so defined that unions which overtly discriminated were certain to triumph.[45]

There remain other significant differences between National Labor Relations Board and National Mediation Board representation procedures which illustrate shortcomings in the policies of the latter body. Unlike the NLRB, the Mediation Board does not put "no union" on the ballot, so that employees who want to register this preference can do so only by not voting. The NMB will not certify a union if 51 percent of those eligible do not vote. The NLRB certifies on the basis of a majority of those voting. The NLRB procedure encourages voting; the NMB procedure does not. Moreover, the Mediation Board's policies require union representation even if only a minority of employees desire a union. For if one more than 50 percent of the employees vote and 26 percent favor one of two unions, it will be certified. The NMB quite frankly states that its "ballot was drafted to permit employees to secure some form of representation."[46] This is an interpretation of the Railway Labor Act quite inconsistent with the repeated assurances of the framers of the law that "employees shall be free to join any labor union of their choice and *likewise be free to refrain from joining any union if that be their desire. . . .*"[47] Nevertheless, court challenges to this form of ballot have been unsuccessful.[48] The National Mediation Board's policy of promoting unionism even though a majority of employees do not desire to be represented continues unchecked. In this manner, as in many others, freedom of association is sacrified to the hegemony of the standard unions. The assumption used by the NMB to rationalize its restrictions on employee rights is that employees always will prefer some union representation to none. In a society in which 45 percent of the elections requested by unions under the jurisdiction of the NLRB find "no union" in a majority, the rationale of the NMB is as dishonest as it is nonsensical.

Employer Excluded from Proceedings

Another extraordinary position taken by the National Mediation Board is that the employer is not a party to representation proceedings. This effectively denies him a voice in handling cases, in determining the bargaining unit, or in petitioning for an election—rights which the employer enjoys under the Taft-Hartley Act. Since choice of unit can have a profound impact on a carrier's operations, there seems no basis for this rule. Moreover any propensity of the employer to represent employees whose views are inconsistent with those of the prevailing union is thus effectively checked. Yet the Supreme Court has declared this policy solely within the Board's discretion.[49]

The administrative limitations on employee and employer rights imposed by the National Mediation Board are all the more serious because of major defects in the law itself. There is, first of all, no decertification procedure, as exists in the Taft-Hartley Act. Thus, a union which is certified on the basis of a minority in its favor remains certified until ousted by another union. The Court of Appeals for the District of Columbia noted that it seems "inconceivable that the right to reject collective representation vanishes entirely if the employees of a unit once chose collective representation. On its face, this is a most unlikely rule, specifically taking into account the inevitability of substantial turnover of personnel within the unit."[50] Yet it is the rule.

Another NMB policy, aimed at furthering unionism without regard to its other impact, permits a union to ask for an election at any time that it can make "showing of interest"—usually authorization cards for 30 percent of the employees. The employer cannot ask for an election, as he can under the Taft-

Hartley Act, if he is caught in a rival union organizing drive, nor is either a union or an employer provided with a contract bar to an election for a year or more. There is presumably no limit on the number of elections which may be held in any one year.

A final difference of interest here between the Taft-Hartley Act and the Railway Labor Act is that supervisors (including yard and road superintendents, stationmasters, and other management personnel) are "employees" under the latter law but would be excluded by the former. The fact that the Railway Labor Act furthers the unionization of managerial personnel has been severely criticized because it interferes both with managerial effectiveness and with freedom of association of the rank and file who are placed in the same bargaining units with their bosses. As in other matters, the Mediation Board in years past compounded the problem by placing such groups as track laborers, who were predominantly black, in the same unit as track foremen, even while the Brotherhood of Maintenance of Way Employees confined Negroes to nonvoting auxiliaries.[51]

Both the Act itself and the Mediation Board's administration are grossly inadequate in assuring employees full freedom of association. The best solution would be to rewrite the law consistent with the Taft-Hartley Act and to transfer the representation function to the National Labor Relations Board. As a mediation agency, the NMB is structurally incapable of a judicial function. Its record on representation speaks emphatically on this score.

Unfair Labor Practice Procedure

The 1934 amendments set forth a series of unfair labor practices similar to those governing management conduct under the Taft-Hartley Act. The Railway Labor Act, however, provides for criminal penalties instead of administrative enforcement for the "willful failure or refusal of any carrier, its officers or agents to comply with" the law.[52]

Despite the fact that the standard railway unions regarded the insertion into the Railway Labor Act of specific penalties for carriers committing unfair labor practices as a major accomplishment, they have been of little importance except perhaps as restraints on potential violators. There has been only one case brought to trial under this section and no convictions. This is not difficult to explain. In the first place, railroads generally have been willing to recognize unions. Hence the number of cases has not been large. Then, too, company unions were ousted in representation cases rather than in unfair labor proceedings. Finally, in instances where unfair labor practice proceedings might have been appropriate, it was soon discovered that criminal penalties were impractical.

The Act provides penalties for "willful" violations. Willful intent is most difficult to prove ordinarily but perhaps even more difficult in unfair labor practice proceedings, in which subtle actions play so significant a role. Criminal penalties also require trial by jury. The average layman is likely to be unable to comprehend easily what constitutes an unfair labor practice; and even if he does, as a juror he is apt to be hesitant to agree that the offense is serious enough to merit fine or imprisonment. If intent is proved, there is the additional problem of placing the responsibility. It is not easy to demonstrate to a jury that a foreman acted on orders in discriminating against a union member. Moreover, the punishment does not fit the crime in other ways. If an officer of a carrier is convicted of committing an unfair labor practice and jailed or fined, this does not provide affirmative relief for employees who may, for example, have been discriminated against or discharged because of union activity. Effective remedial action requires reinstatement with backpay for the employee not jail for the employer.

On the other hand, the lack of an administrative remedy for unfair labor practices has saved the procedure from being converted into "a tactical weapon used in many situations as a means of harassment"[53]—the fate which in substantial part has befallen the National Labor Relations Act procedure.

Civil Suit Record

Although the criminal penalties have proved relatively unimportant in unfair labor practice proceedings, civil suits have been significant. Following the lead set in the *Texas and New Orleans* case, unions have appealed to the courts for injunctions ordering carriers to bargain and to refrain from coercing or intimidating employees in their choice of a bargaining agent. The courts, in turn, have adapted their rulings to the 1934 amendments. In a number of instances, they have defined "good faith" and ordered carriers to bargain with duly certified unions as the exclusive bargaining agents of a craft or class.[54] Moreover, discharges because of union activity are subject to the grievance procedure and hence can be carried to the compulsory arbitration machinery of the National Railroad Adjustment Board. Further, if a carrier attempts to influence the conduct of a representation election, the Mediation Board may set aside the results.[55]

Prior to 1951, union security and checkoff provisions were unfair labor practices under the Act. The standard unions wanted it this way in 1934, fearing that otherwise company and independent unions would be "frozen in." By 1951, the beneficent features and administration of the Act had all but eliminated these rivals. Accordingly, the standard unions pressed for and won congressional approval to amend the Act in order to permit such agreements which are now virtually universal in the industry. Congress voted to permit such contracts despite testimony which showed the then discriminatory character of union membership provisions. Moreover, unlike the Taft-Hartley Act, the Railway Labor Act makes no provision for union shop deauthorization.[56]

Thus, under the Railway Labor Act, unions have considerable protection against unfair employer influence or coercion. The reverse is not the case. Unlike what the Taft-Hartley amendments added to the National Labor Relations Act, there never were unfair acts for unions added to the Railway Labor Act. It would seem, however, that union coercion or refusal to bargain could be enjoined by the courts just as similar employer acts have been. The Act gives both parties the right of complete "independence" of the other and protects for each the right of self-organization and selection of representatives. On June 1, 1971, the Supreme Court ruled that under certain circumstances, a union can be ordered by a federal district court to refrain from striking and to bargain in good faith.[57]

Application of Railway Labor Act to Air Transport

The air transport industry was placed under the Railway Labor Act in 1936 at the behest of the Air Line Pilots' Association, then the only unionized group in the industry. The industry, which has grown tremendously and has become quite thoroughly unionized, took no position. The record indicates that it is at least questionable to attempt to transfer both a system of collective bargaining and a method of government control developed in one industry to another.

The disputes procedure in the airline industry has had the same effect on collective bargaining as it has had in the railroads. The ability to get an emergency board appointed has inhibited collective bargaining and has resulted in more crises after the emergency board procedure has been exhausted. The first airline emergency board was appointed in 1946, and until the mid-1960's, boards were appointed with increasing frequency. About thirty-five airline emergency boards had been appointed as of June 30, 1970.

The incident which altered government policy and led to a diminution of air carrier emergency board appointments was a forty-three day strike of the Machinists union against five carriers in 1966, precipitated by union rejection of an emergency board settlement and the membership's further rejection of a "mediation" agreement reached in the White House under President Johnson's strong arm.[58] The fact that this strike lasted without undue public hardship showed quite clearly that the use of emergency procedure for disputes in this industry has been a questionable public policy, especially since such procedure discourages settlement and does not proscribe strikes.

Voluntary arbitration under the Railway Labor Act has been utilized by unions and employers in the airline industry to an increasing degree, but such arbitration would be equally available if the industry were not covered by the Act and is also used by many other industries—some more, some less—not covered by the Railway Labor Act.

Mediation as provided under the Railway Labor Act has certainly been of service to the parties in air transport, but its usefulness is limited by the fact that nearly all mediators have had their major experience in the railroad industry. As one executive of a large airline stated: "The mediators know their business, but usually they are so steeped in solutions worked out in the railroad industry that they feel all we have to do is what is done there. I doubt that this attitude is helpful."[59]

It is difficult to believe that the Federal Mediation and Conciliation Service could not supply mediation facilities equal to those now provided. Because of the varied conditions to which FMCS mediators are exposed, it is not improbable that they would be receptive to the special problems of the airlines without relating them to solutions developed in just one industrial environment. On the other hand, the power of the National Mediation Board to hold on to or to freeze cases has been a helpful matter in preventing strikes in the air transport industry. Such power could, of course, be given to FMCS.

In the representation area a firm case exists against the decision which brought the airline industry under the Railway Labor Act. In so doing, Congress decreed that employees must organize by craft or class. In other industries, organization proceeded on a basis determined by employees and, in turn, resulted from various factors inherent in labor market and industrial conditions. Even in the railroads the craft or class rule was not decided until after it was largely a fact, although as written into law and administered, it has become rigid and unmindful of change or employee free choice.

By limiting employee organization to craft or class, federal policy created a number of problems and aggravated others. For example, one result was to establish separate bargaining units of each and every class of flight crews—pilots, flight engineers, radio operators, navigators, and stewards or stewardesses. All but the first and last became, or are becoming, technologically obsolete. Their organization into separate unions aggravated the technological displacement problem, because the demise of the craft means the demise of the union. Several strikes of flight engineers resulted from the attempts of a union to save itself after the problems of its members were met.

Rulings Often Inapplicable

The craft or class problem on the airlines has been aggravated by the rigidity of the National Mediation Board's interpretations and rulings. Basically, the Board applies regulations and policies developed on the railroads, and these are often of questionable applicability on the airlines. For example, the NMB insisted for many years that office, reservation, store, stock, and ramp employees, with other incidental clericals, be lumped into one unit, although the ramp group on many carriers had unionized with mechanical groups. The reason was that this suited the jurisdictional claims of the Brotherhood of Railway Clerks and was railway practice![60]

The airline industry and unions therein may be directed by the National Mediation Board, under Section 205 of the Railway Labor Act, to set up an eight-man bipartisan National Air Transport Adjustment Board. No action has been taken, however, and none is advocated by either side. That all unions and all carriers in this industry will agree on two representatives is not likely. Moreover, each group has observed the operations of the National Railroad Adjustment Board, and its emulation is not likely to be considered desirable.

Grievance settlement in the airline industry has instead followed the more common and satisfactory method. Each airline and union which bargain collectively have established procedures to settle grievances. When they cannot agree on an arbitrator, they usually ask the National Mediation Board to make the appointment. Arbitrators so appointed are compensated by the parties, not by the government. On the other hand, the "system boards" established by the parties in air transport have been ruled by the courts to be statutorily established, with judicial guidance based on legal decisions affecting the National Railroad Adjustment Board rather than arbitration in industry generally.[61] Although case loads are heavier than in industry generally, there is not an enormous backlog nor a feeling of unrest such as that generated by the NRAB. No better argument exists for ceasing public funding of the latter.

Concluding Analysis

The Railway Labor Act involves the most complete form of government control of collective bargaining which has been developed for American industry in peacetime. It is noteworthy that the industries involved also are regulated in a variety of other ways including supervision of pricing, business routes and location, and rights to initiate or abandon service.

The experience of the Railway Labor Act raises serious question whether the government can control collective bargaining without being forced into a position of complete dominance. As the situation now exists, the emergency board procedure has caused the parties to cease bargaining in order to await the appointment of a board. Then a crisis is likely to arise *after* the board has been appointed. Collective bargaining is further inhibited by the Act's machinery to settle grievances and contract interpretations. Grievance arbitrations at public expense, excessive retroactivity, and the subversion of local practice to national rules aand interpretations have combined to stimulate grievance disputes but to paralyze grievance settlements. Unrest, strife, and litigation are the results.

That the Railway Labor Act has enhanced union power should not be surprising. The present law is largely designed to give the standard railway unions what they desire, and it is administered obviously and consciously with that intent. Representation dispute cases are carefully handled to insure success for the standard unions, as are the rules and regulations of the National Railroad Adjustment Board. In all facets of the Act, promotion of collective bargaining has been interpreted to mean enhancement of the position of the standard railway unions.

Despite the fact that the strike record in the railway and airline industries is not bad compared with other industries (although it is no better than the record in other utilities), the Railway Labor Act can claim little credit. Serious threats to public inconvenience have been settled by other forms of intervention—most recently by special acts of Congress. Perhaps if the procedures of the Act which inhibit collective bargaining did not exist, fewer crises would have been created. *Certainly almost no major dispute since 1941 has been settled without intervention beyond the Act's procedures.*

By requiring unions and companies to bargain on a craft basis, enhancing the power of a few unions, and promoting bargaining representation on a minority basis, the Act encourages narrow rather than broad interests and discourages adjustment to change. At a time when transportation policy requires cost reduction and managerial flexibility, the Railway Labor Act encourages adherence to old, high-cost rules, precedent, and the saddling of a new industry and technology with the mistakes of an older one.

The subjection of collective bargaining in the airline industry to the rigidities and inhibitions built into the Railway Labor Act can only be termed a sad error of public policy. This would be true even if the Act had worked without criticism in the railroad industry, where it reflects to some extent a codification of past practice. But the structure and problems of the airlines require a collective bargaining system tailored to airlines own needs, not to those of a different industry. The same might be said concerning suggestions often made to place other industries under the Railway Labor Act, suggestions usually based on little research as to how the Act works in practice.

The Railway Labor Act is, in effect, special-privilege legislation. It confers rights and duties dissimilar to those conferred on the parties in other industries. The railroad industry and unions are specially treated in most other social legislation, including social security, unemployment, and health and safety.

The rationale has always been the special nature of the business and employment conditions.

On the other hand, each industry has its special conditions. Does only the railroad industry deserve special privilege?

Some analysts believe so. One observer, for example, found nine conditions which differentiate railroad employment from that in other industries.[62] William Gomberg, in commenting on these points, noted that far from being unique characteristics, they exist, often in greater severity, in many other industries which overcame equally difficult problems.[63] Perhaps the very existence of special-privilege legislation has so conditioned the parties in the railroad industry to governmentally imposed solutions that they cannot be expected to face up to their problems. The airlines may well be headed in the same direction under the impetus of the Railway Labor Act.

The Nixon Proposals

President Nixon has proposed that the disputes procedure of the Railway Labor Act be scrapped in favor of a new law which would cover all transportation industries. The proposal would incorporate the eighty-day injunction provision of the Taft-Hartley Act. Then if the strike threat were not abated, the President would have three choices: extend the injunction for thirty days, require partial operation for a period as long as six months, or appoint arbitrators who would have to choose the final position of one of the parties in the exact form in which it was presented. The President's proposal also calls for disestablishment of the National Railroad Adjustment Board, resumption of the burden of grievance settlement by the parties, and appointment of a commission to make a comprehensive analysis of labor relations in the transportation industries.

The last two points of the Nixon proposal are so obviously in tune with needs that they require no comment. The disputes proposal must also be commended for being a fresh approach to the country's need of a new labor policy for the transportation industries. The purpose is twofold: to provide a procedure which brings a settlement to a dispute, and to induce the parties to settle disputes by collective bargaining instead of relying on, or even inducing, government intervention. The first objective would be achieved by the Nixon compulsory arbitration proposal; however, the second objective may be harder to obtain.

It seems to be a fact that as long as government machinery to settle disputes exists, it will be used and that withdrawal of the right to strike carries with it a decline in inducement to settle. This has occurred as a result of compulsory arbitration, seizure, fact finding, and a host of other intervenor methods in all democratic countries.[64]

Both railroad and air carriers oppose many points of the Nixon proposals. Most of all they fear they will be the losers if the National Mediation Board (or a successor authority such as the Federal Mediation and Conciliation Service) is stripped of authority to prevent strikes simply by holding or "sitting on" a controversy. Railroads also fear partial operation as a form of whipsawing, and air carriers have some of the same concerns.

A bill embodying the carrier position has been put forth. It also provides for a choice of procedures, with three cabinet secretaries taking actions including possibly compulsory arbitration. The carrier bill would permit such action in any dispute, large or small, thus virtually requiring intervention, with obvious impact on collective bargaining which both rail and air carriers believe is not working. The carrier bill would amend the National Mediation Board's representation duties, requiring that "no union" be put on the ballot and that carriers be a party to the proceedings. Supervisory employees would be removed from coverage of the Railway Labor Act and the National Railroad Adjustment Board would be eliminated as a government agency. Railroad and airline unions oppose these measures as well as the Nixon bill.

Both the Nixon and the carrier proposals would be an improvement over the present situation, for perhaps even more than most disputes machinery, the Railway Labor Act, particularly as administered over the years, has rewarded irresponsibility and intransigence. The wide awareness of this fact is heartening.

Unfortunately, both the Nixon and carrier proposals seem somewhat wide of their aims. Despite improvements in representation procedure and abolishment of tax support of grievance settlement, the carrier's proposal essentially looks to compulsory arbitration for relief. One can sympathize with the position and yet doubt that arbitrators will provide the necessary help. Although the Nixon proposals deserve high marks for ingenuity, and obviously were drawn to discourage third-party intervention, it remains doubtful that the parties might not find it regularly useful to create the emergency rather than to risk the internal organizational political consequences of bargaining in good faith. I believe now, as I have previously suggested, that this result could be avoided by distinguishing between the prevention of the emergency and the settlement of the dispute. This could be accomplished by use of the injunction to prevent the strike and by taxing union dues and company revenues until the parties settle or until they at least cease threatening to create an emergency.[65] Preventing emergencies is the duty of government; settling disputes is the obligation of the parties. Labor and management should be penalized for not settling rather than rewarded by government action when they fail to come to terms. If that were done, both unions and carriers in the railroad and air transport industries might be encouraged to follow up the constructive aspects of the 1971 "selective strikes" by settling their disputes without strikes and without regard to the burdensome procedures of the Railway Labor Act, which should be promptly repealed.

NOTES

1. For summaries of my previous findings, see Herbert R. Northrup and Gordon F. Bloom, *Government and Labor* (Homewood, Ill.: Richard D. Irwin, Inc., 1963), chap. 12; and Herbert R. Northrup, *Compulsory Arbitration and Government Intervention in Labor Disputes* (Washington: Labor Policy Association, Inc., 1966), chap. 5. See also Howard W. Risher, Jr., with foreword by Herbert R. Northrup, "The Railway Labor Act," *Boston College Industrial and Commercial Law Review*, Vol. 12, November 1970, pp. 51-99.

2. Prior legislation included the Arbitration Act of 1888, 25 *Stat.* 501; the Erdman Act of 1898, 30 *Stat.* 424; the Newlands Act of 1913, 38 *Stat.* 103; the Adamson Act of 1916, 38 *Stat.* 721; and the Transportation Act of 1920, 41 *Stat.* 456.

3. William H. Spencer, *The National Railroad Adjustment Board*, Studies in Business Administration, Vol. 8, No. 3 (Chicago: University of Chicago Press, 1938), pp. 11-12.

4. Texas and New Orleans Railroad Co. v. Brotherhood, 281 U.S. 548 (1930).

5. References will be made to the "standard" railway unions in this article. These unions historically have included the Brotherhood of Locomotive Engineers, the Brotherhood of Locomotive Firemen and Enginemen, the Order of Railway Conductors, the Brotherhood of Railroad Trainmen, and the Switchmen's Union in the operating end; and the Brotherhood of Maintenance of Way Employees; the Order of Railroad Telegraphers; the Brotherhood of Railway and Steamship Clerks, Freight Handlers, Express and Station Employees; the American Train Dispatchers' Association; the Brotherhood of Railroad Signalmen; the Brotherhood of Railway Carmen; the International Association of Machinists; the International Brotherhood of Electrical Workers; the Brotherhood of Boilermakers, Shipbuilders, Welders, and Helpers; and the Brotherhood of Firemen and Oilers in the nonoperating part of the industry. The last 4 include unions which now have only a small portion of their membership in the railroad industry; the remainder draw most of their members from the railroad industry. Recent mergers have seen the Firemen, Switchmen, Trainmen and Conductors join to form the United Transportation Union, and the Telegraphers and some smaller unions merge into the Railway Clerks. The Clerks have also added "Airline" to their name and the Machinists "Aerospace" to theirs. Earlier the Blacksmiths merged into the Boilermakers, which added the former craft to its name.

6. For an endorsement and elaboration of this viewpoint, see Howard S. Kaltenborn, *Governmental Adjustment of Labor Disputes* (Chicago: Foundation Press, 1943), p. 52.

7. The Board has reiterated this concern in its recent publication, *Administration of the Railway Labor Act by the National Mediation Board, 1934-1970* (Washington: G.P.O., 1970), pp. 30-31.

8. Data from annual reports of the National Mediation Board.

9. Sumner H. Slichter, "The Great Question in Industrial Relations," *New York Times Magazine*, Apr. 27, 1947, p. 5.

10. This outrageous action was the basis of the landmark case, Steele v. Louisville & Nashville R. R. Co., 323 U.S. 192 (1944), in which the U.S. Supreme Court ruled that a bargaining agent must represent all workers in the bargaining unit without discrimination.

11. For details involving this early period, see Herbert R. Northrup, *Organized Labor and the Negro* (New York: Harper & Row, 1944), chap. 3. For a carefully documented and well-written update of this story, see Howard W. Risher, Jr., *The Negro in the Railroad Industry*, The Racial Policies of American Industry, Report No. 16 (Philadelphia: Industrial Research Unit, Wharton School of Finance and Commerce, University of Pennsylvania, 1971). It was the discovery of this messy racial situation which led me to question the "model law" concept and to challenge it at an early date.

12. For a history of railway labor relations during this period see Herbert R. Northrup, "The Railway Labor Act and Railway Labor Disputes During Wartime," *American Economic Review*, Vol. 36, No. 3 (June 1946), pp. 324-343.

13. For a history of disputes during this period, see David M. Levinson, "Railway Labor Act—The Record of a Decade," *Labor Law Journal*, Vol. 3, No. 6 (June 1952), pp. 13-29; and Jacob J. Kaufman, "Emergency Boards under the Railway Labor Act," *Labor Law Journal*, Vol. 9, No. 12 (December 1958), pp. 910-920, 949.

14. *Report of the Presidential Railroad Commission* (Washington: G.P.O., February 1962).

15. From President Kennedy's news conference of Sept. 12, 1962, as transcribed in the *New York Times*, Sept. 15, 1962, p. 12. See also the editorials in the *New York Times* for Sept. 15, 1962, and in the *Washington Post*, Sept. 16, 1962. It should be noted that the vote procedure in the aerospace case did not obtain the union shop for the unions because the employees voted it down. See Northrup and Bloom, *Government and Labor*, pp. 238-241.

16. Jacob J. Kaufman, "The Railroad Labor Dispute: A Marathon of Maneuver and Improvisation," *Industrial and Labor Relations Review*, Vol. 18, No. 2 (January 1965), p. 210.

17. *Business Week*, Dec. 19, 1970, p. 41.

18. See, for example, the comments of union spokesmen advocating the original 1926 law, reproduced in Kaufman, "Emergency Boards under the Railway Labor Act," pp. 911-912.

19. William M. Leiserson, "Public Policy in Labor Relations," *American Economic Review*, Vol. 36, No. 2 (May 1946), p. 345.

20. This was the actual comment of a union official upon receiving a recommendation of an emergency board in 1948.

21. Quoted in Northrup, *Compulsory Arbitration*, p. 66.

22. *Ibid.*, pp. 66-67.

23. Quoted in Risher, "The Railway Labor Act," pp. 69-70.

24. Lloyd H. Garrison, "The National Railroad Adjustment Board: A Unique Administrative Agency," *Yale Law Journal*, Vol. 46, 1937, p. 567.

25. Herbert R. Northrup and Mark L. Kahn, "Railroad Grievance Machinery: A Critical Analysis," *Industrial and Labor Relations Review*, Vol. 5, No. 3 (April 1952), pp. 370-372. The Secretary of Labor has the duty to determine if a union is eligible. The Brotherhood of Sleeping Car Porters is one nonstandard union found eligible, but the other unions do not permit it representation on the Third Division.

26. The Second Division always has been able to agree on referees, the Fourth generally, the Third occasionally, and the First, which decides 70 to 80% of the cases, almost never. The First Division has jurisdiction over operating employees, the Second over shop employees, the Third over all nonoperating groups except shop, waterborne, and supervisory, and the Fourth over waterborne employees of railroads, supervisory, and miscellaneous groups.

27. *Pub. L. No. 456*, 89th Cong., 2d sess., Part I (June 20, 1966).

28. *Pub. L. No. 234*, 91st Cong., 2d sess., Part I (Apr. 23, 1970).

29. Until recently the NRAB refused to hear cases submitted by individuals, despite clear statutory language to the contrary. This was accomplished by union representatives refusing to accept the cases and created a procedural deadlock which there was no way to break. The First and Second Divisions still do not accept nonstandard union cases, although the Third and Fourth do. This is not too important, since most nonstandard unions will not submit cases to an agency whose labor members are controlled by rivals.

30. For a list of cases, see Northrup and Kahn, "Railroad Grievance Machinery," pp. 373-374. Individual authorization, usually obtained through union constitutions and membership applications, is also required for an award to be binding on employees. Merely being the bargaining agent does not confer the right to represent employees before the NRAB. Elgin Joliet & Eastern Railway Co. v. Burley, 325 U.S. 711 (1945).

31. Thus the courts have denied jurisdiction to the NRAB where the dispute involves a conflict between an employee and his collective bargaining representative, Steele v. Louisville & Nashville Railroad Co., 323 U.S. 192 (1944); between two employees, Long v. Van Osdale, 26 N.E. (2d) 69 (1940); or between a carrier and an employee of another carrier, Stephenson v. N.O. and N.E. Railroad Co., 177 So. 509 (1937).

32. These cases particularly involve the Negro porter-brakemen, porters, and white trainmen and have been extant for 40 years. Black workers still strive for justice without much success. See Northrup, *Organized Labor and the Negro*, pp. 66-71; and Risher, *The Negro in the Railroad Industry*, pp. 148-163.

33. In 1949-1950, for example, 6 of 11 emergency boards actually were concerned with matters properly within the jurisdiction of the NRAB, and one 45-day strike occurred. The Mediation Board noted that a "great amount of time of the [Mediation] Board and its mediators was spent in preventing strikes in such situations." See National Mediation Board, *Sixteenth Annual Report* (Washington: G.P.O., 1950), pp. 24-25.

34. Brotherhood of Railroad Trainmen v. Chicago River Industrial Railroad Co., 353 U.S. 30 (1951). The courts will not enjoin a strike if the case has not been submitted to the NRAB, even though the matter is within the NRAB's jurisdiction (Manion v. Kansas City Terminal Railway Co., 353 U.S. 927 [1956]); but presumably, to obtain an injunction, the carrier may merely submit the matter to the NRAB.

35. Denver and Rio Grande Western Railroad Co. v. Brotherhood of Railroad Trainmen, 185 F. Supp. 369 (1960).

36. See Risher, "The Railway Labor Act," pp. 72-73.

37. *Ibid.*, pp. 82-85.

38. Data are from Garth L. Mangum, "Grievance Procedures for Railroad Operating Employees," *Industrial and Labor Relations Review*, Vol. 15, No. 4 (July 1962), pp. 474-499; and National Mediation Board, *Annual Reports*, various issues.

39. Mangum, "Grievance Procedures for Railroad Operating Employees," p. 491.

40. Sumner H. Slichter, *Union Policies and Industrial Management* (Washington, D.C.: Brookings Institution, 1941), p. 195, n. 80. The courts have been equally caustic about NRAB awards. See Northrup and Kahn, "Railroad Grievance Machinery: A Critical Analysis," Part II, *Industrial and Labor Relations Review*, Vol. 5, No. 4 (July 1952), pp. 549-555, for analysis of awards and court citations.

41. Mangum, "Grievance Procedures for Railroad Operating Employees," p. 496.

42. *Ibid.*, p. 499.

43. *Report of the Presidential Railroad Commission*, p. 185.

44. For a more complete analysis of National Mediation Board representation dispute policy, see Herbert R. Northrup, "The Appropriate Bargaining Unit Question Under the Railway Labor Act," *Quarterly Journal of Economics*, Vol. 60 (February 1946), pp. 250-269; Jacob J. Kaufman, "Representation in the Railroad Industry," *Labor Law Journal*, Vol. 6, No. 7 (July 1955), pp. 437-440, 508-512; and Risher, "The Railway Labor Act," pp. 85-97. In addition, the NMB has published four volumes containing its representation cases and decisions, *Determinations of Craft or Class of the National Mediation Board* (Washington: G.P.O., Vol. I, 1948; Vol. II, 1953; Vol. III, 1961; and Vol. IV, 1968).

45. For cases in point, see Northrup, "The Appropriate Bargaining Unit," and *Organized Labor and the Negro*, pp. 58-62; Risher, "The Railway Labor Act," pp. 92-93, and *The Negro in the Railroad Industry*. The fact that many railway unions have historically denied Negroes membership rights means that the careless policies of the Mediation Board in the early years of its existence contributed substantially to furthering union racial discrimination.

46. National Mediation Board, *Administration of the Railway Labor Act by the National Mediation Board, 1934-1957* (Washington: G.P.O., 1958), pp. 18-19.

47. U.S. Congress, House, Committee on Interstate and Foreign Commerce, *Report on HR 9861*, 23d Cong., 2d sess. (Washington: G.P.O., 1934), p. 2. H.R. 9861 became the 1934 amendments to the Railway Labor Act. In like vein, see the comments of Joseph P. Eastman, then Federal Coordinator of Transportation and draftsman of the House of Representatives hearings on this bill and the comments of the late Senator Robert Wagner of New York on the S. 3266 (the companion bill in the Senate) on p. 12 of U.S. Congress, Senate, Committee on Interstate Commerce, *Hearings on S. 3266*, 23d Cong., 2d sess. (Washington: G.P.O., 1934).

48. Brotherhood of Railway Clerks v. Association for the Benefit of Non-Contract Employees, 380 U.S. 650 (1965).

49. *Ibid.*

50. International Brotherhood of Teamsters v. Brotherhood of Railway Clerks, 402 F.2d 196 (D.C. Cir. 1968).

51. E. Dale and R. L. Raimon, "Management Unionism and Public Policy on the Railroads and the Airlines," *Industrial and Labor Relations Review*, Vol. 11, No. 4 (July 1958), pp. 551-571; and Northrup, "The Appropriate Bargaining Unit."

52. For a more detailed analysis of the Act's unfair labor practice procedure, see Herbert R. Northrup, "Unfair Labor Practice Prevention Under the Railway Labor Act," *Industrial and Labor Relations Review*, Vol. 3, No. 3 (April 1950), pp. 323-340.

53. Committee for Economic Development, *The Public Interest in National Labor Policy* (New York, 1961), p. 82.

54. See, for example, Virginian Railway v. System Federation, 300 U.S. 515 (1937); Long Island R. R. v. Brotherhood of R. R. Trainmen, 185 F. Supp. 358 (E.D. N. Y., 1960); Order of R. R. Telegraphers v. Chicago & N.W. Ry., 362 U.S. 330 (1960). See also Risher, "The Railway Labor Act," pp. 62-64.

55. Chicago and Southern Airlines (Case No. R-1955) and Allegheny Airlines (Case No. R-3470).

56. For other aspects of union security under the Railway Labor Act see D. M. Levinson, "Union Shop Under the Railway Labor Act," *Labor Law Journal*, Vol. 6, No. 7 (July 1955), pp. 462-482, 494.

57. Chicago & North Western Railway Co. v. United Transportation Union, U.S. Supreme Court, June 1, 1971.

58. This contract rejection also made repercussions because it stimulated a rash of rejections by members of the Machinists union in other industries.

59. Personal interview, 1965.

60. See, for example, Cases No. C-1693, C-2252, C-2389, and R-1706. These cases and many other aspects of the application of the Railway Labor Act to air transport are well discussed in the "Symposium on Air Transport Labor Relations," *Journal of Air Law and Commerce*, Vol. 35, Summer 1969, pp. 313-534.

61. See Risher, "The Railway Labor Act," pp. 81-82, for a summary of the findings.

62. Jacob J. Kaufman, "Logic and Meaning of Work Rules on the Railroads," *Proceedings of the Fourteenth Annual Meeting, Industrial Relations Research Association,* 1961, pp. 379-388.

63. William Gomberg, "Discussion," *Proceedings of the Fourteenth Annual Meeting, Industrial Relations Research Association,* 1961, pp. 413-416.

64. For a discussion of such legislation, see Northrup, *Compulsory Arbitration.*

65. *Ibid.,* chap. 11.

Collective Bargaining in the Railroad Industry:
The Beginning of a New Era

James E. Burke †

Events which took place earlier this year altered decisively the course which collective bargaining could take in the railroad industry in the coming decade. It would not be an exaggeration, I believe, to state that the survival of the system will in the future be traced to these events.

In order to project on the ability of collective bargaining to survive the stresses and strains of the coming decade, one must review the events of the past in order to recognize the hurdles that must be overcome. We not only assume the need to maintain effective collective bargaining as a basic fundamental employer-employee relationship, we recognize that certain conditions must be met if this fundamental concept is to work effectively.

It is not necessary here to expound on the right of individual employees to join together in unions for their mutual protection. That right is sufficiently recognized. However, there has been the continuing trend, especially in the railroad industry, to restrict the ultimate rights of these individuals, that of withholding their services when necessary, or the threat thereof, and thereby prohibiting them from effectively bargaining to a conclusion in disputes with their employers.

Beginning with the end of World War II, the government and the courts, at the instigation of the industry, repeatedly took the position that the nation could not and would not tolerate a national railroad strike. Thus with the ultimate weapon in effective collective bargaining destroyed, and the natural incentive to reach agreements with it, the industry could go through the motions of negotiating, without really working toward a negotiated settlement, secure and content in the knowledge that they would not face a shutdown.

More than two decades ago, the President of the United States seized the railroads and ordered the army "to take and assume

---

† James E. Burke is Vice President, United Transportation Union.

possession, control and operation" of the industry in face of a railroad strike. This was the beginning of more than two decades of governmental and court involvement in labor-management relations in the industry.

The effect of that takeover was simply that the industry continued to reap its profits, while the employees were tied to wages and conditions which were long overdue for improvement. Their right to strike having been lost, the employees were left without an effective means of bringing about needed changes. Thereafter it became routine for labor disputes in this industry to drag on and on, from one court to another, from one tribunal to another and each time when the moment of truth arrived, the employees were frustrated again with the philosophy of "this nation cannot stand a national railroad strike."

The instant that this philosophy was initiated was also the starting point from which the time between expiration of old agreements and the institution of new agreements became wider and wider and with it, generally, the tremendous savings to the railroad carriers of the nation brought about only by their ability to stall in these negotiations. During this same period retroactive wage settlements in the industry became a rarity and it was not until the last 8 or 9 years that any type of retroactivity crept back into these settlements and only then through the aggressive leadership of some of the younger labor negotiators who were assuming command of some of the older organizations at that time. The Railway Labor Act by its very basic terms that were designed to provide uninterrupted service during negotiations actually provided the incentive for these particular situations to gain a foothold.

Then, as is the history of oppression of any type, a further step in the eradication of basic rights of employees came about when, at the request of another President, Congress enacted the first compulsory arbitration law in peace time. In August 1963, Public Law 188 was passed establishing Arbitration Board 282, which later dictated the terms of settlement of the protracted work rules or manning dispute. This was the back of the hand treatment that the operating railroad labor organizations received from the government for their cooperation in agreeing to a Presidential Railroad Commission to study the restructuring of wages and job classifications at the behest of the then Labor Secretary, James Mitchell, of the Eisenhower Cabinet. Since then Congress has passed other ad hoc legislation disposing of railroad labor disputes in an arbitrary manner. Less than a year ago it passed Public Law 91-541 which restricted our members' right to strike in a protracted wage rules dispute.

Concurrent with the congressional action, the railroads were successfully foiling, in various courts, our union's attempt to bring about a settlement. At issue was the use of the newly conceived "selective strike" idea of UTU President Charles Luna. Successfully, in the lower court, the railroads argued that the union had no right to the use of such economic strength. Finally, the Supreme Court, by denying certiorari, placed such strikes in a legal category of negotiating weapons and a new era of labor management relations began in the industry.

The courts, having recognized the legality of selective strikes in the railroad industry with respect to disputes that have been the subject previously of national handling, returned to my union the right to utilize this form of negotiating with certain restrictions. As a result, we conducted a fair, responsible, and successful "selective strike" in the industry, although the court permitted the remaining railroads to operate under medieval conditions imposed in complete disregard of the Railway Labor Act. I might add that the carriers accepted and applied these almost universally in as inhumane a manner as you could venture to imagine. It did result, however, in a negotiated settlement the terms of which both sides finally admitted to be reasonable and just.

The significance of the court action granting rights to strike selectively and the results of such selective strikes cannot be overemphasized. The nation learned from experience that a railroad strike does not automatically cause a national emergency. The industry learned that it must be willing to meet its obligations at the bargaining table and that it no longer can hide behind the government and the courts when it fails to do so. Labor, too, learned that with the right to strike comes the obligation to do everything possible to reach a negotiated settlement, for the failure to do so brings great economic sacrifice on its members when they are forced to use their ultimate weapon.

An interesting by-product of all this has also been in evidence of late. The National Mediation Board, which is the administrative agency of the government charged with the operation of the conciliation machinery of the Railway Labor Act, can now eliminate the long delays that it invoked to bring about desperation bargaining before the standard national crisis bargaining that resulted in "ad hoc legislation." It can now eliminate these delays with the elimination of the national emergencies by the "selective strike."

Not only the strike and the lockout, but *the right* to strike and lockout are effective and persuasive instruments in face-to-face negotiations. Each in its own way is the ultimate weapon which opposing sides must consider in their battle plans. Each, to a great degree, keeps the other side honest.

One would think, in view of the outcome of the strike rights sustained by the Supreme Court and used effectively in the solution of the dispute between the carrier and my union just recently, that the right to strike selectively and the value of that right would now be unquestioned. This is not the case.

Presently there are before Congress bills which would not only remove this right, but simply stated, would end collective bargaining in the industry. While the provisions pertaining to conditions of settlement of disputes are well camouflaged in the bills, they boil down to pure and simple compulsory arbitration. One such proposal would give the President, among other tools, the so-called Final Offer Selection. The only thing final about it is the fact that it does assure that a dispute will be settled, but gives no assurance that it will be settled equitably. I believe that most people will agree with me that any form of compulsory arbitration is, at least to some degree, repressive of our traditional free enterprise system, and, specifically, repressive of freedom of contract.

Notwithstanding the events of the recent past, the bills before Congress are still premised on the thought that, whenever there is a national railroad dispute, a national railroad strike is an intolerable national emergency; hence, some modification of the present law is needed. The events I have recited, however, demonstrate graphically that it is now the established law that a selective strike is lawful, that such a strike can be conducted fairly and responsibly, and that it will lead to a collectively bargained disposition of even the most far-reaching and bitter dispute.

In many respects the experience leading up to the disposition of our dispute through the agreement of August 2, 1971, was about as severe a test of the efficacy of collective bargaining as one is likely to find. This is true for a number of reasons. In the first place, the issues in dispute were very important and far-reaching; the wage increases involved were of critical importance to our people at a time when living costs were rising rapidly, and our people had had no wage increases for a long time. On the other hand, the revisions of working conditions that the railroads sought were revolutionary—the railroads thought it was important that they should have them, and our people were equally determined not to suffer retrogression in their working conditions.

From some comments that were made, one might gather that the selective strike gave us dictatorial and oppressive powers— that it put us in a position to enforce any demands we might make and thereby bleed the industry white. I submit that anyone entertaining any such notion does so in complete disregard of the facts. Let there be no mistake about it. The strike was no picnic for our people. They were, however, willing to undergo any sacrifices necessary to secure a fair settlement, but no one man is willing to undergo sacrifice for the sake of being oppressed.

Aside from restoring and preserving the basic freedom of the right to strike, you may wonder what other effect the court decision had. Was the settlement fair is perhaps a good question. I don't see how anyone can dispute the fairness of the wage settlement—the wages we contracted for were exactly those which a Presidential Emergency Board had recommended for the duration of the contract they recommended.

With respect to rules, which was the heart of the problem, the settlement was a fair compromise. With respect to inter-divisional runs, about which there was so much publicity during the strike, we have made many agreements for them in the past on individual railroads and we have constantly expressed willingness to make such agreements to fit the precise requirements of individual railroad operations. Numbers of other rules were involved and some of the rules changes we agreed to would certainly have resulted in hardships to our people if we had not also negotiated fair protective conditions to guard against those hardships.

Perhaps the best evidence of the fairness of the terms comes from industry spokesmen. Mr. Stephen Ailes, President of the Association of American Railroads, stated recently, in advocating enactment of one of the bills which would restrict the right of labor to use a selective strike: "the purpose of the bill is not to protect the railroads from the railroad unions—the recent UTU strike should have made it clear that no such protection is necessary."

Further indicating that the industry was satisfied with the outcome of the negotiations which ended the strike, Mr. B. F. Biaggini, President of the Southern Pacific Railroad, indicated recently that the settlement well justified the suffering involved and made the whole affair worthwhile. Thus one can see that while railroad officials may be against the "selective strike," they are not averse to the end results which came about through tough negotiations brought on because of the strike.

Simply stated, the strike action and the carriers' promulgation of the work rules—in lieu of a lockout—brought pressure on both sides for an agreement. Had not the previous negotiations been carried on under ground rules wherein the railroads felt safe that the ultimate strike weapon could not be used, there is every reason to believe a collectively negotiated agreement could have been reached without strike action. Both sides would have been kept honest, and both sides would have been keenly aware of the ultimate weapon in the hands of the other.

There is no question but that the action taken by the carriers after the strike took effect delayed and complicated the final settlement. From the beginning the railroads' efforts were directed toward forcing a national strike and subsequent congressional ad hoc disposition again. This is shown not only by their persistent efforts to enjoin the selective strikes but also by the fact that they put their proposed rules changes into effect by unilateral promulgation on *all* railroads, including those that had not been struck.

To avoid a national strike under these circumstances called for the highest order of discipline among our people. It meant that many thousands of our people had to work under unacceptable and brutal working conditions, and for earnings far below those normally associated with their jobs. It also meant that before final settlement could be made, not only the issues initially in dispute but also those arising from the rules promulgation had to be resolved and provision made for resolving the grievances arising from working under the promulgated rules.

In the past, the government has not been willing to let collective bargaining run its natural course. The courts have not been willing either. If the Administration were to get its way, new laws would prohibit even selective strikes, and again, collective bargaining would not be able to run its natural course. Changing the law, enacting the Administration's bill, would not bring peace and stability to the industry as some claim. It would, on the other hand, create even more dissension.

By this I do not mean that there is not room for some legal changes in respect to employer and employee relations in the railroad industry. Selective strikes have proved themselves effective in bringing about agreements. Legislative action which might further insure that selective strikes not become national in scope well may be in order. For instance, the prohibition of a national lockout converting a selective strike into a national emergency is possibly essential. Moreover, there may need to be provisions established limiting the extent to which the industry can be struck selectively. Perhaps also there should be provisions requiring both sides to provide any service necessary to the national safety and health.

In conclusion, I should like to sound a note of optimism.

We have experienced, for more than two decades, the tragic consequences that come when government and the judiciary take strong roles against the right of labor to use its ultimate weapon, or the threat of it, in collective bargaining situations. Far from bringing about peace and tranquility in the industry, the aim and goal of such interference, the industry has experienced one of its most turbulent periods in history. Now that the right to strike selectively has been established, with the carriers in a position to take suitable counter actions, there is every reason to believe that both sides will strive more earnestly to reach understandings at the bargaining table.

Compulsory arbitration, or any disguised substitute such as the "arsenal of weapons" approach, or the requirement of "final offer referendum" is only new jargon for old and unsuccessful ideas. Nothing that is before Congress in the form of bills that will force settlements will bring peace and harmony in the industry nearly so quickly or so surely as will the continued right of both sides to use its economic strength, or to be the target of such strength, when that time arrives in any given situation.

I believe that the judicial recognition of the lawfulness of selective strikes and disposition of a far-reaching national dispute through a fair agreement resulting from selective strikes demonstrates forcefully the worthiness of such methods of action. In view of the results, I do not believe that Congress can enact legislation which would alter this proven method of settling disputes.

Given this set of ground rules, I believe that peace and tranquility will come once again to the labor-management battleground in the railroad industry. God knows it is high time.

Union Fragmentation: A Major Cause of Transportation Labor Crises

Edward B. Shils †

In the past decade, there has been increasing evidence that labor laws and the present pattern of bargaining in the transportation industries have not contributed to labor stability. Railroad and airline labor unions are under the jurisdiction of the Railway Labor Act (RLA) of 1926 as amended. Maritime, longshore, and trucking unions fall within the jurisdiction of the Taft-Hartley Act of 1947, as amended. In addition to the several laws which cover labor aspects of transportation, the multiplicity and rivalry of unions in the rail, airline, and shipping industries contribute to labor unrest, crippling strikes, and work stoppages harmful to the economy.

President Nixon, weary of the load of appointing emergency fact-finding boards in rail and air and of the frequency of employing the eighty-day "cooling-off period" in disputes in shipping, longshore, and trucking, advised Congress on February 27, 1970, of the Administration's desire for enactment of the Emergency Public Interest Protection Act of 1970.

The primary purpose of the proposal was to join rail and airline labor unions under the same jurisdiction as maritime and trucking unions. This would result in a more comprehensive National Labor Relations Act by further amending Taft-Hartley and discontinuing the emergency procedures of the Railway Labor Act.

---

† Edward B. Shils is Professor and Chairman of the Department of Industry, Wharton School of Finance and Commerce, University of Pennsylvania.

Reprinted with permission from *Industrial and Labor Relations Review*, Vol. 25, No. 1, October 1971. Copyright © 1971 by Cornell University. All rights reserved.

Use of Emergency Procedures

The President, in evaluating the two national labor laws, took the position of a "plague on both their houses." The emergency provisions of the Railway Labor Act had been invoked 187 times from 1927 to February 1970—an average of four times per year. Work stoppages in the rail and air industries, following the end of the sixty-day "status quo" period, had occurred at the rate of more than one per year since 1947. In addition, Congress had to pass legislation five times since 1947 to terminate major railroad disputes.

While admitting that the Taft-Hartley Act encourages collective bargaining much more than does the Railway Labor Act, nevertheless President Nixon indicted it also. In eight of the twenty-nine instances in which the eighty-day cooling-off period was invoked, a strike or lockout took place after the end of the cooling-off period. All of these instances involved the maritime and longshore industries.

Three Options

The President recommended three new options to Congress: (1) to extend the cooling-off period under Taft-Hartley by an additional thirty days if the President believes it to be necessary, (2) to permit partial operation of a labor-troubled industry, or (3) to invoke the procedure of a "final-offer selection" which would require both parties to submit one or two final offers to the Secretary of Labor. The last option would provide each party with five days to meet and bargain over the final offers. If no agreement was reached, a "final-offer-selector" group of three neutral members would be appointed by the disputants, or if they could not agree on the selection, appointments would be made by the President. The neutrals would choose one of the final offers as the final and binding settlement.

The President's proposals were not enacted in 1970, and he continues to press for their consideration in 1971. Nixon is more concerned with labor problems in transportation than in most other industries. These recommendations have genuine value but, in the writer's opinion, will not solve the transportation labor crisis unless there is a substantial change in the structure of the transportation unions themselves and in the pattern of bargaining.

Seventy-seven transportation unions are listed in the tables in this article. This total includes forty-four railroad unions, sixteen airline unions, sixteen maritime and longshore unions, plus (of course) the International Brotherhood of Teamsters (IBT). This article seeks to show there are too many labor organizations in transportation activities in the United States, and their very number, plus their competitive and often antagonistic interests, causes the public to suffer, from time to time, the serious consequences of labor unrest, walkouts, and strikes.

Not only has the public been inconvenienced, but also business in general and shippers in particular often have been hit very hard. During the past decade, business and the public have been exposed to national maritime, longshore, railroad, and airline strikes. On a few occasions, strikes by the Teamsters have tied up important regions of the United States and contributed to violence and bloodshed.

The multiplicity of unions and their day-to-day jurisdictional rivalries have especially hurt carriers. Bargaining individually or as part of multiemployer bargaining groups, carriers face whipsawing, jurisdictional disputes, varying contract expiration or reopener dates and, confronted with the existing union structure, are unable to develop cohesive labor policies. The fractionalized union structure often contributes to fractionalized responses among employers and employer groups.

Brief comment will be made on the Teamsters, whose union structure is somewhat unique in the transportation industry, but the major portion of this article will deal with railroad, airline, maritime, and longshore unions.

Teamsters

The first effective national contract negotiated by IBT President James R. Hoffa in 1964 was hailed by trucking employers and local Teamster chieftains as providing a new era of stability in the trucking industry. Unlike the situation in the airline, railroad, and maritime industries, trucking was to be in the hands of almost two million teamsters belonging to the same national industrial union.

Even when Hoffa rose to the presidency of IBT in 1958, control over bargaining was largely local and regional. There were few areawide agreements in the major regional councils of the union. Furthermore wages, fringes, work rules, and contract expiration dates in Hoffa's Central States Drivers Council varied greatly from provisions in contracts in the western, southern, and eastern regions. The Teamsters were traditionally a decentralized organization whose internal structure reflected the local and regional product markets in which its members worked. Local autonomy and local leadership were very powerful.

Hoffa exercised increasing centralization of policies, procedures, and contract negotiations until his imprisonment in 1967. The national contract, negotiated that year without him, was repudiated by the Chicago Teamsters and had to be renegotiated after a bitter strike. After the second contract was ratified, several months of strikes and violence took place among the steelhaulers in nine states. The pattern with both the Chicago locals and the steelhaulers was repeated before and after the 1970 national contract negotiations. After the 1970 pact, the Fraternal Order of Steelhaulers applied to the NLRB for disaffiliation from the Brotherhood of Teamsters.

At this point in time, it appears that while IBT is a national industrial union, it reveals the same weaknesses of fragmentation and divisiveness characteristic of the entire transportation labor sector.

Railroad Labor Troubles

Exhibit 1 indicates the scope of craft union representation in the railroad industry. Until 1969 the operating workers were divided into five unions known as the "operating brotherhoods." The engineers are still represented by BLE, but the firemen and helpers (BLFE), conductors (ORCB), trainmen (BRT), and yard foremen, helpers, and switchtenders (SUNA) merged on January 1, 1969, into a new organization, the United Transportation Union (UTU).

To some extent, the merger of the four brotherhoods into UTU has lessened fragmentation, although disputes under the Railway Labor Act continue to be processed by craft. With declining rail employment, "contracting-out," and possible worker displacement due to changing technology, there is evidence of a desire of other union members to strengthen their position by merger or coalition bargaining.

In addition to these brotherhoods, the exhibit shows twenty-eight other labor organizations, which represent nonoperating workers on railroads. Many of these unions are affiliated with the AFL-CIO and traditionally represent the same kind of workers in other industries. Among them are such well known inter-industry unions as IAM, IBEW, IBFO, SMW, TWU, UMW, and USA.

In addition to the operating and nonoperating brotherhoods, Exhibit 1 also shows eleven marine unions which represent deck, engine room, officers, bridgemen, cooks, waiters, chefs, and so forth, on riverboats, tugs, rail ferries, and other units coming under the control of railroads. Only three of these craft unions are also found in the list of nonoperating employees. The balance are primarily important maritime unions which come under the jurisdiction of the Taft-Hartley Act when engaged in shipping or longshore activities.

EXHIBIT 1.   *Operating and Nonoperating Unions*
Involved in Railroad Labor Relations
(as of June 30, 1970)

Operating Brotherhoods (2)

BLE	Brotherhood of Locomotive Engineers
UTU	United Transportation Union
	Includes since 1969 these former separate unions:

	BLFE	Brotherhood of Locomotive Firemen and Enginemen
	ORCB	Order of Railway Conductors
	BRT	Brotherhood of Railroad Trainmen
	SUNA	Switchmen's Union of North America

Nonoperating Unions (28)

AMS	Association of Mechanical Supervisors
BBF	International Brotherhood of Boilermakers, Iron Shipbuilders, Blacksmiths, Forgers and Helpers
BMWE	Brotherhood of Maintenance of Way Employees
BRASC	Brotherhood of Railway, Airline and Steamship Clerks, Freight Handlers, Express and Station Employees
BRC	Brotherhood of Railway Carmen of America
BRS	Brotherhood of Railroad Signalmen
HREU	Hotel and Restaurant Employees and Bartenders International Union
IAM	International Association of Machinists and Aerospace Workers
IARE	International Association of Railway Employees
IBEW	International Brotherhood of Electrical Workers

IBFO	International Brotherhood of Firemen and Oilers
ITDA	Illinois Train Dispatchers Association
LU	Local Union
MDFA	Mechanical Department Foremen's Association
MMSW	International Union of Mine, Mill and Smelter Workers
MRMFA	Milwaukee Road Mechanical Foremen's Association
RASA	American Railway and Airline Supervisors Association
RED	Railway Employees' Department
RYA	Railroad Yardmasters of America
SA	System Association, Committee or Individual
SCP	Brotherhood of Sleeping Car Porters
SMW	Sheet Metal Workers International Association
TDA	American Train Dispatchers Association
TWU	Transport Workers Union of America, Railroad Division
UMW	United Mine Workers of America
USA	United Steelworkers of America
UTSE	United Transport Service Employees
WRSA	Western Railway Supervisors Association

Marine Unions in Railroading (11)

BRASC	Brotherhood of Railway, Airline and Steamship Clerks, Freight Handlers, Express and Station Employees
GLLO	Great Lakes Licensed Officers' Organization
ILA	International Longshoremen's Association
IUOE	International Union of Operating Engineers
MEBA	National Marine Engineers Beneficial Association
MMP	International Organization of Masters, Mates and Pilots
NMU	National Maritime Union of America
SIU	Seafarers International Union of North America
SIU-IUP	Seafarer's International Union-Inland-boatmen's Union of the Pacific
TWU	Transport Workers Union of America, Railroad Division
UMW	United Mine Workers of America, District 50

Source: Thirty-sixth Annual Report of the National Mediation Board (Washington: G.P.O., 1970), pp. 82-83.

All in all, railroads bargain with over forty different unions and brotherhoods. The evolution of craft unions into the current labor relations pattern for the railroad industry does not provide any influence in the direction of industry stability. Let us look at one carrier, the Penn Central Railroad, and review its actual bargaining situation.

It appears impossible for a major railroad such as the Penn Central Transportation Company to have a comprehensive labor relations policy because of the many unions with which it deals. The Penn Central negotiates with fourteen unions representing twenty crafts or classes of employees: BLE (engineers), UTU (firemen and helpers), UTU (conductors), UTU (brakemen, flagmen, and baggagemen), UTU (yard foremen, helpers, and switchtenders), RYA (yardmasters), BRASC (clerical, office, station, and storehouse), BMWE (maintenance of way employees), BRASC (telegraphers), TDA (dispatchers), IAM (machinists), BBF (boilermakers and blacksmiths), SMW (sheet metal workers), IBEW (electrical workers), TWU (carmen and coach cleaners), IBFO (powerhouse employees and shop laborers), BRS (signalmen), RASA (mechanical foremen and supervisors), UTU (dining car stewards), and TWU (dining car cooks and waiters).

Penn Central also bargains with four maritime unions representing seven crafts: SIU (licensed deck employees), NMU (licensed engineroom employees), SIU (unlicensed deck employees), TWU (unlicensed engineroom employees), ILA (captains, lighters and grain boats), ILA (float-watchmen, bridgemen, and bridge operators), SIU (cooks, chefs, waiters).

The situation in which Penn Central must bargain with seventeen national unions on behalf of twenty-seven different bargaining units is the general rule on major railroads. The process of accommodating a companywide labor relations policy to compensation, fringes, and working conditions in twenty-seven different bargaining units is almost impossible. One union local looks to the performance of the next in terms of improved settlements and working arrangements.

Contract reopeners take place throughout the year with very little respite for the railroad personnel representatives. Since all unions are losing membership, they want very much to represent additional units on the railroads. The UTU is now competing with the BLE to represent engineers on a number of roads and is approaching other bargaining units as well. The TWU and the Teamsters would like to gain additional representation. The SIU and NMU compete in the maritime end of railroad operations in as bitter a fashion as they do in the shipping industry.

Representation Cases, Mediation Cases, and Arbitration Activity

Data from the National Mediation Board [1] reveal the fact that the Railway Labor Act operates throughout the year in a continuing round of efforts devoted to grievance adjustment, problems of representation, and hundreds of mediation cases within each craft. In fiscal 1969, most of the representation problems were in the train, engine, and yard service followed by similar activities in the dining car and pullman group. The vast majority of mediation activity was also in train, engine, and yard service, with the clerical and marine crafts running second and third in order of activity.

It is the writer's conviction that the number of adjustments, representation cases, and mediation efforts in railroads is much greater than would be the case if crafts and unions were not so greatly fragmented.

Long before the Railway Labor Act, craft organization was the established pattern on railroads. The first written labor contract was effectuated between the New York Central & Hudson River Railroad and the Locomotive Engineers in 1875. The contract had no termination date and remained in good standing until amended by the parties. (Lack of a specific termination date is still an industry characteristic. Everything agreed to from time to time becomes an amendment to a continuing contract.)

From the latter part of the nineteenth century until the passage of the RLA in 1926 there evolved a pattern of labor-management relationships leading from local bargaining to regional settlements in the East, Southeast, and West. Carriers were responsive to the unions and created regional conferences, and through informal coordination, regional action developed into national committees. The RLA did not change the character of the bargaining pattern. By 1963, when the National Railway Labor Conference was formally established for permanent industrywide bargaining, 95 percent of all railway workers had already been included under national rules and compensation formulas.[2]

The Railway Labor Act of 1926 continued in its "Section 6 notice" the previous practice of making changes in contracts by amendments, thus obviating the need for contract dates. The act also continued the old practice of organization by "craft."

Current bargaining practice emphasizes serving notice upon individual carriers by the major railway labor unions representing all railroad employees on the major carriers. Included in the union notice is the recommendation that if the carrier cannot effectuate the proposal, it join with other railroad companies in a conference committee and respond in negotiations on a national level. Counterproposals or new proposals by the carriers can be taken to national-level bargaining in the same way, provided that local union officials are so advised by the individual carriers. When negotiations take place at the national level, the unions also establish national conference committees.

When specific issues are bargained nationally, the results must be incorporated into the hundreds of individual contracts throughout the nation. In some cases they apply not to the systemwide carrier but to a single unit or division of the railroad. National bargaining cannot solve all railroad labor-management problems, hence contracts are amended frequently by local craft unions on individual carriers.

The nature of the collective bargaining structure in railroads (many craft unions and many bargaining units) has made the Railway Labor Act less responsive to the needs of the industry under changing technology than would be the case with a national labor law attuned to industrial unionism.

The craft approach was at its best during World War I, a time when the technology of the industry was relatively static. For this reason, when the federal government controlled the American rail industry during that war, it was able to nationalize work rules and rates of pay without difficulty. Detailed statements of work jurisdictions for various crafts were implemented, and when the roads returned to private operations, the standard rules were made a lasting part of the railroad contracts—and remain in effect today despite radical changes in rail technology since the 1940's.

The introduction of diesels resulted in more trips, more tonnage, and less mechanical servicing. Automatic signals replaced telegraphy; train movement now utilizes the computer for car classification; improved roadbeds and rails also opened new avenues of productivity. As trucking developed into a mammoth competitor, branch lines were abandoned; airlines and private cars curtailed passenger train service; while mergers, consolidations, and reorganizations also adversely affected craft union membership. Changing technology and reduced passenger and freight service made the craft unions restive. The nonoperating unions also were concerned with job security in the face of increasing "contracting-out" of work considered the "property" of the various crafts, as well as the swift reduction in the number of carriers (from 105 in 1966 to 79 in 1970) because of mergers and bankruptcies.

The Report of the Presidential Railroad Commission in 1962 was followed by the arbitration award of the Seward Board and various federal court reviews antagonistic to interests of the craft unions, which desired to keep work rules static.

Had the railorad industry been served by an industrial union, the varying interests of each craft might have been debated and negotiated in its councils. Instead, craft unions have in recent years begun once more to attack the carriers, craft by craft, in an effort to stabilize declining memberships. In the 1920's, rail employment amounted to 2,000,000. By 1944, it had been reduced to 1,400,000 and by 1969 was down to 575,000.

Reductions in Railroad Employment by Craft

Data from reports of the Interstate Commerce Commission [3] show drastic reductions in the employment of many railroad crafts in the period 1950 to 1969. Dieselization and less passenger and freight service reduced employment of firemen on passenger trains by 73 percent and of freight firemen by 65 percent. The virtual extinction of firemen jobs coupled with a 67 percent reduction in passenger engineers and a 25 percent cutback in freight engineers created bitter dissatisfaction in those crafts, which undermines railroad labor relations today. The 10,600 passenger and freight firemen who still are employed on Class I railroads have little hope for upward movement to the position of engineer, a normal expectation for the past one hundred years.

Along with the decline in passenger service, passenger brakemen's jobs were reduced by 77 percent and those of freight brakemen by 24 percent because of yard automation. This pattern of technological change coupled with displacement was also characteristic of the yards, where the reduction in yard masters amounted to 18 percent; yard brakemen, 21 percent; yard engineers, 12 percent; yard firemen, 65 percent; and switchtenders, 75 percent.

In the shops, the conversion from steam to diesel locomotives reduced operations, and contracting-out resulted in serious displacement of nonoperating employees with these reductions during the two decades: blacksmiths, 73 percent; boilermakers, 84 percent; molders, 90 percent; carmen, 43 percent; machinists, 57 percent; and skilled trades helpers and apprentices, 87 percent.

In communications, employment of clerk-telegraphers fell by 61 percent and of telegraphers by 51 percent. Automation of controls and signal devices rendered these formerly important crafts "unessential"; where employment still exists, the work is largely clerical. The power of the small craft union is demonstrated, however, by what occurred in 1962, when 15,500 employees of the Chicago and North Western Railway honored a picket line set up by the telegraphers on that road. A major tie-up of train service in the Midwest and Great Plains states resulted in a strike lasting thirty days. An arbitration award finally led to a job stabilization plan for telegraphers on the struck road as well as the New York Central Railroad.

The principle of seniority in the various crafts of the rail industry creates serious disagreements and labor unrest when employment is reduced. Job security becomes a highly sensitive issue, and emphasis on traditional work rules impedes management efforts to make changes. As the average age of those retained in employment rises, job security issues become more serious in each craft negotiation.

Craft Rivalry and Whipsawing

For several decades the Railway Labor Executives Association, working closely with the Railway Employes' Department, AFL-CIO, provided the leadership for coordinated bargaining for the many shop-craft unions. During the periodic negotiations which took place on a national basis, the seventeen nonoperating unions often prepared for negotiations by first settling among themselves what the package of demands would be. The negotiation packages for many years satisfied both management and the shop-craft unions by providing the same flat rate cents-per-hour increases for all shop-craft employees. These uniform increases eliminated whipsawing on management but over the years created acute problems of wage compression between skilled and semi-skilled workers, since only percentage increases could maintain the same internal wage equities. About seven years ago, the unions began to feel pressure from members who saw other industries giving much superior compensation rewards to workers with skills similar to their own.

A split occurred among the "nonops" in 1964 when the Railway Employes' Department represented only six of the seventeen shop-craft unions in that year's negotiations, and during the bargaining sessions, the Electrical Workers, Machinists, and Sheet Metal Workers won percentage increases rather than the cents-per-hour adjustments received by the three other unions.

In 1967, the same six nonoperating unions (IAM, BBF, SMW, IBEW, BRC, and IBFO) negotiated together and directed their energies toward rewarding skill and ending wage compression. During the negotiations, however, dissension developed over how to determine the degree of skill and amount of increase for each craft. May 3, 1967, was the date set for a nationwide strike. While legislation was being debated, strikes took place on July 16 and 17. On the latter day, Public Law 90-54 terminated the stoppages. On October 16, 1967, the findings of a Presidential board appointed under the statute confirmed the findings of an earlier board but augmented its award with additional increases for journeymen and mechanics.

A year later, the skill issue caused a further split among the shop-craft unions, and only the IBEW, IAM, SMW, and BBF bargained together. The two other unions (BRC and IBFO) went their separate ways.

After negotiations which extended from November 1968 through October 1969, a Nixon emergency board recommended what appeared to be a satisfactory wage increase and other adjustments to end "compression." With the help of the U.S. Labor Department, postboard negotiations appeared to be on their way to an equitable settlement. To the consternation of the nation, the long-drawn-out agreement was rejected under the unions' unit rule, which provided that none of the unions accept an agreement unless all accept it. Members of the Machinists, Electrical Workers, and Boilermakers unions ratified the settlement; but the Sheet Metal Workers rejected it fearing that jobs eventually might be eliminated because of a work rule change which would permit workers in a particular craft to spend up to 50 percent of their time performing work in another craft. Negotiations were resumed on January 19, 1970.

By March 1970, the negotiators found themselves in a complete impasse, with SMW still blocking a settlement. A strike was set for March 5, 1970, Congress acted almost immediately by passing legislation creating a thirty-seven-day prohibition on work stoppages in the dispute. The law was to expire on April 11, 1970. On April 10, President Nixon signed a new law imposing on all four unions the terms of the December 1969 settlement. The fact that Congress had to deal with unit rule indicates how difficult it is becoming to have uniformity in national bargaining with so many different craft unions involved.

Airline Labor Troubles

Sixteen unions fragment bargaining in airlines. Exhibit 2 shows that all but two airlines bargain with the International Air Line Pilots Association. At American, an insurgent and now autonomous local union, the Allied Pilots Association, took over in 1963. At Trans-International Airlines, Inc., the Teamsters succeeded ALPA in 1970.

Flight engineer bargaining units survive only at American, Eastern, Flying Tiger, National, Northwest, Pan American, Seaboard, Trans-International, Trans World, and Western. The Flight Engineers' International Association represents engineers at American, National, and Pan American, while the pilots (ALPA) have taken over at Eastern, Flying Tiger, TWA, and Western. The Teamsters represent engineers at Seaboard and Trans-International, and the Machinists are in control at Northwest Airlines, Inc. Last year ALPA took over at Flying Tiger by defeating the Teamsters.

In the early 1960's the FEIA was a powerful union, representing personnel at most of the major air carriers, but a series of Presidential emergency board decisions aimed at reducing crew size cut into the power of the union.

A landmark blow against FEIA took place in January 1961, when in Case R-3463 a board ruled that all flight-deck crew members on United Air Lines, Inc. in job classifications of pilot or captain, reserve pilot, copilot, second officer, or flight engineer constituted one craft or class. Following an election, the Pilots' union was certified for this craft or class.[4]

EXHIBIT 2. Employee Representation on Selected Air Carriers
(as of June 30, 1970)

Airline	Pilots	Flight Engineers	Flight Navigators	Flight Dispatchers	Stewardesses and Pursers	Radio and Teletype Operators	Mechanics	Clerical Office, Stores, Fleet and Passenger Service	Stock and Stores
Airlift, International	ALPA		TWU	ALDA	ALPA		AMFA	ALEA*	IBT
Air West, Inc.	ALPA			LU	ALPA		IAM	ALEA*	IAM
Allegheny Airlines, Inc.	APA	FEIA		ALDA	TWU	TWU	IAM		IAM
American Airlines, Inc.	ALPA	FEIA		ADA	ALPA	CWA	IAM	TWU*	TWU
Braniff International	ALPA			ALDA	ALPA		IAM	IBT*	IBT
Continental Airlines, Inc.	ALPA			ALDA			IAM		IAM
Delta Air Lines, Inc.	ALPA								
Eastern Air Lines, Inc.	ALPA	ALPA	TWU	ALDA	TWU	CWA	IAM	IAM*	IAM
Flying Tiger Lines, Inc.	ALPA	ALPA			IBT		IAM		IAM
Frontier Airlines, Inc.	ALPA			ALDA	ALPA		IAM	ALEA	
Los Angeles Airways, Inc.	ALPA			ALDA	ALPA		IBT	IAM*	IBT
Mohawk Airlines, Inc.	ALPA			ALDA	ALPA		IAM		IAM
National Airlines, Inc.	ALPA	FEIA		ALDA	ALPA	CWA	IAM	ALEA*	IAM
North Central Airlines, Inc.	ALPA			ALDA	ALPA		IAM	ALEA*	IAM
Northeast Airlines, Inc.	ALPA		TWU	ALDA	TWU	TWU	IAM	TWU	**
Northwest Airlines, Inc.	ALPA	IAM		ALDA	TWU	TWU	IAM	BRASC*	IAM
Ozark Air Lines, Inc.	ALPA			ALDA	TWU	IBT	IAM	IAM*	IBT
Pan American World Airways, Inc.	ALPA	FEIA		ALDA	TWU		AMFA	IBT*	IBT
Piedmont Airlines, Inc.	ALPA				ALPA		TWU		
Seaboard World Airlines, Inc.	IBT	IBT	TWU	ALDA	IGFA	TWU	TWU		
Southern Airways, Inc.	ALPA			ALDA	TWU		IAM		TWU
Trans-International Airlines, Inc.***	ALPA	IBT	IBT	ALDA	IBT	ALEA	IAM	ALEA*	IAM
Trans World Airlines, Inc.	ALPA		TWU	TWU	TWU	CWA	IAM		IAM
United Air Lines, Inc.	ALPA	ALPA	TWU	ALDA	ALPA	CWA	IAM		IAM
Western Air Lines, Inc.	ALPA	ALPA		ALDA	ALPA	CWA	IBT	BRASC*	IBT

* Only a portion of the craft or class.

** Included in clerical, office, stores, fleet and passenger.

*** Formerly Trans-Texas.

Source: *Thirty-sixth Annual Report of the National Mediation Board* (Washington: G.P.O., 1970), p. 81.

EXHIBIT 3. *All Craft Unions in the Airline Industry*
(as of June 30, 1970)

ADA	Air Transport Dispatchers Association
ALCEA	Air Line Communications Employees Association
ALDA	Air Line Dispatchers Association
ALEA	Air Line Employees Association
ALPA	Air Line Pilots Association
AMFA	Aircraft Mechanics Fraternal Association
APA	Allied Pilots Association
BRASC	Brotherhood of Railway, Airline and Steamship Clerks, Freight Handlers, Express and Station Employees
CWA	Communications Workers of America
FEIA	Flight Engineers' International Association
IAM	International Association of Machinists and Aerospace Workers
IBT	International Brotherhood of Teamsters, Chauffeurs, Warehousemen and Helpers of America
IGFA	International Guild of Flight Attendants
LU	Local Union
OPEIU	Office and Professional Employees International Union
TWU	Transport Workers Union of America

Source: Thirty-sixth Annual Report of the National Mediation Board (Washington: G.P.O., 1970), p. 83.

The rivalry between ALPA and FEIA at United had been going on since 1955, when jurisdictional rivalry between the two resulted in a fifty-one-day strike. Even in the 1950's, United wanted only flight engineers who were trained as pilots.

The 1961 decision at United caused FEIA members at American, Pan American, TWA, Eastern, National, Flying Tiger, and Western to strike in protest of the United decision. This illegal strike by FEIA showed airlines the resistance they could expect from craft unions when technological changes required alteration of work rules.

Exhibit 2 shows that ALPA now represents flight engineers at Eastern Airlines. In 1962, an emergency board at Eastern recommended a gradual reduction in crew size. Angered by the board's report, FEIA went on a long strike against Eastern on June 23, 1962, an action from which the union never recovered. Eastern assigned furloughed pilots to be flight engineers. FEIA complained, without success, to the Federal Aviation Agency that Eastern should not permit pilots to assume flight engineer responsibilities after only sixty hours of engineering training. The strike was ineffective, and picketing went on for several years before the FEIA local at Eastern finally dissolved.

Flight navigators are represented by TWU on six airlines, while the Teamsters control one bargaining unit. Automation is gradually phasing out this craft, but unions bitterly resist change.

Flight dispatchers are generally represented by the Air Line Dispatchers Association (ALDA); TWU also controls a number of similar units; while the Air Transport Dispatchers Association (ADA) is still at Braniff.

Radio operators are fragmented among four competing unions: CWA controls five units; TWU, four; the Teamsters, one; and ALEA, one.

In reviewing the unions representing the clerical, office, stores, fleet and passenger service workers, it becomes obvious that all airline unions are extending their traditional jurisdictions to include crafts they did not originally represent. This creates bitterness, competition, and instability. IAM, which generally bargains for the airline mechanics, also represents clerical groups on three airlines. ALEA controls six clerical units; TWU, two; Teamsters, two; and BRASC, two. The Machinists union also represents stores and stock workers on twelve airlines; while the Teamsters control six units; and TWU, two.

IAM is one of the very powerful unions in the airline industry. It represents machinists on sixteen airlines. TWU bargains for two units; the Teamsters, two; and AMFA, two.

When the stewardesses set up a picket line, planes do not fly! In the early 1960's this group was generally represented by the Air Line Stewards and Stewardesses Association (ALSSA). The pilots (ALPA) now have taken over bargaining rights for the "girls" and stewards on thirteen airlines. TWU bargains for this group on seven airlines. The Teamsters control units on two smaller airlines and IGFA now is reduced to one unit.

There is little similarity in the patterns of the organizing activities of the airline unions. If one compares the data relating to Eastern and Pan American in Exhibit 2, it will be noted that in seven crafts, the two carriers have the same unions only for pilots, stewardesses, and flight dispatchers.

Airline Disputes: Representation and Mediation in 1969

A decade ago thirty-seven representation cases involved only 8,600 airline employees. In 1969, thirty-two representation cases involved 28,200 employees. Data from the National Mediation Board reveal that most of the mediation activity in fiscal 1969 involved the mechanics craft, while most of the representation problems centered on clerical, office, and stores employees. Activities involving pilot, engineer, and stewardess units were relatively low.[5]

Evaluation of the merits of the Nixon proposal to place airlines under the Taft-Hartley Act requires comparison of the present bargaining pattern under the RLA with what might be expected from the change. Carriers have complained for years about the ability of a single union, because of the craft basis of representation, to shut down an airline. There is no doubt that transfer of the industry to Taft-Hartley may weaken the strong national airline unions by "introducing into the airline industry the effect of multitudinous units of representation, which are more the rule under Taft-Hartley, the outlawing of the union shop in 'right-to-work' states, the encouragement of dissidents and minority groups in unions. . . ."[6]

While the fragmentation under RLA is clear, a change in the overriding statute controlling airline labor without a complete change in union structure is not the answer. Would there be more representation disputes under Taft-Hartley? Bargaining presently is based on systemwide bargaining units. Under Taft-Hartley it might be possible that a national carrier such as TWA would face both systemwide bargaining and "bargaining units established on a 'station' basis in some sort of industrial unit organization."[7] Charles Redenius takes the position that even greater proliferation of bargaining units might occur under Taft-Hartley than under the RLA and favors making changes in RLA which would take advantage of the procedures in the act which work well, while improving the governance of disputes. Redenius recognizes that ALPA, BRASC, IAM, and TWU are large and powerful unions and recommends that RLA be amended to include a code of unfair labor practices "[to] be prescribed for airline labor unions," inasmuch as "RLA presently defines and proscribes unfair labor practices for employers." [8]

Over the years there has evolved in the airline industry a single carrier-single union pattern of bargaining which is different from the rail bargaining pattern under the same act. The Machinists' strike against five carriers in 1966 was an exception. Of the thirty-three Presidential emergency boards created in the years 1936 to 1969 to investigate airline disputes, only six had more than one carrier and one union as parties to the dispute.

The dispute pattern has developed partly from the fact that "airline unions have to organize and to represent a relatively small, widely dispersed and heterogeneous labor force." [9] The pressure of automation and changing technology have contributed to a sense of union insecurity and prospects of unemployment.

In the years 1936-1969, thirty-three emergency boards were created in the airline industry, with two thirds of them created in the years 1955-1966. "Most of these coincided with the introduction of the jet plane and centered on work rules for ground employees and manning issues for flight deck personnel. In the last seven airline emergency boards, which were confined to ground crafts, wages was the prime issue." [10]

While there have been few emergency boards over the years, the multiplicity of unions has resulted in 1,465 airline mediation cases, of which only 63, however, required the final step of the procedure. [11]

It appears that there is a considerable difference between "national emergencies" under the Taft-Hartley Act and the use to which airline emergency boards are put under the RLA.

Only five of the fourteen unions which have large memberships have been involved in emergency board procedures: ALPA (eleven times); IAM (eleven times); FEIA (seven times); TWU (seven times); BRASC (two times).

Maritime and Longshore Labor Troubles

Maritime labor (seamen, longshoremen, and tugmen) has been the most volatile of all labor groups during the past twenty-five years. The shipping industry has been brought to a standstill on numerous occasions. The record has been bad over time.

In addition to the application of the Taft-Hartley injunction to maritime strikes, an October 1, 1968, injunction against a strike by East Coast longshoremen represented the seventh consecutive use of the injunctive procedure in this continuously disrupted and chaotic industry.

Labor unions and leaders have had a bitter and competitive history. The labor relations picture in the maritime industry possesses some archaic elements. Bitter interunion rivalries have resulted from wounds left by unsuccessful organizing campaigns and jurisdictional disputes of long ago. Furthermore, the personal ambitions of leaders such as Joseph Curran (NMU), Paul Hall (SIU), Harry Bridges (ILWU), and Thomas W. Gleason (ILA) contribute much to conflict and disorganization. The scope of craft union representation is indicated in Exhibit 4. Employer groups categorized in Exhibit 5 are also greatly fragmented for economic and geographic reasons and tend to further complicate the picture.

Certain craft unions historically have been in ideological conflict with each other. Curran is an ex-CIO leader, and Hall is an heir apparent to George Meany. Moreover, the terms "communist" and "radical" have not been used with restraint in describing certain maritime leaders and organizations. Of major importance to the two principal chiefs, Curran and Hall, is the division and control of a declining number of jobs in the maritime industry. Because of constant job erosion, both the SIU and NMU coalitions are in agreement on the importance of organizing the six hundred-odd, American-owned, "foreign-flag" vessels (mostly tankers and ore carriers) now registered principally in Liberia, Panama, and Honduras and employing alien crews, whose wages are about one quarter of those paid on U.S.-flag vessels.

A decision of the United States Supreme Court on February 18, 1963,[12] overruled prior findings of the National Labor Relations Board and denied to American maritime unions the right to organize crews of foreign flagships because the vessels are American owned or engaged extensively in U.S. trade. Though the adverse Supreme Court decision was a blow to the seafaring unions, attempts have been made (and will continue) to organize these "runaway" vessels through the maritime section of the worldwide International Transportation Federation (ITF), and by constant pressure at home. With automation a distinct possibility, maritime unions prefer to increase their jurisdictions rather than lose membership.

A major difficulty among both employer groups and unions is intense fragmentation which leads to jurisdictional conflict, bitter competition among union leaders, and resulting inability to develop constructive, cohesive labor-management policies. These facts contribute to the decline in the U.S. position as a world maritime power.

Exhibit 4 shows that sixteen maritime labor unions operate in the shipping and longshore field. The number of unions is of less importance than the fact that there are two rival coalitions of unions headed by Paul Hall of SIU and Joseph Curran of NMU.

EXHIBIT 4. *Unions Involved in Maritime Labor Relations (as of June 30, 1970)*

Designation	Maritime Labor Union
AMMSOA	American Merchant Marine Staff Officers Association (purser department on the Atlantic Coast)
ARA	American Radio Association (ship radio officers on the Atlantic, Gulf, and Pacific coasts)
BMO	Brotherhood of Marine Officers (deck and engineering officers on the Atlantic Coast)
ILA	International Longshoremen's Association (dock workers on the Gulf and East coasts and Great Lakes)
ILWU	International Longshoremen's and Warehousemen's Union (dock workers on the West Coast)
MEBA	National Marine Engineers' Beneficial Association (engineering officers on the Atlantic, Gulf, and Pacific coasts)
MCS	Marine Cooks, and Stewards Association (stewards, cooks, etc. on the West Coast—autonomous affiliate of Pacific Coast District of SIU)
MFOW	Pacific Coast Marine Firemen, Oilers, Watertenders and Wipers Association (several departments, including stewards, on the West Coast)
MFU	Marine Firemen's Union (West Coast—autonomous affiliate of Pacific Coast District of SIU)
MMP	International Organization of Masters, Mates and Pilots (masters and deck officers on the Atlantic, Pacific, and Gulf coasts)
NMU	National Maritime Union of America (unlicensed personnel of the deck, engine, and stewards' departments, primarily on the Atlantic and Gulf coasts)
ROU	Radio Officers Union of the Commercial Telegraphers Union (ship radio officers on the Atlantic, Gulf, and Pacific coasts)

Exhibit 4. *(Continued).*

Designation	Maritime Labor Union
SIU	Seafarers International Union of North America (unlicensed personnel of the deck, engine, and stewards' departments on the Atlantic, Gulf, and Pacific coasts)
SOA	Staff Officers' Association of America (pursers on the Atlantic and Gulf coasts)
SUP	Sailors' Union of the Pacific (unlicensed personnel in the deck, engine, and stewards' departments on the West Coast—autonomous affiliate of the Pacific Coast District of SIU)
UMD	United Marine Division of the National Maritime Union (tugboat crews, primarily on the East Coast)

Source: Files and special releases of the U.S. Maritime Administration.

Jurisdictional Disputes in Shipping

Historically, when unions were locked in a bitter jurisdictional dispute, the deck officer, engineer, crew member, and longshore unions lined up with their respective chiefs. Occasionally, however, one satellite would deal with the rival leader, thus complicating the bargaining patterns. Special tradeoffs or advantages would lead a satellite union to leave the coalition. Often the MEBA, the MMP, or the ARA would break away from traditional allies when pressuring for a special advantage.

Traditionally, the ILWU, headed by Bridges, would support the NMU by attempting to negate Hall's powerful SIU leadership on the West Coast. On the East Coast, the ILA was traditionally hostile to Curran's NMU leadership. NMU and ILWU were former CIO allies, while SIU and ILA had a shared AFL tradition. Recently, Gleason's ILA has been supportive of Curran.

Examples of extreme fragmentation are often found aboard the vessels themselves. Several years ago the Veritas Steamship Line was staffed with SIU seamen and ROU radio officers. However, on the Union Sulphur and Oil Company vessels, the SUP (the West Coast organization of SIU) had to work with ARA radiomen. Both lines had MEBA engineers on board. During the same period U.S. Line vessels were staffed with NMU seamen, SOA staff officers, MMP deck officers, ROU radio officers, and

MEBA engineers.[13] Any lineup is possible, and what appears to be a friendly ship can rapidly balkanize because of an adverse arbitration award which sets one union against another and makes for rapidly shifting alliances.

Over the years the "fleetwide" issue has made for trouble. Assume that a vessel with a crew consisting of NMU, ARA, and BMO members belongs to a fleet in which all vessels have the same unions. The single vessel is then sold to a West Coast steamship line with a fleet in which all vessels have crews belonging to SIU-SUP, MEBA, and ROU. What happens? The NMU crew tries to save its membership affiliation and jobs. The case could wind up with the National Labor Relations Board, where a decision could be made to look at the vessel in question as a single bargaining unit despite the maintenance of the "fleetwide" principle by the AFL-CIO internal disputes section. On the West Coast, friction could develop into a waterfront struggle, with the ILWU, Curran's ally, refusing to unload any SIU-led ships in the fleet until the matter was settled.

Exhibit 5 shows that bargaining patterns on a national, coastal, or regional basis predominate. On the East Coast, NMU and SIU integrate many crafts into two organizations. On the West Coast, cooperative bargaining is engaged in by the separate unions representing various categories of unlicensed personnel.

EXHIBIT 5. *Pattern of Bargaining in the U.S. Maritime Industry*

East Coast and Gulf Coast

Employer group:

A. Maritime Service Committee (MSC) (mostly dry cargo, subsidized lines)

   Negotiates with six unions: MMP, MEBA, ARA, ROU, SOA, and NMU

B. Tanker Service Committee (TSC) (tankers)

   Negotiates with six unions: MMP, MEBA, ARA, ROU, SOA, NMU, and with independent labor associations structured on a company basis

C. American Maritime Association (mostly dry cargo, unsubsidized) (East Coast and Gulf)

   Negotiates with four unions: MMP, ARA, ROU, SOA, with special locals of MEBA, and with SIU

West Coast

Employer group:

  A. Pacific Maritime Association (mostly dry cargo)

       Negotiates with eight unions: MMP, MEBA, ARA, SOA, SUP, MFU, MCS, and ILWU

  B. West Coast Tanker Operators (tankers)

       Negotiates *individually* with SUP for all unlicensed seamen on their ships

Source: Files and special releases of the U.S. Maritime Administration.

Employer Associations are Influential

Employer groups have developed as a result of history, geography, and economic influences. On the Atlantic Coast, the American Merchant Marine Institute, which formerly represented the federally subsidized lines, has now been replaced by the Maritime Service Committee (MSC) for dry-cargo ships and the Tanker Service Committee (TSC) for tankers. The two groups are coordinated by a common chairman. MSC and TSC negotiate with MMP, MEBA, ARA, ROU, SOA, NMU, and in the case of tankers, with independent labor associations on a company basis.

The American Maritime Association is an employer group of unsubsidized companies in the dry-cargo field. It negotiates for employers on the Atlantic and Gulf Coasts and was formed as the outcome of informal negotiations by unsubsidized employers with SIU. It negotiates with SIU and MMP, ARA, ROU, and SOA on East and Gulf coasts.

A very formal arrangement is found on the West Coast, with the Pacific Maritime Association including all U.S.-flag dry-cargo operators. This multiemployer group has a bargaining committee which negotiates with MMP, MEBA, ARA, SOA, SUP, MFU, and MSC. Those members who do not go along with the majority in approving the agreement cannot remain in the multiemployer group. The Pacific Maritime Association also negotiates with the ILWU on longshore contracts for its regular membership plus foreign-flag lines and stevedoring companies.

On the East Coast, the New York Shipping Association negotiates with ILA and sets the pattern for all Gulf and East coast ports. Its master agreement, however, must be approved port by port. The union hiring hall, emphasizing seniority, has provided a steady labor force to meet industry requirements for shipping association members. Changing technology, automation, larger tankers, and container ships create employment uncertainties for the unions involved, and they are cognizant that the present 967-ship U.S.-flag fleet will decline to 630 ships by 1980, even with new construction. The expectation is that this will eliminate about 18,000 jobs.[14] As the result, the unions want tightened work rules, better pensions with less service, retraining, and guarantees against displacement. Maritime unions are also considering coalition bargaining on a national basis instead of coastal or regional bargaining. National rather than coastal standards on wages and working conditions may yet be attained. In the face of possible national collective bargaining, the employer groups appear weak and fragmented. On this point William E. Simkin has commented:

> On the employer side, strong employer associations exist in railroads but not in [maritime]. . . . In maritime, the only strong association is the Pacific Maritime Association. . . . It is not just happenstance that both maritime and longshore on the West Coast had a much better record than on the East Coast and Gulf Coast. Much as we dislike bigness, effectual employer organization is essential.[15]

Despite the fact that maritime unions are under the National Labor Relations Act, unions of officers have bargaining rights. This circumstance differs from the legal prohibition on supervisory unions observed in other industries. When masters, mates, engineers, and radio officers get together with unlicensed seamen in a SIU or NMU coalition it suggests that industrial unionism is not far off. Unfortunately, however, the strategy of the two opposing coalitions is "rule or ruin."

Prior to the labor troubles of 1961 and 1962, the NMU coalition led by Joe Curran included MMP, ARA, and ILWU. The unions following Paul Hall of the SIU were the MEBA, ROU, and the ILA. During the 1961 strike, loyalties among employers and union alliances began to shift and contributed adversely to the chance for settlement. Fragmentation of both employer and employee groups made communications difficult. Six employer groups had to be consulted on three different coasts on subjects which varied greatly in their impact on each group. Major differences in attitudes of the various employer groups depended on whether they were subsidized or unsubsidized. For example, the Pacific

Maritime Association, not owning "flag-of-convenience" vessels, readily agreed to a demand by MEBA not to employ nonunion aliens on foreign-flag vessels which they owned or might own. This quick agreement whipsawed eastern employers who were contending on the same issue with the NMU coalition.

In the early period of the labor troubles in 1961, MMP appeared to be in the SIU camp but later returned to the NMU fold. MEBA held to its pact with SIU, and since many NMU crews served on vessels with contracts with MEBA, complex pressures prevented a national contract from being signed at one time. Furthermore, it was evident at one point that the American Merchant Marine Institute and the Tanker Service Committee could come to an agreement with NMU but that such an understanding would have to be deferred until the employers could come to an agreement with ROU and MMP. ROU remained an SIU satellite, while MMP vacillated between the two unions for a long time.

Another complication barring settlement was the whipsawing of nonsubsidized employers. The NMU's major strength was on the scheduled subsidized lines, where approximately 80 percent of the total wage bill was to be paid by Uncle Sam.[16] SIU's strength was on tankers and nonsubsidized West Coast U.S.-flag tramp ships.

Further Evolution of Major Maritime Coalitions

Recently Gleason, the powerful leader of ILA, disassociated himself from the SIU coalition and joined the NMU ranks. This break with AFL tradition appeared to have been caused by several events: (1) growing friendship between SIU's Hall and Anthony Scotto, a Brooklyn officer of ILA, who is opposing Gleason's authority within ILA;[17] (2) a sense of insecurity with respect to port automation which Gleason shares with Bridges of ILWU and concern of both men over impending Teamster competition; and (3) Gleason's resignation as vice-president of the Maritime Trades Department of AFL-CIO chaired by Paul Hall.

On December 5, 1967, a new AFL-CIO Maritime Committee was announced by NMU's Curran[18] which included ARA (1,000 ship officers), ILA (116,000 longshoremen), MMP (11,500 deck officers), MEBA (11,500 engineers), and NMU (55,000 seamen). Also in the coalition were 3,000 Great Lakes' seamen, belonging to the USA (steelworkers), and 70,000 members of the Union of Marine and Shipbuilding Workers. The main product of the Curran federation was the organization of an interunion port council in each major port city. The port council had great power since longshore workers were included in the local confederation.

Meanwhile Paul Hall had not been idle with his own AFL-CIO Maritime Trades Department, which included his traditional SIU coalition of SUP and satellite West Coast unions plus an announced strength of about 6,000,000 members from primarily nonmaritime unions such as retail clerk, laborer, bricklayer, butcher, and carpenter unions. Hall's argument in including nonmaritime unions in his coalition was that all major U.S. unions have a stake in the import-export picture of the United States. Some experts [19] believe that Hall is working closely with nonmaritime unions to strengthen his chances as a possible successor to George Meany.

Conclusions

The fact that the Taft-Hartley Act is given a better evaluation by the Nixon Administration than is the Railway Labor Act does not carry too much weight with this writer. When one reviews the longshore crises since 1962, it is clear that there is potentially as much labor trouble under the Taft-Hartley Act as under the Railway Labor Act.

The preceding discussion has tried to make the point that union fragmentation in the rail, air, and maritime industries contributes heavily to labor unrest and that the craft arrangements in these industries block responsiveness to the need for technological change and create rigid work-rule restrictions. This is true not only in rail and air, where craft and class are emphasized by the Railway Labor Act, but also in maritime which falls under the Taft-Hartley Act. Trucking and the Teamsters are also fragmented, but for a different reason, namely, the gradual disintegration of Hoffa's strong central control over the local units and regional councils.

It is apparent that the Railway Labor Act does not encourage bargaining. The emergency provisions of the act worked well in the early years, but as the representatives of the craft unions and of management realized what was possible, both parties bargained with less good faith. Carriers and unions have assumed the stance that an emergency board will always move in with its own recommendations when a strike is threatened. Why, then, bargain meaningfully? The parties now wait for the board's recommendations and bargain more meaningfully after disclosure. The board device originally was designed to be the last stage of bargaining; now it is the first genuine stage. Furthermore, postboard bargaining is not the end. After the parties disagree once more, they know the federal government will intervene—as it did three times recently in the case of the railroads—by passage of special legislation to stop strikes. The RLA influences the parties to widen rather than narrow the area of bargaining, since it is believed that an emergency panel always will split the difference.

The role of the National Adjustment Board in arbitrating the thousands of annual grievances could better be assumed by the parties themselves by stipulating arbitration as the final step of the grievance procedure in their own contracts. This would save taxpayers a substantial sum and would require a more mature approach to grievance handling by the parties. Rail contracts should have termination dates as in private industry and no longer be amended simply by "notice."

The writer is in favor of one National Labor Relations Act. Eliminating the Railway Labor Act would improve understanding and communication between our citizens and labor-management institutions in transportation. The life of the citizen and businessman is becoming more and more involved in the interruptions to transportation services by all four major segments. The average citizen strives to understand the differences in procedure between the Taft-Hartley and Railway Labor Acts but is frustrated by their complexity.

The National Mediation Board has been overscrupulous in defining "craft" and "class" to match the jurisdictional claims of the standard unions. While the purpose of the board was to create stability and discourage work interruptions by lessening competition for representation in rail and air, it has had the opposite effect. Had the airline pilots chosen to come under the Wagner Act in 1936, there would have been a chance to develop industrial unionism in the airline industry. Instead, the Airline Pilots Association feared the Wagner Act might be declared unconstitutional, as was the National Industrial Recovery Act; hence, they chose the Railway Labor Act of 1926 as their statute.

The fact that the Railway Labor Act has no antifeatherbedding rule, unlike Taft-Hartley, is doubtless partially responsible for the active resistance of rail and airline unions to displacement of firemen on diesels, to the railroad "crew-consist" issue, and to displacement of flight engineers in the nation's airlines.

NMB as Merely a Regulatory Agency?

The Nixon proposal also would deprive the National Mediation Board of its mediation functions, leaving it simply as a regulatory agency. Should the mediation function be transferred to the Federal Mediation and Conciliation Service as recommended?

The writer believes that the consolidation would enrich the mediation resources available. Mediators in transportation disputes have had excessive exposure to rail and air problems and are somewhat "inbred." Each nontransportation industry (steel, automobiles, mining, etc.) has unique characteristics and equally difficult problems. Perhaps mediators have been overly conditioned to the special-privilege legislation of the rail and airline industries. A change which would employ the services of the outstanding FMCS mediators is bound to be beneficial to the labor relations climate in transportation.

Although a consolidated national labor law is a step in the right direction, this change and legislation providing "final-offer selection" will not assure better labor relations in transportation. There has to be a basic change in union structure—from the craft union concept to the industrial union concept.

In the early 1940's, the Air Line Pilots Association announced a plan for affiliation with other craft groups. It proposed an Airline Stewards and Stewardesses Association, an Airline Agents Association, an Air Carriers Flight Engineers Association, an Air Carriers Communication Employees Association, and so on. The master plan failed, and the present fragmentation and whipsawing resulted.

While the unions in the airline industry are generally autonomous, there have been many instances of interunion cooperation. First of all, rarely will union members cross a picket line. There have been examples of considerable financial aid exchanged over the years between FEIA and TWU; between FEIA and the Teamsters, and in 1957, ALPA and IAM signed a mutual-assistance pact.

In 1959, an airline coordinating committee was established to settle jurisdictional disputes, combat the carriers' Mutual Aid Pact, and resist the entrance of the Teamsters into the freight handling activity. The consortium consisted of IAM, TWU, ALPA, FEIA, BRASC, and ALDA.

This indicates there is opportunity for a council arrangement in the airlines similar to the ILGWU and ACWA "joint boards" in the ladies' and men's apparel industries. Recently, the stewardesses at most airlines have joined with ALPA, and there has been some broadening of bargaining units by unions such as ALPA, IBT, TWU, and IAM (as noted in Exhibit 2).

In the railroad industry, there is indication that consideration is being given by the unions to eliminating fragmentation. On January 1, 1969, the United Transportation Union (UTU) was formed, consisting of the former unions—ORCB, BLFE, BRT, and SUNA. On the Penn Central Railroad, UTU now also represents dining car stewards and may continue to add constituencies.

The Presidential Railroad Commission in its report in 1962 stated: "On the side of labor, there is equal need for review and reorganization. . . . The time has come to create by merger one engine service and one train service labor organization." [20]

Other mergers have taken place within the past two years. On February 20, 1969, telegraphers and clerks became part of one organization through the merger of the Transportation-Communication Employees Union into the Brotherhood of Railway, Airline and Steamship Clerks. This increased the membership of BRASC from about 270,000 to over 300,000. The BRASC had earlier (December 1969) incorporated the 2,500-member Railway Patrolmen's Union, and BRASC continues to look for mergers. Also, a recent merger of two national yardmasters' organizations took place.

With continuous reductions in the number of American railroads because of merger or bankruptcy, it is evident the federal government will become more involved—almost to the point of ownership.

After fighting union opposition to its birth, Amtrak (a federally subsidized and administered corporation) emerged from several court battles to take over most of the nation's long-haul passenger rail service on May 1, 1971. Because Amtrak is aiming for profitability, it reduced by one third the number of intercity passenger trains (from 285 to 197), which caused the nation's rail unions to view the new corporation with hatred and distaste. A massive managerial reorganization requires an equally massive labor reorganization. Movement to an industrial union structure is becoming essential, in the opinion of this writer.

Movement Toward Industrial Unionism

From time to time, there appear to be movements toward industrial unionism in the maritime and longshore industries. To some extent, the two coalitions headed by Paul Hall of SIU and Joseph Curran of NMU are confederations. Statements on national maritime unity have been coming regularly from NMU headquarters and are jointly signed with other maritime unions. Curran has indicated he would consider a merger with SIU. In February 1964, SIU and NMU issued a joint resolution aimed at furthering unionization of the Pacific Area Command of the Military Sea Transport Command. Their bitter competition had resulted in a "no union" vote as a result of the split. The union leaders agreed to restrict their activities until members of the bargaining unit by their own expression decided to "go union." This evidence of "statesmanship" between the warring leaders shows what is possible.

There have been other developments foreshadowing change in union structure. On the West Coast, unlicensed unions have obtained contractual concessions for possible jobs on shore, if they agree to reduce jobs on company container ships. Throughout the nation, unions of licensed officers, engineers, deck officers, and radio operators are changing their structures, are eliminating port localism, and are well on their way toward obtaining national working conditions in national contracts. If port localism and coastal arrangements are eliminated, national bargaining agreements with regular expiration dates may help the industry. Maritime bargaining structure has stood in the way of the kind of labor-management cooperation necessary to save the rapidly vanishing U.S. fleet—as competition from other nations forces our freight into foreign ships' holds.

NOTES

1. *Thirty-fifth Annual Report of the National Mediation Board* (Washington: G.P.O., 1969), pp. 77-78.

2. Beatrice M. Burgoon, "Effects of the Structure of Collective Bargaining in Selected Industries: The Railway Industry," *Labor Law Journal,* Vol. 21, No. 8 (August 1970), p. 492.

3. Interstate Commerce Commission, *Wage Statistics of Class I Steam Railroads in the United States* (Washington: G.P.O., 1950), Statement No. M-300, and *ibid.* (1969), Statement No. A-300.

4. Edward B. Shils, "Industrial Unrest in the Nation's Airline Industry," *Labor Law Journal,* Vol. 15, No. 3 (March 1964), p. 148.

5. *Thirty-fifth Annual Report of the National Mediation Board,* p. 78.

6. Asher Schwartz, "The Railway Labor Act and the Airlines," New York University *Twelfth Annual Conference on Labor* (New York: Matthew Bender, 1959), pp. 167-168.

7. "Airlines: The Railway Labor Act or the Labor Management Relations Act?" *Labor Law Journal,* Vol. 20, No. 5 (May 1969), p. 296.

8. *Ibid.,* pp. 299-300.

9. *Ibid.,* p. 303.

10. Michael H. Cimini, "Emergency Boards in the Airline Industry," *Monthly Labor Review* Vol. 93, No. 7 (July 1970), p. 59.

11. *Ibid.*

12. Edward B. Shils, "Transportation's Labor Crisis," *Harvard Business Review,* Vol. 42, No. 3 (May-June 1964), pp. 87-88.

13. *Ibid.,* p. 89.

14. U.S. Congress, House, Committee on Merchant Marine and Fisheries, *Hearings on H.R. 15424, 15425, 15640, The President's Maritime Program,* 91st Cong., 2d sess., Part I (Washington: G.P.O., 1970), pp. 16, 18.

15. Effects of the Structure of Collective Bargaining in Selected Industries," *Labor Law Journal,* Vol. 21, No. 8 (August 1970), p. 515.

16. Edward B. Shils, "Industrial Unrest in the Nation's Maritime Industry," *Labor Law Journal,* Vol. 15, No. 6 (June 1964), pp. 341-343.

17. *New York Times,* Aug. 24, 1967, p. 86.

18. *The NMU Pilot,* Vol. 33, No. 1 (January 1968), p. 2.

19. Helen Bentley in *The Evening Bulletin* (Philadelphia), September 5, 1967, p. 44.

20. *Report of the Presidential Railroad Commission* (Washington, D.C.: Superintendent of Documents, 1962), chap. 13, p. 184.

A Proposal for Reviving Collective Bargaining Under the Railway Labor Act

Everett M. Goulard †

If collective bargaining in the airline industry is to survive the 1970's, a way must be found to create in the minds of the bargainers a sincere and strong desire to resolve the issues between them at the bargaining table—not by resort to invective and threats of the use of economic force—but by detailed examination of the relevant facts, mutual exploration of possible solutions, intelligent modification of initial positions and eventual compromise to the point of agreement. More important, if the air carriers themselves are to survive the 1970's as privately-owned and financially sound enterprises, labor-management differences unresolved through the collective bargaining process must be composed for the most part without resort to economic warfare on the threat thereof. Furthermore, a plan for peaceable and equitable resolution of contract disputes in this highly visible industry is essential to bring a halt to the inflationary spiral which the industry perhaps initiated and surely abetted. While these comments will be directed primarily to the labor-management problems of the airline industry, they apply to a degree to other modes of transportation, particularly railroads.

Proposed legislation has been introduced in both Houses of Congress which its sponsors believe would accomplish these purposes. The Dominick Bill, S. 2060, and the Jarman Bill, H.R. 8898, which are identical, amend the so-called emergency provisions of the Railway Labor Act by replacing the existing Emergency Board provisions with an "arsenal of weapons" approach available for use by the government in any unresolved labor dispute. The proposed legislation is the joint suggestion of railroad and airline managements. They believe that it will give new life to the collective bargaining process in their industries and at the same time provide for the peaceful resolution of any labor dispute which, in the opinion of responsible government

---

† Everett M. Goulard is Counsel, Airline Industrial Relations Conference.

officials, would have a serious impact on the traveling public, on the carrier and its employees or on the economy of the nation as a whole.

Specifically, the airline-railroad proposed legislation substitutes the following procedure for that presently contained in Section 10 of the Railway Labor Act:

1. Upon the failure of the National Mediation Board to successfully resolve *any* dispute by mediation, it must notify the Secretaries of Commerce, Labor and Transportation who are directed to appoint an ad hoc Transportation Labor Panel which shall recommend one of the following procedures for handling the dispute:

   a. take no further action;

   b. appoint a neutral board to make non-binding settlement recommendations;

   c. refer to final and binding arbitration; or

   d. submit to a final offer selection procedure.

2. The Secretaries may either accept or reject the recommendations, but, if the latter, they must themselves select one of the other alternatives.

This specific proposal has been advanced as a result of a thorough study of labor contract settlements in the railroad and airline industries in recent years and a resultant realization of their far reaching impact on the national economy. It permits top Administration officials to take positive action in any dispute, large or small, if they believe that a strike or improvident settlement will endanger health or safety, seriously inconvenience the public, or have a substantial effect on the stability of the economy. As a corollary, it permits those same officials, with full knowledge of the facts, to leave the parties to their own devices, including self-help. A brief review of progressively more disastrous settlements in the airline industry points up the problem which must be remedied if the industry is to survive.

In the summer of 1966, The International Association of Machinists (IAM) struck five large airlines in an avowed attempt to shatter the then-existing Presidential wage guideline of 3.2 percent. During the course of direct negotiations and mediation proceedings, the carriers offered the guideline amount, but this offer was rejected by the union, which derided it and termed it "insincere".

During the "cooling-off" period which follows the termination of formal mediation proceedings under the Railway Act, the then Assistant Secretary of Labor held informal mediation sessions. During them the carriers slightly improved their offer, but the union again rejected it. Thereupon, a Presidential Emergency Board created under Section 10 of the Act conducted lengthy hearings and recommended a settlement estimated at 3.5 percent or 3.6 percent per annum. As has been the almost invariable practice in recent years, these recommendations were promptly accepted by the carriers and just as promptly rejected by the union. In this instance the IAM excoriated them as "the product of nineteenth century thinking," to use the union's words.

During the course of the 43-day strike, which commenced after the termination of the "cooling-off" period, Congress and the Administration gave serious thought to the passage of remedial legislation to end the strike, but in the final analysis instead, urged the parties to renew their bargaining in the White House Annex or "woodshed," as they termed it, under the aegis of President Johnson and Labor Secretary Wirtz. After three days of "woodshed" bargaining, the parties emerged with a 4.7 percent per annum settlement, almost 50 percent in excess of the guidelines.

Although this became known as the Johnson settlement, because it was publicly blessed by the President, it failed of ratification by the membership by a vote of more than 2 to 1. Rejection by the membership proved to be an effective method of exacting an even higher price, for after another "woodshed" session, this time of ten days duration, a settlement was reached estimated at from 5.1 percent to 6 percent per annum, depending on the source, and this eventually was ratified by the membership.

This is a classic example of management, in this case a small group of carriers, being overpowered at the bargaining table by a nationwide union conscious of its overwhelming economic strength and determined to use it to exact its price, however excessive. In this instance, the union set out to defy and destroy Administration policy, and it succeeded in spite of the exhortations and admonitions of high government officials, including the President. It was indifferent to the long-range consequences of its action, and these developed to be most serious.

In the opinion of many informed practitioners, this settlement ignited the fires of inflation which the Administration now seeks to control through its current Economic Stabilization program. Only a few weeks after the IAM-airline settlement, the Transport Workers Union (TWU) forced American and Pan American into settlements priced by the BLS at 6.5 percent annually. These settlements begat ever richer surrenders, with the result that average earnings of airline employees, which rose by 3 percent in 1966, skyrocketed to 5 percent in 1967, 8 percent in 1968, 10 percent in 1969 and 11 percent in 1970. The nadir, one must hope, was reached in August, 1970 when one air carrier settled with a large group of its employees for an average annual increase of 15 percent.

Perhaps even more sobering is the stepping-stone effect of settlements wrested by strong national unions from relatively weak airlines bargaining one-by-one. Thus in the 1969-1970 round of bargaining on airline mechanics contracts, individual carriers settled successively for a journeyman mechanic hourly rate of $5.00, $5.18, $5.23, $5.50, $5.65, $6.35 and $7.00—all these settlements having been reached over a period of slightly more than one year!

The unfortunate fact is that airline managements, large and small, are particularly vulnerable to strikes and strike threats because they cannot stockpile their product nor recapture lost business. They, they are overpowered at the bargaining table, whether they bargain jointly or individually, by nationwide unions willing and anxious to use their economic strength to bludgeon them into higher and higher, and inflationary and super-inflationary, settlements.

The end result can be disaster for the airlines, and perhaps irreparable damage to the economy. For it is now obvious to all that this infection of super-inflationary settlements has spread far beyond airlines, railroads and other modes of transportation. The largest industries, and the giant employers among them, all have succumbed, as witness the settlements in the automobile industry touched off by the ten percent per annum General Motors strike settlement in the fall of 1970, and the even higher settlements reached in the can, aluminum and steel industries this year.

The conclusion is inescapable that transportation bargaining, at least airline bargaining—if that is what the airline and railroad confrontations over contract changes in the past several years can be called—has had a significant impact on labor-management relations throughout industry and on the economy as a whole. One must conclude, also, that the effect has been serious and harmful, and that a remedy is needed.

The fact is that collective bargaining in its true sense does not take place unless the parties to the bargain which must be made possess relatively equal strength. The imbalance of bargaining power in the airline industry has inhibited collective bargaining, and will continue to do so unless the rules are changed. It cannot realistically be expected that a union which is able to achieve all of its objectives through the use or threat of use of its strike weapon will substantially modify its desires and those of its more militant members in response to the logical arguments or pleas of poverty of an embattled management. In practice, it simply does not happen. Fully realizing that it need merely be patient and wait for the procedures of the Railway Labor Act to run their course, the powerful union has no real incentive to bargain or modify its position in any significant respect.

The airline-railroad proposed legislation drastically alters the thought processes at the bargaining table. Both labor and management negotiators would realize that the dispute, if unresolved in direct negotiations or during mediation proceedings, would then be examined by top administration officials, who would determine whether its magnitude in terms of effect on the public or the economy warrant the imposition of special settlement procedures. The resultant uncertainty as to which of the weapons in the arsenal might be employed would provide a powerful stimulus to collective bargaining in its true sense. Management could not sensibly fail to strive for a settlement because it could not be sure that the union would not be permitted to strike. On the other hand, the union no longer could participate in negotiations and mediation proceedings in perfunctory fashion because it could not be sure that it would be allowed to strike.

Contrary to opinions voiced by some arbitrators and educators in the labor relations field, it is the firm conviction of the sponsors of the proposed legislation that the uncertainty as to whether arbitration or final offer selection might be employed, or in fact the virtual certainty that one of them would, greatly enhances the bargaining process.

When it is estimated that in excess of 90 percent of civil litigation is settled before trial, the parties preferring to compose their differences rather than risk exposure to the uncertainties of a trial and eventual determination by a judge or jury, it is difficult to understand the apparently sincere belief of those who feel that the parties will supinely await an arbitration proceeding, if they feel such is possible or likely. The experience of Pan American World Airways belies this. For several years this carrier has had agreements with certain of its unions to arbitrate future unresolved contract disputes. The result has been that a much higher percentage of cases has been resolved in direct negotiations or in mediation than has been true in the absence of such agreements. In fact, a dozen or more contract disputes have been resolved amicably and expeditiously over the bargaining table because of the existence of these agreements to arbitrate, while only two cases have gone to final and binding arbitration. Unfortunately, Pan Am has been able to persuade only a few unions to sign such agreements to arbitrate, while other carriers and their unions have not been able to reach any such agreements.

Even more convincing were developments in the grave-diggers strike in New York City late in 1969. The strike dragged on for many weeks under the "free collective bargaining, self-help" system, until officialdom feared that the number of unburied bodies might be harmful to the health of the living as well as macabre. Finally, the New York legislature enacted a law requiring arbitration of the unresolved issues unless there was a voluntarily bargained settlement within forty-eight hours. Faced with the certainty that the decision-making process would be taken out of their hands, the parties reached a settlement over the bargaining table shortly after the deadline and before the law could be implemented.

To summarize, transportation labor-management confrontations have had their impact on labor contract settlements throughout industry, and on the nation's economy. The impact has been serious and the effect most harmful. A way must be found to encourage fair and reasonable resolutions of labor-management disputes, arrived at peaceably through a genuine collective bargaining process. The proposed airline-railroad legislation is such a way.

From Private to Public:
Labor Relations in Urban Transit

Darold T. Barnum †

During the past 25 years, the urban transit industry has been characterized by rapidly declining fortunes and a consequent shift from private to public ownership. Not surprisingly, the industry's labor relations system has been significantly influenced by these trends. This article examines labor relations in urban transit with emphasis on the changes resulting from the industry's shift to the public sector. After a review of the industrial background, the structure and process of collective bargaining and the settlements resulting therefrom are discussed.

The urban transit industry includes all "companies and systems primarily engaged in local and suburban mass passenger transportation over regular routes and on regular schedules" [1] except commuter railroads and limousine service. The industry now operates primarily rapid rail transit and buses, with a few streetcar and electric bus lines. In 1970, for example, 98.4 percent of the systems reporting to the American Transit Association operated bus lines only and the rest some combination of the modes. Rapid transit, however, carried 27 percent of the industry's 5,932 million revenue passengers in 1970, whereas buses accounted for 68 percent and streetcars and electric buses for 5 percent of the volume. The rapid transit lines were all publicly owned in 1970, as were 90 percent of the electric buses and streetcars and 59 percent of the motor buses.[2]

† Darold T. Barnum is instructor in economics, State University of New York at Brockport. He was research associate in the Industrial Research Unit, Wharton School of Finance and Commerce, University of Pennsylvania, when this article was written. The study was made under a grant from the Urban Mass Transportation Administration, U. S. Department of Transportation.

Industrial Structure and Markets

There are many companies in the industry, but the largest systems carry most of the passengers. In 1970, 1,079 operating transit companies existed, or more than one for every city with a population of 25,000 or more. The systems in the twenty-one largest cities, however, accounted for 71 percent of all revenue passengers.[3] Likewise, the four largest systems accounted for almost 50 percent of all employees, and the New York City Transit Authority alone employed almost 30 percent of the industry's workers.[4] Because a few firms account for a large proportion of the industry's passengers and employment, it is not surprising that collective bargaining in these firms has a major impact on the entire industry.

The large operations were almost all publicly owned by 1970, and the average public company tended to be much larger than the average private company. Of the ten largest systems, eight are now public, and the remaining two appear likely to go public in the near future. The 141 public organizations, excluding the New York City system, have an average of 530 employees, whereas the 938 private companies have an average of 270 employees, about half as many.[5] The different average size of public and private systems is an important consideration when comparing collective bargaining settlements by type of ownership, because large systems tend to have higher wage rates than small systems.[6]

No matter how large it is, a transit firm typically operates in only one metropolitan area. Notable exceptions to this rule include Public Service Coordinated Transport, which operates bus lines over most of New Jersey, and National City Lines, which operates wholly owned subsidiaries in more than twenty cities.[7] There is, however, normally only one system in each SMSA. Even when several firms operate in one urban area, as is true in the largest cities, they seldom have competing routes.

Most transit firms, therefore, can be classified as monopolies, with each monopolist limited to one locality. The systems are only monopolies in the most literal sense, as they do compete with other modes of transportation—the most important being the private automobile. Nevertheless, transit bargaining structure and processes are directly affected by this industrial and market structure.

Unionization

The transit industry is almost completely unionized: approximately 95 percent of companies have collective bargaining contracts with some union.[8] Most workers belong to either the Amalgamated Transit Union (ATU) or the Transport Workers Union (TWU). A small proportion of the employees are organized by the United Transportation Union, various craft unions, or independent unions.

In terms of number of collective bargaining contracts, the ATU is by far the dominant union in the industry. In a sample of 194 organized companies, the ATU accounted for 79 percent of the agreements, the TWU for 10 percent, and various other unions for the remaining 11 percent.[9] The ATU claims about 100,000 members,[10] whereas the TWU has an estimated 45,000 transit workers in its ranks.[11] All nonmanagement employees in the transit industry are eligible for membership in both major unions, including craft employees and office workers. The ATU restricts membership to transit workers, but the TWU accepts members from all transportation facilities, public utilities, and allied industries.

Manpower Requirements

The trends and characteristics of the industry are clearly reflected in its manpower requirements. The fact that the industry delivers its one product, mass transportation, primarily with buses and secondarily with subways has resulted in a work force consisting of 60 percent vehicle operators, 12 percent craftsmen (primarily mechanics and other maintenance workers), and 10 percent office and clerical workers. Approximately 83 percent of all employees are blue-collar workers, and almost 80 percent of these blue-collar workers are classified as "semiskilled operatives."[12] In short, the typical transit employee is a bus driver who, although semiskilled, has a considerable responsibility because of his human cargo.

The transit industry has long been noted as one providing highly stable employment. This was made possible by mild fluctuations in the number of riders and a slowly evolving technology. A tradition of the industry growing out of this stability (apparently instituted by management) was adjustment to declines in total employment needs solely through attrition. The rapid decrease in number of workers needed since World War II has, however, caused some layoffs.

A very important trend in the postwar era has been a change in the racial mix of the industry's workers. Only 3.0 percent of the industry's employees were black in 1940. The proportion increased to 6.4 percent in 1950, 10.9 percent in 1960, and to an estimated 30 percent in 1970.[13] The proportion of blacks is even higher in large cities. In 1970 the systems in Atlanta, Chicago, Detroit, Houston, Los Angeles, New York, Philadelphia, St. Louis, and Washington, D. C. had an average black proportion of 40 percent. Over 50 percent of the transit workers are black in Detroit, and a majority of the workers are either Negro or Puerto Rican in New York.[14] The reasons for the trend are found in the center-city location of the industry and the industry's declining image as a good place to work. Urban transit racial policies, discussed at length in a companion study, have had a major impact on both the unions' internal relationships and their relations with management.[15]

Trends in Ridership, Employment, and Finances

During urban transit's relatively short life, structural changes over time have had an important influence on the industry's labor relations. The transit industry was born, reached its zenith, and declined within 150 years. In 1832 the first urban railway began operating in New York City, and during the 1850's almost all large cities acquired lines.[16] The number of riders increased rapidly up to the 1920's, and the industry's revenues more than doubled each decade between 1890 and 1920.[17] Revenues and number of passengers declined with the depression, then again expanded rapidly during World War II. With the return to a peacetime economy, total volume of activity began a slow but steady decline. Between 1950 and 1970, annual revenue passengers decreased from 13,845 million to 5,932 million, a decline of 57 percent.[18] Although the decline has been steady, it has been relatively smooth, with no sharp fluctuations. This is characteristic of the historical lack of short-term variation in number of transit passengers.

Not only did the total number of passengers decline, but also there was an unfavorable change in their distribution throughout the day. Although transit patronage had always clustered around the home-to-work-and-return trips from 7 to 9 a.m. and

TABLE 1. *The Transit Industry: Financial Data, 1945-1970*

Year	Operating Revenue ($ million)	Percentage of Operating Revenue						Net Operating Income
		Operating Expenses						
		Total	Payroll	Maintenance Materials	Fuel	Other, Including Depreciation	Taxes	
1945	1,384	77.3	45.7	5.6	7.7	18.3	11.9	10.8
1950	1,452	89.3	57.5	6.3	8.2	17.3	6.1	4.6
1955	1,426	89.6	60.6	6.2	6.4	16.4	6.5	3.9
1960	1,407	91.7	60.9	8.1	5.4	17.3	6.2	2.2
1965	1,444	95.2	66.7	7.3	4.8	16.4	5.6	—0.7
1970	1,707	110.8	74.6	8.3	4.8	23.1	6.1	—16.9

Source: Calculations from American Transit Association, *Transit Fact Books* (Washington, 1946, 1951, 1956, 1961, 1966, and 1970), various pages.

4 to 6 p.m., the proportion (although not the number) of passengers riding during these hours has increased. In 1902, the New York Metropolitan Street Railway estimated that 35 percent of its traffic rode during the peak hours. By the 1960's, peak-hour loads represented up to 65 percent of daily transit riders in some systems.[19]

The falling ridership has resulted in a steady decline in employment in the industry: from 240,000 workers in 1950 to 138,-000 in 1970, a decrease of 42 percent in 20 years.[20] This contraction is partly a reflection of changing technology, but decreasing ridership, rather than increasing productivity, is the major cause of reduced labor usage. Between 1950 and 1970, for example, the annual number of revenue passengers per employee actually decreased from 58,000 to 43,000; and the annual revenue vehicle miles per employee increased only slightly, from 12,500 to 13,700.[21]

The effects of the shifts in passenger volume and its distribution throughout the day are also mirrored in the industry's financial data. As Table 1 shows, expenses have increased faster than revenues, resulting in increasingly smaller net profits and, later, increasingly larger net losses. Thus, total expenses increased from 89 percent of total revenue in 1950 to 111 percent of total revenue in 1970. All expenses except fuel increased their share of total revenue. The proportions of total revenue accounted for by payroll, maintenance materials, and other expenses increased by 30, 32, and 34 percent respectively between 1950 and 1970.

Change from Private to Public Ownership

The deteriorating financial position of the industry is the primary reason for the shift to public ownership and the discontinued service. Because of increasing expenses and declining patronage, private companies have found it more and more difficult to provide adequate service at reasonable fares. Hence, as of 1970, private companies rapidly are becoming public, and each year shows major additions to the number of public systems. In the entire decade of the 1950's, for example, twenty-five private systems became publicly owned. In the first half of the 1960's, twenty-seven systems became public, and in the second half of the 1960's, fifty-one systems changed to public ownership.[22] Of the five largest private systems in 1968, three are now public and the two others will likely join the ranks soon. Many systems have discontinued service since the mid-1950's. The number of systems either becoming publicly owned or discontinuing service since 1955 is presented in Table 2.

No city with more than 80,000 people has lost service, although Kansas City, with a 1970 metropolitan area population of 1.25 million, was saved from losing its service in July 1971 by an emergency subsidy. The system already is publicly owned and already has a 50-cent fare. About 94 percent of cities with fewer

TABLE 2. *The Transit Industry: Systems Changing Status, by Size of City and Type of Change, 1955-1969*

| | Systems | | |
Size of City	Becoming Public *	Discontinuing Service †	Total
Less than 25,000	6	51	57
25,000-50,000	15	40	55
Over 50,000	74	9	83
Total	95	100	195

* All systems still in operation in 1969.

† About 7% of these may have been publicly owned.

Source: Data provided by American Transit Association.

than 25,000 people which discontinued service did so *before* 1965, while only 50 percent of cities with more than 25,000 which discontinued service did so before that date. It is notable, however, that at least since 1935 no more than 5 percent of total revenue passengers have been in cities with less than 50,000 inhabitants.

With these facts, several observations can be made about systems which have changed status: over 80 percent of the cities with fewer than 50,000 inhabitants have discontinued service, while over 90 percent of the cities with more than 50,000 have established a public system. Almost all the smallest cities (less than 25,000) lost their systems before the mid-1960's, and the cities with between 25,000 and 50,000 people are currently losing their systems. Finally, the number of revenue passengers lost by the industry because of discontinued service is a very small proportion of its total volume. If present trends continue, the urban mass-transportation industry of the near future will consist entirely of publicly owned systems in cities of at least 50,000 people.

Structure of Collective Bargaining

The aforementioned industrial characteristics significantly influence collective bargaining in the industry. Because the industry is composed of local firms which have a monopoly on their product markets, the bargaining unit is coexistent with the firm. Because the industry supplies an important public service, government interest in collective bargaining has been significant, but until recently, that interest has been exercised primarily by state and municipal bodies. And because of declining patronage and revenues, a shift to public ownership has occurred which has greatly increased government interest in the collective bargaining picture.

In both public and private systems, the bargaining unit generally comprises all organized workers in a given transit company, including operators, maintenance workers, and clerical employees. The industrial form of organization has been furthered by the fact that only a few of the organized employees are not operators. If organization by craft had been followed in any but the largest systems, the craft locals would consist of only a few members each.

The four largest systems do have sufficient workers, however, to make feasible separate bargaining units (and unions) for each craft. Boston and Chicago have craft bargaining, although

Philadelphia and New York do not. In Boston's Massachusetts Bay Transportation Authority there are 27 different bargaining units, ranging in size from the 4,295 member Carman's Union (ATU), which accounts for 74 percent of the organized employees, to Local 4 of the Hoisting and Portable Engineers, which has one member.[23] Chicago has a total of 20 unions, but 88 percent of the unionized employees belong to ATU Divisions 241 and 308.[24] In Philadelphia and New York, however, one union —the TWU—represents virtually all organized employees in the major units of the system. The only exceptions are in minor divisions in which formerly separate companies with different unions merged with the system.

The philosophy of the dominant operators' union has in each case determined the type of organization. The ATU grew up in the craft structure of the AFL; even its original name—the Amalgamated Association of Street, Electric Railway and Motor Coach Employees—denotes a combination of crafts. Hence, when the craft unions brought pressure to bear on the Amalgamated's international office in 1918, President Willaim D. Mahon allowed the craftsmen to join their Boston locals.[25] A similar situation caused craft severance in the 1950's in Chicago.[26]

The TWU, however, has considered itself an industrial union and bitterly fought all attempts at craft severance. The TWU's commitment to industrial unionism is well summarized by one of its early slogans: "One Industry, One Union—One for All, All for One." [27] It achieved this goal in the New York system and in the former Philadelphia Transit Company.

When there are several transit firms in one urban area, bargaining is normally on a company-by-company basis. Although the ATU would prefer to bargain with all area firms simultaneously, to alleviate discontent over wage differentials, there never has been strong pressure for consolidation of bargaining. Because firms seldom have competing lines, they do not compete in the product market, and the multifirm bargaining which a union considers necessary in this circumstance is not required.

The establishment of regional transit authorities has in some cases had the effect of consolidating all the area's bargaining units into one large unit. In Pittsburgh, for example, the Port Authority Transit System consolidated thirty-one firms, resulting in a parallel consolidation of the thirty-one independent bargaining units. Similar consolidations occurred in Boston and St. Louis.

Internal Union Organization for Bargaining

Partly because bargaining is on a local basis, ATU locals have always had the power to formulate their own demands and to control the actual contract bargaining. The shift to public ownership has not affected that power. The local membership must approve the decision to strike and must ratify or reject any proposed contract. The locals exercised their independence, at least through the early 1950's, by typically formulating their own demands, although they normally requested an international officer to help with actual negotiations. In cases which might go to binding arbitration, an international officer and a representative of the Labor Bureau of the Midwest (which for many years has represented ATU bargaining units) were normally requested at the outset.[28]

The small size of the average local and the increasing sophistication of the issues have, since the early 1950's, made it difficult for the local to possess the expertise needed for negotiations. The trend in the last twelve years has been increasing use of international officers in all stages of negotiations. Currently, an international representative is present at about 90 percent of all contract negotiations and, in most cases, acts as chief negotiator.[29]

Because the overwhelming percentage of TWU transit members are located in New York City, national officers always have played a key role in bargaining there. Philadelphia is somewhat more autonomous, but national officials are usually present at negotiations.

Impact of Black Workers on Unions

The increasing proportion of black workers is having an important impact on union organization. In 1969 in New York City, where blacks and Puerto Ricans account for over half the transit work force, Negro transit employees challenged the white leadership to end discrimination and "invigorate the complacent labor bureaucracy."[30] A Negro caucus led by Joseph Carnegie, a black subway conductor, collected signatures for a representation election in an attempt to take bargaining rights away from the TWU. Although they failed to obtain the needed signatures, the group remains active.[31]

Carnegie charged the TWU with undemocratic election procedures, settling for inadequate pay increases, and neglecting to stress safety.[32] Although civil rights is often stressed by dissidents, it appears the real issue is that the ethnic composition of the membership is changing faster than is that of the leadership. Just as the Irish once chose Irish leaders to speak for them, the blacks are now demanding Negro representatives. Although a black dissident union could replace the TWU, it is more likely that Negroes will be elected to leadership positions in the TWU, because the workers are not liable to change unions for fear of losing current benefits.

A similar process is occurring in the Chicago Transit Authority, where ATU's Division 241 represents bus drivers and Division 308 represents rapid transit motormen. A group of blacks dissatisfied with Division 241's leadership instigated two wildcat strikes in 1968 and later began collecting signatures for a recall election.[33] In a recent election for union officers, the dissidents did not win the presidency, but they increased the number of black members on the executive board from three to nine and elected a black financial-secretary and second vice-president.[34]

Division 308 has been less torn by dissension, and in December 1969, a Negro, Leonard Beatty, was elected president of that local.[35] Beatty's outstanding qualifications were his competence and his dedication to the trade union movement.

Similar activity is occurring in many of the larger transit system all over the country. The natural process of changing the leadership to meet the changing demands of the members will almost certainly cause a sharp increase in union militancy until the new leadership is firmly entrenched. Much of this militancy is being and will continue to be felt in the collective bargaining process for the near future.

One factor which is slowing the takeover by Negroes is the provision in the ATU constitution which permits pensioners to vote in union elections. Most pensioners are white and have maintained white leaders in office in such cities as Washington, where whites are fast losing their numerical majority among the active rank and file. Needless to say, this has caused considerable discontent among the black rank and file.

Managements' Approach to Bargaining

In one important respect, management organization for bargaining is similar in both public and private systems: companies traditionally bargain independently with little cooperation or collaboration. Although many firms were members of various

employer organizations, beginning with the American Street Railway Association in 1882 and since 1932 the American Transit
Association, Young noted that "their resolution of labor disputes
and their use or rejection of arbitration remained in the province
of the individual company." [36] Thus, the local transit company
traditionally has faced the local union across the bargaining table.
Although the latter often used the resources and expertise of
the international union and the Labor Bureau of the Midwest,
the company normally relied on its own resources. As will be
shown, this greatly favored the union in contract negotiations.

In a number of ways, however, there are important differences
between public and private systems. First, they are operating
under different goals. The private systems generally are attempting to maximize profits while constrained by imposed fare and
schedule requirements. The public systems are attempting to
maximize "service" (measured by something like passengers or
vehicle hours per day) and minimize fare and are constrained in
nonsubsidized cases by zero profits. In both cases, however, management will attempt to keep wages in line, because increased
wages normally will result in both decreased profits *and* decreased
passengers. [37]

A second difference is the source of management's decision
makers. In most public authorities, the governing board is com-
prised of political appointees. Thus, the potential influence of
political considerations is much greater in public systems. In a
strike, for example, a mayor can put more pressure on his appointees than on a private management. Likewise, pressure to
decrease unprofitable lines clearly will be greater on a profit
maximizer than on a "vote maximizer." On the other hand, since
transit is a regulated industry, political influence never has been
absent.

A third difference is source of funds. Private companies seldom get substantial subsidies from governmental sources. Public
companies vary, but some get help. [38] To the degree that public
companies are subsidized, they are removed from the market
pressures noted earlier. The pressure on them to maintain efficient operations no longer comes from the market but from the
donor of the funds. Efficiency can be diluted by political pressures against layoffs and consolidations or discontinuance of non-
profitable segments of the operation.

Bargaining Process Before 1952

The processes of collective bargaining in the transit industry fall into three distinct types, each identified with a period of time. In the first period, before 1952, collective bargaining was carried out almost as if the industry were publicly owned. In the second period, between 1952 and the mid-1960's, much of the industry used collective bargaining processes similar to other industries in the private sector of the economy. In the third period, beginning in the mid-1960's but just gaining force in the 1970's, the industry (because of its shift to public ownership) is increasingly engaging in fact finding and binding arbitration to resolve collective bargaining impasses.

Before 1952, collective bargaining in the transit industry was dominated by a mixture of public and private techniques. Most systems, as private firms, were subject to the National Labor Relations Act and amendments. Impasses were often settled by voluntary binding arbitration and for a short time, in some states, by compulsory binding arbitration and other governmental intervention techniques. In a sense, these devices were more apropos to the needs in the public sector today.

Although the National Labor Relations Act applied from the beginning to private transit firms carrying passengers across state lines (as in Washington, D.C.), its jurisdiction over private systems operating entirely within one state was not verified until 1943. In a case applying to the Baltimore Transit Company, the Fourth Circuit Court of Appeals ruled that:

> While the vehicles of the company do not cross state lines, there can
> be no question that they carry to and from work thousands of pas-
> sengers who are engaged in the production of goods that flow in
> interstate commerce.[39]

Because interstate commerce would therefore be affected by a strike, the court held that the company was subject to the provisions of the Act. This decision gave transit employees the protection of the Act. Nevertheless, although private transit workers could bargain as any other private employee, the ATU continued to use its traditional impasse resolution device—voluntary arbitration.

The use of voluntary arbitration to settle contract bargaining disputes is one of the most notable features of collective bargaining in the transit industry. Voluntary arbitration was more widely used in transit in its early years than in almost any other industry. Even as early as 1888, arbitration of transit disputes was widely urged by both the unions and the employers, as well as by public officials. It was, however, the ATU, under the leadership of William D. Mahon, president from 1893 to 1946, which did the most to increase use of voluntary arbitration in the transit industry.[40]

Amalgamated Encouragement of Arbitration

In its first constitution in 1892, the Amalgamated stated that one of its objectives was "to encourage the settlement of all disputes between employees and employers by arbitration."[41] It was later made mandatory that the locals offer to arbitrate disputes before striking, a constitutional provision still in effect in 1971.[42]

Unlike the Amalgamated, the TWU never has stressed arbitration. Originally a left-wing organization, it was philosophically opposed to embracing that means of settlement. Mike Quill, its late president, was adept at threatening strikes and thus obtaining settlements. Moreover, the New York City system, in which the TWU has its major strength, already was partially publicly owned when the TWU was organized in the 1930's. At that time and for many years thereafter, the city declined to admit that it had authority to arbitrate.

Arbitration in the industry has been encouraged by the fact that fare changes must often be approved by public utility commissions or equivalent bodies. The transit firms undoubtedly felt that the commissions would be more receptive to rate changes if these increases were needed as a result of an arbitrated rather than negotiated wage increase.[43] Moreover, companies learned at an early date that strikes lost business which could not be regained, in addition to placing them in an unfavorable light with legislators whose support they neded for franchise extension as well as for rate increases.

As a result of ATU pressure and company acquiescence, contract arbitration came into wide use by World War I. It remained a major technique for dispute resolution until the early 1950's, accounting for 43 percent of the impasses resolved in the 1920's, 67 percent in the 1930's, and 41 percent in the 1940's (see Table 3). In short, the transit industry itself instituted strike-avoidance procedures much akin to those being advocated today for public employees.

Decline of Arbitration

The reason use of voluntary arbitration declined after 1952 was that management increasingly found it an unacceptable technique for resolving impasses. Management's primary objections, according to Alfred Kuhn, were that the arbitrators had unlimited powers, the arbitrators were biased, the three-man arbitration boards did not try to determine what was objectively right but engaged in "horse trading" among themselves in order to reach a settlement, it cost too much, and its use impeded collective bargaining.[44] But, as Kuhn points out,

> Of all the objections to the present practice of arbitration, the one which appears most frequently . . . is that the Amalgamated has outsmarted, out-bargained, and in general used more effective strategy than has management.[45]

The main reason was that the ATU had centralized control and a highly professional team of advocates, while management had little coordination and less experience. The ATU's advocates, the Labor Bureau of the Midwest, proved easily superior to management's local counsels. As one employer stated:

> The battle array still presents a highly organized team of specialists lined up on the union side against a capable but overburdened group of managers opposing them. . . . The crux of this: Management unorganized is no match for labor organized.[46]

State Strike-Control Laws

Because urban transit provides a public service, it has been the subject of several experiments designed to prevent "emergency strikes." In 1920, for example, Kansas enacted the country's first state compulsory arbitration law, which was rendered inoperative by court decisions in 1923 and 1925.[47] Although the ATU, like all organized labor, opposed the Kansas law, the ATU apparently saw the law as an opportunity. ATU locals initiated eight of the eighteen cases initiated by unions under the act, using the law as a means to force transit companies to deal with it.[48]

Just as the strikes of World War I led to the Kansas act, so the strike wave after World War II moved a number of states to attempt to prohibit strikes and to provide other means of conflict resolution in those areas where the legislatures believed that strikes caused public emergencies. In 1947, 11 states enacted such legislation, 8 of which provided for compulsory arbitration.

Of the latter, Minnesota's law covered only hospitals and Michigan's legislation was declared unconstitutional on procedural grounds before it became operative. One other state, Pennsylvania, had a compulsory arbitration law which excluded urban transit from its coverage. In the remaining five states—Florida, Indiana, Nebraska, New Jersey, and Wisconsin—urban transit accounted for 25 of the 102 cases.[49]

Transit concerns generally preferred these laws to voluntary arbitration because they set strict standards for arbitrators to follow in setting awards and because they provided methods of selecting arbitrators preferable to the industry. Also, management felt that a state public utility commission could not easily refuse a rate increase necessitated by the arbitration award of another state agency. The ATU strongly opposed these laws, however, apparently because they not only decreased the scope of the arbitrator's discretion by limiting the standards to be used to conditions prevailing in the same or adjoining labor markets but also the standards selected were often less favorable than those the union would have chosen.[50] In fact, it was a case brought by the ATU in 1951 which resulted in most of these laws being declared unconstitutional when the U. S. Supreme Court held that state strike arbitration laws conflicted with rights guaranteed by the Taft-Hartley Act, which preempted the field.[51]

In some industries, state arbitration laws had an inhibiting effect on collective bargaining. In urban transit, however, the influence was somewhat different, as explained by Northrup and Rowan.

> For this industry, it appears that voluntary arbitration has been used as a substitute for collective bargaining. And for a short period compulsory arbitration replaced voluntary arbitration.[52]

Seizure Laws

In addition to the compulsory arbitration statutes, Missouri and Virginia enacted seizure laws in 1947 which covered urban transit, and Maryland followed suit in 1956.[53] (New Jersey's compulsory arbitration law provided for seizure as a prelude to arbitration, and the 1947 Massachusetts "choice-of-procedures" legislation provided for seizure as one alternative but did not cover transit concerns.) Transit firms were even more involved in the laws of Missouri, Virginia, and Maryland than in those providing for compulsory arbitration: fourteen of the twenty seizures in Virginia and Missouri involved transit firms, and the Maryland law was enacted to curb a Baltimore transit strike, which ended before the law could be fully invoked. As in the case of compulsory arbitration, the transit firms welcomed this state intervention, and the ATU bitterly opposed it. Again, it was an ATU-sponsored case which found these laws inoperative in interstate commerce because of conflict with the Taft-Hartley Act.[54]

Fact finding has also been utilized extensively by states, and transit firms frequently have been involved.[55] Decisions affecting fact-finding bodies in Hawaii, Michigan, Massachusetts, and Oklahoma have, however, ended such activity pertaining to transit concerns.[56] Again, the ground was the preemption of the field by the federal government through the Taft-Hartley Act. Thus today, state activity in privately owned transit labor disputes has been limited by judicial decisions to mediation.[57]

Despite some innovative attempts, the state laws to curb transit and public utility strikes appeared to serve more as a substitute for collective bargaining (and, in transit, for voluntary arbitration) than as a safeguard to the public. Only compulsory arbitration provided for settlement, although other laws may have induced the parties to agree. Thus, only compulsory arbitration is sufficient by itself to settle the disputes, but when it replaces the strike, it also replaces collective bargaining *and* rights of the parties to codetermine the terms and conditions of employment. With such major consequences, it obviously should be used only when public welfare exhibits a real need. Experience with the state laws has shown that when compulsory arbitration laws are on the books they will be invoked whether the emergency is real or not. According to Northrup and Rowan, in a discussion of the experience of the states with compulsory arbitration laws,

> Laws designed to protect the public from emergencies were invoked to arbitrate the most minor disputes involving situations where public inconvenience was, at worst, slight. . . . The invalidation of these laws . . . saw . . . no public outcry of a need for reinstatement or additional protection.[58]

These state experiences, nevertheless, are significant because today many public systems operate under similar restrictions.

1952 to the Mid-1960's

The failure of state strike-control laws to meet the test of constitutionality did not result in an immediate return to the voluntary arbitration system of the pre-World War II years in urban transit. Although in large cities the historical settlement-without-a-strike philosophy continued to prevail, transit bargaining generally became similar to that in other private industries. Table 3 shows the transit industry used arbitration less and had a higher incidence of strikes. The industry evidently was both sufficiently jaundiced by its arbitration experience of previous decades and sufficiently desperate because of its ever-worsening economic situation to prefer to fight it out rather than permit third parties to determine its labor costs.

Paradoxically, while the industry was renouncing arbitration, it was being forced back to that process by its inability to survive in private hands. The bargaining system, which lost its unique reliance on voluntary arbitration because the industry was no match for the union at arbitration proceedings, was now becoming a publicly owned facility where strikes were per se illegal in most instances and where arbitration was more often being considered a substitute for strikes!

TABLE 3. *Transit Industry: Arbitration and Strikes, Ten-Year Totals, 1920-1969*

Year	Arbitrations	Strikes *	Total	Percent Arbitrations
1920-1929	117	153	270	43
1930-1939	60	29	89	67
1940-1949	260	375	635	41
1950-1959	74	482	556	13
1960-1969	15	532†	547	3

* Strikes in public agencies included only since 1958; however, it is doubtful if many public strikes occurred before that date.

† Private strikes estimated for 1969.

Source: American Transit Association; Alfred Kuhn, *Arbitration in Transit, An Evaluation of Wage Criteria* (Philadelphia: University of Pennsylvania Press, 1952), pp. 26 and 27; U.S. Bureau of Labor Statistics, "Work Stoppages in Government, 1958-68" (Washington: G.P.O., 1970), Report 348, p. 13; and U.S. Bureau of Labor Statistics, "Analysis of Work Stoppages" (Washington: G.P.O., 1968, 1969, and 1970), Bulletin Nos. 1573, 1611, and 1646.

1970's: Collective Bargaining in Public Employment

When a transit system becomes publicly owned, its collective bargaining is no longer under the jurisdiction of general federal labor legislation. As a public agency, the system's labor relations are normally governed by state labor laws covering public employees in general or by laws specifically covering transit systems.

Although no federal labor law directly covers public transit workers, systems which receive monies under the Mass Transportation Act of 1964, as amended through October 15, 1970, must comply with the labor-protection requirements of Section 13*(c)* of that act.[59] Almost all public systems have received federal aid. Hence, the act's labor provisions cover most of the industry's public sector. Moreover, Section 13*(c)* has had a major influence on state legislation dealing with public transit's labor relations; some states have even included all provisions of the section in their statutes.[60]

As a condition of receiving federal aid, Section 13*(c)* of the Mass Transportation Act, as amended, requires that the Secretary of Labor must be satisfied that the system will (1) maintain the affected employees' rights on the job, including previous wages, working conditions, and fringe benefits; (2) continue collective bargaining rights; and (3) provide, within prescribed minimal requirements, job security for employees affected by monies supplied by the federal government. This section has required new public systems to continue to bargain collectively with representatives of the employees' choosing even in cases where state law makes no such requirement. It does not require than an impasse resolution procedure be agreed on, but five of the eight Section 13*(c)* agreements examined included provisions for binding arbitration of impasses in contract negotiations.

Even without requiring a procedure for impasse resolution, Section 13*(c)* has been a major factor in protecting collective bargaining. In the Report of the International President to the 1969 ATU convention, John Elliot said:

> So far as our membership is concerned, Section 13(c) has made a tremendous contribution in the protection of collective bargaining and arbitration in the public sector of the transit industry. I am pleased to report that we have been almost entirely successful in our efforts to require municipalities involved in assuming public control and ownership of a formerly private system to preserve and continue existing collective bargaining arrangements, even in cases

of abandonments, in order to qualify for federal transit assistance. We need only remember the loss of our collective bargaining rights before passage of this Act in such places as Dallas and San Antonio, Texas, and Dade County, Florida, to realize the importance of this federal protection.[61]

In addition to the protection they received under federal law, public transit workers are normally within the jurisdiction of state public employee relations laws.[62] These statutes typically require either that the public employer negotiate or that he meet and confer with employee representatives. The differences in terminology do not necessarily reflect differences in bargaining requirements placed on the employer, however, and an accurate description of employer duties can be gained only by a reading of the act involved. In the Kansas law, for example, the public employer is required only to "meet and confer" with the representatives of his employees, but lack of mutual agreement can lead to mediation, fact finding, and even a form of arbitration.

Although not always the case, most state laws provide for mediation and fact finding to aid resolution of bargaining impasses. Very few states, however, give the public employees a legal method which *compels* resolution of contract bargaining disputes. Only two states, Hawaii and Pennsylvania, under laws passed in 1970, allow public employees to strike, and even in these states the strike weapon is limited to those cases which do not endanger public welfare.

As transit has traditionally been considered a service vital to the public welfare, it is doubtful that strikes against public transit systems will be allowed legally. In the first test of the Pennsylvania law, for example, a strike against Philadelphia's Southeastern Pennsylvania Transportation Authority was, in fact, enjoined. (The workers, however, ignored the injunction and thus conducted an illegal strike!) [63] The strike, therefore, is not likely to become a commonly used device for resolving transit impasses even in those states whose laws provide for its use.

Another technique for impasse resolution—compulsory arbitration—is mandated in several state laws. A Louisiana statute, limited to public transit employees, requires compulsory arbitration for bargaining impasses, and in 1966 Pennsylvania law orders the public transit employers in towns of 135,000 or smaller to offer to arbitrate any contract bargaining impasses. (As the 1970 law allows public transit employees to strike but provides that the rights guaranteed by the 1966 legislation shall not be "repealed or diminished," it appears that the covered employees can determine whether their demands will be better met by strike or arbitration and act accordingly.) Vermont also provides for compulsory arbitration of impasses, not only for transit workers but also for other public employees as well. Although this list probably is not exhaustive, the paucity of state public employee relations laws which include binding arbitration provisions is evident.

In short, very few general state laws give public transit employees a legal method for resolving their impasses with management. Under most of the laws, in the last analysis, management may implement its decisions unilaterally without employee consent. The employees may, of course, engage in an illegal strike, but such a resolution occurs despite the law not because of it.

In addition to the acts covering public employee labor relations in general, a number of states have included procedures for collective bargaining within the legislation creating public transit systems. The California statutes governing each of the state's major public transportation systems, for example, include measures to aid dispute reconciliation. Under these statutes, the state conciliation service determines the bargaining representation. In some cases, it also supplies voluntary arbitration and fact-finding services.[64] In 1968, for example, state conciliators helped to avert contract strikes in the Los Angeles and Sacramento public transportation systems. But, as with most of the previously discussed laws, the procedures only aid and do not compel settlement.[65]

In a number of enabling laws, however, binding arbitration is mandated for unresolved issues, as illustrated by the state statutes covering the Baltimore and Providence public transit systems. Maryland's code, for example, apparently makes arbitration mandatory in the Baltimore Metropolitan Transit Authority.

> In case of any labor dispute involving the Authority and such employees where collective bargaining does not result in agreement, the Authority *shall* submit such disputes to arbitration.[66]

In the case of the Rhode Island Public Transit Authority, however, the statute states:

> In the case of any labor disputes where collective bargaining does not result in agreement, the authority *shall offer* to submit such disputes to arbitration.[67]

Apparently, the union need not make a similar submission. In none of these special laws, however, has the strike weapon explicitly been granted.

Increased Use of Fact Finding and Arbitration

The shift of transit systems to public ownership, therefore, has also shifted collective bargaining into the jurisdiction of public employee laws. This shift has cost the transit workers their legal right to strike and has replaced the strike weapon with mediation, fact finding, and arbitration procedures. For several reasons, one would expect this shift to result in a sharp increase in the use of these alternatives. Certainly, they will be used in some negotiations which formerly would have been settled by strikes. As history demonstrates, when these methods are available, they are used extensively, although illegal strikes have occurred without serious penalty to the union—a situation unlikely to change.

Perhaps of greater importance, these impasse-resolving techniques also may replace sincere negotiations in some cases, as they provide an easy way out of dilemmas facing the public manager and his union colleague. The public manager must respond to two competing influences. On one side the workers pressure him to grant large wage increases, while on the other the public urges him to keep fares down and service up. Because he is a political appointee, the demands of the public are a very important consideration. The manager can solve his dilemma by agreeing to fact finding or arbitration: this allows the union to receive a competitive increase and permits the manager to direct public ire over potential fare increases to the third party.

Likewise, arbitration is an easy out for union negotiators. They can press unreasonably high demands to please their members and direct blame for the "low" settlement on the arbitrator. Also, arbitration usually is preferred to a strike as it is normally less costly to union members, does not alienate the public against the union, and does not result in the permanent decline in passengers (and hence, transit jobs) which often occurs after a strike. The attractiveness of delegating the decision to a third party can be seen by noting that even in those new public systems surveyed where arbitration or fact finding were not mandated by law, *all* had included binding arbitration provisions in their contracts. Not surprisingly, there has been an upsurge in the use of arbitration to settle contract bargaining impasses. For example, the ATU's strike-to-arbitration record for the two years ending June 30, 1969, shows that the international authorized thirty-four strikes and five arbitrations.[68] All authorized strikes were against private systems, and all arbitrations were with public systems. Likewise, the six systems surveyed which had become publicly owned since 1964 had signed eight contracts, six of which were settled by binding arbitration, while another had involved fact finding. As the number of public agencies continues to grow, it is likely that the number of arbitration cases also will increase.

Arbitration may be used, however, with less frequency once a system's dispute-resolution process matures if the parties decide that they can, with their knowledge of the needs of the system, negotiate an agreement more acceptable to both than a potential arbitration settlement. In any case, the use of arbitration will undoubtedly vary among systems. The Cleveland Transit System, for example, has arbitrated half of its sixteen contracts since 1945, while the Chicago Transit Authority has arbitrated only one contract since 1947.[69]

Compensation [70]

Accounting for 75 percent of total revenues in 1970, employee compensation clearly has a major impact on the American transit industry. Compensation can be divided into four elements: hourly rates, fringe benefits, payment for time not worked, and premium payments.

The industry has a relatively simple hourly rate structure because of its local market, its single product, and a concentration of its manpower in the occupation of vehicle operator. Since most employees are vehicle operators, it is not surprising that this is the key occupation in any wage negotiation. Likewise, because the occupation is semi-skilled and training periods are short, bargaining most often is concerned with the highest wage rate, and disputes over the rate relationships are unimportant or nonexistent. Wage rates are necessarily set on a straight hourly basis, as incentives for "increased" production or "quality of output" would be meaningless.[71]

Fringe benefits in the transit industry are typical, including vacation and holiday pay, pensions, and various kinds of insurance. In a sample of seven public systems, fringe items accounted for an average of 20 percent of the total payroll costs, or 16 percent of total revenues. They ranged, however, from a low of 13 percent to a high of 31 percent of total payroll.[72] The largest single fringe item is pension costs; these averaged 4.4 percent of payroll in a different sample of seven public and private systems [73] and are likely to increase because of the rising age of employees in a declining industry.

The introduction of increased fringe benefits can sometimes affect more than just payroll expenses. For example, in 1968 the TWU and the New York Transit Authority negotiated a provision which allowed workers to retire with twenty years' service at age fifty at half their final year's compensation, including all premiums time payments. This agreement substantially lowered the retirement requirements and started what the New York City actuary, Jesse Feld, called a "rush to the exits." The system lost many of its most skilled maintenance craftsmen and operators, which resulted, according to company spokesmen, in a definite lowering in the system's operating and maintenance performance and may be partly responsible for the system's recent accidents.[74] As new benefits spread rapidly throughout the industry, the New York experience may be well repeated elsewhere.

Although wage rate and fringe issues are relatively simple in the industry, the elements of payment for time not worked and premium payments are comparatively complicated. Payment for time not worked includes such items as report and turn-in time; minimum-time guarantee; travel time to relief points; show-up, stand by, and held time; and numerous others. In one typical system, payment for time not worked amounted to 6 percent of the base rate.[75]

Premium time, which includes overtime and spread-time premiums, is typically paid for at 1.5 times the hourly rate. The spread-time premium is a unique feature of the industry and is caused by the peaks in passenger distribution. Because demand is much heavier during the peak hours, many more drivers are needed during these hours than during the midday "base period." For example, assume spread-time premium is paid for all time over ten hours and assume a certain driver works from 6 to 10 a.m. and from 3 to 7 p.m. Although he has only worked eight hours, his total time from beginning to end is thirteen hours. Thus, he will be paid for five hours at the straight hourly rate and three hours at 1.5 times the hourly rate. Spread-time premium is, therefore, an attempt to compensate those drivers who must work undesirable hours.

Although all four elements of compensation are important to the average transit worker, the most important is undoubtedly the straight hourly rate. Not only is it the easiest element to understand, but also it is the easiest element to compare with other systems and with past rates in a given system. Not surprisingly, the hourly rate is by far the most common element of compensation discussed in union publications. Indicative of its importance is the fact that most local ATU officials carry with them a list of base hourly rates by city.

Average Wage Rates

As the base rate constitutes the major element of compensation, it also is considered very important by management. Because of its preeminence in compensation, because comparable data are available, and because rate comparisons are easier not only for workers but also for researchers, the rest of this section will concentrate on base hourly rates.

As in other industries, transit wages rose rapidly in the postwar period. Between 1949 and 1969, they increased 158 percent, about the same rate of increase received by building journeymen and local truck drivers. Transit wages rose much more rapidly than did the rates of book and job printing workers, however, and substantially faster than the manufacturing average rate. As of July 1, 1969, transit workers earned an hourly average of $3.71. In comparison, the average manufacturing wage was $3.19 per hour in 1969. Transit workers, however, earned less than the $4.01 rate of local truck drivers, yet they have about the same degree of skill and more responsibility (see Table 4).

TABLE 4. *Selected Industries: Average Wage Rates, 1949 and 1969.*

Industry	1949	1969	Percentage Change
Local transit	$1.44	$3.71	158
Building (journeymen)	2.34	5.87	151
Book and job printing	2.08	4.27	105
Local trucking (drivers)	1.55	4.01	159
All manufacturing	1.38	3.19	131

Source: U.S. Bureau of Labor Statistics, *Handbook of Labor Statistics, 1970* (Washington: G.P.O., 1970), Bulletin No. 1666, pp. 111 and 203.

Variation in Wage Rates: Public vs. Private Systems

There are, however, substantial differences among the wage rates of different transit systems. In the first half of 1969, hourly wages for experienced bus operators ranged from $2.60 in Columbus, Georgia, to $4.46 in New York City. About 9 percent of all workers earned less than $3.00 per hour, and 39 percent earned $4.00 per hour or more. Except for New York, where subway operators earn considerably more than bus drivers, bus drivers' hourly earnings are the same as or slightly higher than rapid-transit motormen's rates.

It was hypothesized that part of the variation in wage rates was attributable to the differences in type of ownership. Most systems becoming public have done so because of financial need. Compensation, accounting for 68 percent of expenses, is undoubtedly a prime factor in the systems' financial problems. Therefore, it was felt that public systems, being under somewhat less stringent financial constraints, would pay higher wages.

In order to determine what differences, if any, existed between public and private wage rates, two tests were made. The first test compared the wage rates of experienced bus drivers in public and private systems. There was no significant difference between the wage rates after accounting for the variation caused by differences in labor market conditions and by differences in company size.[76]

The second test compared the trend in wage rates of six systems before and after they became publicly owned. Three of the systems (Los Angeles, Philadelphia, and San Antonio) did have significantly higher wages after becoming public than could be explained by the trend; but two (Dallas and St. Louis) had significantly lower wages than expected, and Providence exhibited no significant difference. All that could be concluded was that if the change from private to public operations affected the wage rate at all, the effect was less than 5 percent.

The conclusion that type of ownership has little if any effect on wage rates should, however, be carefully interpreted. First, an effect may have occurred in the other elements of compensation; it is doubtful, for example, that any private system could afford the pension plan of New York City. (And it may be that the city cannot either, as recent events demonstrate!) [77]

Second, most systems, both public and private, have received almost all their revenues from the fare box. The present movement toward subsidization of operating losses increasingly will remove the public systems from market pressures, making possible wage raises which probably would not have occurred under strict market conditions.

Third, as with public employees in general, public transit workers only recently are beginning to test their power, especially their political power. As they become more adept at using this power, their wage rates may increase at a more rapid pace.

One system which may serve as an example of the industry's future is the Massachusetts Bay Transportation Authority, where the key elements of public control, political power, compulsory arbitration of contract impasses, and subsidization of losses through taxes have been present since at least 1931. In a careful study of the system, Melvin Lurie concluded that these factors, most importantly subsidization, have "been of assistance to the Carman's Union in maintaining its power to increase wages over such a long period of time." [78]

There is another set of circumstances which invariably has led to higher wages when a firm becomes publicly owned. When small transit systems on the periphery of a city have been merged into a regional transit authority, the compensation of their employees has increased. Small suburban firms traditionally have had lower wage scales than their much larger counterparts in central city; when they become part of the larger system, their wage rates have been increased to the level paid to the employees of the central-city system. [79] This has occurred in Pittsburgh, St. Louis, and (to a lesser degree) in Boston.

In summary, it is simplistic to say that public ownership per se leads to higher wages. Other elements, particularly subsidization of losses, are, however, likely to do so.

Conclusion

Once dominated by private systems, the transit industry of the 1970's is becoming one consisting of large public authorities. This transition has removed the industry's collective bargaining processes from the jurisdiction of the federal labor laws for private employees and has placed them under a collection of state and local public employee laws. The federal government has, however, helped shape the new collective negotiation procedures through the labor protection requirements of the Mass Transportation Act of 1964 and its amendments.

Negotiating collectively under public laws is resulting in a substitution of mediation, fact finding, and arbitration for the strike (and often for sincere bargaining as well!). Although illegal strikes do occur, impasses in the public sector are being resolved by alternate means in most cases. Public ownership per se has not appeared to affect wage rates, but it is likely that other factors often accompanying public ownership (such as political control and subsidization) will do so in the future.

NOTES

1. U. S. Bureau of the Budget, *Standard Industrial Classification Manual* (Washington: G.P.O., 1967), pp. 203-205.

2. American Transit Association, *'70-'71 Transit Fact Book* (Washington, 1970), pp. 1, 6, and loose leaf attachment.

3. *Ibid.*, p. 7.

4. Data in author's possession.

5. American Transit Association, loose leaf attachment.

6. See last section of this article.

7. Public Service lost $2.3 million in the first quarter of 1971 (*New York Times*, May 30, 1971), and National City has been divesting transit properties rapidly in recent years.

8. Data from the American Transit Association.

9. *Ibid.*

10. Philip W. Jeffress, "The Negro in the Urban Transit Industry," in Herbert R. Northrup *et al.*, *Negro Employment in Land and Air Transport*, Studies of Negro Employment, Vol. V (Philadelphia: Industrial Research Unit, Wharton School of Finance and Commerce, University of Pennsylvania, 1971), pt. 4, p. 19.

11. Matthew Guinan, *Report of the President, 13th Constitutional Convention, Transport Workers Union of America, AFL-CIO* (New York, 1969), pp. 37-82; and company data.

12. Jeffress, "The Negro in the Urban Transit Industry," pp. 14, 15, and 63.

13. *Ibid.*, pp. 45 and 64.

14. *Ibid.*, p. 64.

15. See Jeffress's study for a careful analysis of the situation.

16. Emerson P. Schmidt, *Industrial Relations in Urban Transportation* (Minneapolis, Minn.: University of Minnesota Press, 1937), pp. 3-5.

17. *Ibid.*, p. 29.

18. American Transit Association, *'70-'71 Transit Fact Book*, p. 6.

19. Lewis M. Schneider, *Marketing Urban Mass Transit* (Boston: Harvard Univeristy, 1965), p. 28.

20. American Transit Association, *'70-'71 Transit Fact Book*, p. 10.

21. *Ibid.*, calculations from data on pages 6, 9, and 10.

22. Data from American Transit Association.

23. Robert B. Carr, "MBTA Must Negotiate 26 Separate Contracts," *Boston Sunday Globe*, Feb. 7, 1971, pp. 29 and 47.

24. Data from Chicago Transit Authority.

25. Interview with Philip A. Brine, Jr., Manager of Labor Relations, Massachusetts Bay Transportation Authority, Boston, Mass. March 1971.

26. Interview with F. C. Knautz, Director of Public and Employee Relations, Chicago Transit Authority, Chicago. Ill., April 1971.

27. Peter Freund, "Labor Relations in the New York City Rapid Transit Industry, 1945-1960" (Ph.D. dissertation, New York University, 1964), p. 45. Also see James J. McGinley, *Labor Relations In the New York Rapid Transit Systems, 1904-1944* (New York: King's Crown Press, 1949), pp. 257-330.

28. Frederic Meyers, "Organization and Collective Bargaining in the Local Mass Transportation Industry in the Southeast," *Southern Economic Journal*, Vol. 15, No. 4 (April 1949), pp. 430-431.

29. Interview with Walter J. Bierwagen, Director of Public Affairs, Amalgamated Transit Union, Washington, D. C., December 1970.

30. Jeffress, "The Negro in the Urban Transit Industry," p. 87.

31. *Ibid.*

32. *Ibid.,* p. 88.

33. *Ibid.,* pp. 88-89.

34. Interview with Warren E. Scholl, President, Division 241, Amalgamated Transit Union, Chicago, Ill., April 1971.

35. Interview with Leonard Beatty, President, Division 308, Amalgamated Transit Union, Chicago, Ill., April 1971.

36. Dallas M. Young, "Fifty Years of Labor Arbitration in Cleveland Transit," *Monthly Labor Review*, Vol. 83, No. 5 (May 1960), p. 464.

37. Increased wages normally necessitate fare increases. Fare increases result in fewer passengers, as discussed in Highway Research Board, "Passenger Transportation," *Highway Research Record*, Number 213 (Washington, 1968).

38. Data from American Transit Association.

39. National Labor Relations Board v. Baltimore Transit Co., 140 F.2d 51 (CA-4, 1944); cert. den., 64 S. Ct. 847 (1944).

40. Emerson P. Schmidt, *Industrial Relations in Urban Transportation* (Minneapolis, Minn.: University of Minnesota Press, 1937), p. 193.

41. *Ibid.*

42. Amalgamated Transit Association, *Constitution and General Laws*, Revised, Amended and Adopted at the Fortieth Convention, September 8-11, 1969 (Washington, 1969), p. 47.

43. Herbert R. Northrup, "Labor Relations in Urban Transit: Bleak Future For the 1970's," speech in a series on *Frontiers of Urban Transportation in the 1970's*, sponsored by the Transportation Studies Center of the Center for Urban Research and Experiment, University of Pennsylvania, Philadelphia, Pa., Feb. 2, 1971.

44. Alfred Kuhn, *Arbitration in Transit, An Evaluation of Wage Criteria* (Philadelphia, Pa.: Labor Relations Council, Wharton School of Finance and Commerce, University of Pennsylvania, 1952), pp. 164-194.

45. *Ibid.,* p. 183.

46. *Ibid.,* p. 185.

47. Wolff Packing Co. v. Court of Industrial Relations, 262 U.S. 522 (1923); 267 U.S. 552 (1925).

48. Domenico Gagliardo, *The Kansas Industrial Court, An Experiment In Compulsory Arbitration* (Lawrence, Kans.: University of Kansas Press, 1941), p. 87.

49. Herbert R. Northrup and Richard L. Rowan, "Arbitration and Collective Bargaining: An Analysis of State Experience," *Labor Law Journal*, Vol. 14, No. 2 (February 1963) (reprinted in Herbert R. Northrup, *Compulsory Arbitration and Government Intervention in Labor Disputes* [Washington: Labor Policy Association, Inc. 1966], pp. 215-234.

50. *Ibid.*

51. Amalgamated Association v. Wisconsin Employment Relations Board, 340 U.S. 383 (1951).

52. Northrup, *Compulsory Arbitration and Government Intervention in Labor Disputes*, p. 221.

53. For an analysis of seizure laws and their impact, see Herbert R. Northrup and Richard L. Rowan, "State Seizure in Public Interest Disputes," *Journal of Business of the University of Chicago*, Vol. 26, April 1963 (reprinted in Northrup, *Compulsory Arbitration and Government Intervention in Labor Disputes*, pp. 235-261).

54. Division 1287, Amalgamated Association v. State of Missouri, 374 U.S. 74 (1963).

55. See Herbert R. Northrup, "Fact-Finding in Labor Disputes: The States' Experience," *Industrial and Labor Relations Review*, Vol. 17, No. 1 (October 1963) (reprinted in Northrup, *Compulsory Arbitration and Government Intervention in Labor Disputes*, pp. 263-293).

56. *Ibid.*, p. 288; Grand Rapids City Coach Lines v. Howlett, 137 F. Supp. 667 (1956); General Electric Co. v. Callahan, 294 F.2d 60 (1962); and Oil Chemical and Atomic Workers v. Arkansas Louisiana Gas Co., 320 F.2d 62 (1964).

57. Federal and state governments have concurrent jurisdiction in mediation. See Herbert R. Northrup and Gordon F. Bloom, *Government and Labor* (Homewood, Ill.: Irwin, 1963), pp. 284-292.

58. Northrup, *Compulsory Arbitration and Government Intervention in Labor Disputes*, pp. 32-33.

59. Urban Mass Transportation Act of 1964, as amended, 49 U.S.C. § 1601 *et seq.*

60. Metropolitan Transit District, as amended, Annotated Code of Maryland, Act 64B § 37 para. *a* (1970).

61. John Elliott, *Report of the International President to the Fortieth Convention of the ATU* (New York: Amalgamated Transit Union, 1969), p. 4.

62. The information about state public employee relations laws came from three sources: Bureau of National Affairs, *Government Employee Relations Report*, Reference File, State and Local Programs, updated to May 17, 1971; Richard S. Rubin, *A Summary of State Collective Bargaining Law in Public Employment* (Ithaca, N. Y.: Cornell University, 1968), Public Employee Relations Report Number 3, p. 17; and Sylvia Weissbrodt, "Changes in State Labor Laws in 1970," *Monthly Labor Review*, Vol. 94, No. 1 (January 1971), pp. 15-16.

63. Fred Smigelski and Don McDonough, "Back-to-Work Order Ignored; $100,000 Fine Doubles Daily," *Inquirer* (Philadelphia, Pa.) Apr. 15, 1971, p. 1.

64. California Department of Industrial Relations, State Conciliation Service, *1968 Annual Report* (San Francisco: California Office of State Printing, 1969), pp. 7-8.

65. *Ibid.*

66. Annotated Code of Maryland, Act 64B § 37 para. *b* (1970) (emphasis added).

67. Acts and Resolves passed at the General Assembly of the State of Rhode Island and Providence Plantations, chap. 210, May 7, 1964, Sec. 39-18-17 (emphasis added).

68. Elliott, *Report of the International President to the Fortieth Convention of the ATU, calculations* from pp. 38-66.

69. Data in author's possession.

70. Unless otherwise noted, the data in this section came from the U.S. Bureau of Labor Statistics annual surveys of wage rates and scheduled hours of work for agreements in four industries: building construction, printing, local transit, and local trucking. These studies present the wage rates in effect on July 1. All other data came from U.S. Bureau of Labor Statistics, *Handbook of Labor Statistics, 1970* (Washington: G.P.O., 1970); or American Transit Association, *Transit Fact Books*, various years.

71. Kuhn, *Arbitration in Transit, An Evaluation of Wage Criteria*, p. ix.

72. Main Lafrentz & Co., *Port Authority of Allegheny County, Seven City Report*, November 1970, p. 11.

73. Wilbur Smith & Associates, *An Evaluation Study of the Properties and Operation of Department of Street Railways, City of Detroit, Michigan*, November 1970, p. 35.

74. Richard Phalon, "City Pension Costs Increase Sharply," *New York Times*, Aug. 2, 1970, pp. 1 and 28.

75. Data in author's possession.

76. Although virtually all the industry is now unionized, Lurie found that a wage differential of between 5 and 20 percent existed between unionized and nonunionized companies at one time. For a detailed analysis, see Melvin Lurie, "The Measurement of the Effect of Unionization on Wages in the Transit Industry" (Ph.D. dissertation, University of Chicago, December 1958).

77. See, for example, Phalon, "City Pension Costs Increase Sharply"; and David K. Shipler, "City Pension Costs Snowballing," *New York Times*, March 15, 1971, pp. 1 and 59.

78. Melvin Lurie, "Government Regulation and Union Power: A Case Study of the Boston Transit Industry," *Journal of Law and Economics*, Vol. 3, October 1960, p. 134.

79. The author is indebted to Thomas Lenthall, transportation consultant, for pointing out this phenomenon to him.

PART IV

B. Equal Employment Opportunity

Can Collective Bargaining Survive Without Protecting the Rights of Minorities and Women?

William H. Brown III †

As an almunus of the University of Pennsylvania, it is a great pleasure to be "home again." And, I am most happy to be at a conference co-sponsored by the Industrial Research Unit. Its report series "Racial Policies of American Industry" and "Studies of Negro Employment" have contributed significantly to the understanding of equal employment opportunity.

I was asked to speak to you today on the subject, "Can Collective Bargaining Protect Minority Employees' Rights?" I would, however, rephrase that question to read: "Can Collective Bargaining Survive Without Protecting the Rights of Minorities and Women?" I suggest to you that the answer to that question is a resounding, "No." Failure to protect employment rights of women and minorities is a violation of the law, and failure to do this will encourage women and minorities, no longer willing to wait for justice, to seek alternatives to collective bargaining for the redress of their grievances. The resulting excessive litigation and unrest will in the long run tend to destroy the fabric of collective bargaining.

Let me review some of the statutes and executive orders which prohibit employment discrimination and may have an effect on the collective bargaining process.

The National Labor Relations Act,[1] administered by the National Labor Relations Board, focuses on collective bargaining and union activity. The Board has ruled on race and sex discrimination in a number of contexts. The Board has held that units based solely on the racial[2] or sexual[3] identity of employees are inappropriate, and that a contract that discriminates by reason of race[4] or sex[5] will not operate as a bar to a new election to determine union representation.

---

† The Honorable William H. Brown III is Chairman of the Equal Employment Opportunity Commission.

Furthermore, the Board has established a number of other leading principles with respect to racial discrimination which appear equally applicable to discrimination based on sex or national origin. It has stated that a union which causes or permits discrimination against employees because of race or other "invidious reasons" violates its duty to represent all members in the unit fairly,[6] that a union's refusal to pursue grievance and arbitration procedure because of race violates the Act,[7] and that racial discrimination by the statutory bargaining representative requires revocation of the union's certification.[8] The Board has recently granted the Commission leave to file an *amicus curiae* brief contesting the certification of a union whose international systematically discriminates against women in its model collective bargaining agreement.[9] Finally, in the recent case of *United Packinghouse Union* v. *NLRB*,[10] the Court found that discrimination based on race and national origin *by an employer* constitutes a violation of the Labor Act.

Title VII of the Civil Rights Act of 1964 prohibits discrimination in all terms, conditions, and privileges of employment by employers, employment agencies, and unions based on race, color, religion, sex and national origin. It is administered by the Equal Employment Opportunity Commission.[11]

The Equal Pay Act, which became generally effective in 1964, is administered by the Wage-Hour Administration in the Department of Labor.[12] The Act requires the payment of equal salaries and wages with regard to sex.

Executive Order 11246, as amended by 11375, prohibits discrimination based on race, color, religion, sex or national origin by federal contractors and subcontractors and on federally assisted construction contracts. It is administered by the Office of Federal Contract Compliance (OFCC) in the Department of Labor. The Philadelphia Plan and like plans are issued pursuant to this Executive Order. The OFCC has recently issued proposed Revised Order No. 4 which would require covered employers to establish goals and timetables for the employment of women [13] as they are currently required to do for minorities.

The remainder of my remarks will focus on the relationship between Title VII and the elimination of employment discrimination through the collective bargaining agreement. I would like to discuss the kinds of provisions which must be eliminated, the means available to redress their past discriminatory effects, and the types of affirmative action programs you may institute for the future.

Title VII of the Civil Rights Act of 1964 became effective on July 2, 1965. It prohibits discrimination in employment on the basis of race, color, religion, sex or national origin, by employers of 25 or more employees,[14] unions with 25 or more members or hiring halls,[15] and employment agencies [16] including the United States Employment Service and the system of state and local employment services receiving federal assistance.[17] The prohibition against discrimination in employment under the Act also extends to any employer, union, or joint labor-management committee controlling apprenticeship or other training or retraining, including on-the-job training programs, and employment in any program established to provide apprenticeship or other training, all of which are to include women and minorities.[18]

It is estimated that about 155,000 collective bargaining agreements covering more than 21.2 million workers were in existence in 1968.[19] Some of the provisions in collective bargaining agreements are discriminatory on their face; others, valid on their face, set up a system whose effect is to perpetuate past discrimination. Both types of situations violate Title VII. With respect to the first type of situation, the Commission and the courts have found that job classifications and seniority lines, segregated on the basis of race or sex, must be eliminated.[20] Similarly, company disability insurance benefit plans which do not include disability resulting from pregnancy on the same terms as other non-occupational disabilities violate the Act.[21] Company retirement and pension plans which differentiate on the basis of race and sex also violate the Act.[22]

The more subtle situation, where the contract provisions appear lawful on their face but have the effect of maintaining a discriminatory system, presents more difficulties. Let's take a typical situation of this kind involving a seniority provision.[23] A collective bargaining agreement provides for promotions and layoffs based on departmental seniority, and loss of seniority on interdepartmental transfers. This seniority system on its face would appear lawful. However, let us assume that in this plant blacks and women were traditionally excluded from certain more desirable departments and, accordingly, never attained seniority in them. In such a situation the effect of the seniority provision would be to perpetuate the past discriminatory system of closed departments. The affected women and blacks would be handicapped in competing on an equal basis with those whites and males hired at the same time into the better departments since without seniority in the new departments the victims of discrimination would be unable to secure promotions and would be more vulnerable to layoffs. In such a situation, the contract provision and seniority system must be changed. Depending upon the particular situation the following may be required:

1. A system of plantwide seniority, where possible.

2. A system of seniority carried forward upon transfer to the new department.

3. Rate-maintenance or "red-circling." This involves paying the victims of discrimination at the wage-rate of their pre-transfer position until they attain a position in the new department which pays as much more, or as much as they would have received had there initially not been any discrimination.

4. The development of special training programs to enable the affected women and blacks to move into jobs above the entry level in the new department.

5. Finally, back pay to compensate the affected female and black employees for the difference in wages or salaries they would have earned but for the maintenance of the discriminatory seniority system.

One of the objects of the collective bargaining process must be the elimination and prevention of all forms of employment discrimination. A most effective way to accomplish this is through the establishment of affirmative action programs. Such programs should include recruitment, management and on-the-job training and apprenticeship programs. This is an area where the company and union can effectively work together in developing such programs.

In one sense the achievement of equal employment opportunity is the kind of problem that labor and management are particularly well prepared to deal with. Only a few years ago, labor and management were spending much time and money training foremen to accept such concepts as seniority versus ability, to recognize the importance of job security, and to strike a balance between job security rights and plant efficiency. They were successful in such efforts. Now, labor and management must rise to a new challenge. They must again be willing to spend time and money to implement the concepts of equal employment opportunity.

If the collective bargaining process fails, there may be other avenues open to the employer or union by which to remedy employment discrimination. Faced with a recalcitrant union, an employer may, in certain circumstances, be able to take unilateral action to change the discriminatory provisions of the collective bargaining agreements, and union efforts to resist such changes may be halted by injunction.[24] Inasmuch as such action may bring on charges of unfair labor practices before the Labor Board, the collective bargaining route is, of course, more preferable.

A union, on the other hand, facing resistance from an employer to change the collective bargaining agreement, may file a charge of employment discrimination against the employer under Title VII.[25] In fact, a union has the affirmative responsibility, as exclusive bargaining representative, to fairly represent all employees in the unit, which includes processing grievances of employment discrimination, seeking to bargain with the employer to remedy unlawful employment discrimination, and filing charges, where necessary.[26] Where discriminatory employment provisions or customs exist, both the union and employer are jointly and severally liable.[27]

Failure or refusal by unions and employers to take those steps necessary to eliminate the effects of present and past discrimination have proven very costly. This is so since suits under Title VII are class actions: by definition they are based on group identity like race or sex.[28] Since the damage awards may involve entire classes of employees, they run into considerable sums. The sooner the employment discrimination is eliminated, the smaller any possible damage awards for past discrimination will be. As a matter of self-interest, employers and unions would do well to act speedily. In a sex discrimination case under Title VII, the Anaconda Aluminum Company agreed to pay $190,000 in back wages and court costs to 276 women who had alleged that the company maintained sex-segregated job classifications.[29] In a case against the Lorillard Company and the plant's union [30] for maintaining a seniority system which perpetuated the effects of past discrimination, a settlement of a half million dollars in back pay and $250,000 in attorney's fees was agreed to. In an Equal Pay case, *Hodgson* v. *Wheaton Glass Co.*, the District Court of

New Jersey ordered the company to pay over $900,000 in back-pay and interest to the 2,000 employees involved.

Without doubt, a great effort will have to be made to eradicate all forms and effects of employment discrimination from the collective bargaining agreement alone. The task is clear, the remedy at times complex. Take the initiative and weed out discrimination. The Commission is willing to supply expertise in helping to solve individual problems. Our Technical Assistance Division in the Office of Voluntary Programs has specialists in labor-management fields able to help develop appropriate remedies in cases involving discriminatory seniority systems, for example. Ask us.

The 1970's will see an avalanche of disputes resulting from the existence of inequality on the basis of race, sex, and national origin in the collective bargaining process and lack of full integration of minorities and women in the union leadership.[31] Militant groups of minority workers, as a consequence, are organizing in order to surface their own problems and interests on the job and as union members.[32] Female workers also are making similar organizational efforts. A recent example is the activities of the Communications Workers of America's (CWA) female rank and file. Alleging that last July's strike settlement agreement between their union and the Bell System perpetuated discriminatory wage rates, they attempted to defeat its ratification.[33] This undercurrent of unrest will most likely become a tidal wave unless labor and management end employment discrimination and enable women and minorities to participate in the positions of leadership which control their employment destinies.

In summary, I would like to leave you with these thoughts: The only permissible collective bargaining concerning employment discrimination is its elimination; unions and employers cannot bargain away the rights of employees to be free of discrimination and compensated for its effects where discrimination has occurred.[34] The sooner these legal obligations are realized, the more certain will be the survival of collective bargaining.

NOTES

1. 29 U.S.C. Sec. 151 *et seq.* (1964).

2. New Deal Cab Co., 159 NLRB 1838 (1966); Andrews Industries, 105 NLRB 946 (1953).

3. United States Baking Co., 165 NLRB 951 (1967); Cuneo Eastern Press, Inc., 106 NLRB 343 (1953).

4. Pioneer Bus Co., 140 NLRB 54 (1962).

5. St. Louis Cordage Mills, 168 NLRB 981 (1967).

6. NLRB v. Local 1367, International Longshoremen's Association, AFL-CIO, 368 F.2d 1010 (5th Cir. 1966); Hughes Tool Co., 147 NLRB 1573 (1964); Miranda Fuel Co., 140 NLRB 181 (1962), *enforcement denied,* 326 F.2d 172 (2d Cir. 1963). *Cf.,* The Emporium and Western Addition Community Organization, 1971 CCH NLRB para. 23299, 192 NLRB— (No. 19) (1971) (dissenting opinion, Jenkins).

7. Local 12, United Rubber Workers v. NLRB, 368 F.2d 12 (5th Cir. 1966). *See* Vaca v. Sipes, 386 U.S. 171 (1967).

8. Hughes Tool Co., 147 NLRB 1573 (1964).

9. American Mailing Corporation and Bookbinders and Bindery Workers Union, Local No. 144, I.B. of B., AFL-CIO, Case No. 5-RC-7726 (NLRB 1971).

10. 416 F.2d 1126 (D.C. Cir. 1969), *remanding* 169 NLRB 290 (1968), *cert. denied,* 396 U.S. 903 (1969), 194 NLRB—(No. 3) (1971) (finding no employer pattern or practice of discrimination).

11. 42 U.S.C. Sec. 2000e *et seq.* (1964).

12. 29 U.S.C. Sec. 206 (d) (1964). The Interpretive Bulletin of the Equal Pay Act appears at 29 C.F.R. 800 *et seq.* (1970).

13. 36 Fed. Reg. 17444 (Aug. 31, 1971).

14. Sec. 703 (a), 42 U.S.C. Sec. 2000e-2(a).

15. Sec. 703 (c), 42 U.S.C. Sec. 2000e-2(c).

16. Sec. 703 (b), 42 U.S.C. Sec. 2000e-2(b).

17. Sec. 701 (b), 42 U.S.C. Sec. 2000e(b).

18. Sec. 703 (d), 42 U.S.C. Sec. 2000e-2(d).

19. U.S. Department of Labor, Directory of National and International Labor Unions in the United States 1969, 78-79 (Bureau of Labor Statistics, 1971).

20. Title VII does, however, permit the hiring of members of one sex in those very few situations where the sexual characteristics of the employee are crucial to the successful performance of the job, as they would be for the position of wet-nurse, or where there is a need for authenticity or genuineness, as in the case of an actor or actress. Rosenfield v. Southern Pacific Co., 444 F.2d 1219, 1224-1225, 3 F.E.P. Cases 604, 607-608 (9th Cir. 1971); Diaz v. Pan American World Airways, Inc., 442 F.2d 385, 3 E.P.D. para. 8166 (5th Cir. 1971).

21. Commission Decision No. 71-1474, 3 F.E.P. Cases 588 (March 19, 1971).

22. Bartmess v. Drewrys U.S.A., Inc., 444 F.2d 1186 (7th Cir. 1971); Rosen v. Public Service Electric and Gas Co., 409 F.2d 775 (3rd Cir. 1969).

23. Robinson v. P. Lorillard Corp., 444 F.2d 791 (1971); Vogler v. Asbestos Workers, 407 F.2d 1047 (5th Cir. 1969); Quarles v. Phillip Morris, 279 F. Supp. 505 (E.D. Va. 1968); Local 189, Papermakers v. U.S., 416 F.2d 980 (5th Cir. 1969); U.S. v. Bethlehem Steel, 446 F.2d 652 (2nd Cir. 1971); Jones v. Lee Way Motor Freight, 431 F.2d 245 (10th Cir. 1970), *cert. den.,* 401 U.S. 954 (1971).

24. *See* U.S. v. Papermakers, Local 189, 282 F. Supp. 39, 42, 45 (E.D. La., 1969), *affirmed,* 416 F.2d 980 (5th Cir. 1969); The Emporium and Western Addition Community Organization, 192 NLRB—(No. 19 at 12) (dissenting opinion, Jenkins). *Cf.* Gould, *Black Power in the Unions: The Impact Upon Collective Bargaining Relationships,* 79 Yale L. J. 46 at 70-71 nn. 104-106 (1969); *Cf.* Peck, *Remedies for Racial Discrimination In Employment: A Comparative Evaluation of Forums,* 46 Wash. L. Rev. 455 at 479 (1971).

25. Pulp, Sulphite and Paper Mill Workers, Local 186 v. Minnesota Mining and Manufacturing Co., 304 F. Supp. 1284 (N.D. Miss. 1969); ICW, Local 795 v. Planters Manufacturing Co., 259 F. Supp. 365 (M.D. Miss. 1966); Commission Decision No. 71-1547, 3 FEP Cases 763 (March 30, 1971).

26. *See, e.g.,* Commission Decision No. 71-1985, 3 F.E.P. Cases 1103 (May 3, 1971).

27. *Cf.* Blanton v. Southern Bell Telephone & Telegraph Co., 2 F.E.P. Cases 602, 49 FRD 162 (D.C. Ga. 1970); U.S. v. Georgia Power Co., —— F. Supp. ——, 3 F.E.P. Cases 767 at 792 (N.D. Ga. 1971) (joint liability for payment of attorney's fees); Robinson v. P. Lorillard Corp., 444 F.2d 791 (4th Cir. 1971).

28. Sprogis v. United Airlines, 444 F.2d 1194, 3 F.E.P. Cases 621, 3 E.P.D. para. 8239 (7th Cir. 1971).

29. EEOC Press Release No. 71-8 (June 30, 1971).

30. Robinson v. Lorillard, 444 F.2d 791 (4th Cir. 1971).

31. *See* Gould, *Black Power in Unions: The Impact on Collective Bargaining Relationships,* 79 Yale L.J. 46 (1969); Gould, *Racial Equality in Jobs and Unions, Collective Bargaining and the Burger Court,* 68 Mich. L. Rev. 237 (1969); Hain, *Black Workers* v. *White Unions: Alternate Strategies in the Construction Industry,* 16 Wayne L. Rev. 37 (1969); J. Jones, Jr., *To Rouse "A Slumbering Giant"—Government Contracting and Equal Employment Initiatives for the 70's* in Labor Law Developments 1971, Proceedings of the 17th American Institute (on Labor Law), at 151 (Southwestern Legal Foundation, Dallas, Texas 1971); Gitlow, *The Trade Union Prospect in the Coming Decade,* 21 Lab. L. J. 131, 148-152 (1970); Dolnick, *The Settlement of Grievances and the "Job Conscious" Theory,* 21 Lab. L. J. 240 (1970); Sviridoff, *The Role Of Unions in the 1970's,* in Proceedings of New York University, Twenty-Third Annual Conference on Labor, at 39 (Christensen and Christensen eds. 1971).

32. Groups like DRUM (the Dodge Revolutionary Union Movement), UBB (the United Black Brothers of Ford Mahwah) and the League of Revolutionary Black Workers at Chrysler continue to organize. See Henle, *Some Reflections on Organized Labor and the New Militants*, 92 Monthly Labor Rev. 20 (1969).

33. Calame, *Liberating "Ma Belle": Female Telephone Workers Hit Labor Pact, Say Men Still Get the Best Jobs, More Pay,* The Wall Street Journal, July 26, 1971, at 22, col. 1.

34. Hodgson v. Sagner, —— F. Supp. ——, 3 EPD para. 8214 (D.C. Md., 1971) (union jointly and severally liable with employer for bargaining away back pay rights of female employees).

Will Greater EEOC Powers Expand Minority Employment?

Herbert R. Northrup †

During the past decade more progress has been made in achieving equal employment opportunity than in any similar previous period. Yet, equality is far from a reality. In particular, high unemployment continues to exist in the black populated areas of the cities, and change in many industries, although evident, seems to occur slowly.

Pride in progress is thus coupled with disappointment and frustration at the lack of more. It is perhaps therefore not surprising that instant solutions are so easily peddled and that the consequences of their creating more frustrations as well as more problems thereby are so lightly ignored. Nevertheless, it seems important to me to raise one small voice against the current wisdom (perhaps I should say religion, so fervently and emotionally is it held) that greater powers for the Equal Employment Opportunity Commission would automatically mean greater job equality; and to emphasize that one can hold such views while firmly supporting equal employment opportunity and continuing efforts of government to insist on such opportunity. In making these remarks, I shall rely heavily on the research now being conducted at the Wharton School under my direction,[1] and my thirty year interest in seeking to make equal employment opportunity a reality.[2]

Greater Power for EEOC?

Current legislation before Congress would give the Equal Employment Opportunity Commission power to issue cease and desist orders on the model of the National Labor Relations Board. An alternate bill opposed by the Democrat majority and

---

† Herbert R. Northrup is Professor of Industry and Director of the Industrial Research Unit, Wharton School, University of Pennsylvania. This paper was delivered at the Spring, 1971 Meeting, Industrial Relations Research Association; reproduced with permission.

its civil rights and labor allies, would instead give EEOC the right to seek court enforcement on its own. Now it has neither power, but it can and does file *amicus*, or supporting briefs, when individuals file cases, and can refer cases to the Department of Justice for action where a "pattern of discrimination" is alleged to exist.

Similar bills have been introduced in each Congress since the Civil Rights Act of 1964 was passed. Title VII, which establishes the EEOC and deals with employment, was charged with being inadequate before it went into effect. Uncritically, this charge became part of the wisdom of our times and agreement thereto the *sine qua non* of minority leadership political support. In the last Congress only a dispute between civil rights leaders and the AFL-CIO over the role of the Office of Federal Contract Compliance, the civil rights coordinating agency for executive branch procurement, seemingly prevented its passage.

It would appear logical to assume that the only rationale for giving government bureaucracy more authority over the decisions of private citizens is that present authority has failed to achieve the results desired by Congress through existing legislation. Yet such a change is difficult to sustain, and most emphatically ignores (1) voluntary compliance; (2) cases brought by individuals; and (3) "pattern of discrimination" cases initiated by the Department of Justice generally at EEOC recommendation. Certainly, the great changes in employment patterns wrought since 1965 must be attributed in part to the average citizen's desire to comport with the law. Fortuitously the law became effective at the height of the greatest boom in our industrial history, and the combination of the two contributed to the great change; but the policy of the law certainly played a major role.

In court enforcement matters, the most significant is probably the pattern cases, but individual cases have achieved key decisional victories. For example, the "rightful place" doctrine, preventing the impact of past discrimination from continuing unabated, was won in an individually brought case [3] supported by EEOC, as was the testing decision involving Duke Power Company.[4] The former doctrine was enhanced and expanded in a pattern of discrimination case;[5] the pattern type cases have been used with effectiveness in several building trades cases [6] and successfully to upset the discriminatory seniority system in a major trucking situation—the first break in the invidious union-management policies found in the key over-the-road trucking industry.[7] Numerous other key cases and litigations could be cited to support the position that EEOC initiated or supported litigation has been far more potent than the supporters of bureaucratically enhanced power would lead one to believe. Indeed, I suggest that the case can be far more easily made that EEOC as now constituted has had significant enforcement success rather than the other way around.

The 1970 Civil Rights Commission Report

Of course, despite the successful litigation involving EEOC and despite the great progress made in the past several years, it has been charged that more progress (and presumably more litigation) would have occurred if the EEOC had had greater powers. The most important document which attempts to relate civil rights enforcement insufficiency as a direct cause of continuing job inequality is the 1970 study of the United States Commission on Civil Rights entitled, *Federal Civil Rights Enforcement Effort*.[8] This bulky 1,115 page report, about which many have commented, but which few have read, delves into all aspects of civil rights interest and concludes uniformly that laws and enforcement procedures are not working well. The reasoning is charmingly simplistic: if any inequality exists, enforcement of rights is a failure.

Approximately 350 pages of the *Report* are devoted to employment. Some quite reasonable suggestions are made, for example, concerning the need for better coordination among enforcement agencies and between such agencies and procurement bodies. In addition, the *Report* acknowledges the effective litigation record of EEOC, noting that the latter "has had noteworthy success in its *amicus* activity in persuading the courts to adopt its position, particularly in the areas of formulating adequate remedies, determining issues of 'standing to sue' and in developing procedures designed to benefit the charging party." [9] The *Report,* however, is primarily concerned with demonstrating EEOC inadequacy. Thus it concludes that "while there have been some overall minority employment gains in the general private labor market, discrimination continues largely unabated six years after Congress ordered equal employment opportunity as organic law." [10]

This conclusion, of course, is not only factually incorrect; it also assumes that job inequality is *per se* the result of continued discrimination, whereas the *Report* authors surely must know such relationships are far more complicated. Of course effective government support is an absolute necessity if we are to achieve equal employment. This has been documented innumerable times. In the Racial Policies of American Industry studies, which now cover experience in 27 industries, this has been repeatedly pointed out. Equally well documented is that such support is insufficient in itself to achieve equality. It cannot overcome inadequate training and education; its effectiveness is limited when employment is declining; it cannot immediately offset a history of discrimination; it cannot move people from one location to jobs in another; and it cannot reorder the job structure of an industry to a marked degree, although it can, and has, recast discriminatory upgrading policies and seniority systems.

Consider, for example, the situation in the aerospace industry. In 1966, I obtained data from 21 of the largest companies in this industry, which then employed 788,022 persons in 127 establishments, or about two-thirds of the industry's total.[11] These companies employed 179,436 professionals in 1966, of whom only 0.8 percent, or 1,435, were black. On the face, this looks like a highly discriminatory pattern of employment. Moreover, in 1968, these same companies had, if conventional ratings are utilized, improved little. Their total professional employment declined a bit to 179,041, their black professional complement increased slightly to 1,598, but the Negro percentage was still only 0.9 percent. On such a basis, a company with a considerably better than average record in these matters than the industry, McDonnell Douglas, was publicly excoriated by the Civil Rights Commission as unfit to receive a key government contract because of its low percentage of black personnel in professional and other top salaried positions.[12]

But if one looks at the total picture, a different situation emerges. In 1966, when 21 companies in the aerospace industry had a professional black ratio of only 0.8 percent, they employed approximately 40 percent of all Negro professionals in manufacturing industry reporting to the EEOC! Data for 1968 on all manufacturing are not available, but I judge from the 1969 all industry data that the proportion of Negro professionals had expanded more rapidly in industry generally than in aerospace. Still, aerospace had a large share of those available.

There is still more to the total picture. Professor Robert Kiehl of the Newark College of Engineering has been keeping a careful record of the demand and supply of Negro engineering talent since the mid-1950's. In his most recent study, released in October 1970, he concludes:

1. Only about 2 percent of engineering students are black, but that percentage is not increasing, and did not increase between 1962 and 1970.

2. Government fair employment practice legislation has greatly aided black engineers in finding jobs, but apparently has not increased the supply.

3. "There seems to be no question but that there are widespread education and employment opportunities for blacks in engineering . . .

4. "The relative lack of information on engineering coupled with employment discrimination of the past seem to be the chief reasons for the apparent lack of interest of blacks in the profession today." [13]

Studies of other professions would undoubtedly yield similar results: opportunities available, but going begging, and slow accretion at best at the supply level. Obviously, giving cease and desist powers to the EEOC would not solve this problem.

Moreover, since 1969, aerospace employment has declined dramatically. Engineers have been especially hard hit by unemployment, and further cuts are likely in view of the liberal-led onslaught on defense and space spending. Wiped out are the jobs for which many Negroes were trained by this industry, which without doubt has developed the outstanding training capacity in the land. Especially to be lamented is the disappearance of high talent positions in the Southeast where aerospace concerns led in breaking the color line, opening up housing to black professionals, and upgrading the indigenous labor force.[14] The almost unanimous support of civil rights leaders to cuts in defense and space spending has cost their race considerable in quality jobs. Advocating more power for the EEOC will not restore what is lost.

If space permitted, analyses could be made of several other industries to show that the problem of inequality could not be cured by greater EEOC enforcement powers where the need is for trained personnel,[15] or where employment is declining,[16] or turnover low,[17] or location (for nonracial reasons) has shifted from cities to areas where few minorities dwell.[18] Far from being a failure, existing civil rights legislation has done wonders in the face of the structual and labor market obstacles which it has faced, and will continue to face whether a greater powers bill is enacted, until all aspects of past discrimination in education, motivation, and other socio-economic factors are eliminated through the efforts of all of us.

To return to the Civil Rights Commission *Report*, its conclusions are not only simplistic, its facts are questionable. The *Report* makes no effort to provide a systematic analysis. Rather, it leapfrogs from industry to industry, area to area, and year to year, to present a grab bag of information designed to support a pre-arrived-at conclusion. Its facts pertain to a five-year period and many probably have changed before published. Using as it does isolated examples, the reader must assume that they are typical. They are not necessarily so. By overwhelming the reader with quantity without qualitative analysis or orientation, the desired effect is obtained.

Moreover, many of the so called facts are gleaned from Commission hearings. These are highly structured affairs, in which witnesses are arranged for beforehand, companies or unions are damned publicly without right of witness cross-examination, and information is accepted from highly partisan sources without appropriate rebuttal. Thus the Commission made great headlines castigating McDonnell Douglas (and probably rescued itself from going out of existence) in St. Louis last year. A principal witness was an individual who had been discharged from the company for chaining people in offices and blocking traffic. The Commission listened sympathetically to his special pleading a short time before a federal judge, noting that violating the law and endangering human lives are not protected activities under the Civil Rights Act, dismissed with prejudice his case for reemployment.[19]

The NLRB Model and the EEOC

A secondary argument adduced by those who argue for more power for EEOC is procedural. They point out quite correctly that complaint procedure under EEOC is clumsy and time consuming, requiring as it does, first, reference to a local or state body if available, then conciliation, and finally seeking redress in courts. Moreover, where cases are referred to the Department of Justice for possible pattern of discrimination charges, the latter has found it necessary to reinvestigate because of the failure of EEOC to supply sufficient evidence.[20]

The procedural problems are compounded by EEOC's inability to handle its case load expeditiously. This is usually blamed on inadequate staffing, but the Civil Rights Commission's *Report* also charged various administrative laxities, a high turnover of personnel, and inexperienced management.[21]

Proponents of more power for EEOC argue that it would be able to settle cases more quickly, that it would be able to handle cases more expeditiously and that it would litigate more successfully if it had more powers.[22] The arguments are neither consistent nor persuasive. To be sure, the procedure is time consuming. But it has not been demonstrated that giving EEOC more authority would speed up the process. Certainly the administrative defects in the agency are not caused by lack of authority. Administrative shortcomings, turnover, and inexperience can be corrected over time, but not by cease and desist orders.

Moreover, consider the NLRB upon which the liberal coalition would model EEOC. Professor Philip Ross, an ardent proponent of enhancing administrative power, found some years ago that nearly two and one-half years elapsed between the filing of an unfair labor practice charge and the issuance of a judicial decree.[23] The current chairman of the NLRB regards the extensive period required to conclude a case under NLRB procedure as his major administrative problem.[24] He and other NLRB members continue to be concerned about long drawn out procedures which in fact seem to be about equal to those of the EEOC in terms of time.[25]

It is possible that if EEOC had enforcement powers more litigants would agree to its proposed conciliation terms. Many do not now, however, because the basis proposed for settlement by EEOC conciliations is unreasonable. Cease and desist orders might increase litigation in such instances, but would not necessarily effectuate the purposes of the Civil Rights Act. Moreover, to be successful in litigation, either under cease and desist orders, or with direct EEOC court filings, EEOC investigators would have to improve their investigatory techniques and fact gathering, and learn more about industry structure, intraplant mobility, bargaining relationships, and a host of other factors involved in evaluating personnel policies. Otherwise, their cases will be lost or justice will miscarry.

The fact of the matter is that no demonstration has been made that increased powers will improve EEOC procedure or results.

Certainly, it will do nothing about the agency's alleged shortage of funds. The claims that it will improve its capacity to dispose of cases rapidly is belied by the NLRB experience. And the assertion that more powers will in itself dispose of cases more satisfactorily or more rapidly is at best a pious hope unsupported by evidence.

From the beginning, the proponents of enhanced bureaucratic power have been unhappy with the EEOC enforcement procedure. Thus when the agency was just beginning operation the current Dean of the Columbia University Law School referred to EEOC as "a poor enfeebled thing . . . [having] the power to conciliate but not to compel." [26] This alleged lack of authority would certainly come as a great surprise to such companies as Philip Morris, Crown Zellerbach, Duke Power, such unions as the United Papermakers, the International Brotherhood of Electrical Workers, the Asbestos Workers, and many other companies and unions. It should also be equally startling to the thousands of black persons now enjoying good jobs because of EEOC's existence. A look at the record instead of one's preconceptions tells a different story.

Actually, the real EEOC enforcement problem is not too little, but too late. There is no reason why its procedures cannot be improved within the current model. The current chairman, Mr. William H. Brown III, has already addressed himself to this problem and is making good progress. President Nixon has proposed an increased budget for next fiscal year. Better training of personnel, improved administrative procedures, better development, and better coordination with other agencies can and will substantially shorten case disposition time and reduce case loads.

The Scope of EEOC Authority

Another reason why I believe that it would be unwise to extend the powers of EEOC is that such extension would give the agency great authority over the selection of corporate management, executives, and even directors. Again, of course, this does not imply either that there are enough black or minority persons in such positions of authority, or that persons of minority heritage are not capable of performing these functions. Nevertheless, one may question whether agencies which are primarily interested in improving the economic status of minorities should be in a position to exercise great authority over each and every promotion and appointment to executive positions in industry. Such review is too likely to be narrowly based. I doubt whether it is in the public interest—including that of minorities—to pressure industry to staff its top ranks with persons who are primarily representative of groups instead of primarily capable of performing functional duties. At the same time, it can clearly be demonstated that current civil rights pressures are increasing the upward mobility of minorities in a reasonably orderly fashion. One, again, can sympathize with impatience at slow progress, but neither reverse discrimination, quota application, nor favoritism of those not qualified will aid in keeping American industry competitive or in improving its capacities to provide jobs for blacks or whites.

OFCC Powers

In addition to EEOC enforcement, the government maintains a potent weapon within its procurement function to enforce equal opportunity. Despite again the comments of the Civil Rights Commission *Report,* this has been a significant factor in inducing change since the Eisenhower Administration. The threat of contract debarment has moved many a company to alter policies and to give oportunities to minorities beyond mere nondiscrimination. Critics who point out that debarment has never occurred [27] fail to envision both the magnitude and the success of the threat in achieving the objectives not only of equal opportunity, but of affirmative action as well.[28]

The Need for New Forms

Instead of considering the problem of EEOC powers within the narrow confines of civil rights problems, it should be discussed within the broad picture of administrative reform. Rather than give this agency further powers, should we not seek to end the conflicting and overlapping, costly and inefficient current bureaucratic regulatory scramble in the labor and employment fields and substitute more workable forms for accomplishing our social objectives? The multitude of agencies concerned with employment now place employer and employee in a jungle maze of a choice of jurisdiction, with potentially contradictory rulings on the same subject, innumerable oportunities for multiple filings on one issue, and litigation that never seems to end. Complex occupational health and safety legislation has recently been added to the legislative supermarket that now includes laws pertaining to civil rights, union relations, minimum wages, and other aspects of the employment relationship. Each of these laws has its own administrative forms and agencies; each is administered without sufficient interest to the total regulatory picture; and each tends to build up a vested interest in the maintenance of the regulatory status quo. Often when new legislation has been enacted, inadequate consideration has been given to the impact on existing laws and the administrative function has not been carefully correlated with established forms and actions.

Actually, the primary *raison d'etre* for the administrative form to exist has not proved valid. It was supposed to provide quicker justice than did the courts. The record demonstrates that this has not occurred. It was supposed to be staffed with personnel highly expert in their fields. The record in many cases here indicates that political appointments are more common. Also, in some cases, the degree of zealousness particularly at the staff level raises some very profound questions of justice, due process, and just plain fairness.[29] In other situations, the rights of third parties have been blatantly ignored so as not to offend key groups which the agencies serve.[30] And, of course, Ralph Nader has had a lot to say about failures of agencies to perform the function for which they were created.

I suggest that the time has come to consider a total reorganization of these agencies, combining them into a single one, functioning more on judicial than administrative lines. What I can envision is a kind of labor court. I do not use the term in the vernacular for a compulsory arbitration agency. Rather, I am thinking of a special court of law which would handle labor and employment matters at the primary jurisdiction level. Within its jurisdiction would be all regulatory functions now vested in such agencies as the Department of Labor, the National Labor Relations Board, the Equal Employment Opportunity Commission, the Department of Justice, etc. It would have its own prosecuting attorneys and judges, set up in regions, and appeal would flow naturally to the various courts of appeals.

My thinking has not reached the stage where I am ready to present a detailed program of reorganization of existing agencies. Such a beginning, however, has been made along these lines by Professor Charles J. Morris as set forth in Part II in this volume.[31] Just as my experience in industry has provided me with insights and concerns regarding the impact and efficacy of current administrative forms, so has Professor Morris's prior service as a union counsel caused him to evaluate realistically the current administrative scene. Moreover, Professor Morris has gained additional insights as editor-in-chief of the comprehensive study of NLRB policy and practice recently issued by the American Bar Association Section of Labor Relations.[32] Regardless of whether his or my suggestions are acceptable, it certainly seems that whatever is done, it would be ill-advised to rush ahead adding to an outworn and inadequate model on the basis of such profoundly misleading information as that generated by the Civil Rights Commission.

Final Comment

At the first meeting of the Industrial Relations Research Association, held in Cleveland in 1948, I read a paper detailing how the Railway Labor Act was working in practice, and pointing out that, far from being a "model law" as conventional wisdom then ordained, it was an extraordinary legal and administrative failure which had destroyed the collective bargaining process without substituting therefor an effective method of dispute settlement. Although no one could challenge my facts, I was virtually booed off the stage as if I were blaspheming the current religion. Time has been kind to me on this issue. But would not the country have been better served if industrial relations students had grappled realisticaly a quarter of a century ago with the issues presented by the breakdown of that then cherished legislation?

Today my views here are undoubtedly equally repugnant to the reigning liberal-academic establishment. Yet I believe that they are also grounded on a firm factual basis, and it is possible —although by no means certain—that they may prove as correct in terms of equal employment opportunity as were the earlier ones in terms of free collective bargaining.

Let me emphasize that the goal which we all seek is the one that I have always sought—equal opportunity for all. But as Professor Charles C. Killingsworth has noted, despite the heritage of slavery and years of discrimination "and despite the continuing necessity for efforts to eliminate racial discrimination, there appears to be a reasonable basis for doubting that this factor is the principal *present* source of economic disadvantage for the Negro. If it is not, then continuing insistence that it is may well divert attention and effort from other more important sources and remedial measures." [33]

NOTES

1. Reference is to the Racial Policies of American Industry report series and to the Studies of Negro Employment. Since 1967, we have produced twenty-six monographs and five volumes detailing the background and present status of Negroes in industry. Additional monographs and volumes are in process.

2. This dates back to the late 1930's and early 1940's when I served as research assistant to Gunnar Myrdal in the preparation of *An American Dilemma,* and published my first book, *Organized Labor and the Negro* (New York: Harper & Brothers, 1944).

3. Quarles v. Philip Morris, Inc., 279 F. Supp. 505 (E.D.Va. 1968).

4. Griggs v. Duke Power Co., U.S. Sup. Ct., March 8, 1971.

5. U.S. v. Local 189, United Papermakers, *et al.,* 282 F. Supp. 39 (E.D. La., 1968), *affirmed,* U.S. Ct. Appeals, 5th Cir., July 29, 1969.

6. Two significant cases are Local 53 v. Vogler, 407 F.2d 1047 (CA 5), 1969; and Dobbins v. Local 212, IBEW, 292 F. Supp. 413 (S.D. Ohio, 1968). For numerous other EEOC and state commission cases, see *Race Relations Law Survey,* various issues.

7. United States v. Roadway Express, Inc., Civil Action No. C-68-321, U.S.D.C., E.D. Ohio, September 1, 1970; *see also* Jones *et al.* v. Lee Way Motor Freight, Inc., 431 F.2d 245 (CA-10), 1970.

8. Washington, 1970. Hereinafter referred to as the Commission's *Report.*

9. *Ibid.,* p. 337.

10. *Ibid.,* p. 57.

11. Herbert R. Northrup, *et al., Negro Employment in Basic Industry,* Studies of Negro Employment, Vol. 1 (Philadelphia: Industrial Research Unit, Wharton School of Finance and Commerce, University of Pennsylvania, 1970), Part Three, pp. 165-166, 172-173; Part Eight, pp. 726-728.

12. This occurred at the 1970 St. Louis hearings of the Commission which were given wide publicity. The Commission's *Report* discusses McDonnell Douglas at length, often with less than total accuracy and always without fairness.

13. Robert Kiehl, *Opportunities for Blacks in the Profession of Engineering,* prepared for the Manpower Administration, U.S. Department of Labor (Newark: Foundation for the Advancement of Graduate Study in Engineering, 1970), pp. 13-14.

14. See Northrup, *op. cit.,* esp. Part Three, pp. 204-214.

15. See Theodore V. Purcell and Daniel P. Mulvey, *The Negro in the Electrical Manufacturing Industry,* The Racial Policies of American Industry, Report No. 27 (Philadelphia: Industrial Research Unit, Wharton School of Finance and Commerce, University of Pennsylvania, 1971); and Herbert R. Northrup, *et al., The Negro in the Air Transport Industry,* The Racial Policies of American Industry, Report No. 23 (Philadelphia: Industrial Research Unit, Wharton School of Finance and Commerce, University of Pennsylvania, 1971).

16. Northrup, *Negro Employment in Basic Industry, op. cit.*, Part Five (Rubber Tires); Herbert R. Northrup and Richard L. Rowan, *et al.*, *Negro Employment in Southern Industry*, Studies of Negro Employment Vol. IV (Philadelphia: Industrial Research Unit, Wharton School of Finance and Commerce, University of Pennsylvania, 1970), Part Three (Tobacco).

17. Northrup, Rowan, *Negro Employment in Southern Industry, op. cit.*, Part One (Paper).

18. Walter A. Fogel, *The Negro in the Meat Industry*, The Racial Policies of American Industry, Report No. 12 (Philadelphia: Industrial Research Unit, Wharton School of Finance and Commerce, University of Pennsylvania, 1970). A forthcoming study by Professor Robert Ozanne on the farm equipment and construction machinery industry will likewise show the great impact of location on minority opportunity, as do many of the Racial Policies monographs.

19. Percy H. Green v. McDonnell Douglas Corporation. Case No. 68-C-187 (2), U.S.D.C. E.D. Mo., September 25, 1970. Said the court, "To order the rehiring of plaintiff, who has been guilty of such serious acts of misconduct, cannot reasonably be said proper action to effectuate the policies of Title VII. To hold that plaintiff is entitled to be rehired is to put a premium on misconduct of this type and to encourage like conduct of others. The purpose of the Act is to secure effective redress of employees' rights, to secure for them the right to exercise their lawful civil rights without discrimination because of their exercise, not to license them to commit unlawful or tortuous acts or to protect them from the consequences of unlawful conduct against their employers."

20. U.S. Commission on Civil Rights, *Report*, p. 341.

21. *Ibid.*, pp. 327-341.

22. *Ibid.*, pp. 342-344.

23. Philip Ross, *The Government as a Source of Union Power* (Providence: Brown University Press, 1965), p. 171.

24. See the remarks of Edward B. Miller, Chairman, NLRB, *Daily Labor Report*, October 16, 1970, pp. D-1 to D-4.

25. See the remarks of John Fanning, NLRB member, "Some Reflections on Remedies under the NLRA," *Daily Labor Report*, January 19, 1971, p. D-3.

26. Michael Sovern, *Legal Restraints on Racial Discrimination in Employment* (New York: Twentieth Century Fund, 1966), p. 205.

27. Debarment would put most companies out of business for it would prevent them from doing business with other federal contractors as well as with the government. It is thus in affect too great a penalty to utilize in any situation where improvement is possible, and inevitable improvement has been achieved.

28. The Nixon Administration's role in these situations has been maligned, not told. At a future opportunity I intend to deal factually with the Nixon record in equal employment opportunity.

29. Among the areas which would merit investigation on this point are the Office of the General Counsel of the NLRB, the administration of the Davis-Bacon Act by the Department of Labor, and the format and conduct of hearings, issuances of reports, and control of staff of the U.S. Commission on Civil Rights.

30. A good example here is the record of the National Mediation Board and the National Railroad Adjustment Board in aiding and abetting the virulent discrimination against Negroes in the industry. See Northrup, *Organized Labor and the Negro, op. cit.,* Chapter III; and Howard W. Risher, Jr., *The Negro in the Railroad Industry,* The Racial Policies of American Industry, Report No. 16 (Philadelphia: Industrial Research Unit, Wharton School of Finance and Commerce, University of Pennsylvania, 1971).

31. See "The Need for New and Coherent Regulatory Mechanisms," Part II in this volume.

32. Charles J. Morris (editor-in-chief), *The Developing Labor Law* (Washington, D.C.: The Bureau of National Affairs, Inc., 1971).

33. Charles C. Killingsworth, *Jobs and Income for Negroes* (Washington: National Manpower Policy Task Force and University of Michigan, 1968), pp. 31-32.

Educating the Employed Disadvantaged
for Upgrading

Richard L. Rowan †

The Civil Rights Act of 1964 issues a clear mandate for equal employment opportunity in American industry. Although the Act leaves no doubt about Congressional intent in protecting the rights of those employed after July 1964, a question has arisen in regard to those hired before said date. Is the employer obligated to remove the present effects of past discrimination? In a landmark decision in 1968, the U.S. District Court in New Orleans, Louisiana answered the question in the affirmative in a case involving the Crown Zellerbach Company.[1]

The Crown decision, which was upheld on appeal, was critical for the southern paper industry since Negro employment conditions were very similar among the various companies. Many blacks were hired in the past under discriminatory employment standards which allowed them to be assigned only to specific tasks wherein the opportunity for upgrading into better paying positions was denied. Under the court order, these people became a part of an "affected class"—the employed disadvantaged —and it was incumbent upon employers to develop plans by which equal employment opportunities could be achieved.

It is the purpose of this paper to examine specific adult basic education programs utilized by four southern paper companies for the purpose of providing better job opportunities for those employees who were hired as laborers and until new expectancies were created believed they would remain in such jobs all of their

† Richard L. Rowan is Associate Professor of Industry and Associate Director of the Industrial Research Unit, Wharton School, University of Pennsylvania. This paper was prepared for delivery at the Winter 1971 meeting of the Industrial Relations Research Association, reproduced with permission. The author wishes to thank Mr. Michael Johns for assistance in the preparation. It is based on a larger study supported by grant No. 81-42-71-02 from the Office of Research & Development, Manpower Administration, U.S. Department of Labor. The opinions expressed here are the author's and do not necessarily represent the Department's official opinions or policy.

working lives. The basic questions that the study attempts to answer are: (1) What educational results were achieved by the programs in terms of improvement in reading and math skills? and (2) What job results were attained by the program graduates? The latter question is particularly crucial and one that has been relatively unexplored by those concerned with in-plant educational training programs.

Research Methodology

The data analyzed herein were collected from the companies shown in Table 1 during the period of December 1970 through October 1971. Company personnel directly involved with the programs were interviewed at the plant site. These individuals included industrial relations directors and their assistants, plant managers, and instructors/monitors in the courses.

All of the companies studied are located in the deep South states of Georgia and Louisiana where segregated patterns of education and employment have historically led to the disadvantaged status of blacks. Low income, poor educational achievement, and an inferior labor force position relative to whites characterize the Negro communities in the locations studied.

Data in Table 2 reflect the mean performance, as measured by the Stanford Achievement Tests, of the program graduates in the affected and non-affected classes. Statistical analysis was employed to determine whether or not there was any significant change in the difference of mean performance before and after program administration among those in the affected and non-affected classes, the promoted and unpromoted in the affected class, and the promoted and unpromoted among all program graduates.

Programs Studied

As indicated in Table 1, the following two adult basic education programs were used by the companies studied: [2]

1. Methods of Intellectual Development (MIND) began in mid-1964 as a pilot research study of the National Association of Manufacturers to determine the feasibility of developing human resource programs in private industry. It became a wholly-owned subsidiary of CPC International (Corn Products, Inc.) in February 1967 and more recently it has been operated by a

TABLE 1 *Basic Data for Companies Studied*

Company	Location	Adult Education Program	Dates of Operation	Number in Affected Class[a]	Program Graduates in Affected Class
Crown Zellerbach	Bogalusa, La.	MIND	11/69-8/70	186	7
Continental Can	Hodge, La.	MIND	4/68-Present	69	10
Union Camp	Savannah, Ga.	MIND	6/68-Present	629	26
Georgia Kraft	Rome & Macon, Ga.	USR&D	3/69-12/70	130	71

[a] The affected class is defined in the companies as follows: (1) Crown Zellerbach: All Negro employees hired prior to 1/16/66 and 13 others hired under special conditions prior to 2/14/68; (2) Continental Can: Negro employees hired before 12/10/64 in the Shipping and Stockroom and Millyard Departments; (3) Union Camp: Minority employees hired prior to 12/31/69 who were initially placed in a job from which there was little movement, or were placed in jobs in which minority group employees constituted more than 50% of the incumbents; (4) Georgia Kraft: Negro employees who have remained in entry-level positions for a long period of time who have either not taken the company's pre-employment tests or who have taken them and failed to make a qualifying score.

private consulting firm in New York City. MIND operates a variety of programs teaching occupational skills such as typing and stenography in addition to an Adult Basic Education Program that was implemented by Continental Can, Crown Zellerbach, and Union Camp. Fundamental philosophy, based on a self-learning concept, and training methods that include programmed instruction are similar for all MIND programs.

The two basic components of the Adult Basic Education Program, reading and mathematics, are part of a carefully structured course. The materials which are sold to each client, while undergoing revisions from time to time, are not specifically tailored to a given company or group of employees even though there are wide variations both in the uses to which the program is put and in the backgrounds of employees. Participants in the MIND program study in an informal atmosphere with an effort being made to change the learning environment from the traditional schoolroom setting to one where each person is able to proceed at his or her own pace. Monitors, chosen from among the employees in the plant, rather than professional teachers, are employed to work with the trainees.

MIND projects that a student functioning initially between grade levels 4.5 and 8.5 should be able to progress 3 to 5 grade levels in the standard course of 160 hours of training offered on a two hour a day, five day a week, basis. Trainees are generally given the Stanford Achievement Test at the beginning of the program to determine reading and math grade levels, and these tests are readministered at the end of the course to establish progress. MIND claims that adults who score below grade 4.5 initially have participated with varying degrees of success although it advises that these individuals be given additional tutoring. A special language program has been developed for those who score below fourth grade; however, it has resulted in limited success.

2. United States Research and Development Corporation (USR&D) was founded in 1967 by former staff of the Peace Corps and other federal programs, and it has expanded widely in the adult basic education field. A special program was developed for the Georgia Kraft Company's affected class members.

USR&D, like MIND, emphasizes programmed instruction in math and reading. The course is offered for a maximum of 216 hours in which trainees can attend six hours a week for 36 weeks. Unlike MIND, however, USR&D does not train company

TABLE 2 *Comparative Performance of Selected Graduates of Adult Basic Education Programs in Four Companies*

	Mean Performance		Difference in Standard Units	Mean Performance		Difference in Standard Units	Mean Performance		Difference in Standard Units
	Affected Class	Non-affected Class		Promoted Affected Class	Unpromoted Affected Class		Promoted	Unpromoted	
Crown Zellerbach									
	[t.10,15df= ±1.75]			[t.10,4df= ±2.18]			[t.10,15df= ±1.75]		
Reading Score (Before Program)	4.78	6.40	−1.35	4.15	6.05	−2.21*	5.44	6.38	−0.79
Reading Score (After Program)	5.28	7.20	−1.67	4.80	6.25	−2.31*	5.97	7.31	−1.18
Math Score (Before Program)	4.08	5.66	−1.54	4.35	3.55	0.76	4.67	5.73	−1.04
Math Score (After Program)	6.80	7.85	−0.84	6.97	6.45	0.20	7.03	8.13	−0.90
Change in Reading Score	0.50	0.80	−0.50	0.65	0.20	1.73	0.53	0.93	−0.71
Change in Math Score	2.72	2.19	0.58	2.63	2.90	−0.15	2.36	2.40	−0.04
Stated Education	8.67	9.64	−0.86	9.25	7.50	1.40	0.53	0.92	0.01
Age	42	42	−0.91	39	47	−1.30	42	41	0.23
Continental Can									
	[t.10,69df= ±1.67]						[t.10,69df= ±1.67]		
Reading Score (Before Program)	3.30	5.11	−1.72*	4.00	3.22		5.81	4.74	0.92
Reading Score (After Program)	4.80	7.14	−2.26*	5.60	4.71		7.91	6.67	1.06
Math Score (Before Program)	2.72	5.08	−2.38*	3.80	2.60		5.55	4.64	0.81
Math Score (After Program)	4.26	6.98	−2.66*	5.40	4.13		7.45	6.48	0.83
Change in Reading Score	1.50	2.03	−1.63	1.60	1.48		2.10	1.93	0.46
Change in Math Score	1.54	1.89	−1.20	1.60	1.53		1.90	1.84	0.17

Union Camp

	[t.10,24df= ±1.71]				[t.10,20df= ±1.72]				[t.10,24df= ±1.71]	
Reading Score (Before Program)	3.96	9.15	−7.03*	4.60	3.66	1.60	4.60	4.82	−0.21
Reading Score (After Program)	4.80	12.82	−9.01*	5.53	4.47	1.50	5.53	6.14	−0.44
Math Score (Before Program)	3.65	5.72	−2.72	4.11	3.43	1.19	4.11	3.92	0.28
Math Score (After Program)	4.92	10.58	−11.12*	5.31	4.73	1.38	5.31	5.96	−0.65
Change in Reading Score	0.84	8.28	−4.81*	0.93	0.81	0.43	0.93	1.33	−0.68
Change in Math Score	1.27	4.85	5.08*	1.20	1.30	−0.21	1.20	2.05	−1.03

Georgia Kraft

	[t.10,46df= ±1.68]		
Reading Score (Before Program)	2.92	2.93	0.03
Reading Score (After Program)	4.59	4.63	0.09
Math Score (Before Program)	3.81	3.44	0.22
Math Score (After Program)	5.37	5.43	0.13
Change in Reading Score	1.67	1.70	0.06
Change in Math Score	2.06	1.99	−0.15
Stated Education	7.31	8.56	1.67
Age	40	38	−0.66

* Significant at the .10 level.

Notes: (1) Data were insufficient to compute age and stated education levels at Continental Can and Union Camp.

(2) Continental Can had only one promoted affected class member, and this is not enough information to make the statistical comparison.

(3) Georgia Kraft had no non-affected class members in the programs.

personnel as instructors but rather supplies the total staff including administrators, secretaries, training directors, and group leaders. The concept of a teacher is much more important to the USR&D program than in the MIND operation.

Educational materials used by USR&D are quite similar to those used by MIND and similar problems have arisen. Employees who are functioning below the fourth grade level as determined by the Stanford Achievement Tests appear to have difficulty in relating to both programs, and neither seems to have solved the problem of the nonreader or the person who has only a limited vocabulary.

Analysis of Results

The following sections pertain to the educational and job advancements attained by employees in the affected class who graduated from the MIND and USR&D programs. The analysis is based on data shown in Table 2.

Educational Results

One of the major goals of the adult basic education programs referred to herein was to improve the functional literacy of the employed disadvantaged. Scores on the Stanford Achievement Tests administered before and after the programs indicate low levels of functional literacy. Before the programs, employees were functioning at about the third or fourth grade level) in reading and mathematics. Educational improvement after 160 hours in the MIND program and about 216 hours in the USR&D program was slight.

Under the MIND program, changes in reading were 0.50 grade levels at Crown, 1.50 grades at Continental Can, and 0.84 grades at Union Camp. In mathematics, improvement was somewhat greater with advancements of 2.72 grades at Crown, 1.54 grades at Continental Can, and 1.27 grades at Union Camp. In the USR&D program at Georgia Kraft, improvement in reading was 1.67 grades and in mathematics, 2.06 grades. Advancement in each category and in each company was considerably less than the 3 to 4 grades projected by the MIND and USR&D programs. Black employees in the affected class consistently register more improvement in math than reading. This probably results from past environmental influences. Negro males, who attended segregated schools in the rural South until they dropped out between the sixth and eighth grades, did not gain a wide vocabulary and reading skill. It apparently is much more difficult to compensate at a later age for a deficiency in language skills than in mathematics.

As noted in Table 2, there was no significant difference in the change in reading and math scores of the affected class and non-affected class members in the MIND program except at Union Camp. The exception may be quite important. It suggests that the program has widened the gap between the most severely disadvantaged and other employees in the plant. If it is true that employees with the greatest functional literacy are given better opportunities for upgrading, then the program, at least at Union Camp, may make it more difficult for the affected class members to progress in the future.

The poor educational results of the two programs indicate that they have not been effective in the in-plant environment of the southern paper industry where functional literacy is at a low level. Advancement of only one to two grade levels after 160 to 216 hours of instruction raises fundamental questions about the programs and the context into which they have been introduced. Course materials obviously were not designed to reach the most seriously disadvantaged employee who may be functioning at or below the fourth grade level in reading and mathematics. Both of the programs have failed, in particular, to provide a solution to the problem of the nonreader. The courses offered are neither sufficiently engrossing nor taught in a manner necessary to provide a breakthrough for the functional illiterate.

Lack of success in the programs may be attributed in large measure to course content and teaching methodology. Much of the reading material is not relevant to the southern, small town experience. Stories that relate to the unemployed in the large, metropolitan, eastern cities are not likely to stir the imagination of the long-term employed people in Bogalusa and Hodge, Louisiana and Rome and Savannah, Georgia who are disadvantaged by prior discrimination but nevertheless have had steady employment over the past 20 years, relatively good wages, and considerable status among their peer groups. A narrative on a trip to New Orleans or Atlanta would more likely motivate workers in Louisiana or Georgia than a story pertaining to a visit to New York City. The use of a programmed learning device that employs taped cassettes also may limit the effectiveness of the program for those who need it the most.

MIND and USR&D differ somewhat in their outlook as to the use of a teacher. MIND conscientiously avoids using a teacher or instructor in the traditional sense by employing a monitor who performs an administrative and/or personal service function of simply maintaining records and assisting the trainees in using cassettes. The monitor is usually a female employee who has been working in the plant. In contrast to MIND, USR&D utilizes trained instructors in its courses.

In a somewhat more discouraging light, it may be that the failure of these programs to upgrade educational skills of participants lies more in the characteristics of the employed disadvantaged than in shortcomings of the programs themselves. The typical affected class member is a forty-year-old Negro man who was employed under a highly discriminatory system in the paper industry in a small southern town fifteen to twenty years ago. His stated eduaction is about eighth grade, and he was functioning at about the fourth grade or less before the adult basic education program. He has lived in a segregated community all of his life with little or no oral communication between himself and his white counterpart. He now holds a steady job at good wages. It may be that no basic education program can be devised to deal with this person in a significant manner if the goal is to raise his educational level by four or five grades.

Job Results

One of the basic questions in this study pertains to the job results of the adult basic education programs. Were affected class members upgraded as a result of preformance in the educational programs?

Data presented in Table 2 indicate clearly that within the affected class group and among those in both the affected and non-affected class groups there were no significant differences in the improvement in math and reading between the promoted and unpromoted employees. On balance, it appears that educational advancement was not a crucial factor in the upgrading decision.

Since there appears to be very little, if any, relationship between the improvement in functional literacy and in-plant promotion, other factors must explain the decision to upgrade. Traditional routes for employee advancement apparently still prevail in the companies studied. Seniority and initial job placement appear to determine largely the upward mobility of individuals in the plant. It needs to be pointed out that some employees among the disadvantaged, who did not participate in one of the programs, moved into better jobs as a result of a change in rules regulating job transfer. These movements occurred regardless of improvements in functional literacy and this fact raises the question once more as to the value of educational improvement as a major means of in-plant upgrading.

Concluding Remarks

This study was concerned with two adult basic education programs—Methods of Intellectual Development (MIND) and United States Research and Development Corporation (USR&D)—utilized by four southern paper companies to provide upgrading opportunities to the employed disadvantaged workers. The study concludes that only minimal educational results were achieved; in most cases, improvement was only one or two grades in math and reading. In regard to job improvement or upgrading, very few program graduates made any advancement and there was no significant difference in the mean performance of those promoted and those not promoted. Educational improvement did not appear to be a major factor in the upgrading decision of the companies studied.

The study strongly suggests the need for new thinking about the approach to eliminate the present effects of past discrimination. It is not clear that there was any understanding by the companies of the relationship between functional literacy (which is the thing that MIND and USR&D claim, and have demonstrated, that they can improve) and promotion on the job. It is, of course, likely that an improvement in reading and mathematics skills is valuable to an employee, but how valuable is this to jobs in a paper mill? This is a question that appears to have been neglected in early planning stages between MIND, USR&D, and the companies. Also, how much of an improvement is necessary to further qualify an employee for promotion in a job? In a job sense, of what significance is the fact that participants in the programs advanced educationally by 1.2 grade levels or by 2.3 grade levels? Perhaps the difficulty with these questions lies in the fact that no one has determined conclusively what combination of education and training is necessary for promotion through the various lines of progression in a paper mill.

Among the major factors that distinguish white employees, who have made considerable progress up a promotion ladder, from employed disadvantaged black workers are not stated educational levels and functional literacy but rather many years of training and preferential treatment in early job placement. The gap is not likely to be bridged by a given number of hours spent in an adult basic education program. A more sensible approach may be to offer blacks an opportunity to move into lines of promotion where richer opportunities lie and to offer the requisite training and privileges to allow them to progress in as short of a period of time as possible. But since this is so difficult to do in terms of firmly entrenched seniority systems, white expectancies in the plant, and black unwillingness to accept new conditions of in-plant job transfers after so many years of discrimination, the most we can hope for is that the sins against the fathers will not be visited on the children. And there is reason to have faith. New entrants are being hired and assigned to all departments in the southern paper industry regardless of race. In the meantime, older, disadvantaged employees may remain part of the cruel cost involved in operating a segregated and highly discriminatory society of which employment is only one aspect.

NOTES

1. United States v. Local 189, United Papermakers and Paperworkers, Crown Zellerbach Corp. et al., 282 F. Supp 39 (E.D. La. 1968), *affirmed* —— F.2d —— (C.A. 5, 1969). *See also* Quarles v. Philip Morris, 279 F. Supp. 305 (E.D. Va. 1968).

2. A detailed statement on these two programs pertinent to their origin, philosophy, and objectives can be found in a forthcoming larger study, Richard L. Rowan and Herbert R. Northrup, *Educating the Employed Disadvantaged for Upgrading* (Philadelphia: Industrial Research Unit, Wharton School of Finance and Commerce, University of Pennsylvania, 1972).

PART IV

C. Welfare and Pensions

Public Support for Strikers

Armand J. Thieblot, Jr.†

I. Introduction

With mounting emphasis during the past five years, a number of organizations and individuals have been actively campaigning to encourage people who do not really need public assistance to seek and accept it as an alternative to self reliance. Among those being so encouraged are participants in labor disputes; the result has been a movement toward public support of strikers through the welfare system.

This has created a burgeoning public expense; and even though the dollar amounts involved are but fractions of total program spending for welfare, they are already at this early stage of development more than marginally significant and growing rapidly. Welfare for strikers has potential for economic influence far beyond the dollar amounts of benefits distributed. It is a public thumb on the balance of collective bargaining and may well affect the future viability of the collective bargaining system.[1]

As an example of the use of public support for strikers, let us look back to one of the most important strikes of recent years —the General Electric strike of late 1969—which idled 143,000 workers. The GE strike was a hard-fought one; both sides campaigned with bumper stickers, newspaper ads, and political involvements. The union staged public rallies and instituted a consumer boycott against the company's products during the Christmas shopping season. The company responded with an extensive letter writing and personal contact campaign to invite the strikers to return to work.

The strike lasted for 100 days, but it is neither this fact nor the activities just noted that sets this particular strike apart. What differentiates it from others is the way in which the strikers were able to support themselves during it, and the lack of back-pressures to settle which usually build up from individual strikers as the pinch of paylessness begins to hurt.

---

† Armand J. Thieblot, Jr. is an Assistant Professor, University of Maryland.

With the advantages afforded by hindsight, it is now clear that what allowed strikers and their families to shrug off so easily more than two full months without wages was the massive and trend-setting use in a labor dispute of the machinery and benefits of the publically financed welfare system. One GE striker summed it up quite succinctly when interviewed toward the end of the strike about how he was getting along. "Ah," he said, "there's always help from welfare if you need it." [2]

How much was the GE strike lengthened or its settlement made more costly by the fact that many of the strikers were receiving public assistance benefits? Although it is impossible to tell precisely, there can be little doubt that it had some effect by greatly reducing the harsh economic pressures usually associated with a long strike. There can be no doubt that public assistance use makes at least some strikes longer or costlier. And there can be no doubt that the traditional bargaining powers of the parties to the dispute are undergoing a change with ramifications not yet fully determined. [3]

The flavor of the situation may be gained by considering the following examples:

1. In Massachusetts, where GE has major plants at Lynn and Pittsfield, at least 15 percent of the more than 20,000 strikers received some form of public assistance support from either the state surplus food program or the state welfare and relief program.

2. In New York state, after the seventh week, 92 percent of the strikers were receiving unemployment compensation and drawing more than $1.2 million per week from that employer-funded program. At least a thousand strikers were drawing welfare payments from the Aid to Families with Dependent Children program, and others were receiving surplus food.

3. In various states, strikers sought and received benefits from Aid to Families with Dependent Children, General Public Assistance, Food Stamps, Commodity Distributions, the Veterans Administration, Unemployment Compensation, Social Security, and emergency county or city relief. Those receiving public assistance were also often eligible for the "fringe benefits" of mortgage payment support, free lunch programs, and free medical care.

II. Extent of Public Support

Taken all together, the amount of public contributions to strikers support at GE was significant. We have it on no less authority than that of Mr. Leo Perlis, Director of the AFL-CIO "Community Services Activities" that: "Community benefits average $50 per striker per week, bringing the *weekly* outlay by voluntary and public agencies well above the *$5 million mark.*" [4]

The use of public monies to support GE strikers was massive enough, successful enough, and well enough publicized to establish a precedent; unlike the steel strike of 1959, it was not an isolated incident. The General Motors and Westinghouse strikes, the copper and teamster strikes, and the longshore and telephone strikes which have taken place in the two years since the General Electric strike was settled have all been characterized by public support, as have been smaller strikes in increasing numbers.

These and other strike situations are analyzed more fully in our forthcoming book, *Welfare and Strikes.*[5] For our purposes here, it will suffice to say that a trend has been established. Encouraging this trend, organized labor has lobbied hard—both nationally and at the state and local levels—to liberalize eligibility requirements and promote legislation and administrative changes to make more public monies more easily available to strikers. At the same time, unions are working to educate the rank and file that public funds are available and to persuade them that there is nothing degrading, dehumanizing, or wrong with temporarily becoming a ward of the state by receiving welfare.

New strike organization booklets reflect this. In one, titled "How to Organize a Strike Assistance Program," published by Mr. Perlis' Community Service Activities group for use by individual AFL-CIO locals, we find that the first step, after establishing a strike planning committee is to conduct a "survey of the services and assistance available from public and voluntary agencies." This same widely distributed booklet, by the way, also recommends that "an effort should be made . . . to have eligibility requirements for public assistance liberalized for strikers." [6]

Thus, we can see that public support for strikers through welfare and relief programs does, in fact, take place on a large and rapidly expanding scale. There is no reason to suppose that it will not continue to grow until it becomes a standard factor in labor disputes—one which will have to be countered in every strike situation. There is no doubt in my mind that its use will seriously threaten the precarious balances of economic power which are necessary for the American system of free collective bargaining to function. Let us look more closely at the welfare programs currently available to strikers which are creating this threat.

III. The Public Assistance System

The total social welfare system in this country is mystifyingly complex, as might be expected of a system which, overall, accounts for 20 percent of our trillion dollar gross national product.[7] Of present or potential use by strikers there are perhaps a half-dozen programs which might be called major and as many minor ones. Major programs include Food Stamps and Commodity Distributions, Aid to Families with Dependent Children (with its fringe benefits of medical assistance), State General Assistance or Relief, and Unemployment Insurance. Although these are all key measures, deserving of critical review, the relative importance of Food Stamps and AFDC compels our individual attention here.

Food Stamps

The Food Stamp program was established on a permanent basis only in 1964. It is an entirely federally funded program under the Department of Agriculture in which the state contributes only administrative costs. It is not a "welfare" program as such. The reasons for its establishment include a number of factors such as strengthening the agricultural economy and finding better uses for surplus foods, as well as providing improved levels of nutrition for low income households. It works this way: in participating communities, persons whose incomes are below a prescribed limit can buy, for a small amount, a special script worth a larger amount when presented at the local food store. The amount paid for the stamps depends on the family size and economic status of the purchaser.[8]

Food Stamps were originally thought of as an imaginative and less restrictive alternative to the surplus commodity distribution programs. They have been immensely successful. During fiscal year 1971, the yearly average of almost 9.5 million persons participating in the program was more than three times as many as two years earlier. Coupons were spent encompassing a federal subsidy to food purchasers of $1.5 billion.[9] The average monthly bonus per family was $47.22. Because of changes in the scale of benefits, this bonus amount was almost twice as great as one year earlier.

Designed to be the least degrading of all public assistance programs, food stamps carry with them the fewest conditions which must be met for eligibility. Although some groups—notably communes—are specially excluded from participation, strikers are not; they are eligible immediately after the strike starts. It is for this reason, perhaps, that food stamps found relatively early use by strikers, who seemed able to differentiate between receiving them and "going on relief."

We characterize food stamps as the marijuana to the heroin of Aid for Families with Dependent Children. Food stamps provide the route by which strikers are eased into the welfare system where, if they are not careful, they can be lulled into even greater dependency on the Barmecide of "free" money.

In specific strike situations, we have usually found food stamps to be the most heavily utilized form of public support. In Wayne County, Michigan, for example, during the GM strike in October of 1970, almost 50 percent of the idled workforce received them.[10]

In Delaware County, Pennsylvania, during the 1970-71 Westinghouse strike, estimates made by the county welfare office were that upward of 91 percent of strikers who lived in that county were certified for food stamps. Although this estimate seems a bit high, it can leave little doubt that food stamps are heavily used during strikes.

Aid to Families with Dependent Children

The second of the major programs now being used by strikers is Aid to Families with Dependent Children. This program was part of the Social Security Act and so has been part of the welfare system since 1936. The reasons for its existence were taken from predecessor programs dating from the turn of the century and are based upon two important sociological assumptions: first, that women are not normally workforce participants, and second, that women with young children should not be out of the home during the day. Therefore, participation in this program was predicated on the condition that a woman recipient was deprived both of her husband's support and also any means of her own support. Not until 1961, under a temporary program, could aid be granted to an existing intact family unit whose breadwinner was unemployed. It is under the Unemployed Parent program, made permanent in 1968, that strikers have been included for welfare benefits in almost all of the major industrial states.

AFDC is a large and rapidly growing welfare program. In 1950, there were 2.25 million recipients (including children) who received somewhat over $500 million in aid. By 1960, the number of recipients had risen to three million and total payments had reached just over a billion dollars. Then between 1960 and 1970, AFDC use skyrocketed in a way which cannot be accounted for by the economic pattern of the decade; by 1970, the number of recipients had more than tripled, to 9.5 million, and the costs had increased from one billion to almost five. Average monthly payments to families in 1970 exceeded $180.

Participation in AFDC carries with it certain fringe benefits —notably, free medical care and automatic food stamp certification, if desired. We have not yet been able to calculate the precise value of the medical benefits, but a crude estimate using available statistics indicates the amount may be upward of 40 percent of direct benefits—perhaps $75 per family per month.

During the General Motors strike, strikers residing in Michigan made use of the AFDC program, and the approximately 13 percent who qualified received an average monthly benefit of $95.[11] State residents—and, through the federal government, the rest of us—contributed almost $4.5 million in direct payment support to strikers in this state alone under this one program.

Welfare receipt experience varied considerably from location to location. In Los Angeles County, for example, where GM has an assembly plant, a smaller proportion of strikers qualified for AFDC. But the financial assistance afforded each was considerably greater. The average of $721.19 for each of the recipients over the 58 day strike was more than twice as high as Michigan.[12]

IV.   Benefits and Costs of Public Support for Strikers

The benefits arising from public support for strikers accrue principally to two identifiable groups. First, of course, are the strikers and their families. Second are the unions of which the strikers are members.

Depending on his particular circumstances, the direct benefits to a striker can be great. In 1971, a striker with a non-working wife, two children, and less than $1,500 in liquid assets could, during the first month of the strike, apply for and probably obtain food stamps. If we assume his income consisted only of $80 per month in strike benefits from his union, the food stamp program would allow him to buy $106 in food for $19. With this $87 tax free bonus, his monthly purchasing power would be $167.

During the second month of the strike, he would also become eligible in many states for Aid to Families with Dependent Children. The 1970 nationwide average benefit payment for a family with two children was $180. Depending on where he lived, how much he paid for housing, and a number of other factors, this amount would be reduced by some, but not all, of the $80 monthly strike benefits, and the bonus premium from food stamps would also decrease. Even so, total monthly income from strike payments and welfare would exceed $250, which is substantial.[13]

To see the potential benefits to the unions here, we must only consider that if the $80 monthly strike payment is removed, welfare benefits rise accordingly, and make up a large part of the difference. Eliminating the $80 union strike benefit diminishes total striker support by only $10. Undoubtedly, this is the reason for a trend we have already noticed and which, no doubt, will continue—for unions to halt strike benefits to members receiving welfare.

Now, $254 per month translates directly to an equivalent hourly wage of some $1.59, but one would have to work at a considerably higher wage rate to arrive at this figure for take-home pay. It is net of federal, state, and city taxes, social security, disability insurance, and union dues. Without going to the trouble of working this backwards, I think we can agree that, for the average worker, being on strike is monetarily equivalent to working forty hours per week for at least the minimum wage.

These are very conservative figures, and may do injustice to the ingenuity of strikers and the magnanimity of welfare officials. These figures use a small family size. They do not take into account medical benefits, usually granted for six months once a person is certified for AFDC, from which a striker could quite easily derive $500 or more in benefits. We have also noticed several instances where it appears that initial certifications for welfare payments were made for a three or six month period, so that strikers could continue to receive the entire benefit amount for some time after the strike terminated; in any event, they almost always received payments for the entire month during which the strike ended. Mortgage payments and extra emergency benefits also are sometimes made by the welfare offices, and can be quite large.

As the numbers demonstrate, public assistance benefits can be substantial. We have noted cases where they totaled 80 percent of pre-strike wages without even considering the "fringe benefits." Certainly, with such an income possible on strike, the privations necessary are greatly reduced and the impetus to settle diminished.[14]

Costs

Naturally, there is a cost associated with the benefits. That cost comes in several forms. First, there is the dollar cost. Unless there are some surprises resulting from the continuing international economic crises, or from the wage and price controls, or some other drastic change in the economy, we can probably expect 5,700 to 6,000 strikes per year in the next few years, idling something on the order of three million men.[15] If we assume that these strikers will be off the job for periods similar to those in past years; that the same but no higher proportion of strikers will receive food stamps and AFDC as received those benefits in the large strikes of 1970; that waiting periods are followed and no welfare payments continue beyond the end of the month in which the strike occurred; and that strikers receive benefits at the current average rates for each program for families of four, then we can conclude that the cost of public support for strikers next year alone will exceed $150,000,000 in direct payments.

This figure must be considered tentative but it can also be considered quite conservative. It does not include administrative costs or the costs of spreading unemployment which will increase in proportion as strikers are out longer because of public support. It does not include the cost in self respect to hundreds of thousands of workers who had thought themselves independent enough to be "better than welfare." It does not include the costs to the country of an inflation fueled both by the spending on public support for strikers and also by the costlier strike settlements wihch will probably be their result. If the use of welfare support by strikers lengthened the GM strike by one single day, that one day cost $32.4 million in lost wages, profits, and taxes. If the settlement agreed to was one cent higher, the cost over the contract period exceeds $29 million, much of which will probably have to be made up by higher prices.

V.   Conclusions

Now that we are beginning to comprehend the magnitude of public support for strikers and its potential costs in even the very near future, we begin to appreciate the amount of work involved in bringing it about. Not only did welfare administrators and policy formulators have to be pursuaded that programs clearly designed for other purposes should be expanded to include the temporarily and voluntarily needy strikers, but the strikers themselves had to be convinced that receiving welfare and public assistance is not admission of defeat—not degrading, not harmful to self esteem—but instead a right to be demanded.

But while I am impressed, I am not pursuaded that paying income taxes gives strikers or anyone else a "right to welfare" simply because they fall within the contrived definitions of "need" included in the legislation. AFDC, certainly, and most other public assistance programs, were clearly designed to meet specific catastrophies beyond the control of the potential recipient. To the degree that they no longer do so they have been prostituted and their ideals defeated. Those who have sponsored their misuse have accelerated the rate of moral decay which already imperils the country.

Strikers did not starve before AFDC and Food Stamps became available. They do not starve now in those states where welfare remains unavailable. They will not starve in the future if those benefits are again unavailable. I think we must agree that labor's relative bargaining power before food stamps was great enough to be influential. The additional power which $150,000,000 per year can buy may well overbalance the relative bargaining positions of unions and management so greatly that the fundamental structure of collective bargaining will be at least seriously threatened. All of us will pay the costs—directly through higher taxes and higher prices, or indirectly through increased governmental deficit spending and inflation. The benefits accrue to a group which does not really need them and has but tenuous claim to them. They should not continue.

NOTES

1. Whenever the normal "calculus of economics" is removed from industrial conflicts, grave questions arise as to the continued utility of collective bargaining in the particular situation. Examples arise under the Railway Labor Act and with public employees (as under the Taylor Act). See Gordon F. Bloom and Herbert R. Northrup, *Economics of Labor Relations* (6th ed.; Homewood, Ill.: Richard D. Irwin, Inc., 1969), p. 700.

2. "Now the Real War Begins," *Newsweek*, January 19, 1970, p. 70.

3. For a simplified explanation of the collective bargaining process showing the necessity of some degree of equality between the parties and the consequences of unbalanced economic power, see Clark Kerr, "The Bargaining Process," *Unions, Management, and the Public*, ed. E. Wight Bakke, Clark Kerr, and Charles W. Anrod (2d ed.; New York: Harcourt, Brace and World, 1960), p. 285.

4. "Public Agencies Rally Support to GE Strikers," *Seafarers Log*, January 1970.

5. Armand J. Thieblot, Jr., and Ronald M. Cowin, *Welfare and Strikes: The Use of Public Funds to Support Strikers*, Labor Relations and Public Policy Report No. 7 (Philadelphia: Industrial Research Unit, Wharton School of Finance and Commerce, University of Pennsylvania, Spring, 1972).

6. *How to Organize a Strike Assistance Program*, AFL-CIO Community Services Activities (privately published), p. 5.

7. This figure includes all social welfare expenditures from federal, state, and local public revenue, trust funds, and other expenditures under public law. Includes cost of construction of schools, etc. U.S. Department of Health, Education, and Welfare, *Social Security Bulletin*, Annual Statistical Supplement, Table 1. Total spending in the Aid to Families with Dependent Children program was less than one-quarter of one percent of gross national product, but was nevertheless $4,852,000,000 during calendar year 1970—exclusive of administrative costs and fringe benefits. This was $23.57 per living inhabitant of the country. These amounts can be found in U.S. Department of Agriculture, *Public Assistance Statistics*, No. (SRS) 72-03100, National Center for Social Statistics, Report A-2 (monthly).

8. Local administration and certification of purchasers is a state and local responsibility, but must be in accordance with a new uniform national standard. See *Federal Register*, "Food Stamp Program," Vol. XXXVI, No. 146, Part 11, July 29, 1971.

9. Total food purchased with coupons exceeded $2.7 billion, but this includes the purchase price of the stamps.

10. In October, 35,673 were on strike in Wayne County. Recipient figures taken from interviews with Wayne County, Michigan, Department of Social Services officials, February 1971, show 18,102 were authorized to receive food stamps.

11. Of an estimated 177,000 Michigan residents on strike against General Motors in October, 22,797 received AFDC-U payments. Recipient figures from State of Michigan, Department of Social Services, *Social Service Statistics* (monthly); Publication No. 67.

12. A letter from the Chief Executive Officer of the County of Los Angeles (California), July 2, 1971, shows 309 employees on strike from General Motors received assistance totaling $222,848.

13. For a compendium of how the individual state plans vary (but not how they are applied to strike cases) see: U.S. Department of Health, Education, and Welfare, *Characteristics of State Public Assistance Plans under the Social Security Act*, Public Assistance Report No. 50, General Provisions—Eligibility, Assistance, Administration, 1970 edition.

14. As George W. Taylor has pointed out, when inducements to agree to strike settlement are diminished or the penalties for failing to agree waived, "even more [than normally] devastating consequences result." See George W. Taylor, "Is Compulsory Arbitration Inevitable?" *Readings in Labor Economics and Labor Relations*, ed. Richard L. Rowan and Herbert R. Northrup (Homewood, Ill.: Richard D. Irwin, Inc., 1968), p. 369.

15. Developed by projection of trend of data contained in: U.S. Bureau of Labor Statistics, *Handbook of Labor Statistics 1969*, BLS Bulletin 1930, Table 149; and *Monthly Labor Review*, Vol. XCIV (August 1971), Table 32.

Welfare Payment to Strikers

Ray Andrus †

The matter of welfare payments to strikers and their families
(dependents) has, during the past few years, increasingly become an issue under attack from the far right, certain organizations representing business, some elements of the public media,
anti-labor congressmen, some of the totally uninformed and some
of the only partially informed. Why all of this concern? What
is it all about? Answers to each question are basic and easy
to comprehend. Those who are raising these voices of protest
are generally found to be pro-business, pro-management, and
anti-organized labor. A careful examination of their actions, expressions and policy positions in the past will indicate this is
true in a substantial majority of cases. It is all about whether
or not the family and dependents of a worker on strike are entitled to the same treatment, when in need, that is accorded
every other person in this nation.

It would take a callous individual indeed to advocate denial
of welfare assistance to a needy, hungry family—all of us must
agree that hunger and starvation are dreadful plagues to those
who are directly confronted. Why then would any person of
good conscience energetically strive to deny strikers, their wives,
children, and other dependents (elderly parents, foster children,
etc.) such forms of public assistance as food stamps or welfare
allotments when they become otherwise eligible to receive same?
In response we get the well-stereotyped business oriented answer that: (1) the needy striker and his family are depriving
other needy people of welfare assistance; (2) the striker volunteered to place himself in this present situation; and (3) permitting the "needy" striker and family to obtain any form of
tax supported welfare is placing the government in the position
of aiding one side (unions) involved in the collective bargaining process. This, they state, also tends to lengthen the duration of the strike and influence greater demands from the union.

---

† Ray Andrus is on the staff of the Community Services Committee of the
  AFL-CIO.

At first blush, all of these arguments seem rather plausible and persuasive. They should because no doubt some thought and preparation went into their development as a justification for such a "class" denial of assistance which is otherwise open to all individuals within our society who meet the economic eligibility standards.

To begin with, we in the AFL-CIO believe that "need" alone is the criterion for determining whether assistance should be provided. The hungry child faced with malnutrition or the pregnant mother with little food on the table should not be denied food whatever the cause of their plight, be it unemployment, business foreclosure, war, family breadwinner in prison, or strikes. Regardless of the reason, it would take an inhumane society or an individual hardened and immune to feeling to deny relief to either case. So to repeat—our position is and has been that "need" should be the sole criterion for public assistance and all recipients should be treated alike.

However, despite this compelling argument, we can also prove the validity and justification of our position by showing the fallacy, one sidedness, and lack of equity in the arguments generally used which have been previously quoted.

1. Other needy people are deprived of assistance. This argument is often advanced by those who, in the first place, were opposed to providing welfare to anyone. They use their "so called" concern over other needy people being deprived by the needy striker and his family as an excuse to justify denial of welfare when truthfully it is because they are even more anti-union than they are anti-welfare. It would be interesting to know the percentage (if any) of welfare recipients that have been dropped from the rolls because someone on strike replaced them. It is just not the practice to do so under any welfare program. Besides all welfare assistance should be provided on the basis of need for everyone who qualifies and should not contain punitive penalties aimed at a class or group.

2. The striker volunteered to bring about his present predicament by choosing to strike. This automatically assumes that management had no part in setting the conditions that caused the striker to arrive at his "choice." It absolves management of any blame even though acceptance of highly unsatisfactory wages and working conditions were the other

alternatives. It absolves the public, Congress, the President and all other persons, groups, or factors that may have contributed to an economy that created the conditions which may have made the choice for the striker.

3. Aiding one side involved in the collective bargaining process by use of tax revenue. This charge also fails to reveal the other side of the proverbial coin. What about all of the special tax exemptions that are applied to business? Are they discontinued during the period of the strike? Are all contracts financed by tax dollars cancelled when a company is struck? Are companies on strike allowed to obtain new contracts which are underwritten by tax dollars? Are tax dollars used to purchase products from a company while it is involved in a strike? Of course the answer is no to each of the above, and this is well known to all of us. Yet none of these welfare watch dogs raises even a whisper about continuing or giving this type of tax dollar supported assistance to a company involved in a strike. In addition, a review of strike history and statistics does not show any increase in the length of strikes within established organized basic industries. Over the last thirty years there have been up and down periods and this same pattern or trend is continuing.

However it is not necessary to refute the biased charges of those who would permit other human beings—women, little children, and the dependent elderly—to starve for the sake of aiding corporate interest in a labor dispute. There are many reasons based upon equity and principle, reasonableness, and humanity that support the right of the "needy" striker to receive public welfare.

1. Strikers are taxpayers. They also give generously to private agencies and community causes. In fact what other identifiable group pays more taxes than the 20,000,000 members of organized labor and their families? As taxpayers they should be entitled to the same rights as other taxpayers.

2. Tax dollars are used to provide food for hungry people in other countries—even in some where our aid is accepted in one breath and our country criticized in the next. Are these hungry people more entitled to such assistance than

hungry loyal tax-paying Americans who are engaged in a strike?

3. Even criminals in prison, including the convicted murderer on death row, are fed, clothed, sheltered and given medical assistance. Their families are not disqualified from food stamps or welfare. Aren't needy strikers and their families entitled to at least the same consideration! Some sources have voiced the almost ridiculous argument of the striker having a choice and voluntarily causing his need as opposed to the lack of choice on the part of the criminal. This statement is almost too ridiculous to answer except in the interest of refutation. It must be emphasized that if any point is to be made the criminal had more of a choice than the striker. He could easily have elected not to commit the crime. The criminal action which caused his incarceration was certainly a voluntary act on his part.

4. We use tax dollars to provide food, clothing, shelter, and medical care for enemy prisoners of war. Is the loyal fellow American striker engaged in economic industrial warfare entitled to less? Should he be treated more harshly than an enemy soldier because he confronts big business?

5. No one has an incentive to strike or hold out on strike for the prospect of continuing a welfare level standard of living. Under such standards debts accumulate, installments of mortgage payments that can be postponed must be met later (or the property is repossessed) and such items as food and clothing are less in quantity and quality. Any worker with a family would be highly unlikely to continue a strike under these conditions unless there was some compelling justification in his opinion for him to do otherwise. The company is run by management. It has all the rights and privileges of a person but does not have any physiological needs. A corporation does not have hunger pangs for lack of food, freeze for lack of shelter, or develop a fever for lack of medical attention. Management which acts for the company and makes its decisions continues to draw pay during a strike. Consequently none of these physical needs ever confront the corporation. The "pinch" on the corporation from loss of profits during a strike does not equal the physical pinch upon the striker and his family who face an indefinite period of living at welfare standards.

6. Finally—all strikes do eventually end. As a matter of good business is the company better off by having a deeply imbedded feeling of hate and disloyalty on the part of its employees for having attempted to starve them into submission—or would it not be better with the settlement of the strike to have an atmosphere of respect with a desire to improve employee-employer relations as the foundation upon which to build?

In concluding this presentation, a final reference must be made to the management allegation that welfare for needy strikers gives unions an unfair advantage in the collective bargaining process. This statement is just about as sound as one saying that "Big" David had an advantage over "Little" Goliath.

Pension Opportunities and Problems: Issues in Collective Bargaining and Government Regulation

E. S. Willis †

It has become fashionable today in introducing a subject, to first report on the "good news" and then to sweep it away with the "bad news." Fortunately in pensions there is "good news" (in the shape of opportunities) and there is some "bad news" but at the moment the latter is only in the shape of problem areas.

At the outset, it should be noted that private pension plans today are making an ever increasing contribution to the economy and to individual retirement security. Unless they are smothered with governmental kindness in the form of excessive regulation, they will continue to make an even greater contribution. Further, we can expect this growth to continue as it has in the past in conjunction with the collective-bargaining process. Now there will be areas for dispute where the questions will be ones of priorities and balance. How much, how large, to whom, what is the cost, and in lieu of what other benefits will be the major issues.

I. Background

While pension plans were first adopted by industry as early as 1875, they began their major growth in the 1940's and 1950's. As Table 1 indicates, they are now making a significant and major contribution not only to retirement security but to the capital market. The data indicate further that 30 years ago only 9 percent of the work force was covered by private pension plans (insured and non-insured) whereas 50 percent of the work force is covered today. Pension reserves have jumped from $2.4 billion in 1940 to $137.0 billion today, while pension benefit payments have increased from $100 million to $6 billion per year.

---

† E. S. Willis is Manager, Employee Benefits, General Electric Company.

TABLE 1. *Private Pension Plans*

Year	Coverage[a]	Percent of Work Force	Number of Pensioners	Reserves[b]	Benefits
	(millions)		(thousands)	(billions)	(millions)
1940	4.1	9	200	$ 2,400	$ 100
1950	9.8	22	450	12,000	370
1960	21.2	42	1,780	52,000	1,750
1970	over 30.0	50	4,200	137,000	6,000

[a] Based on Social Security Bulletin, April 1971 and Department of Commerce Data.

[b] Insured and non-insured pension funds.

Projections indicate continued growth of private pension plan assets. By 1980, reserves (insured and non-insured funds) are expected to exceed $215 billion and more than 7.0 million people will be receiving over $11.0 billion a year in benefits. This clearly adds up to a major and growing institution making a significant contribution to the nation's economy and the financial system. It is against these data that we will examine the current "hot" pension issues in collective bargaining and the pitfalls to be avoided in over-regulating pension plans.

II. Collective Bargaining Issues

In the pension negotiation area, two continuing developments stand out sharply: the high flat-rate minimums negotiated in recent major settlements, and the pattern, particularly in public employee pension plans (but also in some industry plans) of liberal early retirement benefits.

The rubber industry settlement in 1970 provided a basic pension rate of $7.75 per month for each year of service—up more than 40 percent from the previous basic rate of $5.50. Later in 1970, the auto industry settlement increased basic pension rates in that industry from $5.50, $5.75 and $6.00 to $7.25, $7.50 and $7.75 depending on earnings. This was a lower percentage increase and stayed within the top $7.75 rate established by the rubber settlement.

In 1971, however, the can companies, in the first of the major steelworker settlements, went to a basic pension rate of $8.50

per month for each year of service—up about 30 percent from
the previous $6.50 rate and setting a new high for a major set-
tlement. This was further increased to a basic rate of $9.00 in
the aluminum settlement—up 38 percent over the previous $6.50
rate. Finally, the basic steel settlement provided minimum pensions of $8.00 per month for each of the first 15 years of service;
$9.00 per month for each of the next 15 years and $10.00 per
month for each year of service over 30. Also, the basic earnings
related pension in the steel industry was increased to 1.1 percent of final 10 year average earnings for each of the first 30
years of service and 1.2 percent of such earnings for each year
of service over 30. An employee retiring at age 65, after 35
years of credited service, would receive total retirement income
including estimated primary social security benefits equal to the
percentage of final 5 year average earnings as shown in Table 2.

Table 2 is not meant as a comparison of the various pension
plans since other provisions, such as optional retirement and
disability and death benefits, would have to be taken into account for a valid comparison. Rather, the data are presented
as a means of illustrating the extent to which these new higher
minimums, when combined with increased Social Security benefits, replace earnings for employees retiring at age 65 with 35
years of service. It is likely that in some cases, the after tax
income following retirement will exceed take home pay immediately before retirement. If allowance is made for decreased
expense in areas such as transportation and work clothes and
Social Security spouse benefits, it is clear that some employees

TABLE 2. *Total Retirement Income as Percent of*
Final Five-Year Earnings

Final Five-year Average Earnings	Est. Soc. Sec. as Percent of Final Five-year Earnings	Industry				
		Rubber	Auto	Can	Aluminum	Steel[a]
$ 6,500	38	88	85	93	96	94
7,500	34	77	75	82	84	83
9,000	29	65	64	69	71	70
10,000	26	59	59	62	64	63

[a] Based on flat rate minimum.

will enjoy an increase in living standards upon retirement. Where a business adopts a high minimum without considering its own pay levels, the ratio to fiscal pay could produce even worse results.

Obviously, we are nearing the end of the road in flat rate minimums in terms of current wage rates. Future improvements are, of course, still possible and in many cases desirable at the higher income levels, but some limitations or restrictions will be necessary at the lower levels if we are to avoid situations where an employee can no longer afford to work because he would receive more income in a non-productive, retired status than as a productive worker.

The retirement income levels referred to above assume retirement at age 65. There is, however, heavy pressure for earlier and earlier retirement. It is being exerted in both the public employee and private employee sectors. The success achieved by unions in the non-profit areas of government, which are not subject to profit restraints, are now spilling over into the private sector where profits have a definite voice in controlling actions.

In government, we find sanitation men, policemen, subway operators, and firemen all insisting, and unfortunately getting retirement at half pay after twenty and twenty-five years. Last year the Patrolmen's Benevolent Association in New York announced it wanted *full* pay pension after twenty-five years and, incidentally, with a minimum salary of $16,000 a year; and the New York firemen naturally followed a few days later with the same demand. They had already achieved full pay at thirty-five years in the present plan.

In the private sector, of course, one of the key issues in the UAW strike against GM was retirement after thirty years of service plus a financial bonus to retire. Many companies have been lowering the retirement age to fifty-five; some with and without actuarial or other reduction. The popularity of this lower age is hard to explain. It seems likely that for many younger companies it is a no cost item now. For others, it helps reduce their work force—a very short range view—and others acquiesce to union demands for various reasons of their own. Some even go down to age fifty; some have age and service formulae based on no discernible rationale but that of eighty-five or eighty or seventy-five points.

These trends all have serious economic repercussions. I am sure that man, ever since he walked upright and reasoned, has enjoyed leisure. The amount of leisure, however, has been generally dictated by how fast he could get the essentials of existence cared for, after which he could relax. Today, the time to take care of existence has been shortened, but not to the extreme limits some would seem to think, and possibly not at the economic cost involved in these arrangements.

Ted Kheel, who initially mediated a number of New York settlements between the city and its employees, has stated that the settlements on early retirement plans (half pay at twenty years for transit men, sanitation workers, policemen and firemen) were causing a critical exodus of skilled workers sorely needed to maintain city services. The *Times* has pointed out that New York City's pension costs have sharply increased from $342 million contribution in 1966 to $518 million in 1970 and it will be $750 million by 1975. Some of this increase is due to rising salary scales and numbers of employees, but a large share comes from more pension at shorter service and lower employee age at retirement. The wave of early retirement reportedly swamped at least one city pension system.

Turning to broader problems, I do not know on what basis our economy can function, but we are certainly pushing toward serious economic problems if an ever smaller base of producers must support more and more nonproducers, or—more likely—must support more cost to the economy as the effective pay of many producers is virtually doubled by paying pensions to people who do not actually leave the labor force.

We cannot expect a rise in productivity to offset either of these unnecessary drains on the economy. The Bureau of Labor Statistics (BLS) predicts that the annual increase in productivity in the 1970's will be about 3 percent, which is slightly *below* the annual rate since the war. A 3 percent rate is more than offset by the annual rates of increase in pay being granted to labor. Therefore, if the productive base of our economy is to be further compressed, it is going to have to run much, much faster. We are all, of course, hopeful that the current wage freeze programs will start a drastic turn-around.

The entire area of payments for time not worked, which includes not only pensioned time but holidays, vacations, and sick pay time provides an illustration of the impact of certain so-called fringe benefits on production. Using General Electric's schedule and including no more liberalizations than those already announced, assuming we have an individual starting to work at twenty and working to age sixty-five, he will have worked only 88 percent of the total available work days and been paid—but not worked—12 percent of the total. To illustrate this another way, this is equivalent to working a steady thirty-five hour week. Now, if he retired at sixty, his productive time is reduced to 79 percent of the total available, equal to a steady thirty-one and a half hour week. If he were to retire at age fifty-five, productive work is only two-thirds of the total available, a twenty-seven hour week. That leisure of 33 percent of the time has to be paid for from a 67 percent productive base. Think what that means if it applied to every employee! And think what age fifty would mean; that is, a man who was twenty when starting to work retiring after thirty years. If he really retired, he would have worked only 42 percent of his available productive time. This certainly would place the economy on a pretty small axis. Or think how much more productive he must become if we are to pay him nearly double for the next fifteen to twenty years.

Some Department of Labor figures[1] claim a slight reduction in labor force participation in age 55-59 from around 91 percent to 90 percent and it is claimed that auto pension plans have reduced the age of that industry's work force accordingly, and it is claimed "to a more limited extent, these provisions have also encouraged complete retirement from the labor force." It is claimed further that this occurs because of the pension benefit formula which curtails benefits if the pensioner earns more than is permitted under a formula. I believe, and I know some auto management people concur, that the Department is putting undue weight in the pure operation of that formula. There may have been some retirements from the labor force, but generally only among those few disabled enough to find work almost impossible. With inflation, and its ensuing rising living costs, the tendency is simply to take a pension and work elsewhere at rates probably not far below their old rates, thus building a good increase in income.

In the auto industry negotiations last fall, the UAW demands included full retirement benefits at any age after 30 years of service. The final settlement did not go that far, but it did provide that beginning October 1, 1971, employees with 30 years of service could retire at age 58 with an initial pension of $500 per month. The pension reduces at age 62 to $450 per month and reduces further at age 65 to an average

$189 per month for 30-year employees. On October 1, 1972, the age 58 requirement will reduce to age 56.

The wage-price freeze and the slow economic recovery and other factors cloud any assessment of the impact of the new early retirement benefits on the exodus of workers. Published figures indicate that at Ford, of 7,800 workers with 30 or more years of service, of whom about 2,600 were age 58 or over, about 650 retired on October 1. It may be assumed that most of the 650 retirements were from the 2,600 employees age 58, or over, and that the percentage of retirements from this group was, therefore fairly high. Current data are colored by the recession we have had, with higher layoffs and fewer job opportunities.

General Motors has published some data concerning results under the previous pension plan which contained a $400 per month allowance. They reported that in three months—just three months—after their $400 allowance program for early retirees went into effect, 5,800 employees retired early. This was 17 percent of the eligibles—a high figure. Perhaps equally significant, 21 percent of these retirees were skilled tradesmen who could find jobs at equal or higher rates by simply applying elsewhere, or even go into business themselves with a guaranteed income from pensions. The loss rate of skilled workers in the steel industry where early retirement is available, but without special subsidy, is closely comparable. It is perhaps significant that in steel, of the retirement on a thirty-year basis for a six-month period, almost 19 percent were *under* age 56, and for a four and a half year period, the total was 15 percent. It is stretching the imagination to believe that any significant number of these permanently leave the work force!

In spite of the claims of some that older people retire from the work force, our own figures dispute this. If many companies put in 30 years-and-out programs, there would be one grand round of retirements and hirings going on—all at the unnecessary expense of the economy. Some recent figures on our experience shows that we already had over 2,200 employees aged fifty-five ond over who had less than five years of service, over one-quarter of whom were aged sixty to sixty-four and were therefore hired at ages 55 to 59. Five hundred of these 2,200 short-service people—nearly one-quarter—were in the skilled category. Obviously, we hired them after they left some other employer—there are no data as to whether they are on pension, but the figures indicate a high employment rate for people in this age and skill bracket.

Everyone engaged in the various aspects of designing benefits has an important part to play in assuring that there is a sound balance in this tug of war between the provision of leisure earned by the work force and the overly costly inflation of economic costs by unsound programs. It is in the best interests of labor, management and the country as a whole that we seriously study and maintain this balance.

III.   On Government Regulation

In the past year, the critics of private pension plans have opened up all stops to discredit the private system, but it is a pretty tough bird and there is still plenty of fight and life left.[2]   In fact, especially if those in business who favor the private pension plan can further intensify efforts to communicate the values of the private system, we can fight off detractors for quite a while and maybe indefinitely.   But those on the other side are hard at work.

While there have been many bills introduced by many sponsors in Congress since the early 1960's calling for additional pension plan regulation, there are now pending two measures which together incorporate all of the major recommendations that have been made.   They are: (1) H.R. 1269—the "Employee Benefit Security Act" introduced in January 1971 by Chairman Dent of the House Labor Subcommittee, and S. 2—the "Pension and Employee Benefit Act" introduced in January 1971 by Senator Jacob Javits.   The Administration appears about ready to introduce its 1972 proposals covering broadened disclosure, fiduciary responsibility, and vesting.

Congressman Dent concluded, on April 28, 1971, the second of two days of hearings on pending legislation. He heard only from Senator Javits, Mr. I. W. Abel (Steelworkers) and Mr. Leonard Woodcock (UAW).   Mr. Dent had held extensive hearings in the House in earlier years on pension plan legislation containing essentially the same features found in H.R. 1269 (Dent) and S. 2 (Javits).   Mr. Dent's Subcommittee has just received authority to conduct more studies with a $100,000 appropriation, so we will be hearing more from Mr. Dent next year and at least he wraps in government plans.

On March 31, 1971 the Senate Labor Subcommittee issued its now famous—or infamous—report on pension plans. This set off a wholesale indictment of the private pension system. *New York Times* editorial writers, scenting blood, or carried away with journalistic flair, reported in banner headlines: "Phantom Pensions in Industry." The Senior Senator from New York, who is acting as kind of majority chairman of the Senate Labor Subcommittee, under Chairman Harrison Williams, was quoted as saying, "Only a relative handful of the tens of millions of workers will ever get anything . . . ." This highly erroneous and misleading report and the recent horror hearings before the Subcommittee have set the tone for the current press coverage which all too often is decrying private plans. The hearings, it is said, are held with sufficient regularity to keep the press stirred up and build up legislative support for "reform." The "other" side does not communicate and it should. Unfortunately, business as usual is spending a lot of time arguing with itself.

Now I am sure anyone in industry is for reform where reform performs a constructive function, and this includes curing abuses and even taking that extra step to make sure that pension plans do not cut the corners. It is hard to believe, however, that a destructive campaign of villification and abuse is the way to go about it; the obviously misleading figures released by the Subcommittee are really a considerable cut below what should be expected as a release. The Report is critical of vesting, yet today a large share of plans have, or are adopting, vesting and actually the Subcommittee figures when carefully analyzed demonstrate to a surprising degree the usage of vesting and other pension provisions. But we do need even faster voluntary action in this area.

Now, what is at stake? Well, as noted earlier, we are talking about a private retirement security system that now covers over 50 percent of the work force or 30.0 million people. We are talking about a private system that in 1940 had 200,000 pensioners drawing benefits—now 4.5 million people and rising rapidly despite the fact that some have the notion no one is receiving benefits. More importantly, we are also talking about an entirely private voluntary system, voluntary unilaterally or by bargaining, that makes a significant and growing contribution to the nation's economy and financial system.

Pensions are first of all a human rights program. But the contribution to our economy and accordingly to job expansion and development are vitally important. We should make sure that in our legislative goals and recommendations we do not curtail the growth and that the contribution they make is not impaired.

Here is a brief check list on what I like to consider to be reasonable goals for private plans:

First   To encourage—not discourage—expansion of private plans so as to cover not by fiat the 50 percent of the working population not fortunate enough to have pensions yet.

Second The next obligation is to protect beneficiaries of plans. This presumes full and adequate communication and employee understanding as to the nature of the pension promise.

Third   Investment of assets to protect pension promises to beneficiaries. The primary social responsibility of the plans is to meet the pension promise. Uneconomical diversion of funds for some other social purpose should not undermine this responsibility.

A major objective should be to make sure that in proposals for new legislation the present flexibilities in investment are not handicapped. The free flow of capital from expanding pension funds to where it is needed in the economy must be assured for future economic growth.

Now, with respect to plans after they are established, there are certain specific recommendations that would be responsive to legislative pressures and not violate these objectives. I believe they could contribute to an improved system with government influence channeled along constructive ways.

1. A federal fiduciary responsibility provision should be established. This would require that persons handling funds of plans do so as fiduciaries in a prudent manner. Existing remedies through many state or federal courts are inadequate or not well-defined.

2. Some additional disclosure of pension plan operations would be helpful as long as it avoids burdensome, nonproductive effort. Disclosure to a full airing is a very great disinfectant. Also, the Secretary of Labor should be able to obtain, on an individual basis, additional data

as needed to carry out the purposes of the Disclosure Act. Annual auditing requirements would seem appropriate.

These recommendations are contained in existing proposals, although there may be minor differences in language. I would hope that these essentially non-controversial proposals could be enacted without further delay. Additionally, there are other recommendations that are receiving serious study.

1. There is a matter of vesting. The issue is not whether vesting per se is good or bad—it is a valuable feature of modern pension plans. There is a clear trend towards almost universal adoption of vesting without compulsion. While recognizing the risks of mandating plan provisions, I believe that employers can support the requirement of such a provision on a reasonable and sound basis, especially if they do not move up on it fast enough on their own. If a vesting requirement is enacted, it should apply to all types of plans—single employer and multi-employer plans. A dual standard exempting multi-employer plans would be unconscionable. Vesting, however, does not require funding regulation.

2. On funding, it seems to me that compulsory funding can only lead to such strict control of pension fund investments as to seriously limit their important contribution, both in the capital markets and in the fullest use to help provide to the optimum degree, the ever larger pensions being paid. There is no demonstrated necessity for funding regulation, and it would also restrict the flexibilities that employers now have to postpone, for a period, a particular funding obligation, perhaps in order to stay in business.

3. A brief comment on portability. This concept of a central clearing house for transferring pension credits when an employee changes jobs has a surface appeal. Most experts believe that such transfer devices are so exceedingly complex as to be impractical and would disrupt the normal operation of pensions and investment of pension funds and would certainly add nothing to the pensions themselves. In any event, the rapid adoption of vesting makes portability clearly academic, since from a practical stand-

point, vesting is tantamount to portability. If employers exercise their initiative as they should in the vesting area, the lack of need for portability will become even clearer.

4. On Pension Plan termination insurance ("Re-insurance"), there are numerous proposals to insure the termination of pension plans. The arguments are too detailed for comprehensive review here. The term has undeniable appeal but most observers agree that the practical drawbacks offset the semantics. They are not sure this is an insurable risk. Also guarantees like this could discourage adequate funding. The stable funds would shoulder the load for the improvident. In doing so, they would also have to spend money that would otherwise be available for pensions. The problem of loss of pension benefits due to plan termination appears minimal and based on sketchy data. The data showing numbers of terminations fail to indicate the fact that in most terminations there was only a transfer of pension credits to other organizations.

IV.   Goals and Objectives

In sum, we should make sure that our legislative recommendations square with basic goals and objectives which should be to: (1) encourage further growth of coverage of private pension plans; and (2) encourage the growth contribution that private pension funds, where there are plans, are making to the well-being of retired employees, to the economy and to our capital formation process.

NOTES

1. Dr. Goeffrey Moore, Commissioner of Labor Statistics, "The Economic Impact of Employee Benefits," October 1970.

2. This discussion is based in part on a paper presented at the 8th Annual Pension Conference, Donaldson, Lufkin and Jenrette, New York City.

Private Pensions and Public Policy

Dan M. McGill†

The private pension institution has turned out to be a vigorous outgrowth of our modern technological society. The first plans of this genre were established in this country almost one hundred years ago but the movement did not gain momentum until World War II when a combination of factors encouraged rapid growth. Today private pension plans cover an estimated thirty-two million employees, or approximately one-half of the private, non-agricultural workforce. Four million retired individuals are receiving $7 billion per year in benefits from private pension plans. Banks, insurance companies, and private trustees hold $140 billion in assets to ensure payment of the benefits accruing under these plans. The private pension institution is clearly a major force in providing old-age economic security.

Yet there are certain facets of this institution that have been undergoing intensive scrutiny over the last several years, leading to a rash of legislative proposals. This paper will examine the three features—funding, plan termination insurance, and vesting —that have received the most legislative attention, and another feature—early retirement—that seems to be high on the priority list of many labor unions.

Funding

Funding has reference to the setting aside of assets in trust or under the terms of a group annuity contract in advance of the time that they will be needed to meet the benefit obligations of a pension plan. The concept of funding is vitally significant to the security aspirations of pension plan participants since the overwhelming majority of pension plans stipulate that benefit payments will be made only out of assets set aside by the employer or other plan sponsor in respect of the plan obligations.

† Dan M. McGill is Frederick H. Ecker Professor of Life Insurance and Research Director, Pension Research Council, Wharton School, University of Pennsylvania.

In other words, pensions in the typical case are not a claim against the corporate assets of the employer. The ultimate objective of every pension plan should be the holding of a dollar of assets for every dollar of accrued liability.

There is no law that requires a pension plan to accumulate assets equal to its liabilities. At present the only legal requirements pertaining to funding are found in the regulations of the Internal Revenue Service which stipulate that during the first few years of a plan's existence contributions must be at least equal to the normal cost plus interest on the initial supplemental cost. The IRS has interpreted this provision to impose the described minimum standard of funding during the first ten years of a plan's existence, and most plan administrators operate on the assumption that the standard must be met at all times, i.e., beyond the initial ten years. The IRS has no statutory authority to concern itself with the actuarial soundness of pension plans, the minimum funding standard presently in force being designed to ensure that plans are not established for the primary purpose of providing benefits to persons retiring within the next few years, especially stockholders, officers, supervisors, and highly paid employees. In fact, the IRS is more concerned with over-funding than underfunding.

Despite the lack of governmental pressure toward adequate funding, there is evidence that most employers are following financial practices that will lead to a completely satisfactory level of funding. The most comprehensive and technically precise study of funding among private pension plans was that carried out by the Pension Research Council of the Wharton School a few years ago. The Council studied a sample of over 1,000 plans, representing a good cross-section of the universe except for collectively bargained multi-employer plans and single employer plans funded through individual contracts of life insurance companies. The basic objective was to compare the market value of plan assets with the actuarial liability associated with accrued benefits, computed on the assumption that the plans were terminating as of the date of valuation. The mid-point of the study, which extended over three years, was 1966. The study showed that in the aggregate, plan assets almost exactly offset accrued liabilities, which for the sample aggregated about $22 billion. More important, it showed that 90 per cent of the plans were being funded more rapidly than would be the case under a standard calling for the funding of normal costs currently and supplemental costs over a thirty-year period. Many plans had more than enough assets, valued at market, to cover their liabilities in the event of plan termination. Multi-employer plans included in the study tended to fund only normal costs and interest on the initial supplemental cost, a funding policy that will generally not lead to a satisfactory level of funding measured against the benchmark of plan termination.

Many persons both inside and outside the government have felt—and continue to feel—that funding is too important a matter to be left to the discretion of the plan administrator. They have urged that as a condition for continued qualification under the Internal Revenue Code and supporting regulations pension plans be required to conform to a standard of funding that in the long run would assure a sufficiency of assets to meet benefit claims in the event of plan termination. Some of the bills now before Congress would impose such a standard.

These bills are generally opposed by both management and labor, as well as some of the professional groups that service pension plans. Management opposes higher funding standards primarily on the grounds that they would impair the financial flexibility needed by corporate managements in meeting the considerable burden of pension plans. Unions oppose higher standards because they might frustrate their efforts to obtain ever larger benefit promises. This is particularly true for multi-employer plans which for any given period must provide benefits out of a finite sum of money—anticipated contributions from employers plus investment earnings. Actuaries as a group oppose mandatory standards of funding out of a fear that the regulatory agency might take it upon itself to specify actuarial assumptions generally thought to be the special province of the actuarial profession.

I have long advocated more realistic funding standards and feel that they could be imposed without undue encroachment on the flexibility of corporate financial policy, the bargaining strategy of organized labor, and the professional prerogatives of actuarial practitioners. A requirement that normal costs be met currently and supplemental costs be funded over a period of not more than thirty years would appear to be reasonable, especially if some leeway were to be provided in meeting the annual funding requirements. Such a requirement should be applicable to both single employer and multi-employer plans. This is only a slightly more rigorous standard than that now being applied by the ac-

counting profession in the recognition of accruing pension costs.
There would be no need for the regulatory agency to stipulate
the assumptions with respect to the various elements of cost. As
a matter of fact, it would be impracticable for the agency to do
so. It would be sufficient for the law to specify the funding objective and then accept annual certifications from qualified actuaries that the funding standard is being followed. This would
involve some mechanism for official accreditation of actuaries,
who are not presently regulated and have no standing in the eyes
of the law. I would suggest that membership in the American
Academy of Actuaries be accepted as satisfactory evidence of
professional qualification to certify compliance with the mandatory funding standard.

Plan Termination Insurance

If a pension plan terminates before it has reached a fully
funded state, the benefit expectations of some or all of the plan
participants will be frustrated. Thousands of plans have terminated for one reason or the other and in most cases there has
been some loss of expected benefits. Studies have shown that
most plans that terminate cover fewer than twenty-five employees
and have been in operation less than five years. A substantial
percentage—as many as a third—are terminated because of
mergers or because of conversion to some other type of plan,
such as profit-sharing. Nevertheless, the loss of benefits that
usually accompanies a plan termination has caused many people
to seek an insurance mechanism that would ensure payment of
accrued benefits irrespective of the adequacy of plan assets.

The idea of plan termination seems to have originated in this
country with the United Automobile Workers after a number of
firms with which it had bargaining agreements discontinued
their pension plans before the assets had matched the liabilities.
The most spectacular case of this type was the termination of
the plan covering the employees of the Studebaker Corporation
at its South Bend, Indiana plant when in 1964 the plant was
closed. The Studebaker Corporation had met its funding commitment to the letter but only those employees aged sixty and
over received their benefits in full. The other participants received
only 15 percent of their accrued benefits. The unfortunate consequences of this termination prompted Senator Vance Hartke
of Indiana to introduce a bill that would create a so-called rein-

surance program for private pension plans. The original bill was introduced in 1964 and has been reintroduced in modified form in each subsequent session of Congress. The proposal has been contained in other bills, including one sponsored by the Department of Labor.

In a monograph published in late 1970, entitled *Guaranty Fund for Private Pension Obligations,* I traced the legislative history of the concept and analyzed the problems that would be involved in the successful implementation of the idea. At the conclusion of the analysis, I outlined what I regarded to be the essential elements in a minimum program of plan termination insurance. I felt that the undertaking should be limited to the insurance of vested benefits and should be further limited to instances of total plan termination by a firm undergoing bankruptcy, insolvency, or other form of dissolution. The guaranty fund would assume responsibility for paying all guaranteed benefits, irrespective of the reason for the insufficiency of assets. It would, of course, take over all assets of the terminated plans. Premiums would be based on the unfunded accrued liability for guaranteed vested benefits and would be charged at a uniform rate. The program would have to be accompanied by mandatory standards of funding and vesting.

The Department of Labor is currently in process of preparing legislation that would establish a program of plan termination insurance which would not be superimposed on a mandatory funding standard. This stratagem is being invoked to avoid a confrontation with those groups that oppose externally imposed standards of funding. The plan under consideration would cover claims arising out of partial plan terminations, as defined, as well as those stemming from total terminations. All terminations would be covered, irrespective of cause, including those situations in which the sponsoring firm continued in existence. The adverse selection that could arise out of such broad coverage would be countered by imposing a contingent liability on the continuing firm to make up any deficiency in plan assets at the time of termination. The firm would be required to make up the deficiency in uniform annual installments over the next twenty years, except that the payment in any particular year would be limited to some specified percentage, such as 25 percent, of pretax profits. Any deficit remaining at the end of twenty years because of the profit limitation would be forgiven. The obligation to make the funding payments would be treated as a general claim against the assets of the firm, with a priority in the event of insolvency or bankruptcy subordinate to that of general creditors. The subordinate position of these claims is designed to protect the credit status of the firm during a time when it might be experiencing some financial difficulties. Only benefits that vest through the normal operation of the plan—as opposed to those that vest only by virtue of plan termination—would be guaranteed and there would be an upper limit, such as, $800 per month, on the benefits that would be assumed by the guarantor on behalf of any one participant. Multi-employer plans would be brought within the scope of the program, but special criteria for partial terminations would apply to such plans.

Management is generally opposed to any proposals for plan termination insurance, principally on the grounds that (1) there is no demonstrated need for such a program and (2) the idea is not technically feasible. Opponents argue that the program could be abused by unscrupulous employers and unions and that it would be inequitable for the premium *rate* to be the same for all plans, as is generally proposed.

Unions generally support the notion of plan termination insurance, not only because of the social benefits that would supposedly flow from it, but because it might pave the way to higher benefits for the same employer contributions. In other ways, it would ease some of the pressure on full funding, especially if the program should be established without funding standards. The United Automobile Workers and the United Steelworkers are particularly aggressive in the pursuit of plan termination insurance and have reputedly told the Department of Labor that they will not support any pension legislation, including the fiduciary bill, that does not include the insurance feature.

I personally believe that plan termination insurance is technically feasible, especially if the program is structured along the lines that I recommended in my book. Two programs, one in Sweden and one in Finland, have been functioning successfully for the last ten years. The economic environment in those countries is admittedly different from that of the United States but we can learn something from their experience. I am not convinced that an equitable plan can be devised without mandatory standards of funding, although the two existing systems operate in conjunction with pay-as-you go financing. It is, of course, possible that the imposition of a contingent liability on the employer who terminates his plan may take the place of mandatory funding. The undertaking is made much more complex when partial terminations are included, but the Labor Department officials feel that any plan that does not cover the Studebaker type of situation will not be politically acceptable.

There does not appear to be an overwhelming need for plan termination insurance at the present time. However, the existence of such a program, properly structured and financed, could only serve to strengthen the private pension institution. I think that the fashioning of such a program would be a worthy project for all those interested in supporting the private approach to social and economic problems.

Vesting

There is intense interest in vesting at the present time, stemming in some degree from the emphasis placed on the concept in the *Report of the President's Committee on Corporate Pension Funds* in 1965. During the last ten to fifteen years, vesting provisions in pension plans have been greatly liberalized, in part through voluntary action by employers and in part in response to pressure from organized labor. Nevertheless, some groups are dissatisfied with the pace of progress in this area and are urging legislation to establish minimum standards of vesting. Several legislative proposals are currently pending in Congress.

The matter is of such critical concern and so subject to misconceptions and misunderstandings that I have undertaken the preparation of an entire book on the subject. The book, which will run to about four hundred pages, is finished and will be published by the Pension Research Council in the spring of 1972 under the title of *Preservation of Pension Benefit Rights*. Even the title has generated controversy among individuals who have read the book in manuscript form. The title suggests—and was intended to do so by the author—that vesting preserves a benefit right that existed in inchoate form before vesting, while the critics allege that vesting creates a right that did not previously exist, namely, the right to receive a retirement benefit not conditioned on service to the point of retirement. My original reaction was that the argument was essentially a matter of semantics but I am willing to concede that an issue of substance may be involved.

The book deals with the concept of vesting, current practices, public policy issues, the cost of vesting, the extent of vesting, reciprocity, vesting and reciprocity in public employee plans, and vesting and reciprocity in other countries. I can only skim the surface of the subject in this paper. I will confine my remarks to the arguments for and against vesting, the cost of vesting, and the extent to which present participants in pension plans can expect to realize benefits.

Arguments For and Against Vesting

Those who argue for more liberal vesting base their position primarily on the issue of equity. They state that pensions are deferred wages and having given up something in the way of cash wages, employees are entitled to expect the rough equivalent of foregone wages in retirement benefits. If an employee has to remain in a pension plan until retirement age before qualifying for a pension, the probability of receiving a deferred benefit for the waiving of a cash wage increase is greatly diminished. It is the tontine principle all over again, even though New York State outlawed that concept for insurance purposes as long ago as 1906. Proponents of vesting also point out that it facilitates mobility of labor, encourages inefficient or disgruntled workers to leave, and enhances the role of private pension plans in providing old-age economic security.

Those who would not force employers to provide for vesting prior to early or normal retirement age question whether equity is on the side of early vesting. They argue that with a finite amount of money going into a pension plan it is simply a question of who has the greater moral claim to benefits. They contend that long-service employees may have a greater moral claim because of contributions to their employer, craft, or industry that were not reflected in cash wages. Under this concept, a pension is a *differential* wage, not simply a *deferred* wage. Management and labor, it is argued, should have the prerogative of deciding whether a large number of individuals will get a small benefit or a smaller number will get a greater benefit. There is no moral law which says that pension benefits must be linked to each year of service, however short the aggregate period of employment. These observers also see a legitimate exercise of managerial discretion in the use of late vesting provisions to hold valued employees—the classic argument for the withholding of vesting. Moreover, they question whether *private* pension plans have a social role to play, in addition to serving management and union objectives. They reserve their strongest objections to the cost of vesting.

Cost of Vesting

Unfortunately, there is much confusion over the cost of vesting. Some people seem to think that there is one ascertainable figure which can be applied indiscriminately to all plans, irrespective of their age, sex, and service composition. Certain governmental officials have suffered from this delusion, frantically searching for *the* cost of vesting.

In the long run, the cost of vesting is represented by, and is measured in terms of, the benefits that are paid out to individuals that would not have been paid in the absence of vesting. This can be termed the *real* cost of vesting, unadulterated by consideration of such factors as actuarial cost methods and interest assumptions. The real cost of any particular vesting provision is influenced to some extent by all the factors that affect benefit payments in general but it is primarily a function of the employees' entry age distribution, the rate of termination among employees whose benefits have already vested, and the distribution of retirement ages. The rate of termination among vested employees is the most important of these cost determinants.

There will usually be some effect on benefit payments within the first few years after the introduction of vesting, the impact growing with the passage of time. However, the true long-run cost of a particular vesting provision will emerge only when the plan has reached a mature state, i.e., when the age distribution of the plan population (active employees, terminated vested employees, and retired employees) has stabilized. Once the population matures, the real cost of vesting, as represented by the increase in actual benefit outlays, will be apparent in one year's experience and will be constant over the years, barring any changes in the benefit formula or the vesting provision.

In reality, a pension plan seldom, if ever, matures in the sense described above. Over time, plan provisions are modified, benefit formulas are changed and salaries on which benefits are based respond to inflationary pressures. In any event, an employer would be reluctant to wait until the plan matures to assess the cost impact of a vesting provision under consideration. Thus, in practice, it is necessary to estimate the real cost of the provision by projecting the relevant cost factors over a realistic period of time, such as one generation of plan participants. These estimates are, of course, subject to a wide margin of error, primarily because of the difficulty of predicting the ages of entry into the plan and the rates of withdrawal among employees with vested benefits.

Under the foregoing method of measuring the cost of vesting, the cost is expressed as the *percentage increase* in anticipated benefit payments. A more meaningful approach for many purposes is to determine the percentage increase in the *present value* of anticipated benefit payments. This approach is identical to the first except that it utilizes a discount function. The percentage increase in the present value of the real cost of a vesting provision is determined by a fraction the *numerator* of which is the present value, according to the relevant assumptions, of the benefit payments that will be made only as a consequence of pre-retirement vesting, and the *denominator* of which is the present value of the benefit payments that would have been made in the absence of pre-retirement vesting. The computation takes into account all prospective benefits whether they have already accrued or are to be credited in the future. It likewise recognizes benefits that have already vested as well as those that are expected to vest in the future. The result, whether computed in respect to one individual or the entire plan, is a composite percentage undifferentiated as to the normal cost and accrued liability of the plan.

Dr. Howard Winklevoss, an Assistant Professor of Insurance at the Wharton School, has developed a computer model which he has used to estimate the cost impact of the three principal legislative proposals for mandated vesting: the Dent Bill, the Javits Bill, and the Administration's Rule of 50. The Dent Bill would require full and immediate vesting after ten years of credited service, irrespective of attained age, subject to certain transitional modifications. The Javits Bill would vest 10 percent of accrued benefits after six years of credited service and an additional 10 percent each year thereafter, with 100 percent vesting being achieved at the end of fifteen years. Under the Administration's proposal, 50 percent of the accrued benefits of a participant would vest when any combination of attained age and service equals fifty, with an additional 10 percent of the benefits vesting each year thereafter. Under each of these proposals, only benefits that accrue in the future would be subject to these vesting requirements, although prior service would be recognized in determining satisfaction of the service requirement.

In estimating the cost of these vesting standards, Dr. Winklevoss assumed that the pension plan under consideration provided for a uniform increment of benefit for each year of service; entry into the plan at ages ranging from twenty to fifty and averaging twenty-nine; retirement at age sixty-five; and an annual growth rate in the plan population grading down from 5 percent in the first year to zero at the end of fifty years. The employer was assumed to bear the entire cost of the plan, there being no employee contributions. The plan was assumed to contain a provision permitting early retirement age age fifty-five with twenty years of service. Thus, all terminations after age fifty-five and twenty years of service were treated as retirements rather than vested terminations.

Three separate plan populations were generated by holding all other factors constant and assuming withdrawals in accordance with a light, moderate, and heavy scale, respectively. All calculations were based upon the assumption that the vesting standards under consideration had been in effect from the time that the first employees were hired and entered the plan. This would produce the ultimate, long-run cost of the vesting provisions. Costs were reflected not only for active employees but also for terminated vested employees and retired employees. Costs were simulated over an eighty year period, reflecting plan populations in varying stages of maturity.

Dr. Winklevoss found that in the fortieth year of simulation, when the plan was approaching a mature state, the percentage increase in benefit outlays (real cost) because of vesting would, according to his assumptions, be as portrayed in Table 1.

TABLE 1. *Percentage Increase in Benefit Outlays*
Attributable to Vesting

Vesting Standard	Withdrawal Assumptions		
	Light	Moderate	Heavy
Dent Bill	7%	12%	19%
Javits Bill	6	12	19
Administration Bill	6	12	23

It will be noted that the estimated cost of the three proposed vesting standards is about the same for any particular withdrawal assumption. For the moderate withdrawal assumption, perhaps the most realistic, the estimated percentage increase in benefit outlays is the same for all three proposals, namely, 12 percent. As might be expected, a higher percentage of the participants would achieve a vested status under the Javits Bill but a smaller proportion of their accrued benefits would be vested at any given point in time because full vesting is achieved only after fifteen years.

The estimated cost of vesting, as measured in terms of the percentage increase in the *present value* of benefit outlays, is shown in Table 2. The benefits are discounted at 6 percent interest.

TABLE 2. *Percentage Increase in Present Value of Benefit Outlays Attributable to Vesting*

| | Withdrawal Assumption | | |
Vesting Standard	Light	Moderate	Heavy
Dent Bill	10%	18%	29%
Javits Bill	9	18	28
Administration Bill	8	16	28

This basis of measurement likewise produces similar estimates of the cost of vesting under the three proposed standards. The estimates range from a low of 8 percent to a high of 29 percent. With a moderate withdrawal assumption, the estimated cost of the three proposed standards runs from 16 to 18 percent.

It should be observed that the cost figures in the illustration show what the cost of vesting would be, as compared to no vesting prior to retirement. Most plans already provide some type of pre-retirement vesting. Thus, the *additional* cost of providing for vesting in accordance with the various legislative proposals is likely to be less than the figures shown in Tables 1 and 2 for plans whose characteristics and experience conform to the hypotheses of the illustrative case. Moreover, the tables depict what the cost of vesting would be in the fortieth year of a plan's operation had the vesting provision been in effect from the beginning. The cost of adopting a vesting provision at some point after the plan has gone into operation, with or without recognition of all prior service of active employers, would be less than the figures shown because of the non-recognition of the service of employees who terminated before the vesting provision was adopted.

Extent of Vesting

In their zeal to obtain legislative approval of minimum vesting standards, certain Congressmen and Senators have issued questionable statements about the present extent of vesting and the chances that a current participant in a pension plan will ever draw any benefits. Congressman Dent of Pennsylvania has given wide currency to a prediction that only one out of ten participants will ever qualify for benefits. On the basis of a questionnaire prepared and interpreted by the staff of the Subcommittee on Labor of the Senate Committee on Education and Labor, Senators Javits and Williams of New York and New Jersey, respectively, have drawn some startling conclusions. The questionnaire was sent to a sample of 1,500 plans in late 1970, asking for the respective turnover data for the last twenty years and the last five years. Preliminary results have been released on eighty-seven plans, fifty-one of which provided for no vesting or vesting only after eleven or more years of service. This group is designated herein as the A group. The other thirty-six plans, designated herein as the B group, provided for vesting within ten years.

The tabulated results for these plans show that 92 percent of the participants in the A group during the twenty-year period left the plans without any benefits, while 77 percent of the participants in the B group left without benefits. The comparable figures for the last five years were 85 and 83 percent, respectively. These figures led Senators Javits and Williams to call a press conference and announce that the chances that the typical plan participant would ever draw a benefit from the plan is extremely remote. One statistic that received wide publicity was that for every person who leaves a plan with a vested benefit, 223 leave without any rights.

The survey was faulty in several respects, including the fact that a participant was counted each time that he left a plan and no account was taken of those still in covered employment with vested benefits. Nevertheless, the results could be inter-

preted to show a very satisfactory state of affairs. Among the
terminations occurring during the last five years (the more meaningful period), 84 percent of the individuals in the A group and
80 percent of those in the B group had less than five years of
service. Utilizing the turnover data for the last five years, one
can determine that the probability that a terminating employee
will leave with a vested benefit is as follows:

Years of Service	A Group	B Group
Five years or more	57%	51%
Ten years or more	77	98
Fifteen years or more	88	99

Excluding the experience of the first *five* years of employment
(when turnover is typically high), less than 5 percent of the
terminating members of the B group *failed* to receive an immediate or deferred benefit during the most recent five years of
experience.

Additional light was thrown on the subject by a study made
for the Treasury Department by Richard Keating of the A. S.
Hansen firm. Mr. Keating analyzed all of the 864 plans serviced
by A. S. Hansen, Inc.—an employee benefit consulting firm—
which at the time of the study covered 881,281 active employees
and 132,466 individuals retired or terminated with vested benefits. The plans were broken down by size, class of employee
covered, industry, whether negotiated or unilaterally established,
and whether contributory or non-contributory. Mr. Keating
found that 30 percent of all the active employees had already
satisfied the vesting requirements and another 36 percent were
expected to become vested before terminating their service. In
the aggregate, two-thirds of the active employees by head count
had either vested or could be expected to vest before termination. Two-thirds of all active employees over age forty-five had
already vested.

In the Pension Research Council study of funding, referred
to earlier, a question was asked concerning the vesting provisions in the plans. Analysis of the responses to this question
revealed that in terms of actuarial value, 81 percent of all accrued benefits in the plans reported had already vested. This is
a higher percentage than one would find in terms of the dollar
value of accrued benefits, since the employees closest to retirement would tend to hold the vested benefits, but it is still im-

pressive evidence of the extent to which plan participants are qualifying for benefits. The fact that four million persons are currently drawing benefits from private pension plans also suggests that the gloomy prediction of Senators Javits and Williams are far off the target.

Despite the encouraging spread of vesting over the last ten years, it may be necessary to mandate a minimum level of vesting to achieve the social and political goals that the private pension movement should be seeking. If vesting is to be mandated, it should be based upon the so-called Rule of 50, but with *full vesting* occurring when any combination of age and service equals fifty, rather than the graded vested proposal of the Administration. This is a more flexible standard than one based on age or service alone. It would assure all individuals fortunate enough to be covered by private pension plans the opportunity to build up at least twenty years of creditable service at a point in their careers when compensation is at its peak. A possible objection to the arrangement is that it would discourage the hiring of older workers.

Early Retirement

Pension plan participants have long been interested in the possibility of retiring before the normal retirement age and most plans permit a participant, under certain circumstances, to retire up to five to ten years prior to the normal retirement age, subject to an appropriate reduction in benefits. In recent years, there has been growing interest in a plan provision that would permit a participant to retire after a specified period of service *with full benefits*, irrespective of the participant's attained age. This feature has traditionally been associated with retirement systems for the military, policemen, and firemen, whose jobs require physical endurance and dexterity. Typically, these individuals can retire after twenty years of service with a pension equal to 50 percent of their compensation at time of retirement. Recently, this feature has been incorporated in plans negotiated by the United Automobile Workers, the Steelworkers Union, the transit workers of New York City, and the sanitation employees of New York City, and other unions are considering adding the feature to their list of bargaining demands.

Retirement with full benefits after twenty, twenty-five, or thirty years of service irrespective of age, can hardly be considered "early retirement" in the traditional sense. It would be more appropriate to call such an arrangement a "pre-retirement pension." There is no pretense nor presumption in most cases that the individuals are going to retire from the labor force. (The Supplemental Allowance negotiated by UAW for workers retiring prior to age sixty-two is payable only so long as the "pensioner" does not earn more than the amount of earnings permitted a retired person under the Social Security Act.) To the contrary, it must be presumed that most individuals receiving a pre-retirement pension will seek other employment.

Unfortunately, information on post-retirement employment is fragmentary. The most comprehensive information on this phenomenon is that assembled for military personnel by the Hubbell Commission. The Hubbell Commission, which was constituted to study military pay and retirement, found that the average age at retirement from the military service for fiscal year 1966 was 42.9 for enlisted personnel and 47.3 for commissioned personnel. On the average, enlisted men retired with 21.3 years of service and officers with 23.3 years. The percentage distribution of retirements by years of active service for fiscal years 1963 through 1966 was as follows:

Year of Active Service	Officers		Enlisted Men	
	Percent	Cumulative Percent	Percent	Cumulative Percent
20	27.4	27.4	52.6	62.8
21	20.8	48.2	16.7	79.5
22	15.3	63.5	9.8	89.3
23	10.7	74.2	4.6	93.9
24	7.9	82.1	2.0	95.9
25	3.9	86.0	0.9	96.8

The individuals with the highest skills were found to be the most likely to retire early, since they can most easily find jobs in the civilian labor market. A very high percentage of individuals who retire early do enter the civilian job market. As might be expected, the younger the individual at the time he leaves military service, the more likely he is to enter the civilian labor market. The following exhibit is instructive on that score.

Age of Termination from Military Service	Labor Force Participation Rate	
	Officers	Enlisted Men
35-44	97.1%	98.8%
45-54	94.5	97.4
55-59	84.6	88.9
60-64	72.3	71.9
65+	39.3	31.9

Among the New York City police force, one-third of the individuals retire at the end of twenty years and 60 percent leave by the third year of their eligibility for retirement. Among the New York City firemen, 15 percent retire at the end of twenty years and 28 percent are gone by the third year of eligibility. Within two years after twenty-year retirement became available to the employees of the Transit Authority of New York City, 68.8 percent of the car maintenance employees had retired, causing a maintenance crisis.

Since 1964, automobile workers aged fifty-eight and over with thirty years of service have been permitted to retire with a $400 monthly Supplemental Allowance payable to age sixty-two. (The Supplemental Allowance was increased to $500 per month effective September, 1971.) The experience under this provision has varied from year to year but the broad range of experience for employees of General Motors is shown below:

Age of Retirement	Percent of Employees Retiring
58	7
59	8
60	20-25
61	10-15
62	35-58
63	15-20
64	15-20
65	Less than 10

It will be noted that less than 10 percent of the workers have remained on the job until age sixty-five. The heavy concentration of retirement at age sixty-two reflects the availability of Social Security benefits (reduced) at that age.

There seems to be an absolute level of early retirement that occurs irrespective of the level of retirement benefits available. The health factor probably plays a dominant role. Above that basic rate of early retirement, the retirement decision appears to be heavily influenced by the size of the pension. The experience of the steel industry illustrates this point. Since 1966, a steelworker with thirty years of service has been permitted to retire with a full benefit, regardless of age. However, the benefit is rather modest—$6.50 per month for each year of service. As a result, early retirement rates have been relatively low. On an overall basis, the annual rates have ranged from 7 to 12 percent. The number retiring before sixty has been negligible. According to Murray Latimer, Actuary for the United Steel Workers Union, the rates of retirement for the industry as a whole in recent years has been as follows:

Age of Retirement	Percentage Retiring
61	10
62	30
63	25
64	22
65 and over	13

Pre-retirement pensions have potential consequences that deserve serious study. The cost to the employer of training replacements may be burdensome, especially if the terminating employees are skilled or semi-skilled—as they are likely to be. The additional cost of providing a full pension at a much earlier age than anticipated is also a major consideration. On a 3.5 percent interest basis, it costs more than four times as much to provide a pension of a given amount at age fifty as it does at age sixty-five, and three times more at age fifty-five. The cost of a pension at age sixty is one and a half times that of the same benefit at age sixty-five. With higher interest assumptions, the additional costs are much greater than indicated.

A high rate of utilization of the early retirement privilege can bring about a drastic change in the composition of the union membership, posing a threat to the union leadership. Older, more conservative members will be replaced by younger, less secure— and hence more militant—members. The union position on many matters, including the vesting and funding of pensions, may have to be altered to fit the shifting attitudes of the membership. If a large proportion of the persons who retire early seek other employment, wage rates in the affected occupations may be depressed. An individual with a generous pension may be willing to accept employment at a much lower level of compensation than his pensionless counterpart.

Finally, society and the economy as a whole may be adversely affected through the loss of valuable skills and manpower, which would be reflected in a loss of production. Sid Willis of the General Electric Company has estimated that universal retirement at age sixty would be the equivalent of a three and one half hour work week for a labor force that works until age sixty-five. Universal retirement at age fifty-five would produce the equivalent of a 27 hour work week. Under such circumstances, leisure time of 32 percent of the total work hours available would have to be supported out of a production base of 68 percent. Such a loss of manpower cannot possibly be offset by the productivity gains of recent years and those expected in the foreseeable future. This new development may have to be brought under public scrutiny.

PART IV

D. Occupational Health and Safety

The Occupational Safety and Health Act and Industrial Relations

Robert D. Moran †

The first section of the Occupational Safety and Health Act of 1970 contains the enacting clause and the name by which the Act may be cited. The very next section sets forth thirteen different Congressional policies and purposes sought to be achieved by the new law's enactment. At least four of these have possible collective bargaining implications as presented below. The purpose of Congress in enacting this law is to assure working men and women safe and healthful working conditions

(1) by encouraging employers and employees in their efforts to reduce the number of occupational safety and health hazards at their palces of employment, and to stimulate employers and employees to institute new and to perfect existing programs for providing safe and healthful working conditions;

(2) by providing that employers and employees have separate but dependent responsibilities and rights with respect to achieving safe and healthful working conditions;

(3) by building upon advances already made through employer and employee initiative for providing safe and healthful working conditions, and

(4) by encouraging joint labor-management efforts to reduce injuries and diseases arising out of employment.[1]

Even before Congress enacted this far-reaching new law, the question whether occupational safety and health was an appropriate subject for collective bargaining had been settled by the courts.[2] Accordingly, we really cannot say at this time that the Williams-Steiger Act has created any "new" subjects for negotiations, but comments by various persons involved in the collective bargaining process indicate that some of the old subjects now have new dimensions and, as I will discuss later, new urgency.[3]

---

† Robert D. Moran is Chairman, Occupational Health and Safety Review Commission.

The Executive Secretary of the AFL-CIO Standing Committee on Safety and Occupational Health, George H. R. Taylor, informs me that:

1. A number of international unions—Steelworkers, Asbestos Workers, International Brotherhood of Electrical Workers, Rubber Workers, Pulp and Sulphite Workers among others, [bargain for] safety clauses as [a matter of course]. Such contract language . . . does not at present, with the exception of the Rubber Workers contract with B. F. Goodrich, reflect the new Act.

2. Many international unions, including the ones mentioned above, have developed or are developing, revised safety clauses for future contract negotiations which will reflect the provisions of the Act. * * * The Pulp and Sulphite Workers have developed a new suggested clause which is contained in their recent handbook (Project III—Occupational Safety and Health) which has been given general distribution among their locals.

3. The extent to which the health and safety clause in a contract should be the main vehicle in protecting workers in work environments is presently the subject of considerable internal discussion in organized labor. The issue is the extent to which governmental regulatory action should be relied upon in work environmental situations, particularly as a supplement or substitute to grievance proceedings arising out of collective bargaining.

    A major reason for such discussion is Sec. 11(c) of the Act—the so-called non-discrimination provision. The question arises over whether remedy for alleged discriminations arising from the use of the provisions of this Act by a worker, should be sought through the Section 11(c) route, or by means of established grievance procedures in a contract.

4. At any rate, it is my opinion that this Act will have massive implications on the whole field of industrial relations, similar in scope to the changes in labor-management relations after enactment of the Labor-Management Act of 1947.[4]

Before leaving George Taylor's comments, I want to amplify a bit on the latter 2 points. Section 11(c) of the Act provides in part that "No person shall discharge or in any manner discriminate against any employee . . . because of the exercise by such employee on behalf of himself or others of any right afforded by this Act."[5] It goes on to set up a procedure under which the Secretary of Labor may investigate any employee complaint of discrimination pursuant to this provision and to seek relief in a U.S. District Court if he determines that a violation has taken place. Perhaps it should be noted that this protection extends only to rights granted employees by the Act itself and not to any rights they may have pursuant to a collective bargaining agreement.

Taylor also expresses the opinion that the new Act will have massive implications on the whole field of industrial relations. I do not see how anyone who is acquainted with the law can disagree with this point. This, of course, was the reason there was so much contention over the several competing occupational safety bills considered by the Congress during 1969 and 1970. I see no useful purpose in rehashing this battle but, by way of emphasizing the point, I would like to quote an apt statement which appeared in the *New York Times* on November 25, 1970:

> The safety legislation has generated the most intensive confrontation between organized labor and business interests since the abortive effort to repeal right-to-work legislation in 1966. Labor leaders and businessmen, led by the United States Chamber of Commerce, have lobbied incessantly on the measure for nearly three years.

Let me return now to what organized labor has been doing since enactment of the new safety law.

The United Steelworkers of America, AFL-CIO, is *inter alia,* seeking to negotiate pollution control and employer recognition of alcoholism and drug addiction as health matters.[6] I am informed that the Steelworkers have successfully negotiated contracts this year providing for the establishment of joint "productivity committees" which may address themselves to individual employee's alcohol and drug abuse problems. This year they have also added the subjects of noise and toxic materials to their standard health and safety provisions, provided for expedited handling of grievances based upon matters affecting safety and health, and established joint "safety and health committees" empowered to conduct investigatory hearings in connection with accidents.[7] Another union [8] is seeking periodic medical examinations and the establishment of a "special health and safety fund," financed by management, for research in connection with health and safety hazards. Most locals of that union, we are informed, successfully negotiated for some parts of the package, but none has succeeded in securing the fund. Such a fund was obtained by the Rubber Workers from at least one employer. In the current longshoremen dispute with the Pacific Maritime Association, the Union is seeking revision of the Pacific Coast Marine Safety Code including *inter alia,* monoxide-free equipment in confined spaces, noise abatement and a "special penalty rate" paid employees in certain circumstances.

Thus, it is clear that the subject matter of collective bargaining has been expanded into an area limited only by the negotiators' imagination, capacity for innovation, and sophostication in specialized matters affecting safety and health. In short, the outer limits of the "new dimensions" mentioned earlier are nowhere in sight.

Turning to the "new urgency" mentioned above, I refer specifically to the increased possibility of work stoppages in connection with hazardous working conditions. The topic is, of course, not "new," having been the subject of not inconsiderable litigation for some years, for example, *NLRB* v. *Washington Aluminum Company,*[9] where the Court agreed with the Labor Board that employees who spontaneously walked out of what they considered to be "miserable" conditions of employment, i.e., "bitter cold," [10] were engaged in concerted activity protected by Section 7 of the National Labor Relations Act.[11] See also, *NLRB* v. *Knight-Morley Corp.*[12] where a walkout precipitated by temperatures of over 100 degrees and an atmosphere full of grit, dust and abrasives in a buffing room with a malfunctioning exhaust blower was found to be protected under Section 502 of the National Labor Relations Act. This particular section of Taft-Hartley undoubtedly has the greatest possible potential for conflict with the Williams-Steiger Act. Section 502 provides in relevant part:

> Nothing in this Act shall be construed to require an individual employee to render labor or service without his consent . . .; nor shall the quitting of labor by an employee or employees in good faith because of abnormally dangerous conditions for work at the place of employment . . . be deemed a strike under this Act.

In the Knight-Morley case, the court held: "That section [502] expressly limits the right of management to require continuance of work under what the employees in good faith believe to be 'abnormally dangerous' conditions." [13]

The Eighth Circuit in its decision in *NLRB* v. *Fruin-Colnon Construction Co.,*[14] while citing and quoting *Knight-Morley,* views the words of Section 502—"abnormally dangerous conditions for work"—as meaning "inherent uncontrollable perils," the existence of which the employees must prove. Absent such proof, employees are engaged in the "unprotected activity of dictating to management their own terms and conditions of employment." [15]

Of course, Section 502 protects the employees from discharge for disciplinary action only. It does not, as does the Steelworkers contract mentioned earlier, guarantee pay for the period during which services are withdrawn because of "abnormally dangerous conditions." Nevertheless, under the Steelworkers contract, the employee ceases work at peril of an arbitrator's subsequent determination that the hazard was nonexistent or insufficient to justify a work stoppage.

Let us consider, however, circumstances suggested by the Occupational Safety and Health Act, Section 13(c) which provides:

> Whenever and as soon as an inspector concludes that conditions or practices described in subsection (a) [such that a danger exists which could . . . be expected to cause death or serious physical harm immediately or before the imminence . . . can be eliminated] exist in any place of employment, he shall inform the affected employees and employers of the danger and that he is recommending to the Secretary that relief [a restraining order] be sought.

At least one commentator believes that this and other "government-by publicity" provisions "invite activists to charge the employer with bad faith in his safety/health program, or to discourage employees from continuing to work in what has been officially ruled to be a hazardous area." [16]

It would certainly seem that, in most cases, the "peril" of employees proving unable to sustain the basis for reliance upon Section 502 of the Labor Act or upon a similar contract provision would be removed by the inspector's informing them of the hazard or by the employer's posting of a citation as required by the Act.[17]

I suggest that the final answer to the question posed by such stoppages will lie in the courts' interpretation of the words of OSHA—"a danger . . . which could reasonably be expected to cause death or serious injury"—and Section 502 of the Labor Act—"abnormally dangerous conditions"—and whether these sections are in *pari materia*. In a case involving a contractual right to cease work, the language and purpose of the contract clause will also require interpretation. Parties may, of course, simplify the latter task by utilizing the language of the Labor

Act or OSHA, or both, in the collective bargaining agreement.

Such, apparently, was the case in *Illinois Ruan-Transport Corp.* v. *NLRB.*[18] There, an employee conducted a personal "safety campaign" based upon a collective bargaining agreement that provided, "Under no circumstances will an employee be required or assigned to engage in any activity involving dangerous conditions of work or . . . in violation of any applicable statute or court order, or in violation of a Government regulation relating to safety . . . ." The dissenting judge (Lay), addressing the question of the employee's protected status (germane, only if the court had agreed with the Board as to the reason for discharge) stated, "[We should not] approve an employee's discharge which serves to condone a company's noncompliance with laws enacted not only for the safety of its employees, but for the public as well." [19]

There was another NLRB case in the Second Circuit [20] where an employee's protests concerning his employer's failure to abide by a New York City fire regulation, and the collective bargaining agreement which incorporated that regulation, was held to be activity protected by Section 7 of the National Labor Relations Act.[21] The court also mentioned, but found it unnecessary to rule upon, the same employee's protests concerning his employer's arguably unsafe method of moving a boiler on the job.[22]

In any case, between statutes and contractual provisions, the complaining employee, or the employees who "wildcat" because of what they conceive to be a hazardous condition in the workplace, appear to be protected in greater measure than ever before contemplated by many persons within industry. Add to this fact an effective and unrelenting campaign for industrial safety by the Federal and State governments, by labor organizations, news media and self-protective management, and it is plain that the American workforce will never again allow itself to be subjected to conditions of employment that represent less than the optimum in safety and health protection. Resistance to this thesis may be costly indeed.

As mentioned earlier, there may—and may not—be some mileage in the OSHA. Consider the terms of subsections 8(e) and 8(f). Section 8(f) permits any employee or employee representative to request an inspection whenever he believes that a violation of a safety or health standard exists which threatens physical harm. If the Secretary's representative agrees with the allegations of such a complaint, this section requires him to "make a special inspection . . . as soon as practicable." If he does not agree with such allegations, "he shall notify the employees or representative of the employees in writing of such determination."

Section 8(e) grants the famous (or infamous) "walk around" rights to management and employees, that is, representatives of both may accompany the Secretary's representative during his inspection. Where there is no "authorized employee representative," the Secretary's agent is required to "consult with a reasonable number of employees concerning matters of health and safety in the workplace." It is entirely within the realm of possibility that the "walk around" permitted or the consultation required by Section 8(e) whether initiated by the complaint procedures in 8(f) or not, can become the occasion for "blowing the whistle on the company" or, however it is perceived by management and employees, a venting of fears or emotions or the calculated use of a procedure intended to assist in the orderly administration of a statute for purposes other than those contemplated by the responsible Federal agency.

I do not suggest that it falls into the latter category, but consider the case of *International Ladies Garment Workers* v. *NLRB*,[23] where an employee brought down the State Health Department on her employer for "deficiencies of the ladies' restroom at the plant." Flushed with success on her first venture into improving the "sanitary conditions" at her workplace, she complained once more. This time, the State's inspector found that conditions "met the necessary health standards." The company, learning the identity of the complainant, fired her. That her activity was eventually found to be "concerted, protected activity" under Section 7 of the Labor Act [24] might be regarded as irrelevant today, since she would surely be protected by Section 8(f) of OSHA, regardless of whether her action was concerted.

In an apparent effort to obviate the possibility of harassment of this sort under the provisions of Section 8(f), the Secretary's complaint form [25] provides some interesting material. First, the employee is required to set forth the alleged violation with particularity and, on the second page, to respond to the question of whether the violation has "been the subject of any . . . grievance or otherwise called . . . to the attention of, or discussed . . . with the employer or any representative thereof?" Will the Secretary's requirements preclude or lessen harassment?   Is the above question appropriate for any other purpose?   I do not know.

In any event, these are some very preliminary observations on possible impact of the Occupational Safety and Health Act upon industrial relations.   I am sorry that I have no answers to give you and have raised only a very few of the questions already being asked.   About the only thing I can say with reasonable certainty at this time is that the new law has added some new dimensions to the ever-expanding industrial relations universe.

NOTES

1. 29 U.S.C.A. § 651.

2. N.L.R.B. v. Gulf Power Co., 384 F.2d 822, 824-825 (5th Cir. 1967); N.L.R.B. v. Miller Brewing Company, 408 F.2d 12, 14 (9th Cir. 1969).

3. *See* Teplow, "Sample Occupational Safety and Health Provisions in Selected Collective Bargaining Agreements," *New Dimensions in Occupational Safety and Health*, Organization Resources Counselors, Inc., 1970, p. 59.

4. Letter dated September 16, 1971, to Robert D. Moran, Chairman OSHRC.

5. 29 U.S.C.A. § 660.

6. *Industrial Safety and Health Report*, Center for Political Research, July 1971, pp. 12-26.

7. Telephone conversation of October 21, 1971, between Bernard Kleiman, General Counsel of the Steelworkers and staff member of the Commission. Paraphrased with Mr. Kleiman's permission.

8. Oil Chemical and Atomic Workers International Union, AFL-CIO.

9. 370 U.S. 12 (1962).

10. *Id.* at 15.

11. In pertinent part:
    > employees shall have the right . . . to engage in . . . concerted activities for the purpose of collective bargaining or other mutual aid or protection . . . .

    29 U.S.C. § 157.

12. 251 F.2d 753 (6th Cir. 1957), *cert. denied*, 357 U.S. 927 (1958).

13. 251 F.2d at 759.

14. 330 F.2d 885 (8th Cir. 1964).

15. *Id.* at 892.

16. Teplow, *supra* note 2.

17. Sections 8, 13.

18. 404 F.2d 274 (8th Cir. 1968) *(enforcement denied on other grounds)*.

19. *Id.* at 290.

20. *Cf.* N.L.R.B. v. Interboro Contractors, Inc., 388 F.2d 495 (2d Cir. 1967).

21. *Id.* at 497, 500.

22. *Id.* at 498. *See also* C & I Air Conditioning, Inc., McKeon Construction, 193 N.L.R.B. No. 132, 78 L.R.R.M. 1417 (1971), where the Board affirmed its trial examiner's conclusion that Section 7 protected an *unconcerted* protest by an employee based upon arguably unsafe conditions on the jobsite and grounded upon a contract clause which incorporated by reference the General Safety Orders of the State authorities. *Compare* Occupational Safety and Health Act, § 11(c)(1), 29 U.S.C.A. 660(c)(1).

23. 299 F.2d 114 (D.C. Cir. 1962).

24. *Enforced after remand, sub nom.*, Walls Manufacturing Co., Inc. v. N.L.R.B., 321 F.2d 753 (D.C. Cir. 1963), *cert. denied*, 375 U.S. 923 (1963).

25. OSHA—7, OMB No. 044R449, GPO 911-005.

Impact of the Occupational Safety and Health Act on Collective Bargaining

Leo Teplow †

The theme of this Conference is the basic question as to the survival of collective bargaining as an institution. On that level, it cannot be said that the impact of the Occupational Safety and Health Act of 1970 will be decisive. Nevertheless, the Act does have an appreciable impact on the thrust of collective bargaining in the future; and consideration of the impact of the Act may contribute to an understanding of collective bargaining and the circumlocutions it involves.

To begin with, it might be appropriate to identify those characteristics of the Act that are likely to determine its impact on collective bargaining. The Act authorizes the most extensive Federal intervention in day-to-day plant operations of any previous legislation—and of a nature that is bound to have substantial employee relations and union relations impact. Federal inspectors (Occupational Safety and Health Compliance Officers) may raise questions concerning not only compliance with old or new safety and health standards in the workplace: they may also look into the employer's safety program, training and enforcement of the company's own regulations among management as well as rank and file employees, since good faith is a factor to be weighed in setting a proposed penalty for violation of standards or the employer's general duty obligation to provide a safe place to work. Such questions are especially likely to arise when the inspection is triggered by a report (required within 48 hours of the event) of an accident involving a fatality or multiple hospitalizations.

A second characteristic of the Act is that it provides an extensive network of new employee and union rights that did not previously exist.[1] Of major import in this connection are: employee (and union) right to be informed of inspections, observed violations or appeals from Federal inspectors' findings of viola-

---

† Leo Teplow is Special Consultant, Organization Resources Counselors, New York.

tions, as well as of exposure to excessive concentrations of contaminants; the right to invoke a federal inspection of the workplace by a Compliance Officer or an HEW evaluation of a suspected hazard; the right to be informed concerning the existence of an imminent danger; the right to monitor the measurement of contaminants, and to be informed of the results of such measurements; and the right to contest a Compliance Officer's judgment as to the period of time within which an observed violation is to be abated.

A third characteristic of the Act is the extent to which it initiates employee participation in matters heretofore regarded as primarily employer or government responsibilities. For example, when a Federal Compliance Officer makes an inspection of a workplace, whether it be in response to a complaint or as part of routine inspection, employees have a right to have an "authorized representative" accompany the Officer on his inspection tour, to bring to his attention matters of special concern to employees, or to uncover possible employer attempts to cover up hazards.

If the Federal Inspector finds more than de minimis violations, he issues a citation against the employer, and such citation must be posted forthwith in the work area to which the citation pertains, so that all employees are alerted to the alleged violation even though the violation may have been abated the moment the employer was informed of it. Employees (and their unions) have the right to appeal (or "contest") the length of time allowed the employer to correct the violation. If the employer contests the citation or the period of time allowed to correct it or the penalty imposed, employees have an opportunity to be made parties to the case before an independent agency—the Occupational Safety and Health Review Commission.

In case the Federal Officer finds a situation which he interprets as an imminent hazard, he must inform the employees of it. And if the Secretary of Labor does not see fit to sue for a restraining order, under some circumstances employees are given the right to initiate a suit for mandamus against the Secretary to force him to file for a restraining order. This extraordinary liberality in the use of an extraordinary legal remedy may well encourage litigation in labor relations.

A fourth characteristic of the Act is its imposition of responsibility on the employee "to comply with occupational safety

and health standards and all rules, regulations and orders issued pursuant to this Act which are applicable to his own actions and conduct." [2]   While this obligation is limited, and
while the Act provides no sanctions in case of employee violation
of this obligation, its inclusion in the law will affect employee-
employer relations and management-union relations.

Since the employer is held responsible for the violation of
standards even when the violation results from employee failure to follow specific company rules—i.e., piling material where
it obstructs passageways—it can be anticipated that companies
will review and strengthen their discipline policies (where other
measures fail) for violation of safety rules.   Strengthened discipline policies, in turn, may be contested by the union.   But
if the violation is covered by the Act's prohibition, neither the
union nor the employee would be in good position to fight the
application of such discipline, especially in case the issue winds
up in arbitration.

Organized labor's attitude with respect to occupational safety
and health is the result of three major factors: embarrassment
because of historical neglect of the issue; the adversary nature of the legislative history of the Act; and profound consideration of political goals.   While organized labor has on
occasion become concerned about specific situations involving
safety and health, it has not historically given this subject a
high priority either in its legislative nor its collective bargaining
goals.   Safety and health have never been pushed in collective
bargaining on a par with, say, the guaranteed annual wage or
pensions—or even rest periods.[3]

When public concern and legislative activity became evident
in 1968, and especially after the Farmington coal-mining disaster in November 1968 and the well-publicized campaign to prevent "black lung" (coalminers' pneumoconiosis), organized labor,
stung by criticism of prior neglect of occupational safety and
health, sought to regain a leadership position by pushing for
far-reaching, punitive legislation rather than emphasize the un-
glamorous but essential task of promoting safety and health
programs at the plant and company levels.

Despite the obvious fact that labor and management have a
basic, common interest in the promotion of occupational safety
and health, the essentially adversary position assumed by organized labor during the legislative battles preceding passage
of the Act have continued and still largely characterize labor's

approach. Characteristic of the adversary approach were: prohibition of advance notice of a Compliance Officer's visit (the malefactor must be caught redhanded); requirement that a Compliance Officer's citation of violation of a safety or health standard be posted for all employees to see (even if the violation were corrected as soon as it was brought to management's attention); and grant of authority to the Compliance Officer to close down an operation and order employees to leave the job in case of imminent danger (eliminated from the draft prior to enactment). Continuation of the adversary attitude of organized labor (at least, at the national level) will necessarily be reflected in collective bargaining problems and frustrations, while contributing little to occupational safety and health.

The AFL-CIO and a number of international unions have mounted extensive campaigns to encourage their members to file complaints with the Department of Labor, when the issue might have been settled more promptly if the complaints were first directed to management—and safe conditions restored. One union spokesman went so far as to recommend: "Declare a form of guerrilla warfare on management if necessary to show industry that we mean business about the protection of our members from occupational safety and health hazards." [4]

Political considerations also loom importantly in organized labor's approach to occupational safety and health. This seems especially notable in relation to organized labor's stance with respect to the U. S. Department of Labor. During the legislative debates, organized labor urged that all administrative and enforcement authority be vested in the Department of Labor. Labor praise for the Department is to be found repeatedly in the record of hearings. [5] During the course of the past year, however, organized labor's attitude has been sharply different. The Department is castigated for moving too slowly, for not requesting an adequate budget, and for failing to hire union members as Compliance Officers. [6] One cannot but conclude that this sudden change in attitude is, in large part, a reflection of organized labor's all-out effort to capture the Democratic Party and defeat the Republican Administration in 1972, even if such action defers effective promotion of occupational safety and health.

Collective bargaining with respect to occupational safety and health provisions in union contracts has been going on for years even though, as pointed out above, it has been given a relatively low union priority in the past. That has now changed. Occupational safety and health is now—and will be for years to come—a major issue in collective bargaining.

Undoubtedly the greatest emphasis both in collective bargaining and in the administration of the Act will be put on the health part of the Act. This is because less is known about the health impact of working conditions and work environment, and occupational health programs are not nearly as far advanced or understood as are the more traditional safety programs. Of special interest, therefore, are those agreements which indicate a manner of dealing with such problems. Probably the most important of these is the agreement negotiated in 1970 by major tire manufacturers with the United Rubber Workers, setting up a joint occupational health program which relies heavily on epidemiological studies to be conducted by one or more eminent schools of public health. While the rubber company agreements call for the financing of such research to be done by the companies (up to 0.5 cents per hour worked), it is reasonable to assume that in the future such research, dealing with major industries or health problems, might be financed by funds allocated for that purpose by HEW's new National Institute of Occupational Safety and Health.

Another possible portent for the future is the agreement negotiated last summer between Deere & Co. and the UAW. Under that agreement the company recognizes a union safety representative at each of its twenty-one plants in the United States, with the company agreeing to provide up to three months of special safety training, and providing up to 40 hours of pay during each four-week period to enable such safety representative to carry out his stated duties. These duties include the making of a joint investigation when a safety grievance has not been satisfactorily resolved in the first step. The Deere & Co. agreement sets out a basic policy that "all reasonable shop rules and all laws governing health, safety appliances and sanitary conditions shall be complied with by the company, the employees and the union," and a joint safety committee is set up to help implement that policy.[7]

Joint safety committees, utilized for decades either as a result of collective bargaining or company policy, will undoubtedly have increased emphasis and responsibilities. Joint safety and health committees constitute one mechanism by which employees and unions can be more actively involved in the promotion of safety and health. Perhaps the greatest deterrent to their adoption is the attempt on the part of some unions to give such joint committees responsibility for the administration of the program—a sharing of responsibility that management is understandably reluctant to undertake.

Some union demands in occupational safety and health illustrate the zeal of a new convert. Repeated demands are made for a complete listing of all hazardous or toxic substances utilized at work or occurring in the work environment, although in many cases no one knows at what concentrations such substances begin to be harmful. Some unions press for the adoption of an extensive and detailed program for joint committee activity, including some 30 items for the agenda of such joint committee meetings.

As in the past, union demands in the occupational safety and health sector will sometimes be made for the primary purpose of winning concessions in other sectors. But all demands will be taken seriously; and progressive management will utilize current and future union and employee interest in this area to improve occupational safety and health programs. Mindful that union or employee dissatisfaction with safety or health conditions can trigger a federal inspection—an inspection that may uncover violations of mechanical standards no matter how effective the program—progressive managements will not only improve their programs and seek to involve unions and employees in them but will also take pains that employees and unions are fully aware of these programs and their results.

In the last few months, a new factor has appeared which is sure to encourage collective bargaining negotiations on safety and health. The wage-price freeze and its aftermath will undoubtedly make unions seek "noneconomic" issues to make up for the limits imposed on wages and fringes. Few issues today have the appeal of safety and health as a substitute for traditional union concentration on money items.

Despite the sophistication that collective bargaining has attained in recent decades, it is still regarded largely as a matter of company reaction to union demands. When it comes to safety and health, however, it can be anticipated that companies will make proposals dealing with such items as identification of the "employee representative" authorized to accompany the Compliance Officer on his inspection tour; union and employee cooperation in case of the discovery of imminent hazard; reference of complaints to the company before complaining to outside authorities; consideration of the special problems of trade secret areas; agreement on objectives of various forms of company-union cooperation; research on issues as to which views differ; and acceptance of obligations by company, union and employees.

The emphasis on occupational safety and health will not be limited to those matters which are now contemplated by that term. Some concept of the greatly broadened areas which will be encompassed in future negotiations may be gathered from the content of a resolution on occupational hazards adopted by a recent International Federation of Chemical and General Workers Unions' Rubber and Plastics Conference. As reported by the BNA *Occupational Safety and Health Reporter,* one part of that resolution

> Demands that new joint union-management negotiations be undertaken on programs to study and introduce changes in traditional work patterns, working days, and job elements and structure, which contribute to destructive boredom, alienation, threaten emotional stability and render impossible a calm and stable home and family life, especially if wives as well as husbands are working.[8]

A reading of the entire resolution should be an antidote for those who assume that safety negotiations primarily involve the wearing of safety shoes, hard hats, safety goggles and earplugs.

In conclusion, it is obvious that circumstances have combined with the enactment of the Occupational Safety and Health Act of 1970 to move occupational safety and health from the back burner very much up front as a subject for collective bargaining. The new emphasis on safety and health is made even stronger as a result of the limitations on wage bargaining imposed by the current wage-price controls.

Second, negotiations on safety and health for the next few years are likely to be characterized by:

a) emphasis on research on the effect of the working environment on employee health;

b) exploration of a variety of activities and uses of joint committees;

c) greatly expanded concept of what is included under the general term "occupational safety and health"; and

d) employer proposals for clauses to be included in the health and safety clauses of the agreement.

Third, the sudden impetus given collective bargaining in the safety and health area is more than a temporary phenomenon. By their very nature, safety and health provisions will become more inclusive in scope and more complex.

Fourth, once organized labor gets over its unproductive adversary approach, occupational safety and health may well be the means for helping both parties to recognize their basic identity of interests and signal a freshly cooperative approach that might not only achieve higher levels of safety and health but lead to greater cooperation in other areas as well.

NOTES

1. See *NAM Reports*, April 19, 1971, p. 10.

2. Occupational Safety and Health Act of 1970, § 5 (b).

3. Jack Suarez, Health and Safety Director, International Union of Electrical, Radio and Machine Workers, AFL-CIO, remarked, "In negotiating a contract, it appears that safety and health clauses come after coffee breaks." *Occupational Safety and Health Act of 1969: Hearings Before the Select Subcomm. on Labor of the House Comm. on Education and Labor,* 91st Cong., 1st Sess., at 244 (1968). For additional evidence of labor recognition of prior lack of "affirmative Action" in the health and safety area, see ORC Management Memo "New Dimensions in Management in Occupational Safety and Health," issued by Organization Resources Counselors, New York, 1970, pp. 25-29.

4. Remarks attributed to Tony Mazzocchi, Washington representative of Oil, Chemical and Atomic Workers Union, Bureau of National Affairs, *Occupational Safety and Health Reporter,* Current Report, May 6, 1971, p. 11.

5. See, for example, *Occupational Safety and Health Act of 1969: Hearings Before the Select Subcomm. on Labor of the Comm. on Education and Labor, supra* note 3, statement of Andrew Biemiller, at 641.

6. Bureau of National Affairs, *Occupational Safety and Health Reporter,* October 21, 1971, p. 483, quotes a resolution adopted by the Industrial Union Department, AFL-CIO which states in part: "Clearly the purpose of the Department of Labor is to avoid utilization of qualified trade union people."

7. See *UAW Solidarity*, June 1971, p. 3.

8. Bureau of National Affairs, *Occupational Safety and Health Reporter,* October 14, 1971, p. 460.

Seeds of Humble Origin Produce a Tree of Life

Peter Bommarito and Louis S. Belicsky †

I. History

Safety and health reference found its way into labor agreements in the early history of the United Rubber, Cork, Linoleum and Plastic Workers of America, AFL-CIO, CLC. Early contractual language covered safety under clauses such as "The Company should maintain a clean workplace." These words were simple, but broad in scope, and were planted in bargaining agreements which led to more specific consideration for future arrangements at the bargaining table in the beginning of the 1940's. An Agreement signed in January of 1941 by URW Local Union No. 101 and the United States Rubber Company contained the following language:

> All employees are expected to cooperate to the best of their ability in the prevention of accidents to themselves and fellow workmen. The dispatchers and supervisors shall be furnished a list of hazardous jobs on which they are not to send a man alone.

Later that year, Local No. 207 entered into an Agreement with the Master Tire and Rubber Company. Its reference to safety was:

> A Plant Safety and Sanitation Committee shall be established, composed of two (2) employees selected by the Union and two (2) representatives of Management. The functions of the Committee are to investigate all complaints concerning Safety and Sanitation, and to make regular inspection tours of the factory and to initiate and propose ways and means of improving the health and safety of employees.

---

† Peter Bommarito is President of the International United Rubber, Cork, Linoleum and Plastic Workers of America and Louis S. Belicsky (M.S., MPH) is Director of Industrial Hygiene, URW International Union.

411

The October 28, 1941 Agreement between Local No. 26 and the Kelly-Springfield Tire Company contained the following general rule:

> The Company shall continue to make reasonable provisions for the health and safety of its employees during the hours of their employment. The Company and the Union agree to cooperate in practicing and carrying out safety rules.

The Goodyear Local No. 2 Agreement supplemented the above a year later with:

> . . . The Company shall provide protective devices and other equipment necessary to protect the employees from injury and sickness.

During World War II, and by the mid-1940's, more reference to safety and health could be found in locals in companies large and small scattered throughout the country and eventually in Canada.

These humble beginnings began to provide for the formation of Joint Labor-Management Safety Committees. The reluctance of the companies to recognize and solve health and safety problems was saliently evidenced by organized action of our local unions through necessary grievance procedure which, more often than not, was stalemated by refusal of the companies to act in good faith. It became obvious that company management was evaluating health and safety by their own denominator—"dollars and cents," and often was quoted as saying, "We know we should correct these situations, but it would cost us too much money to do it." The United Rubber, Cork, Linoleum and Plastic Workers of America soon became aware that if they wanted a safe and healthful working environment, they could only meet the compaines through strong, binding, and forceful language in their bargaining agreement. They further hoped that their respective state laws would assist in the protection of health of the members through meaningful and effective enforcement.

Even in the 1950's and early 1960's, health and safety clauses played only a minor role in the overall bargaining agreement. Unfortunately, one may even say that sometimes matters of health and safety were items of concession to be traded for other more obvious monetary or other bargaining agreement considerations. At this time, URW Trade Union Movement began to get a sense of "awareness" that health and safety was more than just a negotiable item. It became a matter of concrete, positive awareness that they no longer had to consider dust, fumes, noise, heat, unexplained illness, accidents, and even work related deaths as just part and parcel of their job. Their new-found awareness indicated that the "dollars and cents" in pay for work provided did not compensate them for the many lung diseases, serious skin problems, blood, liver, and kidney conditions that confronted them. They soon realized that ill-health was not necessarily part of the job, nor did they feel that these were fringe benefits.

A few of the large companies began self-evaluation programs. They, too, began to realize that ill-health was not part of the job, because it began to hurt them financially from excessive accident and illness claims, out-of-court settlements for permanent disability, forced health-related early retirement, and increased insurance and workmen's compensation premiums. Too few companies, unfortunately, began to realize that good health and safety programs in their plants would save them the "dollars and cents" about which they were so concerned. The thinking of corporate management representatives went so far as to consider increased health and safety problems as specifically unique and an acceptable part of their industry and promoted this archaic thinking to workers at the bargaining table, with a further comment, "If you don't like the health and safety conditions here . . . get a job somewhere else."

In the mid-1960's, some of the locals began to take a good look at the health and safety of their individual members. Their so-called "awareness" now became a matter of stark reality. They compared their accident frequency and severity rates and increased incidence of systemic, lung, and skin disorders and disease with other locals in their own union, and then with other international unions. They now had a "shocked" awareness— workers in their plants did have severe and even fatal health problems far above those encountered elsewhere. Their self-valuation program did not look too good either. At this point, it was no longer a simple matter of laying the blame—something had to be done. The International President was requested to provide assistance and personally to intercede at negotiations aimed at providing immediate corrective action. International President Peter Bommarito also had the awareness of the problems which confronted his members. He had already been personally involved with the acute and serious problems at one of the Wisconsin locals, where hundreds of workers were involved with a unique upper respiratory involvement (URI), which seriously affected the workers to the point where they became totally incapacitated, unable to work and provide for their families, and totally dependent on medical and nursing care.

II. Growth of the Seeds which Grew the Tree of Life— The URM Joint Occupational Health Program

The seeds of "shocked" awareness were nurtured by early death, disease, and unpleasant, unsafe, physically and physiologically unhealthful work conditions. The seeds did not produce a tree of resplendant foliage, but grew as the "Bonsai" tree, with gnarled roots and trunk, stunted and ageless and bent by fruit that is never bourne, a tree nurtured by wisdom, trauma, and constant care. Now began the study of other Locals at large and small companies. The picture was the same. International President Peter Bommarito solicited the aid of a reknowned occupational epidemiologist, Dr. Thomas Mancuso, who had conducted an epidemiological study of Ohio's rubber industry. Together they reviewed a sampling of industry represented by the United Rubber, Cork, Linoleum and Plastic Workers of America. Armed with the facts and information provided by their initial study, the two pleaded their cause throughout the locals in this country. They changed "shocked" awareness to "enlightened" awareness. The health problems in the plants were now being recognized. A possible solution to in-plant environmental health conditions was presented to the bargaining committees of URW locals representing the large corporate structures covered by Master Bargaining Agreements: B. F. Goodrich, Goodyear, Uniroyal, Firestone, and General Tire.

The two-man team organized the crusade for a comprehensive Joint Occupational Health Program which would provide for the first time in history a complete study of the environmental in-plant health problems. This would shed light on numerous health variables, parameters, and hazards confronting the quarter-million membership of the United Rubber Workers of America. The battle commenced, each side adamant in its stand. Stalemate brought on plant closures to demonstrate the Union's unyielding stand. The two-year fight culminated in "right" (workers' health) overpowering "might" of the corporate giants. In June 1970, the large rubber companies mentioned above reluctantly signed the Joint Occupational Health Program, and set aside 0.5 cents per hour worked per employee to be used for a long-range program to be conducted at a recognized School of Public Health. The historic tripartite (URW, Company, and School of Public Health) agreement is to be found in the Appendix A of this article.

The URW has and/or will sign agreements with either the Harvard or University of North Carolina School of Public Health for a minimum of a five-year program, for a comprehensive Epidemiological, Industrial Hygiene, Industrial Medical, and Toxicological Study of all the plants involved in Master Agreement Contracts. From this monumental undertaking will result the recognition, evaluation, and control of health situations and conditions which confront the membership of the URW.

The Joint Occupational Health Program is a *first*—other international unions have attempted such undertakings in collective bargaining, but have not been successful. Not only present members, but also countless others not covered by the Master Contract, and future members will be helped.

This tree of life can now flourish and will bear the fruit of hard work and dedication in the form of better and more healthful working conditions, and perhaps add a few extra years of life after retirement as a direct benefit of the study. The hard won gains at the bargaining table obviously do not reflect a magnanimous gesture on the part of the companies involved. However, since the Joint Occupational Health Program has become a reality, one has gotten the impression that the companies feel that the program was conceived entirely by themselves.

III. **The Impact of the Occupational Safety and Health Act of 1970 on United Rubber, Cork, Linoleum and Plastic Workers of America Bargaining Agreements**

As mentioned earlier, even though strong language regarding safety and health was included in local contracts, it was hoped that state laws and codes would provide the necessary enforcement, without which even strong agreements become next to ineffective. As early as 1951, Senator Hubert H. Humphrey (D-Minn.) and others tried unsuccessfully to provide the workingman with the necessary tools of enforcement. For many years, bills similar to Humphrey's got nowhere. The 1968 Amendment of the Walsh-Healey Act was more farcical than effective. The Daniels Bill was defeated and labor was left frustrated when they realized the futility of their efforts to obtain the uniform enforcement which was unavailable through state programs. The URW was forced to do it on their own, and so they fought for and won their Joint Occupational Health Program.

The Occupational Safety and Health Act (OSHA) was promulgated and became effective in December 1970, about six months after the Tripartite Agreements were signed. The URW program was a prelude to the OSHA program. The advent of the Federal laws dove-tailed with the URW Joint Occupational Health Program and did put teeth into bargaining agreements not covered by the Master Contracts. For the first time in labor history, working people were provided with concrete assistance. If properly administered and maintained, OSHA will change the attitude of management which has never been forced to provide a safe and healthful environment for its sixty million employees. It now becomes a relatively simple matter to incorporate OSHA into the locals' bargaining agreements, and this is the approach the URW is proposing to its local union presidents.

Recently released, and found in Appendix B, is the tentative cursory Memorandum of Agreement which shall be incorporated into local bargaining agreements. Certain portions may be modified for incorporation into existing programs.

OSHA should minimize any reluctance at the bargaining table for full cooperative effort. Companies now realized the full impact of the Act. Through Local Union Safety Committee actions seeking the Department of Labor's assistance, companies respect the penalties and are aware of the public relations image created by OSHA citations.

The United Rubber, Cork, Linoleum and Plastic Workers of America International Union approach is not indiscriminately to wave OSHA as a club, but it will do so when management's attitude precludes any other action. Support from the Department of Labor has been commendable in certain areas, and not only the URW, but also other international unions, will continue to act as watchdogs, interminable in their efforts to keep OSHA from becoming just another paper tiger ornament on the United Rubber, Cork, Linoleum and Plastic Workers of America "tree of life."

APPENDIX A

Sample URW Agreement

Joint Occupational Health Program

THIS MEMORANDUM OF AGREEMENT entered into this .... day of ...., 19...., by and between URCLPWA Local Union No. ...., hereinafter referred to as the "Union," and (Name of Company), located in (City) (State), hereinafter referred to as the "Company."

WHEREAS: It is recognized that the Union and the Company have concern for the protection and preservation of the health and welfare of all those employed under this Agreement, just as it is recognized that all employees have a responsibility to follow safe work procedures; and

WHEREAS: A useful purpose can be served by an independent industrial health survey of the working environment by a recognized school of public health to determine whether any relationship exists between this environment and occupational illness or disease; and

WHEREAS: It is recognized that a firm and continuous commitment to a sound industrial health program is in the best interests of the worker, the Company and society; and

WHEREAS: It is the desire of the parties to promote cooperation and understanding in their approach to the study and prevention of occupational illnesses,

NOW THEREFORE, the parties hereby mutually agree as follows:

1. To establish at (Name of School of Public Health), (City) (State), or an equivalent school of public health, an Occupational Research Study Group to undertake an epidemiological study of the employees covered by this Agreement.

2. To appoint as soon as practicable following the conclusion of the negotiations of the 19.... Labor Agreement, an Occupational Health Committee which shall be composed of three representatives from the Company and three representatives from the Union. The salaries and/or expenses incurred by Company and Union representatives to this Committee shall be paid by the respective party whom they represent.

3. Such school of public health designated under Paragraph 1 of this Agreement shall appoint from its staff an individual who is technically qualified and experienced in the field of epidemiological studies to serve as the Director of the Occupational Research Study Group. This Director shall also serve as chief consultant to the Occupational Health Committee established pursuant to this Agreement and as such, shall act solely in an advisory capacity to this Committee.

4. The functions of the Occupational Health Committee shall be as follows:

   (a) To make recommendations for the implementation of the findings of the Occupational Research Study Group.

   (b) To review occupational health questions referred to it by local plant Health and Safety Committees established under Article .... of the Labor Agreement after all local procedures for handling such questions have been exhausted.

   (c) To recommend methods for obtaining necessary statistical data and information required by the Occupational Research Study Group relative to the sickness and accident and life insurance coverage and experience thereunder. This Committee will also develop uniform record keeping procedures.

   (d) To record and maintain for future reference all findings of the Occupational Research Study Group and to disseminate the reports and findings of this Group to the parties; and

   (e) To recommend procedures for the early identification and detection of potentially toxic and hazardous agents and their use thereof in the plants.

5. The functions of the Occupational Research Study Group shall be as follows:

   (a) To make a preliminary study as to the appropriate procedures for conducting an epidemiological study into potential environmental health problems which might affect employees under this Agreement and to formulate long range programs based upon the results of this study.

   (b) To assist the Company in the development of safe standards for occupational environments.

   (c) To recommend uniform methods of record keeping to assist in the prevention and detection of environmental diseases.

   (d) To act as consultant to the Occupational Health Committee on matters referred to that Committee for consideration.

   (e) To assist in the development of appropriate environmental controls of (1) new chemicals and processes introduced into the Company's operations covered hereby, (2) chemicals and dusts of already recognized toxicity, and (3) other working conditions as appropriate.

6. The Occupational Research Study Group shall make annual reports to the Occupational Health Committee summarizing the work completed during the previous calendar year and the works in progress at the completion of the calendar year.

7. Where existing data and other information available to the Occupational Research Study Group is inadequate for the purposes of carrying out its epidemiological survey pursuant to Paragraph 5 (a) of this Agreement, the Occupational Research Study Group shall have the right to make independent studies at Company locations covered by this Agreement. Such studies shall be conducted wherever possible in a manner which will not interfere with the normal production of the plant.

8. The Company shall, to the extent its legal and contractual obligations permit, make available to the Occupational Research Study Group such data and other information the

Occupational Research Study Group needs in connection with its surveys conducted pursuant to this Agreement.

9. Information submitted by the Company to the Occupational Research Study Group pursuant to this Agreement shall be treated as privileged and confidential and shall not be released to any party, including the Occupational Health Committee, without the prior written approval of the Company. The Company shall have no obligation to submit information or data to the Occupational Health Committee which the Company, in its sole judgment, deems to be confidential.

10. The Company shall periodically report to the Occupational Health Committee what actions, if any, it has undertaken to implement the recommendations of the Occupational Research Study Group or the Occupational Health Committee.

11. The Company retains the sole discretion to determine what action, if any, it should take regarding the recommendations and/or findings of the Occupational Research Study Group and the Occupational Health Committee. The Company's failure to act on the recommendations and/or findings shall not constitute a breach of this or any other Agreement between the parties.

12. Whenever a potential or actual health hazard is recognized by the Occupational Health Committee which requires immediate inevstigation the Committee shall immediately request the Director of the Occupational Research Study Group to designate a qualified expert in order to determine what pertinent data or other information already exists and to recommend what, if any, additional investigation may be needed.

13. Recommendations by the Occupational Research Study Group under this Agreement shall be made on a confidential basis to the parties and shall not be released to anyone not a party to this Agreement without the prior written approval of the Company.

14. Except as provided in Paragraph 2, all necessary expenses incurred in the implementation of this Program not to exceed the equivalent of ½¢ per hour for each hour

worked by employees covered hereby, shall be borne by the Company, including the expenses of the Occupational Research Study Group and the salary of its Director.

15. On or before the ....(.......) day of ...., 19...., and at three (3) month intervals thereafter the Company shall furnish the Union a written statement indicating the number of hours for which covered employees worked for the Company during the preceding three (3) month period and with respect to such hours the Company has a commitment under Paragraph 14 of this Agreement and the total expenditures to date.

16. This Agreement will become effective on the .... (.......) day of ...., 19.....

IN WITNESS WHEREOF THE PARTIES HERETO HAVE HEREUNTO SET THEIR HANDS THIS .... (.......) day of .... 19.....

LOCAL UNION NO. ....
UNITED RUBBER, CORK, LINOLEUM
AND PLASTIC WORKERS OF AMERICA   COMPANY

------------------------------------   ------------------------------------

------------------------------------   ------------------------------------

------------------------------------   ------------------------------------

------------------------------------   ------------------------------------

------------------------------------   ------------------------------------

NOTE: Drafted as two (2) party Agreement (Local Union and Company). Where three (3) party Agreement (including the International Union) is in effect, this Agreement must be revised to reflect the three (3) parties.

APPENDIX B

Article on Safety and Health

Section 1—Safety and Health

(a) The purpose of this Safety and Health Article is to provide effective machinery for the elimination of all work conditions hazardous or potentially hazardous to the health or safety of the employees.

(b) The Company agrees to furnish each employee employment and a place of employment free from all recognized hazards that are causing or are likely to cause physical harm to the employee. The Company further agrees that the General Duty Clause (Section 5) of the Occupational Safety and Health Act of 1970 and all standards promulgated under Section 6 of said Act shall constitute minimum acceptable practice except where an applicable state standard may exceed Federal standards.

(c) The Company and the Local Union shall appoint a joint Labor-Management Safety Committee. The Committee shall be composed of at least three representatives of Management and at least three representatives of the Local Union. The Union representatives shall be selected by the Local Union. Union and Company membership on the Committee shall be of equal numbers.

The Committee shall:

1. Meet at least once a week on a definitely established schedule.

2. Make periodic inspections of the plant but not less frequently than twice every month.

3. Make recommendations for the correction of unsafe or harmful conditions and the elimination of unsafe or harmful work practices. A designated official of the Company shall be responsible for the enforcement of the joint Labor-Management Safety Committee's recommendations. All such recommendations shall include a target date for abatement of hazardous condition or practice.

4. Review and analyze all reports of industrial injury or illness, investigate causes of same, and recommend rules and procedures for the prevention of accidents and dis-

eases and for the promotion of the health and safety of the employees.

5. Subject to grievance procedure of the basic Agreement, negotiate and adjust all disputes arising under the Health and Safety Clauses of this contract.

6. Promote health and safety education.

7. Safety Committee members will be paid Average Hourly Earnings for all lost time when meeting jointly with management and for any inspection or investigation of safety and health problems in the plant.

8. Minutes shall be kept of all Joint Committee meetings, and a written report shall be prepared for review at the next Committee meeting.

9. The Company shall furnish Safety Committee members with annual passes for the purpose of entering the plant and investigating safety conditions which arise within the plant.

10. Members of the Safety Committee shall be permitted to attend grievance meetings regarding safety and health problems.

(d) Accident, Injury and Illness records shall be kept and maintained by the Company and shall be made available upon request to the Union Members of the Joint Safety Committee. These reports shall include all reports required by the Department of Labor under the Occupational Health and Safety Act of 1970, specifically including DOL Forms 101, 102, and 103, or other appropriately designated DOL Forms.

(e) The Company agrees to make available to the Committee upon request an up-to-date list of all compounds and substances used in the plant. This list shall include all chemicals as well as definition or chemical breakdown of trade name descriptions.

(f) The Union members of the Committee may seek the counsel and assistance of representatives of the URCLPWA International Union and such representatives shall be granted the right to accompany the Committee on inspections, attend meetings of the Committee, and make recommendations to the Committee and shall be permitted to make such investigations and physical examinations as may be reasonably connected with the purposes of the Committee.

(g) The Company shall furnish competent medical services and supply adequate facilities for the proper first aid treatment of cases resulting from injury or physical impairments or afflictions obtained while in the plant. Copies of the reports of the medical findings made by the Company's medical service or reports of outside medical services used by the Company shall be furnished to the employee as well as to the Local Union. The Company shall provide necessary mutually acceptable biological studies where indicated by potentially hazardous materials.

(h) No employee or group of employees shall be required to work on a job or machine while its safety is being questioned by the joint Labor-Management Safety Committee. During such time the employee or group of employees shall receive their regular average hourly earnings.

(i) No employee shall be required to work on any job in the plant with which he is unfamiliar until he shall have received adequate safety training instructions in the performance of the operation.

(j) The Union agrees to make every reasonable effort to have its members observe all safety and health rules promulgated under this agreement and to use all safety and protective equipment furnished for this purpose. It is recognized that protective equipment and clothing are temporary measures for relief of conditions which must be subject to further corrective measures through engineering changes or elimination of the hazard involved.

(k) All disputes arising under this Article and not resolved by the Committee shall be considered proper subjects for adjustment under the grievance procedure including arbitration as set forth in Article — of this Agreement. Any such grievance filed by the Union shall be introduced at the level immediately preceding arbitration.

PART IV

E. Construction

Reflections on Collective Bargaining:
Politics and Construction

Arthur A. Fletcher †

I think that the collective bargaining system in America is in trouble and has been in trouble ever since 1966 when the Machinists' Union forced the airlines to accept a settlement far above what was negotiated under President Johnson's direction. The reason is that the unions do a much better and smarter political job than does management—and they do it before, during, and after elections. Most of this audience is composed of management personnel. And you know I am correct.

Unions obtained the authority and power which they now possess from government. They got it because they are the best politicians in the country. And they have no intention of giving it up. They are not going to let that power be taken away from them. When the President froze wages, Mr. Meany turned and called 137 lawyers to Washington, D.C. for one weekend and threatened the entire government. Here is a guy who can sit down and in one weekend have 137 lawyers in Washington, D.C. and say we came to take the Congress on; we came to take the White House on; and, if necessary, we came to challenge the courts. And you are going to sit here and tell me that there is a way that you can get the government to do what you want it to do without recognizing that that is where the ballgame is really won or lost?

I maintain that management does not play very good politics. You certainly do not play it as well as the unions do because they have beaten you for the last forty years at the state, county, and local levels. That is my most direct remark. I will lighten up a little bit now. You see, I had to struggle with unions the last three years trying to get them to be fair where minorities are concerned in the construction industry. And time and time again I would have someone from the management side of the table say to me, "Well, you know, if we get too rough

---

† Arthur A. Fletcher is former Assistant Secretary of Labor.

with them, they will take it out on us." So I think that you really ought to put the facts on the table if you really are going to talk about collective bargaining, and know where it is won and lost, and where it can be retrieved if it can be retrieved.

In the construction industry, which is the biggest industry in the country—$90 billion a year—there were two places in which the battle was lost. First, management in the construction industry gave up the right altogether to decide who could work for them. Any time you contract that responsibility out, and want no responsibility for training, or for recruiting, etc., then you have given it all away. When you cannot control the flow of manpower, then you have given it all away.

The reason that this is so much of an issue for minorities is because, whether you realize it or not, the minority community and business community are on the same side of the track. Twenty years ago, long before any mention of the Civil Rights Act of 1964, we started trying (I was involved in that) to get federal legislation on the books to deal with equal employment opportunity where federal contracts were concerned, and it worked temporarily during World War II. We tried to get that legislation turned into a permanent act in 1948 but management took the position that for the federal government to regulate employment, especially in such a way as to insure employment for minorities, would be taking away from management its right to decide whom it hired. And that was the argument basically that was put forth for almost two decades—to have the federal or state governments involved in this would be to deny management its divine right to decide who works for them.

Now while they were fighting this in the Congress, they were sitting down at the bargaining table and bargaining it away. And, over a two decade period, they completely bargained away the right to hire, train, etc. The interesting part about this is today, in order to control cost, particularly in the construction industry, one of the key factors is to increase the supply of manpower. But, when you bargain that responsibility away, as you have from the management side of the table, you are giving it to the unions. The unions know one way to keep those leap-frog settlements going is to keep the manpower supply small; you are not about to get them to train anybody. That is what they have been waiting on.

Interestingly enough, the minorities are saying the relief for us is to get a job, get into the labor supply, get in the work force, and management is saying the relief for us in terms of cost is to bring some more people into the labor supply. Therein lies the dilemma. When we talk about government and the way it comes down to remedies, look at the manpower act of '62. This was an act put on the books to increase the labor supply, to train the untrained and bring them into the labor market. Now that was taxpayer's money. Now what did I find when I got to the Labor Department? I found that here was an act, with millions of dollars appropriated to train American citizens, to bring them into the labor market, and eventually into the work force. And what did it say? The regulation said you cannot use manpower money to train people to work in the construction industry. You can train them anywhere else but do not use any manpower money to train anybody to work in the construction industry. And, interestingly enough, the same unions that went out and championed the manpower act, championed the budget, went over to the Labor Department and said, "Wait just a minute. Don't get carried away. Make sure the regulations that enforce this thing do not include money to train people to work in the construction industry."

The point that I am making here and now is that they played good politics getting that legislation on the books and they played the same quality of politics after it was brought into being. They went over to the agency where it was going to be administered and made sure it was going to be administered in such a fashion as not to hurt what they had already built up.

If you are not willing to play politics that way, then do not look to government for a remedy. Do not look to government for a remedy unless you are willing to play 24 hours a day, 365 days a year and be where the action is and have some knowledgeable people. Otherwise, they will beat you. It is that simple. Now, in terms of the Davis-Bacon wage panel boards, I did not get a chance to control them, although they should have been under my control when I was in the Labor Department. The feeling over at 16th and I was that I was unreasonable. I learned from them; I learned that they got where they did by being unreasonable.

Let me deal with this unreasonableness a bit because this is something else that I do not understand. These fellows who are leading the labor movement get paid fabulous salaries for being business agents, presidents, etc. Now when that Machinists' airline labor agreement that I talked about was presented to the members and they voted it down, at that point, the leadership lost the right to be reasonable. From there on out, they said, "We cannot afford to be reasonable. If we put a reasonable agreement on the table and agree to it, and take it back to the membership and they vote it down, they will not only vote it down but vote us out of office. So, we have got to be unreasonable."

The thing that amazes me is that I see people in high places understanding this saying, "We understand. You do not have to be reasonable, just come in here and demand anything and somehow when the moment of truth comes we will bite the nail and stand in front of the gun in your behalf." This extends that license to be even more unreasonable, and that license for them to come up with all that rhetoric to make their membership think they are actually leading. Let me say again now that their membership is given a license to believe that all this nasty loud talk—calling the President a dictator and things of this nature—is really leadership. It is not leadership; you know it is not and I know it is not. But they can go through with that bluffing, thinking that that is what seventeen million members want done. As long as the rest of the work force—and please understand that seventeen to twenty million workers or members is not the majority of the nation's work force which numbers eighty-six million—thinks that that is the way to get things done, then all you are really doing is encouraging others who are not now organized to get organized because it seems to be the way to get results.

I am just watching the ecology kids who are really beginning to spend the ecology budget. I am just watching to see what management does about that one. Garbage collectors are being organized now; as soon as they get those salaries up high enough, they will quit being collectors and start being sanitary engineers. The federal government will be paying the whole budget and I am curious to see if the union organizers will organize the garbage workers in such a way that the blacks cannot pass the standards to pick up the garbage. I am just going to watch and see what kind of tests they are going to have to take in order to pick up the can and dump it.

Anyway, it seems to me that the collective bargaining process is lost and has been lost because management and the public at large lost the battle in the political arena. I guess the greatest example of that is Davis-Bacon. When I used to administer the

Davis-Bacon Act, I remember along with others persuading the President to suspend the thing for a while only to discover that the unions were smart enough to have little Davis-Bacon Acts all over the country, which said the same things the big Davis-Bacon Act said. And so we really had not done anything but confuse the situation, which forced us into the Construction Pay Panel that we set up, which incidentally I believe was the forerunner to the price freeze.

When we began to monitor those contracts and set up the means to demonstrate through monitoring and through setting some kind of guidelines and then insisting that some of the settlements that were going on were beyond what we could reasonably expect, we began to get to settlements that were less than 18, 19, 20 percent. They were coming down around 8, 9, 10, 12 percent. That was not the reduction we had in mind, but as a result of monitoring the contracts and surfacing the issues in such a fashion as to put the pressure on some of the unions who were asking for these outrageous demands we began to be able to deal with them.

The problem I have with the Construction Panel and the problem I am going to have with the present price freeze is the political aspect of it. I am led to believe that few people really understand it. I am certain that the everyday voter who votes people into office does not understand it. I am sure, for example, that there are those who do not quite understand why the President takes one posture in the wage-freeze and why a committee in the Congress would vote for a resolution to pay all those retroactive contracts. That confuses the average lay citizen; he is led to believe that something must be wrong, something is unfair. He does not understand that the Committee has a lot of labor representation on it—Congressmen who are going to get their money from labor to run again. Half of the fellows on both sides of the aisle in both parties get their money to run for reelection from labor. And when the moment of truth comes, what I call the basic nitty and the fundamental gritty, you know where their votes are going to be. So, I do not have a lot of confidence as long as the opposition to the trend does not play the game as well as those who are riding with the trend. Right now you do not play it as well as they do.

Coming back to the manpower issue, as I look at the Labor Department, I look at the apprenticeship training program. Here again is a fancy way supposedly to train the people, but it is very clear that management does not run that training program. When it is all said and done, it is run by the various labor locals that belong to it. They decide who gets in, they decide when you get out, they decide how long you can stay, and they can use the apprenticeship program to control the flow of manpower into the unions and into the various crafts and onto the job. That is the reason why, in the Philadelphia Plan, instead of trying to repair the collective bargaining system and do something with it, when we found out that labor had full control of it and management did not have enough courage to try and turn it around, we found another way to bring about equal employment opportunity in the construction industry where federal contracts were concerned. And what we did (for you lawyers in the room) was to put a new burden on contract law. We decided that we should make use of the bid specifications, so that the contractor agrees to allocate a certain amount of man hours and man years of work to minorities as a bid specification. It is not something that is worked out after the contract. Again, I found out that the union lawyers are some of the best lawyers in the business. The very first thing that they do is take a look at whatever is in the contract and determine whether it is legally binding. Will it stand up? If it will stand up they will usually tell their business agents that "you better go ahead and do this." If there is any doubt about whether it will stand up or not, they will say, "Let's find out how much guts they have got. But that is it!!!" So what we did was put the use of minorities into the contract as bid specifications. For example, if the contract is to create a certain number of man hours of work over a period of three or four years, and if there are a certain number of minorities in the labor market and a certain number in the labor supply for that industry, we then go one step further and say that a percentage of these man hours of work must be shared with these minorities. And so the contractors are under the gun.

What the contractor will usually do is come back and say "I've got a collective bargaining agreement with the union and I must get my manpower from them." The appellate ruling in Philadelphia was that if a contractor felt that his collective bargaining agreement with the unions stood in his way of fulfilling his commitment with the federal government, then he should not bid. Now the unions understood that. They told the contractor to go ahead with the bid and they would see if they could work something out. But as long as I was in the Labor Department I could not work anything out; I was just as unreasonable as they are. I used the legal club the same as you do.

Anyway this is what this is really all about now. We pinned this burden on the procurement system because we did not feel that we could repair the collective bargaining system. We did not feel we could get government to do what it was supposed to do where the Manpower Training Act was concerned and where the apprenticeship act was concerned. I personally do not feel that the unions will give up anything they have been able to take or get any way they took it. They have gotten themselves in a power position and I do not believe they are going to volunteer to give it up. That is what is wrong with the hometown solutions—this "volunterism." I have never seen anybody volunteer to give up power, especially when it is economic power.

Now, finally, I think that the construction pay board will work for a while. I would hope that it would work throughout the rest of the decade while we get busy and do something about training the poor whites of Appalachia, the Indians on the reservation, and the blacks in all these ghettos, so that they can be productive citizens in the work market. The only way this is going to happen is to stop things right where they are, train them, and get them into a position to come into the work force in a productive fashion.

Federal, state, private, and public funds of all kinds should be used for the purpose of taking adults, training them, and bringing them into the labor market. In addition to that, I am at a loss to understand why the trade, technical, and vocational schools that are training youngsters cannot get apprenticeship credit. Yet there is state after state where a youngster can go through a very good technical training school and get no apprenticeship credit whatsoever. You must come out and start all over again and do apprenticeship and on-the-job training. Now there is something wrong about that.

If you really want to deal with the collective bargaining system, if you really want to deal with inflation, if you really want to deal with increase and spiral of prices, etc., then you must begin to concentrate on ways to bring more people into the work force. No question about it. There are those out there who want to come in. But they have found that when they have paid the price to prepare themselves, they have either found the system stacked against them, government stacked against them, or the rules and regulations working in such a way that they do not benefit them after that preparation.

It bothers me, for example, for any particular segment of government to have such control over federal funds that they can veto the training of an American citizen with taxpayers' money. I do not think the taxpayers ever had that in mind.

So when you are talking about cosmetics, there is no cosmetic remedy for this—you have got to get down to the basic part of it. And where government is concerned, the government's role is training people, the government's role is seeing to it that they have an opportunity for employment, the government's role is drafting and carrying out laws which control the work force.

And for awhile, again, I think controls will work. I hope they will work. I feel that they will work, possibly '73, '74, and possibly '75, at which time I think you will relax your muscles. I think you will get so busy doing other things, that you will think it will carry on from its own momentum. And the minute you go to sleep, it is going to start deteriorating. And when it does, we are going to be right back where we were again. And so it is improving the labor supply and playing the game in the political arena 24 hours a day, the same way they do; seeing to it that the laws put on the books and the rules and regulations and guidelines for enforcing those laws are consistent with the intent of the legislation. It is very easy to frustrate legislation by coming up with conflicting rules and regulations. You can lose it in the halls of Congress and win it all back with the rules, regulations, and guidelines for implementing the intent of the legislation. Unless you are willing to play in all those places, then you are not going to be where the action is.

Construction Bargaining and the Public Interest

Michael H. Moskow †

I would like to speak today about two areas in which the Department of Labor is intimately involved with the construction industry. Both of these areas represent a major extension of governmental concern for what may be labeled "normal industry processes." Both activities attempt to modify these processes to reflect more what is judged to be the public interest. One represents an economic concern—the other, a more contemporary concern, a social concern.

Specifically, I will discuss the establishment of the Construction Industry Stabilization Committee for stabilizing wages in the construction industry and programs to achieve equal employment opportunity in construction. I shall attempt to provide an overview of the pressures government responds to in developing policy and the kinds of day-to-day decisions officials make to keep policies continuously responsive to the public interest.

Of course, we all know that the true impact of a policy can be assessed only in the long run—and then imperfectly because the impact of one decision becomes influenced by that of others made by different persons, at later periods, with different assumptions, goals, and objectives. Moreover, the public interest changes over time. Virtues and vices have a habit of changing relationships and the theories and concerns of we economists are perhaps not a poor example of the vagaries associated with time. Finally, we know that the public interest is an abstract term representing a combination of numerous personal interests some of which have no affinity to the resulting sum. Let me then label these observations that I make today "The View from Partway to Somewhere"—without any intent at humor.

The construction industry, as all of you know, is a very large and important industry. New construction and maintenance and repair activities account for about 10 percent of Gross National Product. Nearly 3.3 million workers are employed in the

† Michael H. Moskow is Deputy Under Secretary, U. S. Department of Labor.

industry on an average annual basis, and upwards of 7.5 million persons obtain employment at some time during the typical year. There are numerous branches of the industry such as residential, highway, heavy, industrial, commercial, and pipeline. Labor is typically mobile across these lines, but there are often markedly different conditions of competition in the product market for these various types of construction services.

The unions in the industry are organized into 18 major crafts and are composed of highly skilled and fiercely independent persons. Local union processes tend to be highly democratic at least in terms of member influence on decisions of import. Business agents are typically elected for two-year periods and bargaining committees have their accomplishments ratified by local memberships. Needless to say, an agent's tenure is highly dependent upon how well he measures "up to and beyond" other agents of other crafts in the area, bargaining and dealing with management.

Contractors in the industry are typically organized into employer associations. These associations may be of general contractors, who have responsibility for the overall progress of a project, and of specialty contractors, such as electrical contractors, plumbing contractors, and mason contractors. Often a community of interest exists between a craft and a contractor; many contractors are former union members and officials.

Employment contracts in the industry commit a worker to an employer for a finite period, perhaps as little as one or two hours. The employer can discharge the man without any real difficulty, particularly if there is no work. Consequently, the only stable force in the industry is the craft union. It is incumbent upon the union to supply what the employer cannot supply—security or, at least, an income flow resembling what other workers receive. The union, thus, has to negotiate a wage rate which cumulatively will supply an average journeyman an annual income commensurate with an acceptable life style in his community. As a result, the local union, if at all possible, will try to limit the size of its membership to the number of craftsmen who can get enough union work to receive a reasonable annual income. In practice, the easiest way a worker can get a permanent and often exclusive attachment to the construction labor market is to obtain a union card.

Craft unions in construction will try to spread the union scale to as many projects as is economically possible. This provides more work for their members and helps to increase the opportunity to members to receive a secure annual income. Prevailing wage laws are an important means of spreading the union scale and increasing work opportunities. The Davis-Bacon Act, passed in 1931, is the most famous of these laws, but it covers only direct federal construction. There are another 55 statutes relating to federally-assisted construction that require the payment of prevailing wages. In addition, 38 states have "little" Davis-Bacon Acts covering state construction.

Collective bargaining is fragmented on a geographic, as well as craft, basis particularly in the North Central and Northeast states. Each branch of the industry may bargain in a different geographic scope, with wage zones common in the heavy and highway segments. An intricate web of wage relationships exists between crafts usually within metropolitan areas, but also between areas. It is not uncommon for twelve to fifteen bargaining agreements to expire within a geographic area at one time, or better, in staccato fashion.

In the summer and fall of 1970, the staccato rhythm of wage settlements in construction was on the upbeat. The average first-year increase in major collective bargaining agreements (1,000 or more workers) for construction was rising rapidly, especially in comparison to manufacturing. Average increases in construction and manufacturing rose from 7.6 percent and 6.4 percent, respectively, in the first quarter of 1969, to 21.3 percent and 6.9 percent by the final quarter of 1970. Telegrams and letters from concerned citizens, state and local government officials, Congressmen and Senators, construction contractors and employer associations, as well as employers in other industries, were received in bundles at the Department—many forwarded from the White House. The letters often contained newspaper reports of local unions demanding and obtaining annual average wage settlements of from 15 to 25 percent. The authors of this often-spontaneous flow demanded action—any action—to restore rationality to wage determinations in the industry. Employers in other industries worried about the impact of construction settlements on wage demands of their workers.

Discussions with national officials of construction labor and management indicated a sense of helplessness in dealing with the deteriorating situation. Although large numbers of building tradesmen were unemployed, the sense of inequity engendered by the relationships between local craft wage scales and scales in

other areas reduced the ability of both local business agents
and national construction leaders to influence the wage-making
process. Moreover, national union leaders were concerned about
the inroads open shop or merit shop contractors were making
into traditional union volume. In addition, officials of other unions operating in more competitive labor markets were probably
voicing concern for the restiveness of their members engendered
by the high construction settlements. Clearly, the situation in
late 1970 indicated that the industry—labor and management—
had lost control of the situation and lacked authority to "set
things right."

Our response to the situation is well known to you. On March
29, 1971, President Nixon signed Executive Order 11588 establishing the Construction Industry Stabilization Committee for
the purpose of stabilizing wages in the construction industry.
Another portion of the Order provided for the establishment of
an Interagency Committee on Construction to develop criteria
for reasonable prices and white-collar compensation. The path
from concern to a formal stabilization mechanism was rocky
and paved with false starts. Political imperatives of the participating tripartite parties had to be responded to which often
gave the path a kind of carnival-like "fun-house" quality, particularly when viewed through the eyes of the ubiquitous, though
often near-sighted, press. The concerns of the technicians for
long-run implications on factor markets, allocations of resources,
and rising unemployment indicators had somehow to be consolidated with those of the pulse readers whose eyes were on the
letters and cards from home. In the end, the Order was signed
and the nation had its first major stabilization mechanism since
the Korean War period.

More rational wage settlements in the construction industry
were not the sole objective sought by the architects of the stabilization program. A policy which achieved non-inflationary
wage settlements while sacrificing essential freedom in bargaining would hardly be in the public interest. Yet, of course, we
could not be purists either. A stabilization mechanism with
enough clout to influence a decentralized, or better, fragmented,
bargaining structure, would require a review process, criteria
for acceptable settlements, and viable enforcement measures.
None of these components can be reconciled with classic interpretations of free collective bargaining. Thus, the structure and
processes were designed to strike a balance between maximum

local participation and determination, while assuring results in the public interest.

The process works like this: the parties bargain locally with an eye to the local economic situation and the criteria established in the Order. The criteria state that settlements may reflect cost of living, productivity improvements and equity adjustments. Equity is defined as adjustments to restore traditional relationships among crafts in a single locality and within the same craft in surrounding localities. Completed settlements are forwarded to an appropriate joint labor-management Craft Dispute Board along with supporting data. The Board is composed usually of national representatives of the local bargaining parties. The settlements are reviewed by the Board in the light of the published criteria and precedents, and either forwarded to the tripartite Stabilization Committee for final review, or returned to the parties with advice and assistance offered.

The Stabilization Committee is composed of four public, four labor, and four management members. The Committee reviews each contract and finds it acceptable, unacceptable, or remands it to the appropriate Craft Dispute Board with an explanation of why it was not approved. The Board, in turn, contacts the parties, and offers advice and assistance.

Several things about this structure and process of stabilization reflect major policy decisions and have a direct bearing on the degree of freedom retained by the local parties in the bargaining process. First, the criteria are purposely nebulous. Part—but by no means all—of the reason for this is that it preserves considerable freedom of bargaining. Ceiling percentage increases may have simplified administration, but it also would have set goals for some trades. A ceiling rate would of necessity had to have been high, acknowledging the gross equity that may develop among wage rates over five years of heightening rates of inflation. A ceiling percentage increase, however, would have destroyed free bargaining in the industry, rendering it a shakled process. Second, the local parties and their national representatives make the major decisions in the wage determination process. Only at the apex of the review process is the public interest specifically introduced, and then by four public members only, representing but one-third the vote of a body of twelve.

Penalties for noncompliance with provisions of the Order are consistent with a design maximizing continued freedom of bargaining. Unacceptable wage settlements are published in the Federal Register and cannot be used in calculating prevailing wage determinations. To assure that unacceptable rates are not utilized in Federal or federally-related construction, Federal agencies must review their future plans and current construction projects for areas where unacceptable rates are being paid to ascertain whether the planning can continue, and contracts approved or projects continued. Finally, the Secretary of Labor may take any other action authorized by law to carry out the purposes and policy of the Order.

The results of the tripartite Committee's decisions to date have been gratifying. The average annual increase in contract settlements in 1970 was in excess of 15.2 percent. Under the stabilization program, the annual increase in settlements (measured similarly) have been lowered to 10.8 percent. Moreover, the duration of new contracts has shortened considerably, from 29 months in 1970, to 17.5 months in 1971. This means that a lot of the equity considerations have been accounted for in these short term contracts, and that next year the "screw may be tightened" further. The full-employment years between 1965 and 1969 destroyed the historic wage relationships of construction crafts within and between areas. Crafts had signed 3, 4, and occasionally 5-year contracts only to have brother crafts in subsequent years adopt higher annual settlements. The Stabilization Committee has attempted to restore to a great degree the historic equity relationships between crafts.

Another indicator of the success of the stabilization effort is the reduced number of strikes. Historically, nearly one contract expiration in three in the industry ends in a work stoppage for economic reasons. This statistic has been significantly modified. Less than one-half as many strikes have taken place in 1971 as in 1970, affecting less than one-third as many workers. The duration of each work stoppage has also been reduced by one-third. For the first time since 1966, man-hours lost through work stoppages in the construction industry will decline—and the decline will be of significant proportions.

Statistics on declining wage settlements and the incidence of work stoppages, although gratifying in themselves, provide a quantitative assessment of the stabilization program. Of perhaps equal importance are the new relationships that are developing in the industry which may have long-term impact on bargaining and provide insight into how the public interest may be better preserved.

One "qualitative aspect" of import relates to the functions of Craft Dispute Boards. The overly narrow geographic bargaining areas in the industry coupled with the political sensitivity of the business agents often necessitates a parochial view of member interests. Competition between business agents, as well as inadequate labor supplies and labor market mechanisms, has been a driving force behind higher wage settlements. Clearly, regional and national interests have frequently been overlooked in the wage determination process.

The Craft Dispute Boards are composed of national representatives of construction labor and management. These boards —18 of which have been established—are the "tier of first review" for settlements reached after March 29, 1971. Another major board function is to advise and assist local parties in arriving at settlements responsive to the wage criteria contained in the Order. Originally, most boards were way-stations before agreements were shuttled to the tripartite Committee. This situation has changed. More and more contracts are being returned to the local parties by the boards. The quality of "mediation" services provided by the boards—though it varies— has also trended toward higher sophistication. The boards' emerging role of segment-wide disputes settlement augurs well for a greater concern for the regional and national interests of unions and employers alike. In short, these are neophyte national dispute settlement boards. Although their origin is not organic, the prognosis for the graft is salutary.

Another qualitative import of construction stabilization activities has been the development of a reservoir of information about the geographic structure of the industry. Only the bare outlines of reality are visible when more than 5,000 agreements exist in an industry. These by-product data lend encouragement to another idea which many believe would extend the public interest—an expansion of the geographic scope of bargaining in the construction industry.

Narrow bargaining areas by craft promote instability in bargaining—particularly in times of full employment. Workers on strike can journey to a neighboring jurisdiction to escape the economic pressures of unemployment. Moreover, fragmented geographical units keep localities from having a proper perspective of regional and national interests. "Leapfrogging" settlements—the wage escalation caused by one group of persons basing their negotiations on those in the same or neighboring localities—also serves to aggravate problems in the industry.

The Construction Industry Collective Bargaining Commission —a tripartite construction industry mechanism established by President Nixon in September 1969—has been actively seeking an approach to expanding the geographic scope of bargaining in the industry. The work of the Stabilization Committee has helped sharpen the industry's awareness of the fragmentation in bargaining. The Collective Bargaining Commission would hope to build on the new awareness and develop a common consensus between management and labor for reforming the geographic scope of bargaining. The course to regional bargaining in construction is fraught with legal and political complexities but its potential for expanding the public interest is equally encouraging.

Let me move now briefly to the area of Equal Employment Opportunity (EEO) in the construction industry. As many of you know, this is not my area of prime responsibility. We have many persons in the Department who are better versed than I on this subject. My short sojourn in government, and particularly in the Labor Department, has heightened my awareness of the problem, not only in construction but in all industries. I have been impressed by the commitment of my fellow workers to achieve the goal of EEO.

The Department of Labor has developed two approaches to achieving EEO in the construction industry. One of these approaches is to impose a plan on a geographic area. This plan— the prototype was established in Philadelphia in 1969—requires federal contractors to make substantial effort to achieve certain proportions of man-hours of minority employment on all of their projects, public and private. The proportions are developed after a public hearing which ascertains the extent of underutilization of minorities, if any, by trade, as well as other data. Enforcement is assured primarily through the threat of debarment should the contractor not achieve the goal, or demonstrate sufficient intent. A collective bargaining agreement which includes an exclusive hiring hall provision is not sufficient in itself to absolve the federal contractor from the obligation. The Department has about five operational imposed plans at this time.

The second major strategy was designed to overcome many of the weaknesses associated with the first. The Department gives blanket approval to contractors and trades that negotiate and enter into a tripartite agreement including representatives of the minority community. This approach obliges crafts that may be a party to the plan to commit themselves in the agreement to certain numbers of minority workers over stated intervals of time. The major advantages of this approach—the so-called "Home Town Plan"—is that the commitment by craft is applied area-wide, rather than exclusively to federal contractors, and that union membership is assured for minorities accepted into the plan. Labor and management cooperation in the "Home Town Plan" means that a manpower support contract to recruit, train, and place minorities can be extended with a reasonable chance of achieving success. In practice, these contracts are generally awarded on a prime or subcontract basis to a minority organization. Chicago was the site of the first "Home Town Plan." More than 30 "Home Town Plans" have been given tentative or final approval by the Department.

Since each of these strategies was inaugurated, the employment picture in construction has turned sour. The extent of the influence of this situation on the success of either approach is uncertain. Departmental evaluation of the approaches shows some solid successes and some failures. My own feeling is that the specific impact of the plans differs by locality, because of such factors as the extent of federally-aided construction, level of overall construction activity, degree of organization of the minority community, hostility between white and black communities generally, quality of the manpower support activity—and numerous other factors.

The public interest is clear. Minorities must take their rightful place and share equally the employment as well as the unemployment in all industries, at all levels of endeavor. Often times, however, this goal could perhaps be better achieved if a greater degree of flexibility in the choice of approaches were possible. For example, if an imposed plan or "Home Town Plan" lacked reasonable success, a modified approach may be within the best interests of all concerned. Needless to say, however, any approach once instituted develops vested interests whether they be in management, labor, or the community. Attempts to introduce alternative approaches are considerably more difficult.

With these problems in mind, the Department is now considering experimental programs which we will utilize in certain, very limited, circumstances where their chances of success appear favorable. The experimental programs will continue to provide for minority participation in ways that will enhance the achievement of EEO, but will retain great flexibility. In most cases, experimental programs will continue minority participation in manpower support contracts incident to the compliance program. We believe that this wider variety of programs will open up a whole range of new choices in the EEO field, for selection in those instances where an alternative to an imposed or "Home Town Plan" may better reflect the public interest.

The subject areas I have discussed today—wage stabilization and equal employment opportunity—represent a considerable shift in the involvement of government in things of the private world. This may please some of you, not others. Policies in these areas are, however, necessary and dynamic responses to a changing world, made up of people with developing ideas and goals. In both of these areas—"partway to somewhere"—the uncertainties presented by our policy choices will surely present the next generation of policy makers with suitable challenge.

PART V

COLLECTIVE BARGAINING AND
THE NEW ECONOMIC POLICY

Price and Wage Control:
The Sickness of an Overgoverned Society

W. Allen Wallis †

The New Economic Policy that took effect on August 15 by presidential edict and went into its second phase last Sunday, has two main thrusts, one domestic and one foreign. Each of these two thrusts in turn has two parts, one dealing in the short run with pricing aspects of the economy, the other dealing in the longer run with real economic activities.

On the domestic front, the wage and price controls have an immediate impact on the nominal or measurement aspects of producing and distributing real goods and services. The proposals with regard to taxes and productivity are designed to increase the amount of goods and services produced, by stimulating fuller employment of resources and by stimulating more efficient use of resources, but it will take some time for them to be adopted and then to affect the economy.

Similarly, on the international front, floating exchange rates and the ten percent surcharge on imports have an immediate effect on prices. Efforts to bring about revisions in the trade policies of other countries are intended to shift the pattern of real economic activities, but this cannot happen quickly.

Thus, on both the domestic and foreign fronts, there are price measures intended to have an immediate impact, and there are real measures intended to improve underlying economic conditions in the long run. The short-run domestic measures are exactly the opposite of the short-run international measures. Internationally, the prescription is to replace rigidity and bureaucracy with flexibility and freedom, that is, to go from governmental price-fixing to free markets for international currencies. Domestically, the prescription has been to replace flexibility and freedom with rigidity and bureaucracy, that is, to go from free markets to governmental price-fixing for wages and prices. The long-run measures, however, are alike on the domestic and international fronts, in that both depend on the ability of the Ad-

---

† W. Allen Wallis is Chancellor, University of Rochester.

ministration to obtain cooperation by persuasion or inducement
of unsympathetic bodies, namely the United States Congress for
the domestic economy and foreign governments for international
trade.

I shall discuss only the domestic thrust of the New Economic
Policy, and only the wage and price controls. Concerning these,
I shall discuss, first, the prospects for success; second, why they
came about; and third, when they will go away.

First, the prospects that wage and price controls will succeed
in checking inflation are nil. Wage and price controls will affect
many things, but inflation is not among them. It can be asserted
with assurance—an assurance growing not only from economic
analysis but from thousands of years of history in many countries and civilizations—that if effective demand exceeds supply
at the prevailing price level, the purchasing power of the dollar
cannot be maintained by any means.

Saying that effective demand exceeds supply at prevailing
prices is simply another way of saying that there are not enough
goods and services to be matched up with all the dollars, if as
many units of goods go with each dollar as is specified by prevailing prices. Some dollars are left over; there are no goods
to match with them. Unless fewer goods and services are assigned to each dollar—that is to say, unless prices rise—the only
alternative is some kind of rationing scheme, formal or informal,
to decide which dollars will be the potent ones that get the goods
and services. Thus, some of the dollars become sterile and lose
their purchasing power altogether for lack of ration points, cer-
tificates of priority, influence, friends, gray-market power, getting in line soon enough and waiting long enough, or whatever
consideration it is that determines which dollars are allowed to
remain potent. The dollars that are reinforced by the required
supplementary consideration buy the same amount as before.
Notice, however, that the potent dollars by themselves did not
command the goods, but dollars *plus* something else; so as a
practical matter the purchasing power of even a potent dollar is
no longer as great as when it alone could command the goods.
Notice also that when the sterile dollars that can command
nothing are averaged with the potent dollars, the average amount
of goods commanded by all the dollars has declined. The only
possible way to maintain the purchasing power of the dollar is
to maintain a balance between total monetary demand and total
supply of goods and services.

Inflation can be generated only by the government. Business firms, labor unions, or consumers with excessive market power can do many objectionable things that are contrary to the public interest; but one objectionable thing that they cannot do is to cause inflation—or, for that matter, prevent it. Within our government the only important power to cause or prevent inflation lies with the Federal Reserve Board. If the government has a large deficit, this will not cause inflation unless funds are supplied for financing the deficit; correspondingly, a surplus will not cause deflation unless the money supply is allowed to lag. There is one, and only one, way to achieve the price stability at which the wage and price controls aim, and that is to control the rate of growth in the stock of money and credit.

Some subsidiary devices are available, to be sure, for influencing the size of the effective demand that results from a given stock of money, taxes being the most important, but these are distinctly subsidiary to monetary policy—indeed they are simply one of the things monetary policy has to reckon with in judging the proper rate of growth in the stock of money. Price and wage controls, whether they are effective or not, will not make a bit of difference in inflation.

This is not to deny that some prices and wages will be lower because of the controls. But to the extent that a price is lower because of controls, the money that in the absence of controls would be spent on that product or service becomes available for spending on something else, and the increase in demand for other goods causes their prices to rise.

Not only will wage and price controls fail to check inflation, they will in fact be harmful to the economy. There is a strong tendency to regard prices simply as incomes to those who receive them. Indeed, this fallacy is reflected in the use of the term "incomes policy" to refer to wage and price control. The same prices that constitute incomes to those who receive them constitute costs to those who pay them. More generally, prices are the coordinating device of the economy, and economic efficiency is strongly dependent on them.

Prices coordinate and organize the economy in two ways. First, they transmit vital information, for the prices that consumers will pay for various products reveal the intensity of their desire for more of those products, and the prices being charged for raw materials and labor reflect the importance of conserving or utilizing them. Second, prices serve as an incentive to advance the public interest by producing the things that are most wanted and consuming the things that are least needed, thereby earning a profit.

Thus, injury to the public interest can result from a price being too low, quite as much as from its being too high. If there is a large increase in the demand for a commodity, to give one illustration, a rise in its price serves the public interest in several ways. First, the price rise induces users to consume the commodity sparingly, especially if it is of little significance to them or easily replaced, so that the supply is left for those to whom it is significant and who cannot easily find substitutes. Second, the price rise induces producers to expand output, by offering higher rewards to the suppliers of its inputs—including labor. Third, the higher price makes production of the commodity still more profitable, and thus induces more firms to seek to enter the field. These and similar effects are all in the public interest, for they result in the public being supplied with what it most wants and they open up new opportunities for labor and for producers of raw materials to earn more. Correspondingly, a wage rate can be too low for the public interest, whether or not the worker "needs" more income.

If effective demand exceeds the supply of goods and services, the Government can best serve the public interest by not attempting to interfere with the rise in the level of wages and prices that is then inevitable. The Government's intervention through wage and price controls will not be without consequences; those consequences will be to lower the efficiency of the economy and to cause inequities and injustice, but not to maintain the purchasing power of the dollar.

Please note that I have *not* said that the Government can best serve the public interest by allowing inflation. In my judgment, inflation is probably contrary to the public interest. What I have said is that *if* there is inflation, it is contrary to the public interest to attempt to supress the symptoms. Analogously, it is contrary to an individual's welfare to have a pronounced tremor in his hands; but if he does have such a tremor, it is against his welfare to eliminate it by fastening his hands firmly into rigid stocks.

Not only do wage and price controls reduce economic efficiency, they are a major restriction on personal freedom. We intellectuals, who earn our livings by writing and talking, are inclined to rate economic freedom as distinctly secondary to freedom of expression. Freedom of expression, however, *is* our economic freedom. For the overwhelming majority of the population, restrictions on what they can buy or sell, and on what terms, have far greater impact on their personal lives than restrictions on expression. It is as easy for us intellectuals to write and speak admonishing the rest of the population to sacrifice economic freedom in the public interest as it is for the nonintellectuals to tell us to shut up or else say and write only those things that are in the public interest. We, of course, would respond eloquently and passionately that it is in the true public interest for us to say whatever we please, even if it contradicts official policy and received doctrine—in fact, *especially* if it contradicts them. The nonintellectuals—those who earn their livings by making and doing rather than by writing and talking—being less facile with words and ideas, may actually be led to believe that sacrificing their freedom is in the public interest.

There is one way in which wage and price controls might happen to prove useful. That would occur if they were invoked simultaneously with an abrupt retardation in the rate of inflation. In our economy innumerable commitments and contracts are made every day that will be fulfilled in the future—leases, labor contracts, sales agreements, and catalogues that must be printed in advance are examples. In making these forward commitments it is necessary to allow for possible changes in the price level. If prices have been rising for some time at 4 to 6 percent per year, as in fact they have for the past 6 years, it is prudent to project a continuation of that rate of inflation in making commitments for the future. Should there be a sharp reduction in the rate of inflation, such commitments might cause hardship. For example, if a wage commitment were predicated on a 5 percent rate of inflation and inflation were to halt, unemployment would probably result.

Thus, if the government knew that inflation was about to halt and the public did not know it, the government might protect people from their ignorance or folly by prohibiting price and wage increases for a period long enough to let the public see that inflation had stopped. Thereafter, the public could be left to its own discretion.

This is an extraordinarily fine-spun theory. It amounts to saying that people do not believe that the government is going to arrest inflation, so the government will force them to act the way they would act if they did believe it. The paternalistic co-

ercion needs to last only long enough for the government to stop
inflation and for people to revise their expectations and consequently their actions. Actually, the government does not know
whether it is going to stop inflation, only whether it hopes and
intends to stop inflation. Comparison of the instructions about
the money supply given by the Open Market Committee of the
Federal Reserve Board with the actual behavior of the money
supply makes it at least doubtful that the government knows
much more than the public does about how government policies
will work. Furthermore, even if the government had the capacity to produce an abrupt deceleration in the rate of inflation,
it seems scarcely likely that it would do so. The unemployment
that would result from abruptness would be too objectionable.

It is notable that while the money supply grew during the
first half of this year at an annual rate in excess of 10 percent, it has grown little or not at all since the New Economic
Policy was adopted. Obviously the rate will not be held so low
much longer, because of the unemployment consequences. But
it is not impossible, though it is improbable, that monetary
policy will be tight enough so that a year from now the rate of
rise in the official price indexes will have fallen to the 2.5 percent rate that officials have recently promised. (That will depend in part upon the diligence with which the Price Commission disciplines the specific prices that enter the index; these
prices are always subject to special attention under price control.) The odds are that monetary policy will not be restrictive
in 1972 but expansionary, partly to stimulate employment and
partly to keep interest rates from rising too much in the face
of a large Federal deficit.

In the unlikely event that monetary policy does bring the rate
of inflation down to the target rate within a year, the long-run
consequences might be unfortunate, for the public would have
learned a false lesson. The public would conclude that price
control is an effective cure for inflation, and Price Commissions
would become a permanent, or at least a recurrent, feature of
the economy.

Since monetary policy probably will not, and should not, be
so restrictive as to haul the rate of inflation down to the level
some Administration spokesmen are anticipating, the Pay Board
and the Price Commission are likely to encounter increasingly
rough weather. The 5.5 percent rate of increase in wages that
is being allowed may be consistent with price stability and full

employment now, since productivity increases rapidly in the early stages of cyclical recovery. But the rate of increases in productivity declines as the economy expands, so it will presumably be felt necessary in due course to lower the allowable rate of rise in wages. Anticipating this, employers and employees both are likely to press for the maximum allowable wage increases now, for fear that they will not be permissable later. But this would make the recovery less vigorous than it otherwise would be, since it would reduce the rise in profits that results from the lag of wages behind productivity and thereby strengthens the expansion.

Similarly, the Price Commission should be able to adhere for a while to the 2.5 percent annual rate of price increase that it is allowing. At the rate of inflation prevailing when the price freeze took effect on August 15, 2.5 percent would cover the increase for six or seven months, that is until about March, if 2.5 percent per year is interpreted as 2.5 percent now and no further increase for a year. After that—or a little earlier or later depending on the growth of the money supply—pressures will begin to build, but they might not become unmanageable for another three or four months, just as they did not in the recent 90 day freeze. Eventually, further increases in the ceilings will be required; but if they come just when the allowable rate of rise in wages is being reduced, the apparent inequity will put a great political strain on the whole system— and at a time when the political atmosphere will already be highly charged.

How did we get into this mess? Or, as a *Wall Street Journal* editorial put it a few days ago, "What's a nice country like this doing here?" All the objections to wage and price control that I have mentioned, and many that I have not mentioned, are known and thoroughly understood by the economic leaders of the Administration, including George Shultz, Paul McCracken, Herbert Stein, and—above all—Richard Nixon.

While I have not discussed with those gentlemen, or with anyone else in the Administration, the reasons for the New Economic Policy, I have a conjecture that seems to me highly probable. My conjecture is that the pressures for wage and price control were so universal and so powerful that they became irresistible. The head of a country in which 70 to 80 percent of the population believes in witchcraft, simply has to practice a little sorcery. Or as a friend of mine put it, "When all the world is mad, 'tis folly to be sane." Public opinion polls show that more than 70 percent of the voters believe in wage and price control as a means of controlling inflation.

Indeed, I believe that the President did a good job in staving off controls as long as he did. In the late spring and early summer of 1970 there was a powerful drive for controls by leading newspapers, television commentators, and members of Congress; and in apparent response to that the President established the National Commission on Productivity in the summer of 1970. In August of 1970 Congress passed the bill giving the President power to invoke wage and price controls, and thereafter kept up a steady barrage of criticism because he did not invoke them.

In the late spring and summer of 1971 a heavier and more sustained attack occurred. The attack by liberal Democrats in Congress was joined by twelve influential Republican Senators. The Committee on Economic Development (CED) came out swinging for controls. The President's own appointee as Chairman of the Federal Reserve Board, long one of the most trenchant and devastating critics of price control, publicly urged an "incomes policy," as he had begun to do soon after taking office. In July 1971, in a nationwide TV interview, the President of the AFL-CIO said, ". . . if I was in [the President's] position, I would impose controls at this time. I don't see any other way that this situation is going to get under control."

Thus, leaders of business, labor, Congress, economics, and journalism and most of the public were clamoring for controls. What voice was heard on the other side? Only the President's. Some may think that the President should have ignored everyone but himself, and quoted George Washington: "If to please the people, we offer what we ourselves disapprove, how can we afterward defend our work? Let us raise a standard to which the wise and honest can repair." But George Washington was not President of the United States when he said that. I personally would have liked to see the President ignore everyone's opinion but his own, since I share it; but on the other hand I'm not sure I'd like to live in a country where the President had that much power to ignore public opinion.

Finally, when can we expect wage and price controls to end? I fear that there is nearly an even chance that controls will not end in this century.

There can be no doubt of the Administration's total commitment to ending controls as soon as possible. It is perfectly clear from many statements by Mr. Nixon, some going back a dozen years or more, that he must find the controls totally repugnant. Invoking them in August represented surrender to overwhelming political force after a long, determined, and skillful fight. In the fight the President repeatedly voiced clear and sound analyses of the objections to controls. He has made many statements, going back at least to the period of his Vice Presidency, that show that he objects to price control on grounds of both practice and principle, of both economic efficiency and personal freedom. Politically, he must be keenly aware that he was first elected to public office with one of the only two Republican Congresses in forty-two years, and in both the elections that the Republicans won, antipathy to controls was an important issue and was a major issue.

The conclusion that must be drawn from the President's capitulation is that the forces favoring controls are overwhelming. While these forces will diminish as the inevitable bureaucratic interferences of controls affect more and more people, or as the controls break down, the conclusion many people will draw then is that more extensive and stronger controls are needed, and that present controls are simply being administered badly. It has to be recognized that many liberals believe in controls as a way of life, and welcome any extension of them under whatever pretext. I see no counterforce of any consequence. When a business group as influential as the CED, a labor leader as influential as George Meany, leaders of the economics profession as influential as Arthur Burns and Kenneth Galbraith, Congressional leaders as influential as the twelve Senators, newspapers as influential as the *New York Times* and the *Washington Post,* and a proportion of the voters as influential as three-quarters of them all advocate wage and price controls, then even though from time to time some of these groups may become disillusioned (as Mr. Meany did in little more than a month), we have to recognize a consensus that may make price and wage controls a permanent part of the American way of life.

Furthermore, while life under controls will disillusion many who now favor them, it also will arouse new appetites. When a broad system of controls is in force, it is possible for groups with sufficient political impact to manipulate the controls to their own advantage, for any use of controls inevitably has the effect of taking from some and giving to others. A special control that might be too blantant an act of piracy to survive politically or legally by itself, may survive when it is just one bit of a vast and complex administrative apparatus, and when it can come about by administrative action without legislative enactment or even notice.

Walter Lippmann in his great book, *The Good Society,* written more than a third of a century ago, makes this point: "The attempt to regulate deliberately the transactions of a people multiplies the number of separate, self-conscious appetites and resistances. To establish order among these highly energized fragments, which are like atoms set in violent motion by being heated, a still more elaborate organization is required—but this more elaborate organization can be operated only if there is more intelligence, more insight, more discipline, more disinterestedness, than exists in any ordinary company of men. This is the sickness of an over-governed society . . . ."

A frightening possibility, suggested by my colleague at the University of Rochester, Professor Karl Brunner, is that our economy may go the South American route. That is, we may run large government deficits, finance them by printing money, and respond to the resulting inflation by direct controls. That is, in fact, exactly what has happened in the past 6 years, which has been a classic example of pure monetary inflation. In the 6 years 1966 through 1971, the public debt (net of debt held by U.S. government agencies and trust funds) has grown by roughly $35 billion, and the amount held by the Federal Reserve Banks has grown by roughly $25 billion. In essence, two-thirds of the deficit has been covered by printing money. The public has liked this apparently costless method of feeding all sorts of appetites at the public trough, but it has not liked the inflation which has resulted. If now it believes that price and wage controls can dissipate inflation, and if experience in the next year seems to confirm that, then we have to fear that the South American way of life might become our way of life. A look at any South American economy can only result in dismay at such a prospect.

I do not want to leave the impression that I am predicting that price and wage controls are here to stay. I do want to leave the impression that the probability of this is too serious for complacency, at least by one who is concerned for the fate of this country and his grandchildren. I fear that there is almost a fifty-fifty chance that some degree of federal price and wage control will outlive the twentieth century and even my grandchildren.

A more optimistic possibility, one that seems to me equally probable, is that the whole apparatus—Cost of Living Council, Pay Board, Price Commission, and IRS field staff—may collapse in a shambles before this time next year. That might happen if at some time the Pay Board takes a firm stand on a wage contract that is important to labor unions. (Note that while less than a quarter of the labor force is organized, all five of the labor members of the Board represent organized labor.) The labor members might then walk out, in which case the Pay Board would presumably collapse and then the Price Commission. Another possibility for collapse of the whole control mechanism is through Congressional intervention, to relieve or provide special privilege for one group or another, or more generally through *de facto* intervention by individual Congressmen and committees and legislation in the day-to-day administration of the controls.

To recapitulate: First, the controls will not check inflation, though if inflation is in fact being checked abruptly right now by monetary policy it is conceivable (though improbable) that a brief period of controls would partly ameliorate the very adverse employment consequences of such an abrupt check. The controls will, to the extent that they have any effects at all, reduce the efficiency of the economy and impair individual freedom. Second, the controls came about as a consequence of an irresistible consensus of an overwhelming majority of the American public. Third, the controls may collapse within a year or they may outlast this century, both alternatives being about equally likely and all other alternatives together being less likely than either of these.

Management Responsibility for Collective Bargaining: What Every Businessman Should Know About Cost-Push Inflation

Virgil B. Day †

There is every reason to expect that control of inflation in a full employment economy will be the dominant problem of the 1970's for the United States. Certainly, even the sweeping "New Economic Program" announced by President Nixon in August has not been acclaimed as a panacea, but merely as a start on dealing with an economic challenge of monumental proportions. I would like to focus on the role of management in helping to meet this challenge.

The business members of the Pay Board have a dual responsibility. We are charged with speaking for management, but must also seek to serve the public interest. Management can claim no innocence with respect to the problems that caused the creation of the Pay Board, and management cannot sit idly by awaiting the correctives which must occur. We are guilty in part of what came to be and we must also help to be the cause of that which is to come.

It is pretty hard to debate the issue of bargaining's failure. Jefferson once said: "They are governed best who are governed least," and that is particularly true of bargaining. The process was designed to operate without outside interference. The justice of all this lay in the fact that the parties to the agreement ought to know best since they have to live with it. But as bargaining's impact on our economy increases, the public's right to be heard with respect to bargaining results increased as well. And when excessive settlements showed that bargaining was failing to respond to our national needs, the public interest was expressed in the form of controls. So, bargaining is to be regulated like a public utility for the time being with all the encumberances such regulation entails.

† Virgil B. Day is Vice President, General Electric Company and a Member of the Pay Board.

458

It took us only about five years to go from collective bargaining that is free to what I will call at least collective bargaining that is "filtered." But the filters may not remove all of the impurities. We spent the first half of the last decade negotiating good settlements; those good for both management and labor. They were good because they let productivity keep pace with wage increases and there was real wage growth. Over the last five years we have seen the ever-upward ratcheting trend of settlements which led us to where we were on August 15.

Admittedly, faulty monetary and fiscal policies were the original culprits, but the "me too" and "can you top this" interrelationship of all settlements hurt as well. Probably the biggest culprit of them all was construction where wages ran rampant and then spilled over to force industrial settlements to dangerous levels.

Maybe we in management could not control monetary or fiscal policies and maybe we were all victims and not villains in the drama of national economic policy. But we had as much an interest as labor in making bargaining work. And when it failed, we failed.

We were not diligent, or vigilant, or indignant. We were slow to recognize spillover, and we were greatly responsible as customers for what happened in construction. We took too narrow a view of the bargaining arena. Our labor friends made Congress their ally. They moved forward with increases in minimum wage and statutory benefits and, more importantly, they tapped the public treasury through use of welfare and food stamps to support their strikes. We, as usual, sat on the sidelines and stayed above politics.

And let's not forget that we, too, caught the inflation euphoria. We did not worry enough about price increases. We just paid what it took to settle and thought we could pass along what it took to pay.

In sum, we in management just have not been smart. We have not tried to do the teaching job with the public or with our employees. We have not sold our good case for the need to compete in world markets. We have not convinced enough people about the value of real wage growth versus the gossamer increases high settlements have produced. We have not moved to dampen rising expectations by showing the cold clear light of day.

We could, I suppose, curse the darkness. I suggest, however, that we repent and reform and not relax. We are in a new ball-game in Phase II, but it is a ball-game in which we still have to bargain and bargain well.

The Pay Board is not going to be that "George" who every-one else wants to let do it. We are going to have to strive for sufficient public understanding to support responsible deci-sions and not just complain about being victimized by economics. The economic lessons are clear but the message must be heard. Let me try today to begin to deliver by starting with what I will call "management's responsibility for collective bargaining failure." My colleagues on the business group of the Pay Board have discussed these ideas and we are in general agreement.

The Compelling Determinatives of Phase I

In retrospect, something corresponding to Phase I was in-evitable at the juncture of the development of the U.S. economy marked roughly by the end of the second quarter of 1971. De-mand-pull inflation had been largely arrested. The unemploy-ment rate was close to its peak level since the last economic expansion began to take hold in 1963, but conspicuous wage settlements kept getting higher and higher and prices kept going up. Our economy was under a sustained attack from wage-push inflation which could not be tamed—in the prevailing political and social climate—by monetary-fiscal restraints. The need to curb wage-push inflation was compelling. So something corresponding to Phase I was inevitable.

A second determinative force was the accelerating deteriora-tion of the ability of American business overall to make a creditable showing when it met its international competitors in both foreign and domestic markets. To sell competitively at home, more and more U.S. firms were forced to seek sources from overseas. To sell competitively abroad, more and more U.S. firms were driven to manufacture in foreign facilities. The critical element in many of these decisions was the handi-cap American business suffered in producing at home at grossly uncompetitive wage costs.

Our exports of goods and services exceeded imports by $8.5 billion in 1964. Our imports exceeded exports by $0.5 billion in the second quarter of 1971. Beyond that, there were balance of payments deficits of $23.0 billion on the net liquidity basis and $22.8 billion on the official reserve transactions basis. In early August, the dollar overflow reached crisis proportions. The need to protect our international competitive position became compelling. So, again something corresponding to Phase I was inevitable.

The Inescapable Constraints of Phase II

The compelling determinatives of Phase I are the inescapable constraints for Phase II. The Nixon Administration really had no practical choice but to confirm the inevitable by instituting Phase I. The Pay Board and the Price Commission have no practical choice but to implement the inevitable by determining the paths that will lead to the objectives of Phase II—(1) a 2 to 3 percent inflation rate; (2) to be accomplished by the end of 1972.

Both objectives are imperative. Scaling down the rate of inflation to 2 to 3 percent must be achieved to restore the kind of confidence in our economy that will encourage consumers to spend again, and business to invest again, in the goods and services that will create employment. Reaching this goal over a period of several years might be acceptable if the U.S. were protected by an economic iron curtain. But it is not. The import surcharge tax is temporary—like the other Phase I measures. We cannot have a healthy economy at home by isolating it from the world economy, even if this were possible. Economic isolationism—like political isolationism—has been tried before with disastrous results. Thus, it is essential to restore as quickly as possible the capability of U.S. business to vie with its foreign competitors. The nation cannot afford to postpone the 1972 target date. The deleterious impact of domestic price increases due to rising costs on our international competitive position has made foreign competition an inescapable constraint on how long we can endure cost-push inflation.

Wage-Push Inflation

There is general agreement that what started out as a demand-pull inflation (as the result of the misfinancing of the escalation of the Vietnam war) has now become a cost-push inflation (as the result, among other things, of expectations of future inflation). There are several ways of demonstrating that demand-pull inflation has long since run its course. One way is to examine the "GNP Gap"—the difference between potential [1] output and actual output. A crude measure of demand-pull inflation is the extent to which the economy is operating above its potential. In the first quarter of 1965, GNP was $12.5 billion (in 1958 dollars) below its potential. In the fourth quarter of that year, it was $5.3 billion about its potential. During 1966, it reached $11.5 billion above its potential in both the first and fourth quarters and remained above potential until the second quarter of 1969 when it was $0.1 billion below potential. During 1970, the deficit increased from $26.6 billion to $54.5 billion between the first and fourth quarters. Even in the second quarter of 1971, the economy was still operating $49.7 billion below its potential.

Another measure of demand-pull inflation is the extent to which manufacturing capacity is being utilized. With a base in 1957-59 of 100, the Federal Reserve Board index of the utilization of manufacturing capacity reached its high point in 1966 at 90.5 from which it declined to 73.2 in the second quarter of 1971.

A third indicator of demand-pull inflation is the extent to which we are employing our human resources. But unemployment was dwelling around the 6 percent level in the second quarter of 1971, well above what most economists would characterize as an indicator of full employment.

While economists and statisticians may argue about the precise date at which the predominantly demand-pull inflation changed to a predominantly cost-push inflation (and, indeed, it undoubtedly changed at different times for different sectors of the economy), there seems to be little question that long before the second quarter of 1971, the inflation was predominantly cost-push, and the predominant push in costs came from wage increases.

Despite the *sharp rises in unemployment*, shown by the bars on the left side of Chart 1 (with the rate of unemployment rising from 3.5 percent in 1969 to 6.1 percent in April, 1971 and 5.8 percent in October), increases in the *hourly compensation* of employees throughout the entire private sector of the economy continue above seven percent. Construction workers, teamsters and other strong employee groups received increases double and more than double this national average.

So, we see sharp rises taking place in *both* unemployment and hourly compensation. This runs counter to the normal economic

CHART 1

WHY THE ECONOMY IS IN TROUBLE
(An Economic Paradox)

DESPITE SHARP
INCREASES IN
UNEMPLOYMENT

INCREASES IN
COMPENSATION
CONTINUE HIGH

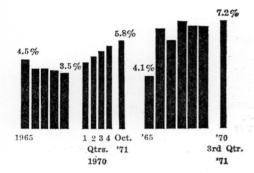

4.5%   3.5%   5.8%   4.1%   7.2%

1965   1 2 3 4 Oct.   '65   '70
        Qtrs. '71   3rd Qtr.
        1970   '71

CHART 2

WHY THE ECONOMY IS IN TROUBLE

PRODUCTIVITY
Down

PRICES
Up

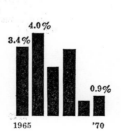

3.4%   4.0%   0.9%

1965   '70

1.7%   5.5%

1965   '70

CHART 3

WHAT'S BEEN HAPPENING
TO PRODUCTIVITY?

Annual Average % Increase
Private Sector

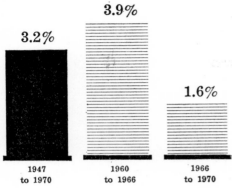

3.9%

3.2%

1.6%

| 1947 | 1960 | 1966 |
| to 1970 | to 1966 | to 1970 |

CHART 4

PERCENTAGE OF
CHANGE IN OUTPUT PER MANHOUR

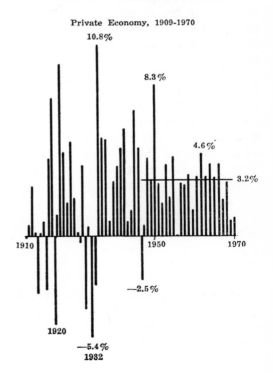

Private Economy, 1909-1970
10.8%

8.3%

4.6%

3.2%

1910   1950   1970

—2.5%

1920

—5.4%
1932

expectation that with a sharp increase in unemployment, the size of wage demands will moderate and unit labor costs and prices will eventually decline. But, the militancy of the individual union member and the political power of the international unions enable union negotiators to impose superinflationary wage increases on the economy despite rising unemployment.

Adding to the wage problem is *the drop in productivity* growth in recent years, as shown in Chart 2. The sharply rising hourly compensation costs and falling productivity improvement rate has resulted in the rapid rise in the general level of *all prices* and still greater increases in consumer prices. Some time ago there had been hope expressed that with a strong pick-up in business activity, productivity would respond with high back-to-back increases in 1971 and 1972. It was suggested that if productivity increases of five percent were achieved, the economy would stand a chance of partially offsetting the excessive wage increases and thus partially offsetting the rise in prices. However in the first three quarters of 1971, the increases in output per man-hour averaged about 3.8 percent over the same quarters of the previous year. This is not much more than the average rise of 3.2 percent from 1947 to 1970, as shown in the first bar on the left of Chart 3. A 3.9 percent increase was experienced from 1960 to 1966, with but a 1.6 percent increase from 1966 to 1970.

While it has been suggested that the *heavy capital investment* in recent years may make possible increases of 5 percent a year for two successive years, we also had substantial, successive annual increases in gross investment per worker starting with 1946. Only the one year of 1950 shows an increase in output per man-hour over 5 percent. Also, the estimate of the Bureau of Labor Statistics for the decade of the 1970's of a 3 percent average annual increase in output per man-hour for the private sector again indicates that *no new productivity factor can be expected to work toward off-setting the high hourly compensation increases now being experienced.*

By way of perspective, note from Chart 4 the percentage increase in output per man-hour for each year since 1909. With wider swings in business activity before World War II we experienced wider swings in output per man-hour. While a strong cyclical upswing in business activity may result in an increase in output per man-hour approaching five percent, it is questionable how much beyond the first six or twelve months of a strong upswing, cyclical forces will maintain output per man-hour at a higher than average level.

Thus, while any increase in productivity will help, *what is primarily needed* to bring down the current rate of increases in prices *is a decrease in the level of the excessive hourly compensation increases.* But, instead of a decrease, wage gains in 1971 were still ratcheting up. The 29.6 cents increase in hourly wages, shown in Chart 5 by the bar on the right for the first quarter of 1971, compares with 22.7 cents last year and 7.7 cents in 1965. The 29.6 cents is the median—the center point in the range of 638 agreements negotiated during the first three months of 1971, based on a study by the Bureau of National Affairs. Construction leads the parade with building-trades unions getting a median increase of 82.2 cents an hour, 12.7 cents higher than a year earlier. In April, the Construction Industry Stabilization Committee got down to work and has been able to lower the average settlement from 15 percent last year to 10.8 percent this year, from April on. Better—but hardly adequate to meet the national needs.

Chart 6, based on the Bureau of Labor Statistics study of major settlements, only covers contracts affecting 1,000 workers or more and breaks them down as between manufacturing and nonmanufacturing. As you see, it shows an 8.1 percent increase in the former and 15.2 percent in the latter for 1970. The 15.4 percent increase reflects the superinflationary wage rate increases won by construction workers and teamsters. As to what rate of hourly compensation increases may be expected in the future, the average estimate of some 28 economists is 5.8 percent for the decade of the 1970's. This estimate was made before the development of the New Economic Program. An hourly compensation increase of 5.8 percent implies about a 3 percent increase in prices during the 1970's, if we assume output per man-hour will provide offsetting cost savings of about 3 percent. And, such a level of annual increases in prices over the next 10 years is a new and disturbing force affecting the competitiveness of U.S. products in the marketplaces of the world.

The *expectation* of an increase in prices at a level of 3 percent and more gave rise to demands for a topless cost-of-living escalator clause, which was negotiated in the auto, can, aluminum and steel settlements. Interestingly enough, George Meany

CHART 5

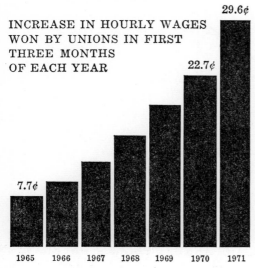

WAGE GAINS ARE
STILL SPEEDING UP

INCREASE IN HOURLY WAGES
WON BY UNIONS IN FIRST
THREE MONTHS
OF EACH YEAR

29.6¢

22.7¢

7.7¢

1965 1966 1967 1968 1969 1970 1971

CHART 6

1st Year Wage Rate Increases
MAJOR SETTLEMENTS

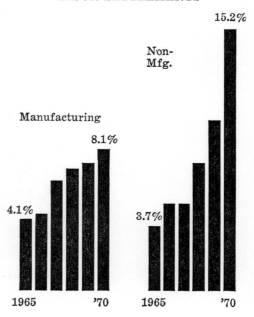

15.2%

Non-
Mfg.

Manufacturing

8.1%

4.1%

3.7%

1965 '70   1965 '70

CHART 7

OUTPUT PER MAN-HOUR AND REAL COMPENSATION
PER MAN-HOUR, TOTAL PRIVATE ECONOMY, 1950-69

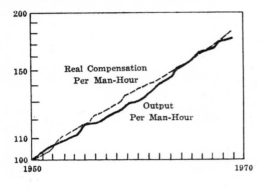

Index 1950=100

CHART 8

AVERAGE ANNUAL PERCENT INCREASE IN
HOURLY COMPENSATION

All Employees in MFG., 1965 - 1970

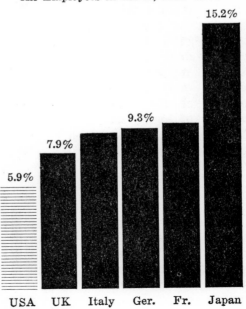

at the end of World War II made the point very well when he said:

> The American Federation of Labor has never agreed to the principle of basing wages on cost of living or on price inflation. The established wage policy of this country has always been based on raising wages as increases in productivity made this possible. This is the only possible basis for an expanding economy with rising living standards.[2]

The soundness of Mr. Meany's observation at that time—of basing wage increases solely on increases in productivity—is illustrated in Chart 7. Here, it is shown that there is a very close relationship over the years between the rise of *real* compensation per man-hour and output per man-hour. Put another way, when the rise in hourly *money* wages is deflated by the rise in prices, the rise in real hourly compensation over a period of years parallels the rise in output per man-hour. Thus, it may be said that hourly compensation increases in excess of output per man-hour are paid for, as the late Walter Reuther put it, in the wooden nickels of inflation.

All of this suggests that nobody would be served better than the American worker by a pay stabilization policy that is tied to the productivity of the American economy.[3] This was the basic concept of the Kennedy-Johnson noninflationary wage-price guideposts, the only peacetime "incomes policy" this country has ever tried in the past, and which, incidentally, seemed to work better than it was given credit for, until it was scuttled by the demand-pull inflation that became conspicuous in 1966. But now we are in a totally different situation where cost-push inflation—not demand-pull—is the primary source of our economic problems. We really have no "Divine Right" to our standard of living, and we must ultimately accept the discipline of wage and price decisions oriented to the 3 percent range of productivity increases in our economy anticipated for the 1970's.

The U.S. Economy's Deteriorating Position in World Competition

The primary objective of the Stabilization Boards of the past, as well as that of Kennedy-Johnson noninflationary wage and price guideposts, was containing inflation. But there is another related but equally urgent objective today of the Nixon Administration, of labor and of business. That is the loss of competitiveness of American products in world markets, the loss of jobs and the vanishing of our trade surplus. It is estimated that exports keep three million Americans working.

Thus, in formulating wage policies for the post-freeze period there is the need not only to contain inflation but also to look forward to the strengthening of our competiveness in markets throughout the world, including American competitiveness in American domestic markets. It might be said that we should be formulating an internationally competitive wage guidepost. This would take account of the wage and productivity trends of other industrial nations, as well as the other determinants of the competitive strength of a nation—and of its individual product lines. Over five years ago, the President's Council of Economic Advisers in its 1966 Report recognized the underlying international charter of a national wage policy. To get an international perspective, it is helpful to examine the hourly compensation, output per man-hour and unit labor cost *trends* of the manufacturing sector of the United States as compared with that of other industrial nations.

Chart 8 shows that the average annual percentage increase in hourly compensation for the United States (the first bar on the left) was 5.9 percent for the five-year period from 1965 to 1970, while in Japan it was 15.2 percent. Chart 9 shows the range of the average annual percentage increase in output per man-hour. It is from 1.8 percent in the United States up to 13.9 percent in Japan. With the greater increase in output per man-hour in the manufacturing sector of other nations offsetting their greater percentage increases in hourly compensation, the average annual increase in unit labor costs ranged from 1.1 percent for Japan to 4 percent for the United States, and 4.6 percent for Italy, as shown in Chart 10.

It is important to note that these are average annual percentage increases from the base year of 1965. The percentage increase is quite different from the absolute dollar amount of hourly compensation (whether it be $1.34 in the steel industry of Japan or over $5.00 in the United States), and the amount of productivity in units of output and the amount of unit labor costs expressed in monetary units. Further, the figures reveal percentage changes for all manufacturing as an average. An average hides the wide range of differences between industries and firms within each industry. This weakness of an "all manufacturing" average is significant in view of the fact that foreign competition is on a product basis not an all manufacturing average.

CHART 9

AVERAGE ANNUAL PERCENT INCREASE IN OUTPUT PER MANHOUR,

Manufacturing, 1965 - 1970

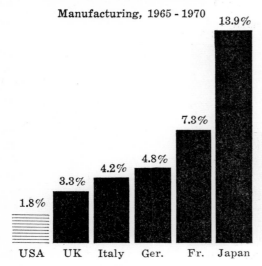

CHART 10

AVERAGE ANNUAL PERCENT INCREASE IN UNIT LABOR COSTS,

Manufacturing, 1965 - 1970

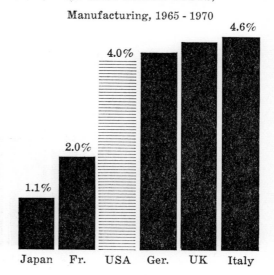

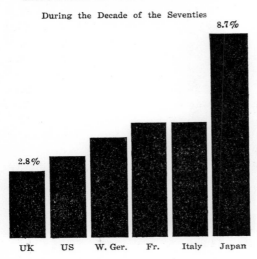

CHART 11

ESTIMATED AVERAGE ANNUAL
PERCENT OF INCREASE IN
GROSS DOMESTIC PRODUCT PER CAPITA

During the Decade of the Seventies

8.7%

2.8%

UK   US   W. Ger.   Fr.   Italy   Japan

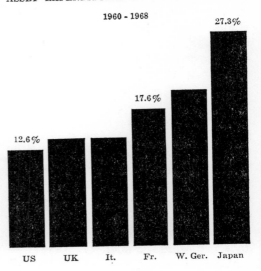

CHART 12

ANNUAL AVERAGE FIXED
ASSET EXPENDITURES AS PERCENT OF GNP

1960 - 1968   27.3%

17.6%

12.6%

US   UK   It.   Fr.   W. Ger.   Japan

As to the future, the European Organization for Economic Cooperation and Development projects the estimated average annual percentage increase in gross domestic product per capita will show a continuation of the wide gap between the increases in productivity of the U.S. and Japan, as well as other major industrial nations. For the United States the projected annual increase is 3.2 percent per capita while that for Japan is 8.7 percent (Chart 11). A significant contributing factor to this relative productivity performance is the annual average fixed asset expenditures of the different nations, shown as a percentage of GNP for the eight years, 1960-1968 (Chart 12). It was 12.6 percent in the United States with other industrial nations shown averaging 14.0, 14.3, 17.6, 19.9 and 27.3 percent respectively. The increase in the average annual manufacturing output per man-hour for these particular nations ranked in the same order as did their fixed asset expenditures.

In addition to the higher rates of fixed asset expenditures, other nations (as cited in the July 1971 Report to the President on the Steel Industry) get more capacity for their investment dollar due mainly to the difference in the cost of labor to construct plants and to install equipment. The Report to the President on the Steel Industry cited a cost of $350 per ton of installed steel-making capacity in the United States with an average cost for Japan of somewhat more than $100 per ton. Another illustration relates to productivity differences in the construction of comparable nuclear power plants in the United States and Japan. The U.S. plant required over 5.4 million skilled craft man-hours; the Japanese plant required 21 percent fewer skilled man-hours, or 4.25 million skilled man-hours. This difference reflected primarily the relative productivity of the work forces rather than any unique requirements of the site, the specifications, the materals or the regulatory authorities.

The greater investment in fixed assets as a percentage of GNP of other nations for the decade of the 1960's, as shown in Chart 13, indicates that American industry has a catch-up problem of long standing which is why our government should maintain a continuing program of depreciation allowances and investment credit competitive with that of other nations. Competitive government is a requisite for competitive industry.

The argument that the current amount of idle plant capacity does not warrant such tax incentives fails to recognize the percentage of plant and equipment in the U.S. that is reported obsolete and which needs modernization to increase productivity. For all manufacturing industries, 15 percent of U.S. plant and equipment is reported to be obsolete.

The most significant conclusion for the Pay Board and the Price Commission that emerges from this analysis is that we are dealing with long-range trends, not transient aberrations. U.S. business is in trouble when it comes up against its foreign competitors in both foreign and domestic markets. It is not just temporarily in trouble. It has been getting into trouble for a long time. It can get out of trouble only by taking drastic, decisive and, above all, prompt and urgent action.

The U.S. working man is also in trouble if we do not solve these problems. In fact, the job before the Price Commission and the Pay Board is really one of protecting the growth in real wages. The wage earner knows that, despite the feverish pace of money wages during the past five years, he is not really making much progress against rising living costs. Until inflation is under control, the growth in real wages will be stunted. The consumer must be king—and that is the name of the game. We should have learned from the 1960-65 experience that inflation can be contained while improving the real wage earned by people in their functions as consumers, producers, and taxpayers.

For the Price Commission then, the job is to identify and to implement vigorously measures which will achieve the President's objective of an inflation rate of 2 to 3 percent by the end of 1972. For the Pay Board, the job is to move courageously and relentlessly to bring pay increases—whether newly-negotiated or deferred—back to the levels which the productivity of our economy can support.

As Arthur Burns has warned:

> The rules of economics are not working in quite the way they used to. Despite extensive unemployment in our country, wage rate increases have not moderated. Despite much idle industrial capacity, commodity prices continue to rise rapidly. And the experience of other industrial countries, particularly Canada and Great Britain, shouts warnings that even a long stretch of high and rising unemployment may not suffice to check the inflationary process. . . . *The problem of cost-push inflation in which escalated wages lead to escalated prices in a never ending circle is the most difficult economic issue of our time.*[4] (Emphasis added.)

The compelling determinatives of Phase I—wage-push inflation and foreign competition—are the inescapable constraints of

Phase II. Any attempt to escape these constraints—or to loosen them for some fleeting comfort—would be to trifle unconscionably with the jobs of American workers, and the standard of living of the American people.

Let me attempt to summarize the points which I and my colleagues on the business group of the Pay Board feel are crucial to an understanding of the situation facing the U.S. economy.

—What had started out as a demand-pull inflation with the Vietnam escalation had become a cost-push inflation.

—Despite sharp increases in unemployment in 1970 and 1971 increases in money wages continue at levels inconsistent with price stability.

—While these compensation gains continued at high levels, productivity improvement dropped off.

—While some increase in productivity over the poor record of recent years may be expected, and is clearly desirable, no new productivity factor can be expected to come close to offsetting the recent level of compensation increases.

—What makes solution of these problems truly urgent is the loss of competitiveness of American products in world markets, the loss of jobs and the vanishing of our trade surplus.

—The ultimate objective of the Stabilization Program is not to stop good wage increases—far from it. The objective is to bring about conditions in which the growth in *real* wages can continue.

Let me close briefly with some comments about the work and the role of the Pay Board. The very fact that the Pay Board exists proves also that high settlements have been a problem. So, this alone can be a source of education for the general public, and also for management and employees. But the Pay Board is going to be too busy to teach economics and certainly will not always be available to repair your bargaining defects. The Pay Board does not exist to save the unwise or foolish from the effects of their folly. At the outset I called the next step "filtered" collective bargaining, not free collective bargaining. Filters have varying sizes of screens, but in all cases, things get through, and if you bargain for more than you can bear, you might just be left to live with it.

The Pay Board will not be a substitute for prudence on your part. I think I speak for all members of the Pay Board when I say that our hope is to go out of business as soon as we can. We all know that won't be tomorrow, but if those here begin to do their job, my current one will end. I can safely say, the sooner the better.

NOTES

1. The potential GNP is a measure of the economy's total output under conditions of "full employment," defined by the Council of Economic Advisers until 1969 as 4 percent unemployment of the labor force, and since then as 3.8 percent.

2. *War-Labor Reports,* 1945.

3. And nobody would be served worse than the American worker—especially the teenager, the minority and the unskilled worker—by the premature 25 percent increase in the minimum wage to $2.00 an hour, as now proposed in a bill before Congress.

4. Statement by Arthur F. Burns, Chairman, Board of Governors, Federal Reserve System, before the Joint Economic Committee, July 23, 1971.

Reflections on Public Sector Bargaining and the Wage-Price Freeze

A. H. Raskin †

It is an axiom of collective bargaining that no one on either side of the table ever lets himself be hemmed in by the theoretical scope of bargaining if that proves disadvantageous. In line with that hallowed tradition of irrelevance, I intend to romp blithely around the unmistakeable limitations of my title to discourse on the altered situation in which all of us find ourselves as a result of President Nixon's astonishing plunge into a semi-regimented economy. That plunge will put both public and private sector bargaining into a common mold of trying to find escape hatches to frustrate the rules, and that gives me all the excuse I need for taking a wide end-run around my supposed topic.

Just as an earnest of good faith in establishing that connection, however, let me point out that "me tooism" is the essence of public sector bargaining as we know it in New York City, the place where unions are perhaps most securely rooted in both strength and statutory safeguards and where they have made the largest strides in pushing up wages, pensions and other benefits. Whatever one union wrings out of a not too resistant municipal administration becomes the jumping off point for an even bigger exaction by the union next in line.

A recent survey by the Bureau of Labor Statistics showed that the old concept of city employes as second-class citizens, paid off in job stability at the price of substandard wages, no longer has much validity in New York or other big cities. In both blue-collar and white-collar occupations, the earnings of unionized civil service employes are way out ahead of those in the private sector. And the same thing is true of holidays, vacations, health insurance and pensions. Earlier this year all our principal industry groups—the State Chamber of Commerce, the Commerce and Industry Association, the Economic Development Council

† A. H. Raskin is Assistant Editor of the Editorial Page, The New York Times.

and the Citizens Budget Commission—joined in a warning to Mayor Lindsay that one of the elements prompting business to move out of New York was the extent to which the city's profligacy at the bargaining table not only was driving up taxes but also was acting as a spur to inflated demands by unions in the private sector. What you do wrong in one sector inevitably spills over into the other. Unfortunately, this is a Gresham's Law concept. It never works in reverse for the things you do right.

Now, I know it's fashionable to insist that New York is *sui generis* and that it makes no sense to describe its experience as a kind of bench mark for what might happen in civilized communities—and least of all for cities that are right at the earliest stage of union recognition for public employes. But we have learned how quickly a city can move from the Year 1 to 1984 in these matters, and we in New York City are still setting bad examples on the bargaining front right at the beginning of Phase II. Just to prove we're not unique on such things I see the City Council here in Philadelphia was all set to go the same route—at least on big wage and pension grabs for itself—till Mayor-elect Rizzo blew the whistle.

My own feeling is that the long-range remedy is going to have to lie in a multi-sided bargaining table—one in which the civil service union and the municipal government don't monopolize all the chairs. The business and labor interests in the outside community should be represented and so should representatives of blacks, Puerto Ricans and all the rest of the decentralized and neighborhood community groups, which have a vital stake in the elements of basic public policy so often determined at the bargaining table these days.

Now, having made that obeisance to my topic, let me push on into a digression that links both public and private bargaining with the viability of our whole economy.

With all due respect to my distinguished fellow-panelist, Virgil Day, I cannot pretend to be excessively sanguine about the life expectancy of the newly promulgated guidelines for wages or prices. That is not because I have reservations about either their basic soundness or the urgent need for some such detour from normal market principles to help stabilize the purchasing power of the dollar. On the contrary, I salute both the Pay Board and the Price Commission for having fulfilled an exceedingly difficult mission with skill and dispatch and, more important still with scrupulous—perhaps even excessive—concern for considerations of equity.

Notwithstanding my admiration for the program's fundamental design, I am skeptical about its success or even its long survival for reasons that can best be summed up by a capsule explanation I got in London two and a half years ago on the reasons for the collapse of the incomes policy which the Wilson Government had started so bravely in 1966 with a view to putting the brakes on a wage-price spiral a good deal less rambunctious than the one we are trying to curb. The explanation was given to me by Ray Gunter, who was then Britain's Minister of Labor, a hearty, down-to-earth fellow out of the railroad unions, very reminiscent of George Meany in appearance and in no-nonsense mode of expression.

I had developed a considerable admiration for Aubrey Jones, the exceptionally talented former industrialist whom Prime Minister Wilson had put in charge of the incomes program, and I was interested in learning from Gunter why, despite the combination of brilliant leadership and the auspices of a Labor Government, the program had so quickly proved a flop. His answer was quite simple:

> We started this program with a six-month freeze, and in that period we were all right. All my old friends from the TUC would come in and say: "Ray, this freeze is very unfair. You know our blokes are entitled to more money. We've got a very good case. Nobody can deny that." And I'd agree with them and tell them I wished I could do something for them, but that I couldn't get them anything, not even a bob.
>
> So they'd go back to their unions and tell them that the Minister of Labor agreed they had a terrific case but they'd just have to wait. Everybody was under a freeze and there couldn't be any exceptions. Well, they could all live with that, but once we came out of the freeze and began to put some flexibility into the program, we were in trouble.
>
> Every increase we authorized, every exception to take note of some inequity or other, brought a hundred demands for the same thing or more. And, of course, everybody could show why his case was better than anybody else's and why his union should get at least double what the other union got, or maybe three times as much, or four times as much. And the same thing was happening on the price side, and pretty soon you couldn't even pretend you had anything left in the way of a program.

I thought it might take 24 hours or perhaps even as long as 48 before the same lugubrious story began unfolding in this country. After all, it was the AFL-CIO which had been calling lustily for controls for fully two years before President Nixon overcame his aversion to the whole idea. There was nobody in labor's high command or in labor's rank and file who wasn't thoroughly aware that workers never came out ahead when the wage-price leapfrog was in wild swing. Just to take New York City as a case in point money wages for factory workers went up by $29 a week in the last half of the 1960's, but the average family head ended up $1.80 behind in what his pay envelope could buy after taxes and inflation had taken their ravenous bite. And this in a time span when on a straight productivity basis the worker should have wound up at least 15 percent ahead for the half-decade.

Given realities of that kind on a countrywide basis you would have thought that our labor movement, which prides itself on its worship of "realism," would have addressed itself with some seriousness to working out a program that would take the water out of the currency and make the wage dollar worth something again. There is not one top leader on the labor side who doesn't know that increased productivity is the root of any real improvement in living standards for workers or anybody else. And, in truth, labor was ready to write into the stabilization prescription all of the proper homilies and even the right numbers, give or take a point or two. But the much more overriding, even obsessive, concern of the union representatives was to couple any formula that emerged with so many loopholes that no self-respecting Swiss cheese would go to market so adorned. In organized labor's book, wage control is not to take hold with any real bite until everybody in the current round has done all the grabbing he could have done if there were no controls.

But in a period of long-term contracts there is no beginning and no end to any contract round. Everybody can justify an endless cycle of inflationary increases on the basis of "tamdem" or "catch-up" or "substandard." And, as all of you know, that is just what has been happening ever since the freeze ended. What's worse, we haven't got anywhere close to the top of the mountain yet. Every tandem has a built-in springboard, as the Pay Board will discover when it gets to the prospective settlements of the West Coast and East Coast longshore strikes. On the West Coast Harry Bridges has a problem with rebel elements, especially in his San Francisco and Seattle locals. For all that, many of us still tend to think of Bridges as the werewolf of the waterfront and scourge of the capitalist system; his own dissidents accuse him of being "in bed" with the employers because of his receptivity to automation and labor mobility in the interest of greater efficiency. Bridges is coming out of two five-year contracts, the result of which was to put West Coast wages a good deal behind those on the East Coast. So there is a strong case in equity to be made for a big pay boost in the new Bridges contract. Even on that basis, however, the 25 percent the Pacific Maritime Association has proposed for a one-year contract would be hard for any Pay Board to swallow.

But suppose Bridges does accept some such figure and the board does pass it, is there anyone in this room who doubts that Teddy Gleason will go to his employers in the Port of New York and insist on getting just as much? Bridges' justification will be a catch-up with the East Coast; Gleason's will be that he is not going to accept a narrowing in the differential between the two coasts, and both will be able to find plenty of elastic in the Pay Board's rules to support their polarized, mutually contradictory rationales.

Much of the same kind of thinking is already beginning to surface on the price side, with everybody looking for ways to get around the ceilings. The auto industry, which is the most coddled of industries under Nixon's New Economic Policy, started it by an attempted end-run to evade advance clearance of its price increases. Now the real estate industry is clamoring for a blanket exemption on rents.

And that is only the beginning. Employers, in general, will be lobbying to get above-ceiling pay increases ok'd in the interest of industrial harmony, then they will rush to the Price Commission for authorization to pass along the increase in higher prices. All of which makes me fear that both industry and labor will be guiding all their conduct in this period by the concept of "look what the other guy is getting away with" and making that the justification for abuses on their own part. No stabilization system can survive on that basis. But neither can any economy that is in as much trouble as ours is. My worry is that in the eagerness of every one of us to operate on the basis of the lowest common denominator of social responsibility when it comes to our economic decisions, we will wind up watching the highest overall standards in history go down the drain of an economy no longer able to hold its own in an ultra competitive world.